"UNITE OR DIE"

Intercolony Relations, 1690–1763

KENNIKAT PRESS

NATIONAL UNIVERSITY PUBLICATIONS

SERIES IN AMERICAN STUDIES

General Editor

JAMES P. SHENTON

Professor of History, Columbia University

HARRY M. WARD

"UNITE OR DIE"
Intercolony Relations 1690-1763

NATIONAL UNIVERSITY PUBLICATIONS
KENNIKAT PRESS
Port Washington, N.Y. // London

Library of Congress Catalog Card Number 72-139362
ISBN 0-8046-9013-8

Manufactured in the United States of America

Published by
Kennikat Press
Port Washington, N.Y./London

To Hiley

PREFACE

Until fifty years ago the span from the Glorious Revolution to the era of the American Revolution was one of those "middle periods" neglected by the historian. Colonial history had been too much the province of the "Whig" or "national" historian, who, for the most part, was concerned with depicting a "spirit of Democracy" or chronicling a "crusade" against the French. Since about 1920, however, we have had a proliferation of able studies of the American colonies in the eighteenth century.

Taken collectively, the works of Osgood, Andrews, Beer, Gipson, Dickerson, Labaree, and others of more specialized interests provide an integrated whole of the institutional growth of the colonies within the framework of the imperial system. Behind the scenes politics at Whitehall and Westminister have been probed by studies of the colonial agency, the colonial American in Britain, and the careers of politicians. In the colonial arena, except for substantial studies of social and intellectual development, the emphasis has been on biography and intra-colony affairs. Recently new vistas have been opened in the study of social and political elites and the role of colonial assemblies. The greater use of demographic methods has added a new dimension to colonial life and institutions, although many historians working exclusively in this vineyard have fallen into the very pitfalls – even to a greater degree – as those they lay to the so-called literary historian. Strangely, one of the most slighted aspects of the colonial "middle period" has been in-depth studies of colonial origins of American constitutionalism – and in particular the area of civil liberty.

One significant void in the historiography of the period has been the origins of American federalism in the colonial experience. American union was not created in a vacuum; an important source was the colonial past. If the acceptance of union during the American Revolution appears as a sudden shift from the colonial position only a few years before, it nevertheless was not accidental. A people are prone, after long endurance and experience in certain forms of political association or government, to modify their institutions, and, if need be, to turn to a new order – even if it entails secession or revolution. Colonial responses – negative and positive – to common problems and mutual interests were instructive in the later establishment of union. It is the purpose, therefore, of this study to investigate a major factor contributing to the formation of American union – intercolony cooperative action.

The road to union before 1763 in the practical sense was largely confined to the linking of the colonial governments in external affairs. The direction came naturally from the colonial governors and magistrates, more often than not in response to crown-initiated actions. The colonial assemblies had little vision during this period. Their interests, as is endemic of all legislative bodies, were primarily economic – finances, land, and protection of commerce and industry. They as yet had not made a common cause of grievances with the home government. Collective action among the colonies would be most useful in coordinating measures for defense and war, and hence in this area responsibility was incumbent upon the executives.

I have limited this study to the forms and instances of intercolony cooperation in external affairs and the problems pointing to the need for cooperation. If intercolony cooperative action has a preponderant aura of military affairs about it, it is precisely that it took a sense of crisis and threat to security to arouse the colonies beyond their narrow and selfish interests. What strides were made came mostly through the executive war powers in the colonies, which is not surprising in view of the fact that the creation and expansion of central authority in America since the colonial period has usually occurred at times of stress in war or other emergency.

Quotations from contemporary sources are left as they are except to eliminate raised letters and to extend other shorthand abbreviations where they obstruct readability. Certain quirks of late seventeenth century spelling have been modernized, such as substituting "v" for "u". No attempt has been made to bring dates before 1752 under the Gregorian calander; the only change has been to take January 1 rather than March 25 as the first day of the year.

I am indebted to the staffs of many libraries. Especially I am grateful for the splendid services of the Virginia State and Southern Illinois University Libraries. A grant from the Virginia Society of the Cincinnati through the University of Richmond has helped to defray research expenses.

University of Richmond *H.M.W.*
March, 1971

CONTENTS

"UNITE OR DIE"

Intercolony Relations, 1690–1763

CHAPTER I

IDEAS OF UNION

Early settlers in America discovered the advantages of cooperation for mutual succor and defense. But they also learned that unification of settlements over a broad area required a sustained common interest and an ideological underpinning as well. Although the colonies shied away from the idea of union as the seventeenth century drew to a close, they still sensed the need for some cooperation in meeting common perils and solving problems of intercolonial rivalry. Beyond cooperation for limited emergencies, however, they would not care to go.

Two kinds of union had already been given a trial by the end of the seventeenth century. One had died a natural death and the other was so distasteful that it fomented revolution.

Fear of foreign and Indian neighbors was the catalyst that called into being the first American confederacy, the United Colonies of New England. The most important constitutional idea of the New England Confederacy was the pooling of executive power in external affairs. Almost without exception the Commissioners of the United Colonies consisted of the governors, deputy governors, or other magistrates.

Lasting half a century, the New England Confederation passed through four phases: (1) quasi-sovereignty in the fields of foreign relations and war and peace; (2) constitutional crises and disuse of the confederation, 1653–1672; (3) revival, under a more limited federal compact, which saw the valuable services of the Commissioners as a general council of war; and (4) the unsuccessful re-establishment of the Confederation after the downfall of the Dominion of New England. By 1690, time had run out for a Puritan defensive league; protection of frontier settlements was now a larger inter-regional concern. It was also expected that the crown would take over from the New England Confederation the responsibility of coordinating military action.

The crown-imposed union of the northern colonies of 1685–89 reflected an ignorance of colonial affairs which would plague British policies throughout the colonial period. Attempting to consolidate the colony governments under one administration and to interfere with local powers of taxation and land policy, the Dominion of New England aroused general antagonism throughout New England. Governor Andros's commission and instructions struck at the heart of local self-government by confining all colony powers to an administrative council, without recognizing the right of the people to legislate their own affairs. Such a brash extension of imperial bureaucracy inevitably caused the people of New England to form lines of constitutional defense in behalf of their liberties and to rise in rebellion. The fault for the complete failure of this consolidated union, however, may well be assigned to William III, who, too anxiously seeking good will, readily deferred to the interests of the theocrat party in New England. A distinguished assessor of the Dominion believes that it would have persisted had William III had the foresight to establish a representative assembly and to appoint a more acceptable governor than Andros.[1]

Yet practical necessity continued to dictate the need for cooperation. But could cooperation be institutionalized into union?

Two illusive dilemmas thwarted the road to union. First of all, from the colonial viewpoint, union threatened local liberties. Whereas united action would be attractive in times of crises, in settled times, pooling of authority would be viewed as oppressive. It would take a sustained and general danger, accompanied by demonstrable benefits of centralized authority, before any real measure of American union could be achieved. Meanwhile, intermittent war crises, intercolonial rivalries, and the less tangible factors such as latent nationalism and awareness of separateness from Great Britain would contribute to a desire to experiment with cooperation.

Secondly, a co-ordinate colonial union would be unacceptable to the mother country.[2] The conception of empire in the eighteenth century could have it no other way. The colonies could probably have been prevailed upon to accept a limited union – confederate and regional to deal with emergencies only. Yet British policy consistently distrusted the idea of encouraging any form of colonial union without first bringing complete uniformity of the colonial governments. The home government had the fear, somewhat justified by seventeenth century colonial experience and in particular from violations of acts of trade and navigation, that once set in motion a co-ordinate rather than a consolidated union dependent upon Parliment would tend toward independence.[3]

What was needed was initiative on the part of the crown. Had the British government promoted limited regional unions, which would not offend colonial autonomy, the colonists would probably have raised no objections and there would have been a more efficient exercise of British authority. But the simultaneous uprisings in the colonies as part of the Glorious Revolution and the sense of insecurity of the new monarchy precluded any immediate experiment in imperial union. To avoid stirring up hornet nests, the policy of the British Government would be to leave alone the existing political institutions in the colonies, but it would seek to establish uniform standards in the operation of these institutions, and, if the opportunity presented itself, to royalize the charter and proprietary colonies.[4] The result would be a rapprochement based upon a dichotomy of royal control, principally in external matters, and of colonial legislative authority over internal matters, to last until Parliament in the 1760's would attempt pell-mell to extend its authority over all colonial affairs.

During the 1690's the New England colonies showed a readiness to send commissioners to join with commissioners of other colonies to concert war policy, but they considered the protection of the frontiers from the French and Indians to be the responsibility of the home government. Public opinion prevailed for the re-establishment of a northern union for military purposes only, but one in which the chief burdens would be on England.[5] Jacob Leisler's ill-starred cooperative venture in 1690 underlined the lack of determination of the northern colonies to help their neighbors against the enemy.[6] Yet the colonies theoretically would support the principle of military coordination under royal control until the American Revolution. In 1698 the Privy Council expressed the colonial position when it stated that the charters of the northern colonies prevented anything other than a military union.[7]

To the man who had already advocated a Parliament of Europe goes the honor of being the first person to propose a general union for the colonies. Certainly William Penn was not motivated simply by the need of a central agency to promote harmonious relations among the colonies. Parliament and Privy Council committees were beginning to attack all semi-independent charters,[8] and Penn undoubtedly realized that colonial union would give protection to the colonial charters.

In a hearing before the Board of Trade on December 11, 1696, Penn complained of New York's impost on ships coming from England, and used this opportunity to suggest an intercolonial congress to determine military quotas.[9] At a later hearing on the overall question of maintaining defense on the New York frontier, Penn was asked to put his views in writing.[10] On February 8, 1697 Penn presented his famous *A Briefe and Plaine Scheam* . . . to the Board of Trade. At this time he argued that the chief benefit of union would be the adjustment of civil matters rather than military.[11]

Penn's Plan proposed that the ten colonies send two delegates to meet in New York at least once a year in wartime and two years in peacetime. The presiding officer would be the King's commissioner, who would be commander in chief of colonial levies against a common enemy. Among broad powers of the intercolonial congress were: (1) jurisdiction over debtors fleeing a colony; (2) apprehending fugitives from justice; (3) preventing discrimination in colonial commerce; and (4) finding means to support the union and to protect it against the common enemy. Lacking in the Plan was specific authority to levy troops and to tax the colonies for their support. Penn's Plan fell on deaf ears, largely because the Board of Trade was preparing to unite the military command of the northern colonies. Penn, however, continued to work for greater comity among the colonies.[12]

In 1698 two other writers turned their thoughts to furthering American unity. After a visit to Governors Bellomont of New York and Nicholson of Virginia to secure backing for his reclaiming public office in New Hampshire, the erstwhile merchant, John Usher, addressed a long letter to William Blathwayt. Usher called for two regional unions of the northern colonies to provide for defense and promote commerce. The New England colonies were to be formed into one government, and New York, Pennsylvania, and the Jerseys would constitute the other. Although Usher did not spell out particulars, he apparently sought to restore the Dominion of New England. Usher's views may be taken simply as those of a frustrated placeman.[13]

Sir Charles D'Avenant, whom Herbert L. Osgood called "the ablest politico-economic writer of the time,"[14] published in London his *Discourses on the Publick Revenues, and on the Trade of England.* D'Avenant proposed both an intercolonial council of trade appointed by Parliament and a national assembly for the northern colonies. Since the colonists had hazarded their lives in coming to America, D'Avenant thought their rights should be left intact. The stronger the colonies would grow, he pointed out, "the more they would benefit the crown and the kingdom; and nothing but such an arbitrary power as shall make them desperate can bring them to rebel."

D'Avenant's main concern was the problem of piracy and breach of trade and navigation acts in the colonies. An intercolonial council, therefore, "can watch that matters relating to our traffick be not neglected or betrayed by our ministers abroad and that important points be not lost for want of courage to assert the interest of England in foreign courts." He suggested that the council "be impowered to correspond with the king's ministers abroad and from time to time to receive an account how the posture of our trade stands and upon what foot we deal with the respective nations where they reside." The proliferation of colonies should be halted, and the mutual dependence of the colonies economically should be encouraged. He thought Americans would not turn to manufacturing for another three or four hundred years. Essentially a mercantilist, D'Avenant felt that leaving the colonists alone in their natural political and economic growth would serve British interests in the long run.[15]

D'Avenant also accepted in essence the provisions of the Penn Plan which he had seen before drawing up his own observations on a national assembly. No proponent of union examined the nature and necessity of such an assembly as did D'Avenent, who considered the preservation and character of the empire at stake.

> What we propose is thus: That their first model of future government should be framed here; that afterwards they may have power to make for themselves such laws as they shall think needful for their better polity; and these laws thus enacted among them, not to be rescinded but by authority of parliament in England.
>
> Without doubt, it would be a great incitement to their industry, and render them more pertinacious in their defence, upon any invasion which may happen, to find themselves a free people and governed by constitutions of their own making.
>
> . . . .
>
> For which reasons, [D'Avenant's reasons for mixed government are omitted here] if it should be thought convenient to set afoot the national assembly here proposed for the northern colonies, early care must be taken to put a stop to the growth of faction, for if that be suffered to reign, it will, in process of time, render what was intended for their good, a burthen to the country.
>
> With good government it is not improbable but that these colonies may become hereafter great nations; upon which account it seems of importance to give them, in their infancy, such politic institutions as may preserve them for many ages in wealth, peace and safety; and in order to [do] this, the nearer they are brought to the model of the English government, will undoubtedly be the better.
>
> These national assemblies, the use of which are here recommended for our northern colonies, will be of little benefit, unless the people, by whose voices they must be chosen, can be kept from being corrupted in their elections; for otherwise they will prove but a false appearance of freedom, which is the worst kind of slavery.
>
> . . . .
>
> And all these points have been here handled, with a design to show, that if it should be thought expedient to regulate the constitutions of the Northern Colonies, and to give them power to govern their affairs

> by a national assembly; they who form a model of this kind, should take care to propose methods of correcting the manners of the people, the mending of which has at all times, and in all free countries, produced wise and just National Assemblies, and in such there have been always reared up able ministers; and from statesmen of that kind there may continually be expected a steady and safe administration, wherein faction shall be rooted out; for the progress of the cure is by the same steps as the disease first grew upon the body politic.[16]

Robert Livingston, leader of the Albany faction in New York politics and the colony's Secretary for Indian Affairs, suggested a tripartite union in his letter to the Board of Trade on May 13, 1701.[17] Livingston's proposal shows the colonial concern for frontier defense and for regional entity. He recommended "that one form of government be established in all the neighboring Colonies on this main Continent." For general administration the colonies should be grouped into "three distinct governments, – to wit, That Virginia and Maryland be annexed to South and North Carolina" and "That some part of Connecticut, New York, East and West Jersey, Pennsylvania and New Castle be added together and that to Massachusetts be added New Hampshire and Rhoad Island and the rest of Connecticut." Quotas of money would be assigned to the colonies to be raised by the local governments, and they would be in effect for a ten year period. Livingston did not spell out particulars. Nevertheless his plan indicates the colonial viewpoint of the time.

The anonymous author (a Virginian and probably Robert Beverley) of *An Essay Upon the Government of the English Plantations on the Continent of America* (London: 1701) contemplated a more national union of the colonies than did previous plans.[18] Among the recommendations were: (1) elimination of proprietary and charter governments and all colonies be made royal colonies; (2) proportionate representation in the general assembly (Virginia, 4; Maryland, 3; New York, 2; Boston, 3; Connecticut, 2; Rhode Island, 2; Pennsylvania, 1; Carolinas and the Jerseys, 1 each); (3) meetings rotated among five towns; and (4) the Governor of the colony where the meeting was held to represent the King. This plan reflected the heated controversy in England at the time over the abolition of the charters of non-royal colonies.

At the end of Queen Anne's War crown officials in America detected the rise of disintegrating forces and became all the more aware that any unification would not come from a colonial impetus. Governor Robert Hunter of New York wrote Secretary St. John that

> the frequent tumults in all parts, and the general aversion to the support of government in most, are sufficient indications that you are pleased to hint of putting all North America under one Uniform plan

> of government, would most certainly be a Sure remedy, but I am afraid it is too lingering a one for the present exigency; the purchasing proprietary governments and taking away usurpations being a work of time and trouble.[19]

That provincial upstart, Colonel Caleb Heathcote, who became surveyor-general of the customs for the northern department of North America in 1715, called upon the British government to void all the charter privileges of the American colonies, to be followed by a consolidate administrative grouping of the colonies. The colonies should bear a customs and excise revenue that would cover the cost of the civil service and of ships assigned to protect the ports. The crown would have control of raising and dispensing this revenue. Thus "all the Governors, & other officers" would "Receive their Bread, & support, from the Hands of the King, without a slavish dependence for it, on the uncertain Humours of assemblys. . . ."[20]

During this period the main efforts of British policy to bring about uniform government in the colonies were concentrated in *quo warranto* proceedings and attempts to secure an act of Parliament to abolish the charters of the corporate and proprietary colonies.[21] Had this attack succeeded, undoubtedly some form of imperial union, if only for military purposes, would have been imposed on the colonies. Indeed, the Board of Trade recognized the royalization of all the colonies as the basis for effective union.[22] Anticipating this possibility, the Board of Trade in 1721, as requested by the king, drew up an elaborate report for a comprehensive union of all the colonies from Nova Scotia to South Carolina. Since John Dalyrimple, a Scottish peer and second Earl of Stair, was offered the post of Captain General under this scheme, the proposal is referred to as the Earl of Stair Plan. Actually, the Earl of Stair probably had little to do with framing it.[23]

Like earlier plans, the Earl of Stair Plan provided for a representative of the crown as the chief administrative officer, assisted by a council, which would hardly be more than a committee of the colonies. Thus " the said captain-general should be constantly attended by two or more councillors deputed from each plantation, he should have a fixed salary, sufficient to support the dignity of so important an employment, independent of the pleasure of the inhabitants . . . ." The General Council would levy taxes and quotas of men on the colonies "in proportion to their respective abilities." It could also establish a postal system, build forts, and regulate colonial trade. The Captain General could appoint all officers of a standing army, whom the crown would commission; remove officers of the colonial militia for cause; command and move militia from one colony to another; suspend governors for cause; and advise the Board of Trade on colonial affairs. The crown could create a navy, supported by the central government and to be commanded by the Captain General. No colonial governor could assume office without royal approval. The chief difference between this plan and others, as O.M. Dickerson has noted, is that the governor-general would occupy the same position to the whole of the colonies as the governors to each colony. Because it was patterned after the government of the Leeward Islands, it was unrealistic for the conditions in America.[24]

Daniel Coxe, son of a wealthy New Jersey proprietor and a Councilor, Superior Court Judge, and Anglican leader in the colony, published in 1722 a treatise on the imperial designs of France in the New World. The preface to *A Description of the English Province of Carolina, by the Spaniards called Florida, and by the French La Louisiane,* details a plan of union. Coxe proposed that "all the Colonies appertaining to the Crown of Great Britain on the Northern Continent of America, be United under a Legal, Regular, and firm Establishment," and that a "lieutenant, or Supreme Governor" be appointed to "Preside on the Spot, to whom the Governors of each Colony shall be Subordinate." Two deputies were to be elected annually by the council and assembly of each colony, "who are to be in the nature of a great council or general convention of the states of the colonies." Although each assembly should levy and raise its own quota of men or money for the "mutual defence", the grand council was to set the quotas, subject to the veto of the governor-general.[25] Coxe's plan did not differ substantially from previous plans, and is in accord with what one would expect from an official of a royal colony.

Standing apart from the plans of union mentioned thus far was the proposal of Martin Bladen, a member of the Board of Trade, submitted to Walpole on December 27, 1739.[26] He thought a two-house legislature should constitute the intercolonial assembly. The upper house should consist of crown-appointed councilors and the lower house of popularly elected delegates. Massachusetts, Nova Scotia, and all the colonies south of New York were to have two councilors and four representatives; Rhode Island, Connecticut, and New Hampshire one half this number. New York, the seat of government, would have four councilors and eight burgesses. The chief benefit of such a union would be military. If the colonies continued

> in the State they are in, divided into so many different Provinces, spread over so immense a Tract of Land, as that from Cape Canso to the River of Saint Mattheo; no less than Fifteen hundred Miles in length, in perpetual Contest with each other, upon the Subject of their Trade and Boundarys; Ruled by so many various Forms of Government; so little concerned for each others Prosperity, and as

> devoid of all Care for the Welfare of the whole, as if they were not the Subjects of the same Prince; a much less force, than their own, might be able to destroy them; A Force that would not dare to meet them, once United in the Field.

The "Plantation Parliament" at New York therefore should

> advise and consult, upon such Methods, to raise such Supplys, and such Number of Forces, from time to time, as may be necessary for the Security and Defence of the said Plantations, And also to Enact such Laws as shall be agreed on by Common Consent, according to the Custom of British Parliaments, for the General Welfare and Advantage. And it is humbly conceived that such an Institution, can never be deemed a violation of the Privileges, granted to the Proprietary or Charter Governments; because within their respective Precincts, their Several Patents would still retain their full effect.

There would also be other advantages of union. The Captain General would be the eyes and ears of the King, sending agents into the colonies to report on the administration of the governors and the "Dispositions of the People."

> He will soon learn to distinguish, between the private Views of particular Colonys, and the Welfare of the whole, between the Interest of America, and that of Great Britain. To dissuade the Planters from the persuit of Manufactures detrimental to their Mother Country, and to direct their Industry to the Improvement of Naval Stores, and of such other Products, as may be profitable to them, and convenient for Us. And above all, to engage them to pay more Respect to the orders of the Crown, more Regard to the Laws of Trade and Navigation, then they have hitherto done . . . .[27]

Archibald Kennedy, who eventually succeeded to a Scottish earldom, came to America about 1715 and became active in the public affairs of New York, most notably as collector of customs and receiver general. As a land speculator he was concerned with the need of preserving the Iroquois alliance. In 1751 he published in New York *The Importance of Gaining and Preserving the Friendship of the Indians to the British Interest, Considered,* which was reprinted in London the following year. "It is high time," said Kennedy, "we should look to our own security, and most unnatural to expect that we should hang for ever upon the breasts of our mother-country." Kennedy wanted to institutionalize the military quota system, which the colonists had never taken seriously. He proposed "That a number of commissioners from all the colonies be appointed to meet yearly" at New York or Albany to fix quotas to be ratified by Parliament. They would also superintend frontier security.[28] In order to stem corruption in Indian affairs and prevent colonial rivalries, Kennedy advocated the appointment of a superintendent of Indian affairs and a smith and two apprentices to be attached to each tribe to teach Indian youths the English language and to supervise the distribution of supplies – both ideas later materialized in the creation of an Indian superintendency by the crown and in the "Plan of 1764". Kennedy hoped that a unification in the administration of military and Indian affairs would have the double benefit of striking fear among the French and securing control of the fur trade for the English.[29]

Before publication, Kennedy submitted his essay to Cadwallader Colden[30] and Benjamin Franklin[31] for their reaction. Both men drew up a lengthy commentary.

Colden confined his remarks to an evaluation of the priority and problems of maintaining the Iroquois alliance. Like Kennedy, he was troubled by the jealousies of the colonies over the Indian trade and the lack of cooperation of the neighboring colonies of New York to share in the burdens of frontier defense. Colden endorsed the specific Indian reforms suggested by Kennedy. But he also linked the cost of defense to a reform of tariff policies. The revenue from a universal impost, such as a tax on importation of wine, could be applied to the frontier costs. Additional revenue should be raised proportionately by the colonies themselves, which required the pressures from "some superior authority."[32]

Franklin agreed with Kennedy and Colden on the emergency nature of Indian and frontier affairs. But he went further in recommending a union of "the several Governments, so as to form a Strength that the Indians may depend on for Protection, in Case of a Rupture with the French; or apprehend great Danger from, if they should break with us." Such a union, Franklin added, could not be attained through the reliance upon cooperation of the governors,[33] who were often on bad terms with each other and would be unwilling or unable to get a legislature to vote appropriations entailed by a union. A viable union could best be formed by the colonies sending men "in the Nature of Ambassadors" to the other colonies, where "they would have the Opportunity of pressing the Affair both in publick and private, obviating Difficulties as they arise, answering Objections as soon as they are made, before they spread and gather Strength in the Minds of the People . . . ." Thus in 1751–2 Franklin favored "a voluntary Union entered into by the Colonies themselves," but at the Albany Congress he thought a plan of union by the colonies should receive the sanction of Parliament. Franklin had no objection to Kennedy's specific proposals. Near the end of his letter of commentary Franklin shirked off the opportunity for a further critique by saying that "I wish I could offer any Thing for the Improvement of the Author's Piece, but I have little Knowledge, and less Experience in these Matters."[34]

In 1752 Governor Dinwiddie of Virginia urged the Lords of Trade to establish two separate confederacies, north and south.[35] Indeed it may be surmised that by the time the Albany Congress opened in 1754, the prevalent thinking of the colonists embraced the idea of regional unions for defense. This may also be ascertained from the other plans presented at the Congress other than Franklin's and the failure of the colonies to ratify a plan of general union.[36] The colonial position in 1754 was not unlike that of 1690.

In response to the threat of war in the New World and the promptings of colonial governors, the Board of Trade in September 1753 sent a circular letter to the Governors of New York, Virginia, Maryland, Pennsylvania, New Jersey, New Hampshire, and Massachusetts requesting that they send commissioners to a meeting at Albany with the Iroquois. The southernmost colonies of the two Carolinas and Georgia were not invited. Virginia and New Jersey refused to send delegates. Lieutenant Governor De Lancey, of New York, upon the death of Governor Sir Danvers Osborne, had the task of organizing the conference. De Lancey invited two additional colonies, Connecticut and Rhode Island, and stated the purpose of the meeting would include drawing up a plan for defense against the French and the Indians.[37] The work of the Albany Conference in Indian and military affairs will be treated in later chapters. Here we are concerned with the Plan of Union and the reasons for the failure to ratify it.

While Franklin had drawn up his "Short Hints" on the way to Albany, other commissioners also had their suggestions for union. It is difficult, and virtually impossible, to determine if any of the commissioners had any influence on Franklin's original plan. L.H. Gipson and Leonard Labaree have fairly well exhausted the pros and cons of Thomas Hutchinson's self-alleged authorship of the main features of the Albany Plan. It is generally agreed that Franklin "projected" an original scheme and had a predominant role in putting the plan into final form.[38]

On June 24, five days after the opening of the conference, a committee was established to "prepare and receive Plans or Schemes" for a union "and to digest them into one general plan for the inspection of this Board."[39] On the same afternoon the committee drew up its own "Short Hints", which were reported in the handwriting of Meshech Weare, who was apparently a disinterested member of the Congress.[40] The essential differences between Franklin's "Short Hints" and those of the committee, except for spelling out provisions in Franklin's outline, were that the committee substituted "A General Union of the British Colonies on the Continent" for Franklin's "scheme for uniting the Northern Colonies", and, while Franklin mentioned that members of the Grand Council were to be chosen by the assemblies, the committee more ambiguously stated that members were to be "at least Chosen by the Representatives of each Colony in Assembly." On July 9 Franklin was directed to draw up the plan as now agreed upon by the committee. The following morning he presented the final draft to the Congress, whereupon after some deliberation it was resolved that the Plan of Union be laid before "their respective constituents for their consideration."[41] The final document called for union of eleven colonies, omitting Delaware, Georgia, and Nova Scotia.[42]

The Albany Plan[43] opens with a "residual powers" clause intended to safeguard the colonial constitutions, which, along with a similar statement towards the end of the document were not in the committee's "Short Hints." The opening clause also reflects Franklin's change of mind in asking for a Parliamentary imposed union rather than a voluntary one, which he earlier had advocated.[44] It reads as follows:

> THAT humble Application be made for an Act of Parliament of Great Britain, by Virtue of which, one General Government may be formed in America, including all the said Colonies, within and under which Government, each Colony may retain its present Constitution, except in the Particulars wherein a Change may be directed by the said Act, as hereafter follows.

A similar clause towards the end reads: "That the Particular Military as well as Civil Establishments in each Colony remain in their present State, this General Constitution Notwithstanding."

The union would consist of a President General, named and supported by the crown, and a Grand Council elected by the colonial assemblies. The Grand Council would have forty-eight delegates, on a proportionate basis: Massachusetts and Virginia, 7; Pennsylvania, 6; Connecticut, 5; New York, Maryland, and each Carolina, 4; New Jersey, 3; New Hampshire and Rhode Island, 2. The amount of representation would be based upon the proportion of funds anticipated from a colony – hence this principle was a departure from the unit representation of previous plans going back to the New England Confederation.

Meetings were to be annual, while the written consent of seven members could call an emergency session of the Grand Council. Members would be paid ten shillings per diem during sessions and journeying to and from. All legislation required the assent of the President General, who was also charged with the execution of the laws. The proposed federal government could regulate the Indian trade, make Indian treaties, make peace or war with the Indians, regulate purchases of land and settlement on the frontier,

> raise and pay Soldiers, and build Forts for the Defence of any of the Colonies, and equip Vessels of Force to Guard the Coasts and Protect the Trade on the Ocean, Lakes, or Great Rivers; But they shall not Impress Men in any Colonies, without the Consent of its Legislature. That for these purposes they have Power to make Laws And lay and Levy such General Duties, Imposts, or Taxes, as to them shall appear most equal and Just, Considering the Ability and other Circumstances of the Inhabitants in the Several Colonies, and such as may be Collected with the least Inconvenience to the People, rather discouraging Luxury, than Loading Industry with unnecessary Burthens.

All military commisions "under this General Constitution" were to be nominated by the President General, but the appointments required the approbation of the Grand Council.

At least three distinct plans came to the attention of the Albany delegates other than the Franklin plan and its subsequent amendments. The Reverend Richard Peters of Pennsylvania presented "A Plan for a General Union of the British Colonies of North America," which proposed that the continental colonies be organized into four geographical divisions, with each contributing to a "union regiment," to be maintained by colonial excise taxes and commanded by officers appointed by the crown.[45] The two plans in the handwriting of Johnathan Trumbull may have been composed after the Albany Plan had been approved by the Congress or were simply copies of plans written by Thomas Hutchinson. The main difference from the Albany Plan was that they proposed only a northern union of the New England colonies and New York and New Jersey. One of the plans states that the President General shall be "The Governour of the Province of the Massachusetts–Bay for the Time being. . . ." Unlike the Albany Plan, both curiously refer to the proposed union as the "The United Colonies", which, with much of the language in the documents, suggests shades of the New England Confederation.[46]

Thomas Pownall, an official observer for the Lords of Trade and not a member of the Congress, submitted at the last session "Considerations toward a General Plan of Measures for the Colonies."[47] William Johnson read a paper on "measures necessary to be taken with the Six Nations for defeating the designs of the French."[48] Both plans were concerned with military cooperation rather than union.

It was a foregone conclusion that the colonies would not themselves accept the Albany Plan – a lack of faith of the delegates in this possibility accounts in large measure for the insertion of the clause that Parliament would have to set it in motion. Yet, after unanimously adopting the Plan, the Congress ordered that no copy of it was to be sent to Parliament. This contradiction of seeking reliance upon Parliament and at the same time refusing it a due respect would make virtually any imperial union impossible and perhaps may be viewed as the first shift towards the protest movement denying Parliamentary authority of the next decade.

It is highly probable that the colonies would have accepted the plan of union on a regional basis – namely, at least three regional groupings of those colonies sharing a common frontier: New England, the Middle colonies, and the Southern colonies.[49] Such regional unions would have met the objections of colonies who feared their men and taxes would be drawn off to defend a frontier in which they had no interest. The two proprietaries, in any event, would have posed the chief obstacles, but, with the insecurity of the Maryland and Pennsylvania charters and mounting popular opposition to the proprietors' rights at a time when the French were invading the Ohio Valley, these two colonies could probably have been brought easily into line. Perhaps the provisions on limiting westward expansion and the broad taxing powers would have had to be softened.

No colonial legislature ratified the document. Although there was dismay from some leaders over the total inattention to the Plan, the reason is not hard to explain when the particularistic objections abounding in the colonial records are noted. Briefly, specific criticism may be listed as follows:

1) a union of councils deemed better than actual union (Mass.)[50]
2) lack of currency in the colonies for taxation (N.J.)[51]
3) "affect our Constitution in its very Vitals"[52]
4) colonial interest in defense, Indian alliance, and regulation of fur trade rather than in union [53]
5) the smaller colonies underrepresented (R.I.)[54]
6) the commissioners betrayed their trust by not committing themselves to any Plan[55]
7) if union were feasible, it could be put into effect by the assemblies rather than by Parliament (Colden)[56]
8) no authority of the commissioners to conclude union (Colden)[57]
9) objection to President General's veto (Conn.)[58]
10) fear territory and population too large for single administration (Mass.)[59]

In instructions to its agent in London, the Massachusetts House of Representatives in December 1754 regarded the Plan of Union as a violation of constitutional rights:

> Several objections were made against the plan, which appeared to be of weight with many of the members of the Court; such as the perpetuity of the proposed union, the great sway which the Southern Colonies would have in all the determinations of the grand council &c.

> But the great and prevailing reason urged against it, was, that in its operation, it would be subversive of the most valuable rights and liberties of the several colonies included in it; as a new civil Government is thereby proposed to be established over them, with great and extraordinary powers to be exercised in times of peace as well as war; such as those of making Laws to be of force in all the Colonies; building forts and ships of war, and purchasing lands at discretion; and for these purposes raising monies from the several colonies in such sums and in such a manner, as the President and Council shall think fit. These powers are in the judgment of the two houses inconsistent with the fundamental rights of those Colonies and would be destructive of our happy constitution.[60]

Of interest is that the plan appears to have been endorsed by some of the colonial councils, which again emphasizes the notion, going back to the days of the New England Confederation, that union involves the linking of executive powers. The Massachusetts Council actually instructed its agent in England "to take the proper Steps for obtaining an Act of Parliament wherby the union proposed in this plan may be carried into Execution . . . ."[61] At least one politician, Chief Justice Stephen Hopkins of Rhode Island, made the Albany Plan a political football. An ardent champion of colonial unity, in his speechmaking he baited the commissioners and the Legislature for doing nothing in regard to the Plan, and won the governorship.[62]

Meanwhile, five days before the Albany Congress began, the Board of Trade directed Secretary Robinson to prepare a "Plan of general concert" for the mutual defense of the continental colonies to be submitted to the governors.[63] The "Plan for the Union of the Colonies" was completed and sent to the king on August 9, 1754. It represents the desire of the home government for a union for military purposes rather than for political federation.[64] The plan would require the colonial governors to appoint commissioners, nominated by the assemblies, to agree upon a military establishment to maintain forts and men on the frontier. Using as a guide colonial expenditures of twenty years past, the commissioners were to make the proper apportionment of charges upon the colonies. The crown would appoint a commander in chief, who would also be commissary general for Indian affairs. The intercolonial assembly could be re-convened in time of emergency.[65] In proposing only a military union, this plan differed from the Albany Plan. Both, however, in G.L. Beer's words, "started from the premise that the colonies should in equity provide for their own regularly established military system."[66] The only feature of the plan that the Board of Trade accepted was the suggestion to send a commander in chief to the colonies. The reasons for the rejection of the major part of the plan was perhaps two-fold: (1) a recognition of the necessity of delay before a union could be established;[67] (2) the difficulty in getting such a measure passed because of the personal enmity between the President of the Board, Lord Halifax, and the head of the ministry, the Duke of Newcastle.[68]

The colonies fell back to the old and tried procedure of concerting action in time of danger through a council of commissioners. The schemes of the Board of Trade had been unimaginative and the colonies lacked the will to create a union. It may also be said that colonial union was killed through leniency on the part of the home government. The colonists sought to shift responsibility for the conduct of war to the crown, and the invitation was accepted. The British government in the last intercolonial war adopted policies of reimbursing the colonies for expenses incurred in the war, putting colonial troops on the royal payroll, and paying for provisions for royal troops in America. The crown thus took over the lion's share of financial responsibility.[69] The British government could well have attempted to establish a permanent fund for colonial defense to which the colonies could have been required to contribute. Having missed the opportunity during the last two colonial wars, after 1763 it would be too late.

A general fund maintained by the colonies was not a new idea. Among earlier advocates of this view was Sir William Keith, Governor of Pennsylvania, who in 1728 recommended to the Board of Trade that all the crown's civil officers be appointed and held accountable to the Board, that a First Lord Commissioner have daily access to the King, and that a Commissioner as Treasurer be in charge of all colonial rents, customs, revenues, and profits. All surplus revenue should then be applied to purchasing proprietary lands, building forts, and extending settlements to the Great Lakes. Keith even favored Parliament extending the English Stamp Act to the colonies.[70]

Archibald Cummings, surveyor and searcher at the port of Boston, suggested in 1723 the levying of universal taxes upon the colonies by Parliament, such as stamp duties, import duties on West Indian products, an excise tax on rum made in the colonies, and a tax on unimproved land. The revenue would help to support a military establishment of some six thousand troops in America.[71] Governor Horatio Sharpe of Maryland thought along the same lines in 1754 when he mentioned a duty on imported liquors and a poll tax as possible schemes for intercolonial cooperation in taxation.[72]

Although colonial governors were urged to work for the establishment of a general fund in the colonies,[73] there was little they could do with the legislatures adhering to selfish and particularistic interests. Nevertheless Governor Shirley did some serious thinking on the matter. He noted in early 1755 that since King George's War the lack of cooperation of other colonies had convinced him of "the necessity not only of a Parliamentary Union, but taxation, for the preservation of His Majesty's dominions upon this Continent, which the several Assemblies have in so great a measure abandon'd the defence of . . . ."[74] Shirley also thought it expedient to have members of colonial councils and all the governors meet in a general assembly, which would be empowered to draw upon the British treasury for funds for colonial defense, which in turn would be raised through a Parliamentary tax on the colonies.[75] Also advocating a colonial general fund was Governor Dinwiddie of Virginia, who recommended an "Act of Parliament to oblige each Colony to raise by a Pole tax of 1S. St'g, or otherways, a proportionate Quota of a Gen'l Sum, to be applied to the pres't Exigency . . . ."[76] Governor Clinton and Cadwallader Colden were among others who favored a general fund supported by Parliament levying import duties.[77]

Arguing from the premise of virtual representation, William McCulloch's pamphlet, published in London (1757), presented a case for colonial responsibility in raising a general fund:

> The Colonies . . . are to be considered with respect to each other as so many independent States; yet they ought to be considered as one with respect to their Mother Country, being under the Protection of the Legislature, and in some Degree in the Character of Wards, or those under the Protection of Guardians; and altho' many Persons in the Colonies have often insisted that they have no proper Representative here, yet this Plea may with equal Reason be urged by many Men of Fortune in this Kingdom; but as both there and here such Persons enjoy the Privileges of Subjects, and the Protection of Laws, they are indispensably bound to conform their Conduct to the Rules and Principles prescribed to them by the Laws and Constitution of this Kingdom.

Therefore, every person in the colonies, age 14–60, should pay a poll tax, 18d. per head, which would yield about £ 50,000 per annum. A commissioner should be appointed to superintend the raising of this revenue. "Bills of Union" would be issued, and would contribute to the paying of provincial troops. Thus the colonies would be united for military and financial purposes.[78]

Nothing new was added to the dialogue on colonial union from 1755 to 1763. It can be said that the watchwords were simply "union of councils", to borrow Governors Shirley's and Clinton's often used phrase, and regional cooperation for mutual defense. The several plans broached by colonists in these few years sounded like old hat. For example, an anonymous plan published in the *Pennsylvania Journal* in 1757 called "for forming a triple Union of our Colonies in North America, in order to retrieve our Losses, and prevent the like for the future." The three divisions would be: (1) Nova Scotia, New England, New York, and New Jersey; (2) Pennsylvania, Maryland, Virginia; and (3) North Carolina, South Carolina, and Georgia. This arrangement would make "three different and distinct Countries" because of the natural boundaries, mutual enemy, and respective climate, soil, and products.[79] In "Questions relating to the Union and Government of the Plantations" enclosed in a letter to the Archbishop of Canterbury in 1760 from Philanglus Americanus [Dr. Samuel Johnson?], we find a proposal to establish a "Vice Roi, or Lord Lieutenant" for the colonies to reside in New York. Each colony would send a delegate each from its assembly and council

> to represent and consult whatever may contribute to the union stability and good of the whole, – Something in the nature of the Amphictyons of the ancient States of Greece? Here the common affairs of war, trade &c might be considered and the confirming or negativing the Laws passed in each government, and the result to be confirmed or negatived by the King.

The author also advised Parliament to provide for one medium of currency in the colonies. He acknowledged the possibility of union leading toward independence, but this could be counteracted by inculcating a stronger fear of God and honor of the King.[80]

If the colonists were not taking the idea of union seriously, the same could be said for the British ministry. Perhaps William Pitt's remarks illustrate the lightness which the matter now assumed. Pitt proposed that Canada might be erected into a kingdom for Prince Edward and possibly another kingdom from the colonies. Such an arrangement would be more natural than the Bourbon family compact because here would be found "the union of two peoples of the same blood, religion, polity, language, laws, honour and genius under the same family."[81]

During the 1760's it was generally acknowledged by the crown servants in America that any cooperative union among the colonies was not in the interests of the empire. Governor Bernard best summed up this viewpoint: "There is in my opinion no System of Government in North America that is fit to be made a module of. The royal Governments are faulty in their constitution .... If therefore there should be a new establishment of the governments in North America upon a true English constitutional bottom, it must be upon a new plan ...."[82]

Before the parting of the way in the 1760's, in view of the growth of colonial legislative right over domestic concerns, it might have been a wise policy for the British government to have offered the colonists representation in Parliament. Benjamin Franklin in 1754 supported the idea provided that the colonies would have "a reasonable number of Representatives" and "that all the old Acts of Parliament restraining the trade or cramping the manufactures of the Colonies, be at the same time repealed, and the British Subjects on this side the water put, in those respects, on the same footing with those in Great Britain, 'till the new Parliament, representing the whole, shall think it for the interest of the whole to re-enact some or all of them." Franklin seems to have been inspired by an ideal of an Atlantic community of Anglo-Americans.

> I think too, that the government of the Colonies by a Parliament, in which they are fairly represented, would be vastly more agreeable to the people, than the method lately attempted to be introduced by Royal Instructions, as well as more agreeable to the nature of an English Constitution, and to English Liberty; and that such laws as now seem to bear hard on the Colonies, would (when judged by such a Parliament for the best interest of the whole) be more chearfully submitted to, and more easily executed.
>
> I hope too, that by such an union, the people of Great Britain and the people of the Colonies would learn to consider themselves, not as belonging to different Communities with different Interests, but to one Community with one Interest, which I imagine would contribute to strengthen the whole, and greatly lessen the danger of future separations.[83]

But, if the colonists were not attracted to the idea of a national assembly, they would hardly favor representation in Parliament. Minority bloc representation in Parliament would be as disadvantageous as having a general assembly subject to the veto of the crown. Yet such a gesture by the home government might have opened the door to fruitful discussion and have gained the respect of the colonies for the intentions of the mother country. As it was, a form of group representation which had characterized other empires in history – the colonial agents in London – had to suffice as quasi-representation to the central government. Agents appeared jointly before the Board of Trade but they pleaded separate causes.[84]

Although the colonial agency does not come within the purview of this study, had the British government seen fit to institutionalize it into a general representative body of the colonists, thereby making it less of a foreign service, some of the constitutional stress that was to lead to

Revolution might have been alleviated. British authorities accepted and even desired colonial agents in England, but they were to make the mistake of trying to control the agency in the fitful decade before the Revolution. Ironically, as a sense of nationality began to appear, Americans pinned less hopes on their agents.

Instead of developing a means for a central representation for the colonies, the British government would soon turn to a far-reaching mercentilism, economic and political. By preserving the colonies as an agricultural region and opening up new regions for settlement, the colonies could be fitted more tightly into an imperial frame. Though the abolition of the proprietary and corporate colony charters was still considered too drastic a step, the colonial governments would be made more dependent on the crown. There would be more stringent enforcement of trade regulations, efforts to make the colonial governors independent of the assemblies, such as a fixed civil list, and an imperial military establishment.[85]

An extensive imperialization of colonial affairs, however, would force the British government to face manifold problems,[86] that to be dealt with squarely would be expensive and would necessitate widespread reform, for which, as time was to prove, the British government would not make an all out effort.

Yet 1763 was a year even more ripe for establishing a union of the colonies than ever before. Intangible factors of union – American pride, consciousness of cultural identity, a rising sense of isolation from Old World problems, prosperity, increased population and mobility, improved communications – were discernible. Fearing the birth of an independence movement, British policy made no efforts to bring the colonies together, which was a blunder since the colonies might have responded to imperial direction of union. Imperial union would have been more beneficial to the mother country than if the colonies were to discover union on their own. Failure to promote union under imperial auspices was compounded by an even worse mistake, namely the negative policies of treading on colonial liberties evolved over a century and a half. James Otis in 1761 and Richard Bland in 1764 appeared as harbingers to remind England of the separateness of the American condition – with the message not sinking in until the Revolution.

By 1763 the colonies were on the threshold of going beyond envisaging union as merely an intercolonial senate, where commissioners would consult as ambassadors plenipotentiary of their respective colonies. The colonies were ready to explore means of institutionalizing a representative consensus that would be subject to no other authority than the right of representation claimed by His Majesty's subjects on the condition of their migrating to the New World.

NOTES

[1] Viola F. Barnes, *The Dominion of New England*, reprint ed. (New York 1960), 275.

[2] See Harold M. Baer, "The Equality of States as a Theory of Britain and America: Imperial Structure at the Time of the American Revolution" (unpubl. Ph.D. diss., Harvard University, 1925).

[3] Louis F. Koontz, *Robert Dinwiddie* (Glendale, Calif., 1941), 22–23.

[4] Lawrence H. Leder, "The Glorious Revolution and the Pattern of Imperial Relationships," *New York History* XLVI (1965), 203–11.

[5] Gov. Fletcher to the Earl of Nottingham, Feb. 14, 1693, *CSP*, XIV, 23. New England, Virginia, and New Jersey agents on Jan. 25, 1697 requested the Board of Trade to establish a northern military union under one governor, as realized in the appointment of Gov. Bellomont. Herbert L. Osgood, *The American Colonies in the Eighteenth Century*, 4 vols., reprint ed. (Gloucester, Mass., 1958), I, 267–68.

[6] See later chapters for the ill-success of intercolonial cooperative action under Leisler's leadership.

[7] See Everett Kimball, *The Public Life of Joseph Dudley,1660–1715 [Harvard Historical Studies*, XV (New York, 1911)], 68ff.

[8] Catherine O. Peare, *William Penn*, reprinted. (Ann Arbor, 1966), 327-28.

[9] See Alison G. Olson, "William Penn, Parliament, and Proprietary Government," *WMQ*, 3d Ser., XVIII (1961), 176–95; "William Penn's Observations on the Proceedings of Governor Fletcher," *NJA*, 1st Ser., II (1881), 132.

[10] In Aug. 1694 an Order in Council restored Penn to his Proprietorship, but denied his military commission. W. Hepworth Dixon, *A History of William Penn* (New York, 1902), 264.

[11] A good analysis of Penn's scheme is found in Edward C. Beatty, *William Penn as a Social Philosopher* (New York, 1939), 86–90. The plan is printed in numerous places, e.g., *NYCD*, IV, 296–97; *CSP*, XV, 354–55; *HSP Memoirs*, VI 264–65; *PMHB*, XI (1887), 495–96; and H. E. Egerton, *Federations and Union within the British Empire* (Oxford, 1911), 112–13.

[12] See later chapters; also Edwin B. Bronner, *William Penn's Holy Experiment* (New York, 1962), 220–21.

[13] See Margaret Kinard, ed., "John Usher's Report on the Northern Colonies, 1698 [Letter of John Usher to William Blathwayt, Sep. 19, 1698]," *WMQ*, 3d Ser., VII (1950), 95–106.

[14] Osgood, *American Colonies*, I, 182.

[15] Charles Whitworth, ed., "Discourses on the Public Revenues and on Trade (part 2)," in *The Political and Commercial Works of Charles D'Avenant* (London, 1771), II, 40–41; Richard Frothingham, *The Rise of the Republic of the United States* (Boston, 1886), 112 and 112n.; Osgood, *American Colonies*, I, 183.

[16] Whitworth, ed., *D'Avenant's Works*, II, 52–74.

[17] Robert Livingston to the Lords of Trade, May 13, 1701, *NYCD*, IV, 870–79. For Livingston's role in New York politics and his other suggestions to the Board of Trade, see Lawrence H. Leder, *Robert Livingston, 1654–1728 and the Politics of Colonial New York* (Chapel Hill, 1961), chapter 10. Other colonial agents and lobbyists in England urged a northern colonial union at this time. See Robert M. Gatke, "Plans of American Colonial Union, 1643–1754" (unpubl. Ph. D. diss., American University, 1925), 104, 109–10.

[18] Louis B. Wright, ed., *An Essay Upon the Government of the English Plantations on the Continent of America (1701): An Anonymous Virginian's Proposals For Liberty Under the British Crown, with Two Memoranda by William Byrd* (San Marino, Calif., 1945), 48–49; Gatke, "Plans" (Ph. D. diss.), 131; Frothingham, *Republic*, 112–13. For a strong case alleging Ralph Wormeley, secretary of Virginia and president of the Council, rather than Beverley as the author of this tract, see Virginia W. Fitz, "Ralph Wormeley: Anonymous Essayist," *WMQ*, 3d Ser., XXVI (1969), 586–95.

[19] Robert Hunter to Sec. St. John, Sep. 17, 1711, *NJA*, 1st Ser., IV, 138–39.

[20] Caleb Heathcote to the Lords Commissioners, Jan. 28, 1716, in Dixon R. Fox, *Caleb Heathcote: The Story of a Career in the Province of New York, 1692–1721* (New York, 1926), 181.

[21] Oliver M. Dickerson, *American Colonial Government, 1696–1765*, reprint ed. (New York, 1962), 212–13. As a result of the constant attack the proprietary rights in the Jerseys and the Carolinas were surrendered.

[22] "Representation . . ." of the Board of Trade to the King, Sep. 8, 1721, *NYCD*, V, 591–630.

[23] Signatories for the Board of Trade were John Chetwynd, Martin Bladen, Paul Docminique, and Edward Ashe.

[24] Dickerson, *American Colonial Government*, 215–17.

[25] Frothingham, *Republic*, 113–14; Breckinridge Long, *Genesis of the Constitution of the United States* (New York, 1926), 120–22; W. H. Bennett, *American Theories of Federalism* (Tuscaloosa, Ala., 1964), *passim*.

[26] Bladen in 1721 proposed, with other members of the Board of Trade, a loose confederacy under a captain general similar to Penn's Plan, and in 1726 recommended a single agency to administer the colonies (attempted in 1748 under Lord Halifax).

[27] See Jack P. Greene, ed., "Martin Bladen's Blueprint for a Colonial Union," *WMQ*, 3d Ser., XVII (1960), 516–30. Document reproduced, 521–30.

[28] See chapters 6 and 10 for Kennedy's recommendations on troop quotas and the frontier.

[29] Archibald Kennedy, *The Importance of Gaining and Preserving the Friendship of the Indians to the British Interest* (London, 1752), 5–28; *FP*, IV, 117 and 117n., 120n.

[30] Archibald Kennedy to Cadwallader Colden, Apr. 15, 1751, *CP*, IV, 264.

[31] Franklin's review of Kennedy's essay was attached to the London edition.

[32] Colden to Clinton, Aug. 8, 1751, *CP*, IV, 271–87.

[33] The governors, e.g. Clinton and Shirley, constantly pled for cooperative action in arranging quotas for men, finances, and supplies. Gov. Thomas of Pennsylvania in Feb. 1746 suggested, without going into detail, union of the colonies. Burton Konkle, *George Bryan and the Constitution of Pennsylvania, 1731–1791* (Philadelphia, 1922), 12.

[34] Franklin to James Parker, Mar. 20, 1751, *FP*, IV, 117–21.

[35] John C. Hammelef, "British and American Attempts to Coordinate the Defenses of the Continental Colonies to Meet French and Northern Indian Attacks" (unpubl. Ph. D. diss., University of Michigan, 1955), 137–38; Lady Edgar, *A Colonial Governor in Maryland: Horatio Sharpe and His Times, 1753–1773* (New York, 1912), 18.

[36] See below.

[37] Lawrence H. Gipson, "Massachusetts Bay and American Colonial Union, 1754," *AASP* (1961), LXXI, 64–65; Lois K. Mathews, "Benjamin Franklin's Plans for a Colonial Union, 1750–1775," *APSR* (1914), VIII, 397–99n.

[38] See Gipson, *ibid.*; Gipson, "Thomas Hutchinson and the Framing of the Albany Plan of Union, 1754," *PMHB* (1950), LXXIV, 6–35; *FP*, V, 344–417; Beverly McAnear, "Personal Accounts of the Albany Congress of 1754," *MVHR* (1953), XXXIX, 727–46.

[39] Quoted in *FP*, V, 357

[40] Weare's copy is printed in *NYPL Bulletin* (1897), I, 149–50 and in *FP*, V, 361–64.

[41] *FP*, V, 360, 374–75.

[42] "Delaware's status was ambiguous: with the same governor and council as Pennsylvania, though with its own unicameral legislature, it was often omitted from lists of the separate colonial governments. The exclusion of Nova Scotia and Georgia can be explained not only because of sparse English-speaking populations in 1754 but more importantly because their civil administrations and military garrisons were supported by annual parliamentary appropriations." *FP*, V, 376n.

[43] This brief resumé of the Albany Plan is based on the copy published in *FP*, V, 387–92. The reader is referred to the thorough annotation on the correlation between the final draft and the committee's "Short Hints" and the various copies.

[44] For Franklin's change of mind see Gipson, "Massachusetts Bay," *AASP*, LXXI, 68–74. Dr. William Clarke of Boston supposedly convinced Franklin of the inability of the colonies to form a union in the midst of intercolonial jealousies.

[45] Gipson, "Thomas Hutchinson," *PMHB*, LXXIV, 6; *FP*, V, 336n. For the proceedings and personnel see the appendices in William Foster, *Stephen Hopkins* (No. 19 of *Rhode Island Historical Tracts* [Providence, 1884]) and Sidney S. Rider, ed., *A True Representation of the Plan Formed at Albany in 1754, for Uniting All the British Northern Colonies*. . ., by Stephen Hopkins (No. 9 of *Rhode Island Historical Tracts* [Providence, 1880]).

[46] *FP*, V, 385. The two plans are found in *The Fitch Papers (CHSC*, XVII [Hartford, 1918]), I, 20–29. All four plans – the two New England plans (Hutchinson or Trumbull?), Franklin's "Short Hints", and the final Albany Plan of Union are printed side by side in four columns for comparison in Gipson, "Thomas Hutchinson," *PMHB*, LXXIV, 29–35.

[47] Gipson, *ibid.*, 6; *FP*, V, 358 and 358n.; Hammelef, "Attempts" (Ph. D. diss.), 114–15.

[48] Pownall's Plan (July 11, 1754) is found in *NYCD*, VI, 893–97, and Johnson's Plan (July 1754) in *ibid.*, 897–99.

[49] Franklin gave six reasons why "partial unions" were rejected. Most importantly particularism of any sort would leave the colonies weaker than general union, and a regional union to which Pennsylvania would belong would be dominated by the Quakers. *FP*, V, 401–2.

[50] See Hammelef, "Attempts" (Ph. D. diss.), 98.

[51] Address of the House of Assembly to the Governor, Oct. 18, 1754, *NJA*, 1st Ser., XVI, 491

[52] *Ibid.*, 492.

[53] See Peter Wraxall, *An Abridgement of the Indian Affairs . . . in the Colony of New York, From the Year 1678 to the Year 1751*, ed. Charles H. McIlwain (*Harvard Historical Studies*, XXI [Cambridge, 1915]), x.

[54] Foster, *Stephen Hopkins*, 40.

[55] *Ibid.*, 43. An indictment of Gov. Hopkins's failure to work for the Plan, along with reasons for its adoption, is found in "A Short Reply to Mr. Stephen Hopkins VINDICATION . . . by Philolethes" (1755), printed in *ibid.*, 46–65.

[56] Colden to Franklin, June 20, 1754, *FP*, V, 354.

[57] *Ibid.*, 355.

[58] "Reasons Concerning the Plan of Union," The Fitch Papers (*CHSC*, XVII), I, 38–39. This detailed document puts forth most of the objections raised in the colonies. The full document is printed on pp. 37–42 (Oct. 2, 1754).

[59] "Report of the Committee Chosen by the General Assembly Respecting the Foregoing Plan of Union," Oct. 1754, *MHSC*, 1st Ser., VII, 207–9. Several of the royal governors vehemently opposed the Plan, chiefly on the grounds that the assemblies would appoint the delegates, whereas the selection of delegates should be considered the prerogative of the governors. The most detailed critique entered by a governor is William Shirley's letter to Sir Thomas Robinson, Dec. 24, 1754, Charles H. Lincoln, ed., *Correspondence of William Shirley*, 1731–60, 2 vols. (New York, 1912), II, 111–18. Hereafter cited as *Shirley Corr.*

[60] Mass. House of Representatives to Agent Bollan, Dec. 31, 1754, Massachusetts Papers, Bancroft Transcripts, NYPL.

[61] Mass. Council, S/ Benjamin Lynde, Dec. 11, 1754, MA, VI, 176.

[62] Speech by Chief Justice Stephen Hopkins (1755) in Albert B. Hart, ed., *American History Told by Contemporaries* (New York, 1899), II, 357–60.

[63] Secretary Robinson to the Lords of Trade, June 14, 1754, *NYCD*, VI, 844.

[64] "The Draught of a Plan or Project for a General Concert . . .," Aug. 9, 1754, *ibid.*, VI, 903–6.

[65] *Ibid.*

[66] George L. Beer, *British Colonial Policy, 1754–65*, rev. ed. (New York, 1933), 24–26.

[67] *Ibid.*, 27.

[68] Alison G. Olson, "The British Government and Colonial Union, 1754," *WMQ*, 3d Ser., XVII (1960), 25. This is an excellent article on the behind-the-scenes politics in Great Britain.

[69] The problems of colonial taxation for the general war effort is discussed in Chapter 7.

[70] Charles P. Keith, *Chronicles of Pennsylvania, 1688–1748*, 2 vols. (Philadelphia, 1917), II, 698.

[71] Beer, *British Colonial Policy*, 46; Osgood, *American Colonies*, II, 319–20.

[72] Horatio Sharpe to Cecil Calvert, Sep. 15, 1754, William H. Brown, ed., *Correspondence of Horatio Sharpe*, 4 vols. (Baltimore, 1888–1911), I, 99. Hereafter cited according to *Md. Archives* vol. number (VI, IX, XIV, XXXI).

[73] Circular letter to the Governors in North America, S/Thomas Robinson, Oct. 26, 1754, *NCCR*, V, 144ff.; see R. H. Hunter's Message to Council and House, Dec. 19, 1754, *PCR*, VI, 203.

[74] Shirley to Sir Thomas Robinson, Feb. 4, 1754, *Shirley Corr.*, II, 124.

[75] Beer, *British Colonial Policy*, 47.

[76] Dinwiddie to Sir Thomas Robinson, June 18, 1754, R. A. Brock, ed., *The Official Records of Robert Dinwiddie*, 2 vols. (Virginia Historical Soc., *Colls.*, III and IV [1883–84]), I, 204. Hereafter cited as *Dinwiddie Corr.*

[77] Beer, *British Colonial Policy*, 41–42.

[78] William McCulloch, *Proposals for Uniting the English Colonies on the Continent of America so as to enable them to act with Force and Vigour Against their Enemies* (London, 1757), 21–22, 27.

[79] *Pennsylvania Journal*, Oct. 13, 1757. Since William Bradford was the publisher of this paper, it is probable that he was the author of the plan.

[80] "Questions relating to the Union and Government of the Plantations..." (1760), *NYCD*, VII, 441–43.

[81] Quoted in Hubert Hall, "Chatham's Colonial Policy," *AHR*, V (1900), 673.

[82] Gov. Bernard to Lord Barrington, Dec. 15, 1761, Edward Channing and Archibald C. Coolidge, eds., *The Barrington-Bernard Correspondence, 1760–70* (*Harvard Historical Studies*, XVII [Cambridge, 1912]), 43.

[83] Franklin to Shirley, Dec. 22, 1754, *FP*, V, 449–50.

[84] See Clyde M. Ferrell, "The Massachusetts Colonial Agents in England" (unpubl. Ph. D. diss., University of Wisconsin, 1923), 145–47; Lawrence H. Gipson, *The British Empire Before the American Revolution*, X (1967), 38–40.

[85] See the mercantilist recommendations of John Rutherford, *The Importance of the Colonies to Great Britain with Some Hints towards making Improvements to their mutual Advantage...*, ed. W. K. Boyd, *NCHR* (1925), II, 351–75; Thomas C. Barrow, ed., "Hints Respecting the Settlement for our American Provinces," probable author William Knox (1763), *WMQ*, 3d Ser., XXIV (1967), 108–126.

[86] For a good essay on the problems and decisions facing imperial administration in 1763, see Gipson, *British Empire*, X, Chapter 1.

CHAPTER II

UNIFIED MILITARY COMMAND

In 1690 the colonists expected to conduct their own defense in military affairs, as before, but in accord with the royal prerogative. The crown would send aid when available, especially in naval assistance. Colonial militia would make up the armies in the field, commanded, if the crown saw fit, by a royal official. Later, when the colonists faced an increasingly formidable threat from foreign and Indian neighbors, they would accept a larger direction from Great Britain.

If the colonists were willing to shift some of the burdens of war to England, they could certainly approve an imperial command system. Before the Seven Years War such an accommodation was haphazard and not demanding. Only when the British Government attempted after 1763 to set up a military establishment in America, on grounds that the colonists had acquiesced in this right in the past, did the colonists, confronted with the new imperial mercantilist policies, discern intentions of coercion.

By 1763 the British Government wanted to have its cake and eat it too. As George Grenville said:. "Protection and obedience are reciprocal. Great Britain protects America; America is bound to yield obedience."[1] But the Americans did not see it this way. To their point of view, war emergencies called for temporary operations. A military establishment, except for frontier defense, should exist only for the duration of a crisis – during which time all efforts, at home and abroad, should be used to defeat the enemy. Americans had a practical bent. But what they did not realize, and future generations have learned only too well, was that recurring wars leave an indelible imprint, furthering the expansion of military power and its centralization.

In the seventeenth century, during emergencies, the northern colonies on their own united for military purposes and appointed commanders in chief. Such was the case during King Philip's War, with Josiah Winslow given the over-all command. The crown had also made efforts to establish a unified military command over the northern colonies. In the 1630's Sir Ferdinando Gorges was named Captain-General, but he never reached America to assume this authority. Sir Edmund Andros, as Governor of the Dominion of New England, was appointed Captain-General of all the military forces of the New England colonies and New York, and in 1688 his command was extended to all territory east of the Delaware River. Viola Barnes observes that this military appointment "brought centralization of command which made possible a comprehensive military campaign, gave opportunity for the fortification of the weakest spots on the frontier at the common expense, and prepared the way for the adoption of a uniform Indian policy, according to which the Indians of the north and east would be able to deal with one powerful governor instead of with a number of more or less inefficient executives."[2] The Dominion of New England "fulfilled the expectations of the Lords of Trade as a solution of the colonial problem of defense." It checked Indian encroachments and strengthened the alliance with the Iroquois. Andros's garrisoning of the frontier and his aggressive military ventures "made New England formidable to its enemies."[3]

When the Dominion of New England collapsed, the new government in England delayed the formulation of imperial policy for the defense of the colonies. The Lords of Trade were insisting on a re-establishment of a consolidated government over the northern colonies (New England, New York, and New Jersey) under a governor-general. However, this plan of reconsolidation was left up in the air because of the effective opposition led by the New England agents in London.[4] Despite the victory of the New England Puritan party in restoring separate colony status, substantial opinion existed for re-establishing the Dominion minus its autocratic features. Forty-five citizens of Massachusetts signed a petition asking the King to appoint "a Governor and Council over us to administer the Government with an elected Assembly . . . and as many of the little provinces as seem good to you may be united under one Governor for mutual defence and security."[5] The new Governor of New York, Henry Sloughter, claiming the backing of the Council and Assembly, expressed the same desire.[6]

Meanwhile, the colonists, faced with the hostility of the French and Indians on an exposed frontier, sought to create a makeshift military union on their own. The French and Indian hostilities along the New York and Maine frontiers in 1689 caught the northern colonies by surprise. To meet the emergency, attempts were made to re-instate a regional military union of much the same sort as the New England Confederation. Governor Bradstreet, speaking for the Massachusetts convention of July 1689, asked the Connecticut authorities to "be ready to yield all necessary assistance when desired according to the rules of our ancient union and confederation."[7] The old Confederation could not be stirred to life; but the New York Congress[8] in May 1690 entrusted a sea invasion of Canada to Governor William Phips of Massachusetts and an overland expedition to Jacob Leisler of New York as commander in chief and Fitz-John Winthrop as deputy commander. Winthrop received charge of the Montreal operation on condition that he obey orders from the New York Committee of Safety and from a five-man council of war headed by Leisler. Connecticut had insisted that Winthrop be given the command of the expedition as the price of cooperation. Everything conceivable that could go wrong with a military expedition did. Having advanced only a hundred miles beyond Albany, Winthrop took the advice of his council of war and returned to camp outside of Albany. Leisler had him placed in confinement, but he was rescued in a few days not by his own Connecticut troops but by a visiting delegation of Indians.[9]

After this fiasco Governor Bradstreet of Massachusetts took the initiative to secure coordinated action for another overland invasion from New York.[10] This project did not materialize, but William Phips, who had been victorious against Acadia, was given the command by Massachusetts of the expedition against Quebec, which was as ill-fated as the Montreal expedition.[11] Besides the New York-New England rivalry, another factor that worked against Leisler's over-all command was the lack of loyalty to his regime on part of the upriver merchants and landlords. His arch-enemy, Robert Livingston, fled to Hartford, where he deferred to New England leadership. Said Livingston:, "We hope we shall have a Governor speedily, but in the mean tyme, it will be very requisite that the united Colonies take Inspection of all affairs with us, since their interest and ours are so inseparable . . . ."[12]

William Phips's commission of 1692 that appointed him the first royal Governor of Massachusetts also named him commander in chief of the militia of all the New England colonies. Phips had difficulty in interesting "able Brisk men" to join a "flying army" for another invasion of Canada. Connecticut and Rhode Island would not allow Phips to recruit from their militia, on grounds that the two charter colonies held the inviolable right to control their own militia. Phips's appeal to duty to His Majesty's command and that "you will not be soe unmindfull of your old neighbours" did not bring any result. The Rhode Island Assembly refused to recognize Phips as commander over the colony's militia and petitioned the crown for recognition of its charter rights. The Attorney General and Committee of Trade agreed to uphold Rhode Island's constitutional stand, but reaffirmed the Attorney General's opinion of 1690 that the crown retained the power to appoint a commander in chief over any part of a colony's forces and in time of invasion to take charge of whatever forces he deemed necessary. New Englanders had had enough of a taste of war for a while, and Phips made no overt move to put an army in the field or to assume command over the militia of the two recalcitrant colonies.[13]

To complicate matters, in May 1693, the crown ordered Governor Fletcher of New York to take command of the Connecticut militia for an expedition against Canada. Phips was told merely to "consult and advise" with Fletcher. The West Jersey militia had already been placed under Fletcher's command. East Jersey and Pennsylvania refused to cooperate with Fletcher's demands for money and troops.[14]

In October 1693, Fletcher, accompanied by two members of the New York Council, journeyed to Hartford to publish his commission as commander of the Connecticut militia and to secure help for the defense of the New York frontier. Having caught wind of Fletcher's intentions earlier, the Connecticut General Court dispatched Fitz-John Winthrop to England to gain confirmation of the full privileges of the charter. The General Court took the position that Fletcher's commission could not supersede the charter powers of the Connecticut government over the militia. "We are still willing to doe our proportion with our neighbours in such public charge wherein we are equally concerned," the Connecticut General Court informed Fletcher, but other colonies must do their share. It was also contended that Connecticut had already done more than her part in contributing to the garrisons at Albany and Deerfield.[15]

Upon returning from Connecticut, Fletcher wrote full accounts of his abortive mission to the Lords of Trade, warning that Connecticut's obstinacy would lead to the French overrunning Albany. To John Trenchard, the Secretary of State, he advised: "These People of Connecticut are In a greate fright the noise of a Quo Warranto or A sharp Letter from theire Majesties will reduce Them the wisest and Richest of them Desire to bee under the Kings imediate Government."[16] The next best thing that Fletcher could do was to call a general conference of the governors and to obtain pledges of troops and financial aid from each colony.[17] The Board of Trade approved Fletcher's call for troops from New York, Rhode Island, Massachusetts, Pennsylvania, Maryland, and Virginia and that the crown should appoint a "Chief Commander" in time of war over the colonies who would act upon advice of the governors. But it was acknowledged, as expressed in a Rhode Island Assembly resolution, that "in time of peace, and when the danger is over, the militia within each of the said provinces ought, as we humbly conceive, to be under the government and disposition of the respective Governors of the Colonies, according to their Charters."[18] The crown ordered the colonies to contribute troops or other assistance upon request of the royal governor of New York. A typical reaction was that of the Maryland House of Delegates, which reluctantly voted a token sum of money and elusively promised future "free gifts."[19]

A priority of the first business of the new Board of Trade was the consideration of establishing a colonial military union. The Board's first report in this area, of September 30, 1696, was largely a response to a recommendation by John Nelson and letters of Governors Fletcher of New York and Nicholson of Maryland. The Board concluded that in wartime colonial militia should be put under one captain general invested with the powers of a royal governor in whichever provinces he should be present. American agents appearing before the Board had split on the issue. New England agents – Edmund Harrison, Henry Ashurst, William Phips – and Daniel Coxe of New York had argued for a governor general with civil as well as military jurisdiction. Fitz-John Winthrop stanchly defended Connecticut's charter rights. Chidley Brooke and William Nicoll of New York opposed union on grounds that Massachusetts and New York were located too far apart and for fear that Boston would be the center of government. Actually Brooke and Nicoll favored a stronger union established on a more thorough basis by Parliament. Doubting the expediency of voiding the charters of Rhode Island and Connecticut without due legal process, the Board of Trade decided to go only so far as to recommend a military union imposed by the crown. In February 1697 an order by the king-in-council directed the establishment of a military union of the four New England colonies, New York, and West New Jersey under a captain general.[20]

This action led to the appointment of Richard Coote, first Earl of Bellomont in the Irish peerage, as Governor of New York, Massachusetts, and New Hamphsire with command over the militia of all the northern colonies during wartime. Bellomont had an inside track to the position because of the backing of William III, Lord Shrewsbury, Sir Henry Ashurst, and other powerful friends. He was acceptable to the New England and New York agents alike. Tall and dignified, looking only fifty of his sixty-two years, Bellomont had won a reputation for integrity and a high sense of duty during his long public career in Parliament and in diplomacy. Bellomont did not reach New York until April 1698 and did not take over the reins of the Massachusetts government until May 1699, at which time he was embroiled in the Captain Kidd affair.[21] He investigated Rhode Island's violations of the Navigation Acts, and had no success in gaining recognition of his military powers in that colony.[22] The factiousness of New York politics and undoing the misrule of his predecessor, Benjamin Fletcher, also took up much of his time. Bellomont might have built up support from the various assemblies for union had he not died suddenly in March 1701.

Although a joint executive for New York and New England was abandoned upon the death of Bellomont, a central military authority for New England was revived on the eve of Queen Anne's War under Joseph Dudley, who received a commission in 1702 as Governor of Massachusetts and New Hampshire, captain general over all the New England militia in time of war, and vice-admiral of Rhode Island.[23] Despite his previous experience in administration and Indian affairs, Dudley found it impossible to wield together an intercolonial military system. New Englanders had an aversion towards him both because of his service as the first governor of the Dominion of New England and also because of his ties with the high church party in England.

Dudley soon discovered that Rhode Island and Connecticut were as insistent as ever on their charter privileges. Connecticut, a safe distance from the eastern war and offended over New York's land claims, refused to send troops beyond the Connecticut Valley frontier during the early phase of Queen Anne's War. Connecticut troops in 1704 disbanded without orders when told to obey the orders of the Massachusetts Governor. In 1706-7 Dudley appealed to Fitz-John Winthrop to use his powers of persuasion to bring Connecticut into a combined expedition to capture Port Royal in Acadia. Winthrop replied that the Connecticut Assembly would not comply because the colony had nothing to gain:

> The temper of our people (tho' very stout) is generally very thoughtfull and cautious; and 'tis possible some may insinuate that tho' wee should succede in the designe, yet if upon the conclusion of a peace (which one would think not far off) it should be restored to them, the honor of our succes will soon be forgotten, and we should much resent that wee have lavisht our blood and treasure.[24]

Rhode Island also denied Dudley's military authority. The issue was dramatized when Dudley in a visit to Rhode Island ordered the militia to parade, but Governor Cranston refused to obey. The Massachusetts Governor's insistence upon reposing all military authority in himself did not set well with the other New England governors.[25] Dudley, however, did leave field command to others, for example Colonel Benjamin Church, who was designated commander in chief of the Massachusetts troops operating along the eastern frontier.[26]

Because of his own failure to organize an effective fighting force, Dudley had the good sense to recommend that the crown take over directly this responsibility. The hasty return of a disparate New England force (without Connecticut militia) that had engaged the enemy only in minor skirmishes at Port Royal underlined this point.[27]

In assuming control of operations against Canada, the crown, however, allowed the command to be fragmented. Samuel Vetch, who since his immigration to America in 1699 had risen to affluence and power in New York, was named to direct an intercolonial offensive on Canada. While Vetch made preparation for an attack by sea, Colonel Francis Nicholson led forces up the Hudson. The cancellation of anticipated English naval support ended both projects, but the next year, in 1710, Nicholson, in command of a joint colonial and British force, took Port Royal.[28] A full scale invasion of Canada under Henry Boyle, the Viscount Shannon, who, as "General of all our land forces," would also command a provincial force, did not get beyond the initial stages of preparation because of the fear of a Stuart invasion of Scotland.

As 1710 drew to a close, Nicholson sailed for England to secure new backing for a grand campaign against Canada. He had no trouble persuading the new Tory ministry, who were anxious to offset the European victories of the Whig Duke of Marlborough. Although the British government committed an army of five thousand and sixty ships and the colonists responded more generously with troops than before, the whole operation of 1711 was a fiasco, which need not be discussed here. Suffice it to say, the overlapping of command played a major role in the ill-success:, General John Hill commanded the British regulars; Sir Hovenden Walker, the British naval units; Samuel Vetch, the colonial troops accompanying the British forces against Quebec; and Francis Nicholson again led a colonial army to approach Montreal.[29]

Anticipating a victory in Canada, the English Whigs planned an expedition to the West Indies under Robert Hunter. But, because of the failure in Canada, the West Indian project was abandoned, and instead Hunter was appointed Governor of New York and New Jersey. Hunter arrived in New York on June 14, 1710, accompanied by British regulars.[30]

Although the British Government took charge of operations in the last years of the war, it did not see fit to establish a universal military system in America. The colonial governors were thought to have sufficient military authority. As commanders in chief in their respective provinces, the governors also had sufficient powers to coordinate military policies of the colonies. No wonder that so many colonial governors were selected on the basis of their military background. It is estimated that sixty per cent of the colonial governors to 1728 had been army career officers. From 1704 to 1709 the principle of military men as governors was reinforced by the ruling Tory party, and the Duke of Marlborough used his influence among the Whig politicians and at court to secure the appointment of soldiers to the colonial governorships[31].

Another detriment to a general military establishment was the fear of the colonists against standing armies; the lessons of the Stuart and Cromwellian periods were as fresh to them as to Englishmen at home. Yet the colonists might have tolerated a substantial British force in America, if the troops were dispersed on the distant frontiers. But the British government did not want to go to this trouble and expense. Only four companies of one hundred each constituted the complement of British troops permanently stationed in the American colonies during Queen Anne's War – their mission being to thwart the invasion routes along the Mohawk and Champlain valleys. These troops were cruelly neglected by the British government. At the end of Queen Anne's War the crown, as Professor Shy has noted, considered leaving troops in the colonies only if three conditions existed: (1) lack of capability for self-defense of a particular colony, (2) definite strategic or financial value, and (3) colonial cooperation in paying part of the costs of maintaining garrisons.[32]

Not until 1721 were other regulars sent to the colonies, when eight infantry regiments were ordered to the New York, Virginia, and Carolina backcountry. But actually the only troops sent to America on a permanent basis were a few companies as reinforcements to the New York garrisons and one hundred "invalids" – pensioners relieved from active duty because of infirmity – who accompanied Governor Nicholson to South Carolina. Nicholson, as governor of a royal colony, could dispose of regulars stationed in his province into garrisons as he saw fit.[33]

A factor also working against a general military establishment was that the idea of a captain general (commander in chief) on a permanent basis was anathema to the colonists. Virginians had held out in the campaigns of 1710 and 1711 because they felt cooperation would be interpreted as support for a captain general over all the colonies and the placing of "military disciplined captains for Councillors, and serjeants and corporalls for Sheriffs and Justices of the Peace."[34]

Nevertheless, a plan for creating a captain general over the colonies was well underway in England and was endorsed by Governors Nicholson and Hunter. After Queen Anne's War it became a persistent recommendation of the Board of Trade.[35] But the only appointment before

1754 of a captain general over the colonies went to the Earl of Stair, who declined.[36] A vestige of the idea continued, however, in the appointment of a single governor for Massachusetts and New Hampshire until 1741 and for New York and New Jersey, 1720-1737. To meet the emergencies of Indian war, Governor Burnet of New York in 1722 was appointed "Captain Generall and Commander in Chief of the Forces by Sea and Land without our colony of Connecticut."[37]

During the twenties the controversy over military authority of the crown in the colonies warmed up, particularly over Massachusetts's reluctance to maintain frontier defense. On April 30, 1725, Lord Townshend, President of the Privy Council, warned Elisha Cooke, Jr., Agent of Massachusetts, who had presented a petition, that

> you will play a very bad game if seeking to be solemnly heard, you have nothing but trifles to offer in excuse of a province that has invaded the kings prerogative in every article of government, both civil and military. You have taken upon you to demolish forts, to march armies, to muster troops and to disband them when you please, without any regard to the king's authority. Depend upon it you will find yourself mistaken, if you think a certificate about one single circumstance will excuse all your undutifulness to the crown . . .[38]

Governor William Burnet, now of Massachusetts, wrote the Lords of Trade shortly before he died in 1729:, "Among the many attempts that the People of this Province have made to be Independent I think the greatest and most dangerous is that of endeavouring to wrest the sword out of the Royal Hand." As Governor Shute, his predecessor, had also complained, Burnet pointed out the Assembly had failed to keep up forts on the frontier and had mustered out the garrison troops. "In this manner it depends on them to strip men of all Military Force at their pleasure, and indeed as it is, the Soldiers and Officers are in fact much more at their command than mine." Burnet recommended that royal troops be dispatched to Massachusetts – two Independent Companies, one to garrison Castle Fort and the other to be stationed in frontier posts.[39]

With the outbreak of war in 1740, once again the thoughts of the British ministry turned to a unified colonial military establishment. Colonel Spotswood was designated commander in chief of troops raised according to colonial quotas until Lord Cathcart, with a regular force, could be sent over as "General and Commander in Chief of all his Majestys Troops sent to, or raised in, America".[40] Nothing came from this arrangement.

During King George's War, Governor William Shirley of Massachusetts, by virtue of his powers as a royal governor, took it upon himself to prepare a colonial expedition against Louisbourg. Though he was unable to enlist other colonies outside of New England in his "extremely wild" scheme because of the lack of sanction for it by the crown, Shirley managed to accomplish the feat with the help of a fleet commanded by Peter Warren. Shirley commissioned William Pepperrell, a Boston merchant and formerly of Kittery, Maine, as Lieutenant General and field commander and Roger Wolcott, businessman and deputy Governor of Connecticut, as Major General.[41] Captain Warren bore a commission from the crown, appointing him Commodore and Commander in Chief of all His Majesty's Ships stationed north of South Carolina. Warren gave most of the credit for the success of the expedition to Shirley:

> the indefatigable pains taken by Governor Shirley, who concerted and carried this great design into a thorough and most successful execution, with the assistance of a very few of the colonies, and a squadron of His Majesty's ships . . . .[42]

The expedition brought forth a sense of pride in colonial strength and mutual self-congratulations.[43]

So emboldened by this success, Shirley planned an invasion of Canada the next year using mainly colonial troops. The Duke of Bedford, however, objected to an all-colonial force because of "the independence it might create in those provinces, when they shall see within themselves so great an army possessed of so great a country by right of conquest".[44]

In 1746 the British Secretary of State ordered the colonial governors to raise as many Independent companies as they could of one thousand each, and those of New York, New Jersey, Pennsylvania, Maryland, and Virginia to be formed into one corps under William Gooch, Lieutenant Governor of Virginia. This force would rendezvous at Albany for a march on Montreal.[45] Admiral Peter Warren met with Shirley in the summer of 1746 to coordinate plans for an invasion of Canada.[46] Various factors combined to prevent the materialization of the planned attack: the lack of enthusiasm of the Pelham ministry, which also did not entertain any fondness for Shirley who had been a Newcastle protégé, the lateness of the season and the usual dilatoriness of the northern colonies other than Massachusetts,and British reverses in the Caribbean.[47]

In the southern theater, Governor Oglethorpe of Georgia, acting as an officer in the British regular army, led expeditions into Florida.[48] After the war, the crown ordered detachments from the three Independent companies in South Carolina to be stationed in Georgia.[49]

As the French and English colonies prepared to fight over the Ohio Valley, military command in America was confused. Governor Cornwallis of Nova Scotia, in 1750, wrote home that it was "evidently the common cause of all the Northern Colonies" that he should "immediately apply to the Governments of the Massachusetts and New Hampshire for assistance."[50] Shirley kept up interest in military preparedness, and would have been the logical choice as commander in chief when the war broke out had not two other placemen – Clinton and Sharpe – greater influence at Whitehall. Shirley's "knowledge and experience in American affairs" was unmatched by any other colonial governor;[51] but he was also getting up in years, and British policy would also favor an appointment acceptable to the southern colonies.

During the preliminary staging of the French and Indian War, colonial unity continued to be frustrated by an overlap of command. Governor Clinton of New York was appointed "Captain-General and Commander in Chief of the militia, and all the forces by sea and land, within the Colony of Connecticut, and of all the forts and places of strength within the same."[52] Robert Dinwiddie, Lieutenant Governor of Virginia, in early 1754 was appointed to the general command of colonial operations against the French in the Ohio Valley. His request for contributions from neighboring colonies, to serve under "my Gen'l Officer," went unheeded by the northern colonies. The Earl of Holderness, however, did order two Independent companies from New York to be placed under Dinwiddie's command along with any troops that might be forthcoming from the other colonies. The two New York companies, as did a contingent of North Carolina militia, arrived too late to help in Washington's encounter with the French. The South Carolina company appeared as scheduled, but Captain Mackay, who held a royal commission, refused to take orders from a provincial colonel, and Washington, therefore, consigned the South Carolina troops to guard the stores in the rear.[53]

To renew the attack against the French later in 1754 the crown appointed Governor Horatio Sharpe of Maryland as commander in chief. Sharpe apparently owed his appointment to a triumvirate in the British cabinet – the Duke of Newcastle, Lord Chancellor Hardwicke, and the Earl of Holderness. The Duke of Newcastle, as Secretary of State for the Southern Department, expected to direct the impending war in America and to win favor at the court by a quick victory. He consulted John Hanbury, a Quaker merchant and banker who was also a member of the Ohio Company. Hanbury suggested Virginia as a base of operations and that Sharpe was the best person in America to take charge of a campaign, even though Sharpe's previous military experience had been undistinguished. Undoubtedly Hanbury hoped for personal gain for his trading concern and landed interests for recommending Sharpe. Newcastle consulted with other lesser known figures, but did not seek out the advice of the two ministers who were most informed on colonial affairs – the Earl of Halifax, the President of the Board of Trade, and the Duke of Cumberland, the commander of the British army.[54] Sharpe's original commission, appointing him a "Lieutenant Colonel of foot in the West Indies" to follow such orders "as you shall receive from us, our Captain-General of Our Forces or any other your Superiour officer according to the Rules and Discipline of War," was soon amended to include "the command of the Combined Forces that shall be Assembled in America to oppose the Hostile Attempts Committed by the French in Different parts of his Majesty's Dominions."[55] Dinwiddie heartily concurred in Sharpe's appointment. Both men worked out plans for an immediate fall campaign. Dinwiddie exhorted neighboring colonial governors and the Lords of Trade to support the proposed expedition, while Sharpe assumed field command over Virginia and Maryland militia. But when the Virginia legislature refused to vote funds the planned campaign was abandoned until the next spring.[56]

With war still undeclared with France, the English government had a hard choice whether to send officers and men and other aid to the colonists, which might be construed an act of war by the French. Late in September, 1754, however, the British ministry resolved to bolster the American defense. Two Irish regiments were to be sent to America under Edward Braddock, a friend of the Duke of Cumberland. In addition, Shirley and Pepperrell were each to raise and command a regiment, with the crown bearing the expense. Braddock's regiments did not embark for America until January, 1755.[57]

Governor Sharpe's appointment as commander in chief proved to be only a nominal title. Colonial governors were directed to correspond directly with Shirley and Pepperrell "upon every thing, relative to the Present Service."[58] And on January 12, 1755, Governor Sharpe received a letter from Sir Thomas Robinson of October 26, 1754 informing him that he had been superseded by a "General Officer of Rank & Capacity" and British regiments were on their way, although Braddock's name was not mentioned.[59]

The royalization of colonial militia serving with regular troops in time of war was put into effect in reference to Braddock's command. Colonial troops in service came under the revised Mutiny Bill, namely that "all Troops in America, whilst in conjunction with the British Forces, under the Command of an officer, bearing His Majesty's immediate Commission, shall be liable to the same Martial Law and Discipline, as the British Forces are."[60]

Although Braddock was commander in chief, in a sense there were two chief commanders. Shirley continued to organize the military force for the north and planned concerted attacks on the French outposts.[61] On his own, he appointed William Johnson "Major General and Commander in chief of the forces now raising" by the governments of Massachusetts, New York, New Hampshire, Connecticut, and Rhode Island "For an Expedition against the French Incroachments at crown point and upon the Lake Champlain."[62] Shirley's plans and actions were approved by Braddock.

The old Massachusetts–New York rivalry, however, flared up over Shirley's northern command. He tried to allay the animosity by securing a Lieutenant General's commission for Johnson from the acting New York Governor, James De Lancey.[63] But Shirley still had to contend with the intrigue of a cabal led by Johnson, De Lancey, and Thomas Pownall, who did all they could to have the Massachusetts Governor recalled. De Lancey represented New Yorkers who were at odds with Shirley for not awarding them lucrative contracts; Johnson resented what he considered Shirley's interfering in Indian affairs; and Pownall, a favorite of Lord Halifax, was in America seeking quick fortune at any costs. As a matter of fact, New York politics was bitterly divided into pro- and anti-Shirley camps. William Smith, John Morin Scott, and William Livingston were his defenders.[64] Johnson refused to correspond with Shirley, and, while at Crown Point he wrote to several of the colonial governors for reinforcements rather than go through Shirley.[65] When Shirley went west to reinforce Oswego, no Indians joined his expedition, for which he blamed Johnson. Shirley's enemies succeeded in discrediting him before the eyes of the British ministry, and especially when he could not mount an attack against the French in New York, it was a demonstrable charge that he had squandered the King's money.[66]

The year 1755 was indeed a dismal one. Braddock lost his life in the defeat of his army on the Monongahela, and Niagara and Crown Point were still in the hands of the French. Shirley, though discredited, intended to keep his position as major general in command of the militia of North America and second in command. After all, he had been the "first proposer" and "principal Promoter" of the military operations in the north and therefore the one who had "his Majestys Service, the Honour of his Arms, and Welfare of his Colonies" most at heart.[67]

Yet the precedent of appointing a regular army officer of general rank over all the military forces in the colonies had been established with Braddock's command and would continue until the Revolution. The powers of the commander in chief steadily encroached upon a governor's military powers within his own province, with the British commander in chief usually regarding the governor of a colony as a mere liaison officer between himself and the assembly.[68] The commander in chief had the advantage of answering only to superior authority in Great Britain, whereas the prerogative powers of the governor were built into a system of checks and balances. The colonial governor found that he did not have military powers separate from his council. When Governor John Reynolds of Georgia during the French and Indian War tried to exercise the royal prerogative independently in military affairs he was rebuked by the British government. The crown considered it more important to secure backing of the influential planter-merchant class during a war than to strengthen the royal prerogative of a governor.[69] But the commander in chief was to have no more success with the assemblies than did the governors. Braddock was only the first to discover that all he could do was to urge the colonial governors to stimulate their assemblies in voting aid. Not only had Braddock found "all want of Union among the Colonies" but the more affluent a colony, as in the case of Pennsylvania, the more it took advantage "of the common Danger in order to encroach upon His Majesty's Prerogative in the Administration of His Government."[70]

The Newcastle ministry, which had found its prestige diminished by the military events in America, decided in January 1756 to create a more unified command in America. Upon the Duke of Cumberland's recommendation and with the backing of other powerful Lords, John Campbell, the fourth Earl of Loudoun, a wealthy lowland Scot and one of the sixteen Scottish peers, was named as commander in chief for the military forces in America. As "Commander in Chief of all and singular our Forces employed or to be employed in North America," he could require the assistance of all colonial governors and "all other Officers Civil or Military" in America. The extraordinary powers in the commission were couched in vague language, as had been the case with Braddock's commission. Thomas Pownall best described the commission: "The general words which made it up mean nothing, or suppose everything, when a justifiable occasion, or perhaps a colourable pretext calls for the exercise of them." Unprecedentedly, Loudoun was instructed to raise a corps of 4,000 troops in the colonies to form a Royal American corps. If for any reason Lord Loudoun could not exercise his command, the commission "should devolve on Our . . . Major General Abercrombie or such other officer bearing Our Commission as shall be next in Rank to the said Major General Abercrombie."[71]

Meanwhile, William Shirley, who had been given a temporary appointment as commander in chief by the Lords Justices after the death of Braddock, was getting into more hot water. Letters written by someone in Pennsylvania under the name of Pierre Fidele to the Duc de Mirepoix revealing secret instructions of Shirley on military and Indian affairs were intercepted. Shirley's judgment and, to some, his loyalty were held in question, and besides he had a French wife. It became imperative for the Newcastle ministry to replace Shirley as commander in chief at once. Since Loudoun was delayed, Webb, and then Abercromby, were sent on ahead. For a few weeks Webb was acting commander in chief until Abercromby arrived. Loudoun did not reach New York until July 1756. Thus in less than two months Americans had three commanders in chief.[72]

The whole system of command in America seemed on the verge of collapse. Shirley continued briefly in the governorship and used his efforts to raise troops from the New England colonies for an expedition against Crown Point, making these available for General Abercromby. Shirley also advised that troops raised in New Jersey and North Carolina could be employed anywhere in America at the discretion of the commander in chief.[73] The remnants of Shirley's and Pepperrell's regiments were disbanded, to be replaced by the Royal American corps.

Loudoun soon had headaches in dealing with the colonies. A special order from England had stated that no provincial officers should rank higher than a senior captain of regulars. If this were followed literally, Johnson, Bradstreet, Washington and other ranking colonials would have been deprived of rank.[74] Virginia protested that her troops were considered as "Irregulars" and that provincial troops should be "regularly enlisted."[75] Massachusetts refused to cooperate with Loudoun on grounds that military powers of the colony derived from the governor's prerogative bestowed by the crown. "They desire or tacitly claim a right to act only under the command of their own Governor [Shirley]," wrote one observer, and "it should appear that They act under their own Governor in no other way than as independent of all Command and Controul of the Crown, either in It's immediate Command or in It's delegated Power to It's Governor."[76] Loudoun complained that a Massachusetts council of war took it upon itself to direct "the Motions of his Majesty's Troops."[77]

By and large the principle of Loudoun's over-all command was acquiesced in by the colonists. As Benjamin Tasker wrote Governor Sharpe:

> The divided State of the Colonies is justly deplored by all sensible Men, who are Interested in their safety, and Prosperity; and animated with an Adequate Zeal for their welfare. The only Provision (amidst the distraction of such various views as are entertained in the different Colonies notwithstanding the Common danger) which has the least

> Tendency towards an Union, or can conduce to an uniform Plan of Mutual assistance and defence, is that by which the Forces raised in the Respective Governments are subjected to an direction in their Military operations.[78]

Although Loudoun's cool-headedness and administrative abilities won respect, his days were numbered. He incurred the enmity of Dinwiddie and Shirley over the embargo[79] and troop deployment. He threatened the colonial legislatures to keep up pay for the troops, and yet pay amounted to six months in arrears.[80] His rigorous billeting and quartering policies in Virginia, Maryland, Pennsylvania, New York, and Massachusetts stirred up popular resentment.[81] But worst of all, he was not a winning general, and, to borrow from the parlance of a later time, he had the "slows." Fort William Henry was captured by the French. He would not attack Louisbourg until every iota of preparation was perfect. Thus Loudoun was censured and recalled.

The Pitt ministry took a firm hand to create a more unified military system in the colonies. All provincial officers were made equal in rank to corresponding officers in the regular army. England would provide munitions and Pitt promised that the King would recommend to Parliament to reimburse the colonies for supplying the men, clothes, and pay for a renewed war effort.[82] Major General James Abercromby – against the wishes of Pitt – was appointed to succeed Loudoun as commander in chief, and at the same time Brigadier General John Forbes was named commander of the Southern District, which included Pennsylvania, Virginia, Maryland, and the Carolinas. Forbes was to operate jointly with Abercromby against the French in the west.[83] A British naval force was to be sent over, and colonial governors were advised to report all intelligence concerning naval affairs to the "Commander in Chief of the King's Ships to North America."[84] Abercromby's second in command was Brigadier General Lord Viscount Howe, who substituted for the commander in chief whenever Abercromby had to absent himself from his headquarters at Albany.[85]

Abercromby entered his command with vigor. He diligently applied to all governors from New Hampshire to North Carolina for assistance.[86] But he had the same difficulty as did Loudoun in obtaining support, and the colonists were reluctant to recognize him as supreme commander. Governor Pownall issued a call for unity but not to much avail:

> Nothing can give the Enemy an Advantage over us, Nothing can hurt and ruin this Country, but a Disunion among the Several Parts of the army, and want of proper subordination to the Supream Command of

> it – I must therefore for the sake of your own Honour and that of the Province for the sake of your Country – for the sake of the Good Cause you are Engaged in Recommend to the troops of my Province, that they do most conscientiously maintain a Spirit of union, and Subordination.[87]

Lieutenant Governor James De Lancey, whose brother Oliver De Lancey commanded the New York troops, likewise deplored the lack of co-operation by provincial officers. Trying to console Abercromby he wrote:

> I am sorry you are so Disturbed with some of the Provincial Troops, who will pay no regard to your Commands, they cannot but know that they are all under your Command. . .in pursuance of His Majestys Commands signified by Mr. Secretary Pitt . . . to proceed with a Body of the Kings Brittish Forces and under the supreme Command of His Majestys Commander in Chief in America: and again the Governors are further directed to have nothing in view but the good of the Kings service and a due subordination of the whole when join'd to His Majestys Commander in Chief in conformity to which after a few directions in relation to the Oeconomy of the New York Regiment, I order Colonel [Oliver] De Lancey to proceed to Albany to put himself under your Command and obey such Orders, as he should from time to time receive from you or the Commander in Chief and it is to be presumed the Provincials of the other Governments have the like Orders from their respective Governors.[88]

Abercromby was not held in high regard by his men. He was, as J.C. Long puts it, "a doddering old fellow, so pettifogging that the colonial troops dubbed him 'Mr. Nambycromby.' "[89] Abercromby's great mistake was to act as field commander for the attack on Fort Ticonderoga. The repulse of his army three times the size of the force manning the French garrison decisively ruined his reputation.

As a result of the catastrophe, Abercromby was recalled to England, and Sir Jeffrey Amherst was named to succeed him. Pitt directed the colonial governors at the time of Amherst's appointment to "apply to and correspond with the Major General Amherst on all Matters relating to the King's Service, and that you do obey such orders, as you shall receive from him . . . ."[90] Amherst was also governor-in-chief of Virginia, as Loudoun had been, but in his circular letters to other governors he did not mention his post as governor.[91] Amherst sent deputies into the colonies to promote recruiting and to supervise the outfitting of men.[92] Because of the Indian crises in the south, Amherst dispatched Brigadier General Monckton with 1300 troops to South Carolina.[93] Pitt himself took general direction of military campaigns, and constantly entreated the governors to use their influence on the councils and assemblies to raise as many men as possible and to move them as Amherst directed.[94]

Virginia, Maryland, and Pennsylvania refused to place their militia under Amherst's command. Instead of continuing the dillydallying for colonial support, Pitt, acting on the recommendations of Amherst, Bouquet, and others, decided to win the war with British troops alone.[95] The victory over Canada vindicated British military authority in America.

At the war's end, Major General Thomas Gage, acting lieutenant governor of the district of Montreal, was promoted to succeed Amherst. Other contenders for the appointment were Governor Robert Monckton of New York and James Murray, afterwards Governor of Canada – both men had the support of Scottish politicians such as Lord Mansfield and Lord Bute. Gage, of course, also had influential connections.[96]

In 1763, Amherst and Welborne Ellis, the Secretary at War, worked out a plan for a peacetime military establishment. Intended as much to "retain the Inhabitants of our antient Provinces in a State of Constitutional Dependance upon Great Britian" as to offer protection against the Indians and to administer the outlying districts, the plan received the endorsement of the British ministry and was put into effect immediately. Ten regiments were to be sent to America – only one of which was to go to an American colony, South Carolina.[97] There were no problems anticipated over the purely military aspect of the establishment, since the colonists had become accustomed to the office of commander in chief and some British regulars had been stationed in America ever since the end of the seventeenth century. But Gage knew the traditional hostility toward a peacetime military establishment, and noted that success depended especially upon "the resolves of the New England governments."[98] The general in chief now would have practically unlimited powers in Indian affairs: to scrutinize the Indian trade and supervise agents and commissaries, including control over all expenditures.[99]

The military establishment of 1763 removed to a degree the competition in military affairs, which Thomas Pownall had earlier characterized as a dichotomy between the commander in chief, the regular army, and British administration on one side and the colonial militia, assemblies, and governors on the other.[100] But one grave shortcoming was the failure to establish some sort of a federal regulated militia, which, given the colonial experience and prejudices, would have been as impractical as it would have been virtually impossible. But a "well framed Militia Law," to appropriate the words of Governor Denny when he tried to firm up the militia in Pennsylvania, "founded on the Principles of an *English* Constitution" and preserving "equally the legal Prerogatives of the Crown, and the just Rights of the People,"[101] enacted by Parliament for the colonies, may have wielded together a greater identity of the colonists to the military establishment.

Nevertheless, what had long been in the planning had become reality. The last years of the war had brought prestige to the office of the commander in chief. By heading a peacetime army in America, the commander in chief, permanently residing in New York City, as Clarence E. Carter points out, "turned out to be the most cohesive element that had yet appeared in the American colonies."[102] It is also significant that the defense of the colonies would now be regarded as a whole rather than as regional entities.

NOTES

1 Quoted in Beer, *British Colonial Policy,* 6n.

2 Barnes, *Dominion of New England,* 216.

3 *Ibid.*, 229. The maintenance of a garrison of regular troops in New England was the joint responsibility of Andros, as Governor, and Sir William Blathwayt, as Secretary of War and Plantations. Garrisons were "intended as much to hold down the New Englanders as to protect them from hostile Indians." Stephen S. Webb, "William Blathwayt: From Popish Plot to Glorious Revolution," *WMQ*, 3d Ser., XXV (1958), 14–15.

4 Barnes, *ibid.*, 262.

5 "Address of divers gentlemen, merchants and others of Boston to the King," Jan. 25, 1691, *CSP*, XIII, 212.

6 Copy of unfinished letter of Gov. Sloughter, – July, 1691, *ibid.*, 514.

7 Order of Simon Bradstreet, Governor by the Mass. Convention, July 17, 1689, CA, Colonial Wars, II, 10.

8 See Chapter 5.

9 Richard S. Dunn, *Puritans and Yankees: The Winthrop Dynasty of New England, 1630–1717* (Princeton, 1962), 290–93.

10 Simon Bradstreet to Robert Treat, Aug. 30, 1690, CA, Colonial Wars, II, 120.

11 See Johnson, *History of the French War*, 94–95; John Wynne, *A General History of the British Empire in America*, 2 vols. (London, 1770), I, 126–27.

12 Robert Livingston to Government of Conn. assembled in Hartford, May 9, 1690, *NYCD* III, 729.

[13] Addington (Sec.) to Gov. Robert Treat and Council of Conn., July 30, 1692, MA, Colonial, II, 211; Phips to Gov. and Council of Conn., Feb. 24, 1693, *ibid.*, 212; Osgood, *American Colonies*, I, 100–103. An opinion rendered by the Attorney General in 1694 stated that during an "extraordinary exigency" the crown could take over civil functions as well as military of a colony. Kimball, *Dudley*, 152, 158.

[14] Blathwayt to Fletcher, Feb. 26, 1693, Blathwayt Papers (photostats), NYHS; Proprietors of West Jersey to Gov. Fletcher, June 1, 1692, *NJA*, 1st Ser., II, 89; Fletcher to Blathwayt, Mar. 8, 1693, *NYCD*, IV, 13; Earl of Nottingham to Sir William Phips, Feb. 22, 1693, Parkman transcripts, Colonial Entry Book (PRO), XXXVI, 92, MHS; Osgood, *American Colonies*, 102–3.

[15] Gov. and Gen. Ct. of Conn. to Gov. Fletcher, Mar. 6, 1695, *Mass. Acts and Resolves*, VII (1892), 418.

[16] Fletcher to John Trenchard, Nov. 10, 1693, PRO, CO, Vol. 1082, LC: Fletcher to Trenchard, Nov. 19, 1694, *ibid.*; John G. Palfrey, *History of New England*, IV (1890), 225–27.

[17] See Chapter 5.

[18] "Minutes of the Board of Trade respecting Assistance from other Colonies to New-York," Apr. 13, 1694, *NYCD*, IV, 101; R. I. Assembly to Privy Council, *RICR*, III, 296.

[19] Mathew P. Andrews, *History of Maryland* (New York, 1929), 209–10.

[20] Journal of Council of Trade and Plantations, Jan. 25, 1697, *CSP*, XV, 318; Memorial of Sir Henry Ashurst and Edmund Harrison, Feb. 11, 1697, *ibid.*, 358; Order of the King in Council, Feb. 25, 1697, *ibid.*, 385; Report of the Board of Trade on the Union of New-York with other colonies, Feb. 25, 1697, *NYCD*, IV, 259–61; Ferrell, Mass."Agents" (Ph. D. diss.), 149–50; Osgood, *American Colonies*, I, 151–52, 267–69.

[21] Journal of Council of Trade and Plantations, Feb. 22, 1697, *CSP*, XV, 380; Archibald Hanna, Jr., "New England Military Institutions, 1693–1750" (unpubl. Ph. D. diss., Yale University, 1951), 223; Arthur Gilman, *The Story of Boston* (New York, 1889), 196; Frederic de Peyster, *The Life and Administration of Richard, Earl of Bellomont* (New York, 1879), 31–32, 57.

[22] For Blathwayt's detailed report to the Privy Council on the irregularities of the R. I. Government, see *RICR*, III (1858), 385–88.

[23] Kimball, *Dudley*, 79, 138–39, 152. Dudley's royal commission reproduced in Appendix A, 211–18.

[24] Quoted in Kimball, *Dudley*, 120.

[25] Kimball, *Dudley*, 75, 135, 143, 145, 147–48; Palfrey, *Hist. of New England*, IV, 359–62; Hammelef, "Attempts to Coordinate the Defenses" (Ph. D. diss.), 46. Actually all commissions of the governors of Mass. from 1691 until after Queen Anne's War contained a provision making the Mass. Governor the commander of the R. I. militia. Mr. Popple to Sir E. Northey, May 1, 1716, *CSP*, XXIX, 71.

[26] *Boston News-Letter,* Aug. 14, 1704, in Weeks, ed., *Hist. Digest*, 118.

[27] *Ibid.*, 119–20; Howard H. Peckham, *The Colonial Wars, 1689–1762* (Chicago, 1964), 66–68.

[28] Address of Richard Ingoldsby to Col. Francis Nicholson, June 3, 1709, *NJA*, 1st Ser., XIII, 352; Peckham, *Colonial Wars*, 70–71; Instructions to Viscount Shannon, July –, 1710, PRO, CO, Vol. 9, LC; see G. M. Waller, *Samuel Vetch: Colonial Enterpriser* (Chapel Hill, 1960), *passim.*

[29] Donald L. Kemmerer, "The Struggle for Self-Government in Colonial New Jersey, 1694–1738" (unpubl. Ph. D. diss., Princeton, 1934), 198; G. M. Waller, "New York's Role in Queen Anne's War, 1702–13," *New York History*, XXXIII (1952), 45; Peckham, *Colonial Wars*, 71–73.

[30] Kemmerer, *ibid.*, 189–90.

[31] Stephen S. Webb, "The Strange Career of Francis Nicholson," *WMQ*, 3d Ser., XXII (1966), 513, 541.

[32] John Shy, *Toward Lexington: The Role of the British Army in the Coming of the American Revolution* (Princeton, 1965), 26–29.

[33] *Ibid.*, 30; *The Statutes at Large of South Carolina*, Feb. 15, 1723, III (1838), 235.

[34] Quoted in Webb, "Francis Nicholson," *WMQ*, 3d Ser., XXII (1966), 543.

[35] *Ibid.*, 542.

[36] See Chapter 1; Dickerson, *American Colonial Government*, 214–15; Clarence E. Carter, "The Office of Commander in Chief: a Phase of Imperial Unity on the Eve of the Revolution," in *The Era of the American Revolution*, ed. Richard B. Morris (New York, 1965), 171–72. The Captain General would be assisted by two or more councilors from each colony and have a fixed salary.

[37] Burnet's commission, July 22, 1730, CA, Colonial Wars, II, 177.

[38] Conference between Elisha Cooke, Jr. and the Privy Council, Apr. 30, 1725, Saltonstall Papers, MHS.

[39] Burnet to Lords of Trade, Mar. 31, 1729, Bancroft transcripts, American Colonies, II; see also John A. Schutz, "Secession Politics in Massachusetts, 1730–41," *WMQ*, 3rd Ser., XV (1958), 508–20.

[40] Duke of Newcastle to Gov. Belcher, Jan. 5, 1740, Massachusetts Papers (New Hampshire Boundary, 1731–42), Force transcripts, LC; Newcastle to Sharpe, Jan. 5, 1740, *Md. Archives*, XXVIII, 199–201.

[41] William Shirley to Roger Wolcott, Mar., 1745, Roger Wolcott Papers, CHS; *New Hampshire Gazette*, July 13, 1759, obituary of William Pepperrell; Edgar J. Fisher, *New Jersey as a Royal Province, 1738–76* (*Columbia University Studies* . . ., XLI [1911]), 324; Fairfax Downey, *Louisbourg: Key to a Continent* (Englewood Cliffs, N. J., 1965), 24.

[42] Admiral Warren to Gov. Wanton, Sep. 13, 1745, *RICR*, V, 144; *Virginia Gazette*, April 18, 1745.

[43] William Shirley's Address to His Officers, Louisbourg, Oct. 9, 1745, Belknap Papers, MHS; Thomas Hancock to William Pepperrell, Dec. 31, 1745, Pepperrell Papers, MHS.

[44] Quoted in Arthur H. Buffington, "The Canada Expedition of 1746," *AHR* (1940), XLV, 555.

[45] Wynne, *A General History* (1770), I, 513; Davidson, *War Comes to Quaker Pa.*, 43–47.

[46] Shirley and Peter Warren to Gov. George Thomas, July 4, 1746, Gratz Collection, Colonial Wars, HSP.

[47] John A. Schutz, "Imperialism in Massachusetts during the Governorship of William Shirley, 1741–56," *The Huntington Library Quarterly*, XXIII (1960), 217–18, 224.

[48] James P. McCain, *Georgia as a Proprietary Province* (Boston, 1917), 86.

[49] Meeting of the Trustees, Feb. 2, 1749, *GCR* I (1904), 525.

[50] Gov. Cornwallis to Lt. Gov. Phips, May 3, 1750, Bancroft transcripts, Colonial Documents, NYPL.

[51] R. H. Morris to Col. Morris, June 23, 1756, Personal Miscellany (Robert Hunter Morris Correspondence), LC.

[52] Quoted in Samuel Peters, *General History of Connecticut* (London, 1781), reprint (New York, 1877), 102.

[53] Dinwiddie to Gov. of Pa., N. C., N. Y., Md., N. J., Mass, – Jan. 1754, *Dinwiddie Corr.*, I, 63–71; to Sec. Robinson, Sep. 23, 1754, *ibid.*, 323; to Earl of Halifax, Mar. 12, 1754, *ibid.*, 100; Lee, *The Lower Cape Fear*, 237; James Veech, *The Monongahela of Old* (Pittsburgh, 1910), 48.

[54] Arthur M. Schlesinger, "Maryland's Share in the Last Intercolonial War," *Md. Hist. Mag.*, VII (1912), 137–37.

[55] *Ibid.*, 137.

[56] *Ibid.*, 134; Dinwiddie to Gov. Glen, Oct. 25, 1754, *Dinwiddie Corr.*, I, 379; Dinwiddie to Lords of Trade, Oct. 25, 1754, *ibid.*, 365; Sharpe to Thomas Robinson, Jan. 12, 1755, Parkman transcripts, XL, MHS; Edgar, *Sharpe*, 24; Brian Connell, *The Savage Years* (New York, 1959), 41.

[57] Thad W. Riker, "The Politics Behind Braddock's Expedition," *AHR*, XIII (1908), 745–52.

[58] Thomas Robinson to Governor of Pa., Oct. 26, 1754, Ettling Revolution Papers, U. S. Manuscripts, 1733–99, HSP.

[59] Schlesinger, "Md. in Last Intercolonial War," *Md. Hist. Mag.*, VII (1912), 148.

[60] Thomas Robinson to Gov. and Co. of Conn., Dec. 31, 1754, Privy Council Orders, 1743–75, CHS; Robinson to Gov. and Co. of Conn., Jan. 23, 1755, Jonathan Trumbull Papers Sr. Papers, CHS.

[61] Shirley to Thomas Robinson, Feb. 18, 1755, Parkman transcripts, XL, MHS.

[62] By His Excellency, William Shirley, Apr. 16, 1755, William Shirley Papers, MHS; Alexander Flick *et al.*, eds., *The Papers of Sir William Johnson*, 13 vols. (Albany, 1921–62), I, 461–62.

[63] James De Lancey to N. Y. Assembly, Apr. 23, 1755, Emmet Collection #4680, NYPL; De Lancey to Johnson, Apr. 16, 1755, Flick *et al.*, *Johnson Papers*, I, 468; Harrison Bird, *Navies in the Mountains: The Battles on the Waters of Lake Champlain and Lake George, 1609–1814* (New York, 1962), 45.

[64] [William Livingston], *A Review of the Military Operations in North America... [1753–56], MHSC,* 1st Ser., VII (1801), 98–99; John R. Alden, *General Gage in America* (Baton Rouge, 1948), 33.

[65] *The Boston Evening Post*, Sep. 22, 1755.

[66] Livingston, *Review of Military Operations, MHSC*, 1st. Ser., VII (1801), 134–40. For a good discussion of the case against Shirley and the various efforts at vilification, see John A. Schutz, *William Shirley: King's Governor of Massachusetts* (Chapel Hill, 1961), 217–18, 232–34. De Lancey went back to the Chief Justiceship under a reprimand for having exceeded his authority by the new Governor, Sir Charles Hardy.

[67] "Circular Letter to the several Governors," Camp at Oswego, Sep. 25, 1755, MA, Colonial, VI, 211; Samuel Niles, *A Summary Historical Narrative of the Wars in New England with the French and Indians..., MHSC*, 4th Ser., V (1861), 391.

[68] Leonard W. Labaree, *Royal Government in America,* reprint ed. (New York, 1958), 108.

[69] W. W. Abbot, *The Royal Governors of Georgia, 1754–75* (Chapel Hill, 1959), 43–44; Trevor R. Reese, *Colonial Georgia: A Study in British Imperial Policy in the Eighteenth Century* (Athens, 1963), 24.

[70] Braddock to Gov. Morris of Pa., Mar. 9, 1755, Loudoun Papers (Huntington Lib.), microfilm, Pa. State Archives, Harrisburg.

[71] Stanley M. Pargellis, *Lord Loudoun in North America* (New Haven, 1923), 38-39. Pownall quote, *ibid.*

[72] *Ibid.*; Earl of Halifax to Sir Charles Hardy, Mar. 19, 1756, "Intercepted Letters to the Duke de Mirepoix, 1756," *Annual Report of the AHA for 1896* (Washington, 1897), 685–86. Halifax was also irked that Shirley was arranging a military campaign without informing authorities in England.

[73] June 27, 1756, Parkman transcripts, XLI, MHS.

[74] A. G. Bradley, *The Fight with France for North America* (Westminister, 1900), 150.

[75] "Remonstrance of Officers of the Va. Regiment to Gov. Dinwiddie," Apr. 16, 1755, John C. Fitzpatrick, ed., *The Writings of George Washington*, I (Washington, D. C., 1931), 26.

[76] "The State of Massachusetts Bay as it stood in the year 1757," Mass. Miscellany Collection, LC, (Thomas Pownall is the probable author); Shirley to Loudoun, Sep. 3, 1756, Parkman transcripts, XLII, MHS.

[77] Extract of a letter from Loudoun to Shirley, Aug. 2, 1756, Parkman transcripts, XLII, MHS.

[78] Benjamin Tasker to Horatio Sharpe, Dec. 16, 1757, PRO, WO: 34, XXXIV, LC.

[79] Loudoun had proclaimed an embargo upon all the colonies in provisions from the colonies to foreign ports. His edict was based upon an act of Parliament and order-in-council, both of 1757. Shirley and the Mass. Council wanted exemption to trade in provisions with southern colonies. Dinwiddie, without Loudoun's consent, lifted the provisions embargo in Virginia; Maryland and Pennsylvania followed suit on grounds that Virginia had broken the "Concert made with the other Provinces." See below, note no. 33 (1757), Chapter 12.

[80] Joseph Shippen to his father, n. d., "Military Letters of Capt. Joseph Shippen," *PMHB* XXXVI, 418.

[81] James High, "The Earl of Loudoun and Horatio Sharpe, 1757–58," *Md. Hist. Mag.*, XLV (1950), 14–15, 24–25.

[82] Koontz, *Dinwiddie*, 38; Johnson, *History of the French War*, 268–71.

[83] Pitt to Gen. Abercromby, Dec. 30, 1757, *Pitt Corr.*, I, 146; Forbes to Gov. Arthur Dobbs, Mar. 21, 1758, A. P. James, ed., *The Writings of General John Forbes* (Madison, 1938), 59–60; Chester H. Sipe, *The Indian Wars of Pennsylvania* (Harrisburg, 1929), 387. Loudoun left Col. John Stanwix to command in Maryland and Pennsylvania.

[84] Pitt to Dep. Gov. of Pa., Dec. 30, 1757, Emmet Collection, #1819, NYPL.

[85] E. g., to meet with Lt. Gov. James De Lancey in New York City. Abercromby to Pitt, Mar. 16, 1758, *Pitt Corr.*, I, 208.

[86] *Ibid.*

[87] Thomas Pownall to Col. Prebble and the Rest of the Colonels of the Mass. Regiments, July 28, 1758, Emmet Collection, #5094, NYPL.

[88] James De Lancey to Abercromby, Aug. 7, 1758, PRO, WO:34, Vol. 29, LC.

[89] J. C. Long, *Mr. Pitt and America's Birthright* (New York, 1940), 282, 295–96.

[90] Pitt to Dep. Gov. of Pa., Sep. 18, 1758, Emmet Collection, #1722, NYPL.

[91] Flippin, *Royal Government in Virginia*, 67–68.

[92] Norkus, "Francis Fauquier" (Ph. D. diss.), 89.

[93] Robert Monckton to Gov. Hamilton, May 17, 1760, Emmet Collection, #4513; Pitt to Amherst, June 14, 1760, *Pitt Corr.*, II, 302.

[94] Circular letter of Pitt to governors of Mass., N. H., Conn., R. I., N. Y., and N. J., Dec. 9, 1758, *NJA*, 1st Ser., IX, 147.

[95] Theodore Thayer, *Pennsylvania Politics and the Growth of Democracy, 1740–76* (Harrisburg, 1953), 82.

[96] John R. Alden, *General Gage in America* (Baton Rouge, 1948), 62.

[97] Shy, *Toward Lexington*, 66; Clarence A. Mowat, "The Southern Brigade: A Sidelight on the British Military Establishment in America, 1763-75," *The Journal of Southern History*, X (1944), 61.

[98] Gage to Governor of R. I., Dec. 6, 1763, *RICR*, VI, 377.

[99] See Clarence E. Carter, "The Significance of the Military Office in America, 1763–75," *AHR*, XXVIII (1923), 475-80.

[100] John A. Schutz, *Thomas Pownall: British Defender of American Liberty* (Glendale, Calif., 1951), 107.

[101] Message of Governor William Denny to the Assembly, Oct. 17, 1757, *Pennsylvania Gazette*, Jan. 12, 1758.

[102] Carter, "Office of Commander in Chief," in Morris, ed., *Era of the American Revolution*, 176.

CHAPTER III

WAR CONFERENCES

The convening of intercolonial conferences on the conduct of war became an essential ingredient of wartime participation of the colonies. General congresses of the governors or specially appointed commissioners were held during each of the colonial wars. The congress would set the initial plan of cooperation as to quotas of men, matériel, and finances. Needless to say, the expectations of proportional contributions were usually higher than the returns, and there would always be several colonies whose legislatures would balk at implementing the pledged contributions that their emissaries had entered into. Each congress was the result of extensive correspondence among the governors and, by and large, the principal endeavor of one or two governors, who envisioned unity, if not union, among the colonies. In addition to the general congresses, there were numerous councils of war of officers representing various colonies and consultations usually of a bilateral nature.

With the threat of a French and Indian war in 1689, the three colonies of the defunct New England Confederation met to revive the Confederation. The session held in Boston lasted September 16–20. The Connecticut commissioners acted as spoilers, claiming that such great diversity in the instructions of the commissioners made it impossible for the delegates to "be accomodated each to other at present so as to make one rule for the Carrying on and defraying the Charge of the said warr," and, therefore, they refused to be committed to a new confederation. At the meeting the commissioners did informally pledge to raise troops on a proportionate basis.[1] When Governor Bradstreet returned to Boston, he sought to raise a New England contingent of troops to relieve Albany from the threat of a French attack.[2]

After the French and Indian raid on Schenectady struck terror throughout the colonies, Jacob Leisler, the usurper of the New York government, petitioned the governors of Massachusetts, Maryland, and

Connecticut for aid. In April, he invited the governors of Massachusetts, Connecticut, Plymouth, Rhode Island, the Jerseys, Pennsylvania, Maryland, and Virginia to send delegates to a conference in New York City on April 24.[3] When the meeting finally began on May 1, seven commissioners represented the three Puritan colonies and New York. Maryland's delegate arrived too late; Virginia was awaiting the arrival of a new governor and hence did not act; Pennsylvania and the Jerseys showed no inclination to participate; and Rhode Island never got around to sending commissioners. Besides authorizing attacks by land and sea, settling command, and arranging quotas, the conference also decided that

> matters of great Concernment be directed and ordered by the Council of War Consisting of the Major with the rest of the Commissioned officers or so many of them as their is opportunity for:[4]

Fitz-John Winthrop, as field commander, did use a council of war in planning operations.[5] Apparently a reason for New England's cooperation in the congress was to stay a revival of the Dominion of New England.[6] But in actually implementing the decisions of the Congress, Connecticut and Plymouth, beset with jealousies toward New York, responded half-heartedly, and Massachusetts preferred to commit her troops to the sea expedition. The chief significance of the congress and at least the pretense of concerted operations is the broadening of intercolonial cooperative action into the idea of regional union, and, with Virginia and Maryland having been invited, a hint of general cooperation of the colonies against a common danger.

When Governor Sloughter of New York requested the aid of New England and Virginia in 1691 to cooperate in an expedition against Canada, he received the reply from Connecticut that plans would have to be worked out by an intercolonial congress of commissioners. It was considered too late in the year (June) to begin preparations, and, therefore, no action was taken.[7]

In 1693, Governor Fletcher of New York received royal instructions to hold a congress at New York with commissioners from the New England colonies, New York, Pennsylvania, Maryland, and Virginia. Fletcher called "for the meeting of Commissioners from all the neighboring Colonies and provinces at New York, to Concerte and agree upon a Quota of men and money for the defense of the frontiers." Phips refused to send commissioners, although earlier in the year he had tried to drum up from the governors of New York, Virginia, Maryland, and Pennsylvania a "Speedy agreement upon a quota of Men or other assistance to be given to

New York by each Province or Colony during the Warr according to her Majesties Royall command." Maryland and Rhode Island claimed they did not have time to select commissioners; and "Pensilvania deny the carnall sword." Only a commissioner from Connecticut and one from Virginia met with the New York commissioners, and these would not act unless there were more full representation. It was agreed, however, that Virginia and Maryland should send money to aid the planned expedition. Fletcher considered the failure of the colonies to participate in a conference to arrange mutual support as justification for his recommendation to unite New York, Pennsylvania, Connecticut, and the Jerseys under one military command.[8]

Because the colonies were unable to get together and have their commissioners determine quotas, an order of the Privy Council went out in August 1694 fixing quotas of aid to New York by each of the colonies.[9] No further efforts were made during King William's War to convene an intercolonial congress, although in 1697 Massachusetts named commissioners to Rhode Island and Connecticut to treat on matters of the war.[10]

During the first part of Queen Anne's War there was some scurrying about for intercolonial negotiation. Commissioners from New York, New Jersey, and Connecticut met briefly in New York on July 13, 1704, but the actual content of the discussions is not known.[11] Governor Nicholson of Virginia also attended the meeting and afterwards went to Boston to confer with Governor Dudley.[12] Massachusetts in December of the same year sent three commissioners to Connecticut to secure pledges of "men and money towards the service, wherein the Queen's subjects of your parts are equally concerned."[13]

Samuel Vetch, as agent for the Queen, by May 1709 had lined up pledges for meeting assigned quotas from each colony for a Canadian expedition. After promising partial reimbursement by the crown for expenses of the campaign, Vetch secured the unanimous vote of the New York Assembly to supply its quota of troops. At Fort Anne, near Albany, Vetch met with representatives of the Council and Assembly intermittantly from May 23 to June 21, 1709 to work out plans for the expedition. Governors Gurdon Saltonstall of Connecticut and Charles Gookin of Pennsylvania attended the conference as interested observers. A main order of business was to select a commander for the overland invasion. Governor Lovelace, the most likely choice, had recently died, and Richard Ingoldesby, the Lieutenant Governor, who had once been considered a possible choice for the command, for whatever reasons was not considered. Vetch asked Ingoldesby, Saltonstall, and Gookin to nominate someone who had demonstrated courage and ability as a military leader, and they named Nicholson.[14] It was also agreed that Colonel Peter Schuyler should be second in command and each of the four participating colonies should have its force organized into a battalion.[15]

With the Canadian expedition stalled at Wood Creek awaiting orders and hopefully news of the arrival of the British fleet and troops, Vetch thought it an apropos time to call a congress at New London. Because of the lack of accommodations at New London, Vetch transferred the site to Newport, but acting Governor Ingoldesby of New York refused to attend, insisting upon New York as the proper site of the conference. The traditional Boston-New York jealousy flared up, and Governor Dudley refused to attend a New York meeting. A logical choice would have been Philadelphia, but Pennsylvania had not cooperated in the expedition. Vetch decided upon Newport, but at the last minute, in order to make it easier for Dudley to attend, he moved the conference site to Rehoboth.

When the congress convened on October 14, 1709, in attendance were Governors Saltonstall, Cranston, Dudley with several persons from their respective councils and assemblies, Speaker Mark Hunting and Councilor Samuel Penhallow of New Hampshire, Colonel Nicholson, Colonel John Moody, and Vetch. After more than a week of discussion, the congress resolved to send an intercolonial force against Port Royal in conjunction with six men of war then in American waters, to maintain the three forts at Wood Creek, and to advise England to obtain Canada and Nova Scotia in the peace negotiations. It was also agreed to send Nicholson to England, accompanied by agents from each colony and five Iroquois chiefs. The three governors, Nicholson, and Vetch signed the resolutions, which were forwarded to England. Except for sending Nicholson and the Indian sachems to London, all the provisions of the congress came to naught. The troops at Wood Creek had to be disbanded and the forts dismantled because of the alleged poverty of the legislatures, and the British ship captains offered various excuses for not cooperating in an attack on Port Royal.[16] The Rehoboth conference was a missed opportunity in colonial union. But it was not to the degree that G. M. Waller, who overlooked the imperial connotation, would have it:

> No doubt it would have become a landmark in the development of colonial co-operation, if all its resolves had been carried out. If even the capture of Port Royal in the fall of 1709 had stemmed from the deliberations, as was intended, that gathering would have marked the initiation of a vigorous and united colonial effort carried through independent of all but the remotest British government supervision. Such an unprecedented effort would have stamped the proceedings as momentous.[17]

In June 1711 Nicholson arrived in Boston with orders from the crown to attack Canada and to hold a conference of governors from colonies north of Pennsylvania. On June 21 he met with Governors Hunter, Dudley, Saltonstall, and Cranston and Colonel Schuyler of Albany at New London. Nicholson presented a plan for a dual attack on Montreal and Quebec (with assistance from the British fleet); and troop quotas were worked out for all colonies north of Maryland.[18] Numerous consultations succeeded the conference. Governor Dudley, for example, frequently met with the British Admiral and General on Noddles Island where the British troops were stationed.[19] Councils of war were held at Annapolis Royal and aboard ship between the British military commanders and Vetch and New England colonels.[20]

Upon the suggestion of Nicholson and Vetch, commissioners from Massachusetts, Connecticut, and New Hampshire met in Boston on November 13, 1711 to draw up a resolution that the crown was neglecting the three hundred miles of "open villages" of the New England frontier while sending British troops to defend New York. The commissioners also considered means how to retain the neutrality of the Five Nations.[21]

As was threatened in 1740, Colonel Alexander Spotswood, formerly Governor of Virginia, in the spring, after meeting with Lieutenant Governor Gooch and Governor Johnston of North Carolina at Williamsburg, undertook a trip to confer with governors of the northern colonies concerning troop quotas, but he died at Annapolis on June 7. Gooch made the tour himself, conferring with several of the northern governors and military authorities.[22]

When news reached America in June 1744 of the British declaration of war upon France, Governors Jonathan Law of Connecticut and William Shirley of Massachusetts immediately arranged an intercolonial congress. Commissioners were named by both colonies to join with representatives of other northern colonies to work out measures for mutual defense and for treating with the Indians. The Albany conferences of 1744 and 1745, which will be treated in a later chapter, were the result.[23]

Governor Shirley went it alone, however, for the Louisbourg expedition of 1745. Instead of calling intercolonial conferences to enlist the support of other colonies, he merely applied through correspondence for aid; hence it is not surprising that the expedition was so much a unilateral affair.[24]

In 1747, commissioners from Connecticut and Massachusetts met with New York commissioners, but nothing was accomplished at the New York meeting except an agreement "to make some representation to his Majesty concerning the neighboring Governments which should refuse to unite with them for the general interest upon this occasion . . . ." A re-scheduling of the conference to convene at Middletown, Connecticut for January 20, 1748 does not appear to have led to another meeting.[25]

Governor Clinton wrote Shirley in April 1748 that "now I conceive that a Congress should be held in this City without delay with Commissioners from your Government and Connecticut and whatever application you think proper to make to the Southern Governments." The result was a congress at Albany on July 13, 1748 with commissioners only from New York and Massachusetts. Although treating primarily with Indian affairs, the commissioners considered military policy and drew up a resolution to the Board of Trade that all colonies be required to contribute to the defense of the New York, Massachusetts, and New Hampshire frontiers.[26]

Military affairs did not come in for attention at a general intercolonial meeting until the Albany Congress of 1754. Because the main purpose of the Congress was to consider a plan of union and the problems of Indian diplomacy,[27] the only military subjects discussed were the war powers of the President General and the Grand Council and fort building on the frontier. Since war with France was not an actual fact, no attempt was made to settle troop quotas or to plan operations, although it was stipulated that future quotas should follow the ratio of representation. Nevertheless a basic assumption by both the Board of Trade and the colonists in convening the Congress was that a colonial union in itself would afford the best means for providing for the common defense.[28]

If the Albany Congress failed to create a union of the colonies, it at least promoted the idea of intercolonial cooperative action. Massachusetts had instructed its commissioners on the eve of the Congress to present to the other delegates the necessity of providing for "stated interviews" and "a steady Union of Counsels" after the meeting had adjourned.[29] Shortly after the Albany Congress, Governor Dinwiddie took steps to arrange another intercolonial meeting in order to concert his planned war operations in the West. In a reply to Dinwiddie, Governor Glen of South Carolina favored an immediate consultation of the governors:

> I do not Comprehend what you mean by saying that you approve of Commissioners from each Government to enquire into the State of the Colonies but that there is no time to be spared for a general Congress. I for my part, could set out at a Weeks warning and I should be ashamed to say that I could send Commissioners who knew the State of this Colony as well as myself. I would propose to make no Parade or Long stay . . . .[30]

In October 1754, Dinwiddie conferred with Governor Dobbs of North Carolina and Sharpe of Maryland at Williamsburg to prepare for a spring campaign aganist Fort Duquesne and other French forts in the Ohio Valley. One thousand men exclusive of the Independent companies were to be assembled. It was also agreed to erect a fort on the Ohio to prevent the French from a southward use of the Ohio and to strengthen Fort Cumberland at Will's Creek as a supply base. Governor Glen was not invited to attend the conference presumably because of the enmity between Virginia and South Carolina over the Cherokee Indian trade. This was Sharpe's only military conference as commander in chief for a western offensive.[31]

As soon as Edward Braddock, the new commander of the colonial and royal forces in America, arrived at Hampton, Virginia in February 1755, he got in touch with Dinwiddie, and after several consultations at Williamsburg both men wrote to the colonial governors from Nova Scotia to South Carolina for contributions to the ensuing campaign.[32]

Braddock summoned the governors of Virginia, Maryland, Pennsylvania, New York, and Massachusetts to a conference at Alexandria to plan operations against the French. Unfortunately, Governor Glen of South Carolina was not invited and did not attend; he could have delivered a contingent of Indians for Braddock's army. On April 3 Braddock and Dinwiddie went to Annapolis, expecting that they might meet Shirley, De Lancey, and Morris there, but when they did not arrive, Braddock and Dinwiddie returned to Alexandria on the 7th. By the 14th all the invited governors had appeared at Alexandria and the conference began. Also attending were Colonel William Johnson, who was designated the commander for an expedition against Crown Point, and Commodore Augustus Keppel, commander in chief of His Majesty's fleet in North America. The conference decided that all the regular troops should be used against Fort Duquesne, except for two regiments which Shirley would deploy with provincials to attack Fort Niagara. William Johnson was to lead a colonial expedition to Crown Point. Surprisingly, such important matters as logistics and manpower received slight attention. Other items discussed at the conference were the crown's request for a common fund in the colonies and the use of Indians in the campaign.[33]

The lack of realism of the Alexandria conference's laying out a grand strategy of three fronts against the French without attending to the necessary details reflects the plan devised by the Duke of Cumberland, who had never been to America. "The Duke was one of those dangerous soldiers who love war for its own sake," comments Arthur Pound, "and who delight in mapping campaign moves as timid clerks delight in solving puzzles. That he knew next to nothing of the American scene, its broken and wooded nature and the sentiments and capacities of its people, hindered him not a whit from dictating a plan which cost dearly."[34]

Because Johnson owed his appointment as head of the Crown Point expedition to the governors conference, the question arose to whom should he turn to as superior commander? He was to operate independently of Braddock's command, and his force would consist entirely of provincials. His new post of Superintendent of Indian Affairs merely underlined his civilian status. Governor De Lancey tried to clarify the matter to Johnson:

> As to all other Matters concerning which you have no particular Instruction herein given you, you are to use your Discretion therein for the Good of his majesties Service always Consulting thereupon with a Councill of War to Consist at least of the Commanding Officer of the Troops of each Province engaged in the Expedition, acquainting me or the Commander in Chief of this Province with your Proceedings as soon as may be.[35]

Johnson followed this advice, which was a wise policy since colonial assemblies sent out commissioners to spy on him. Not having a military staff, he also used the council of war as a means of getting necessary staff work done. Even then, Johnson, who commanded largely New England troops, could note that "My Council of War are playing Politiks upon me."[36] At his camp at Lake George in October a committee was named "to draw up a particular state of this Army" and to report to a council of war, consisting of officers from Massachusetts, Connecticut, New York, and Rhode Island.[37]

After Braddock's death in the disastrous western campaign, William Shirley, as acting commander in chief, called for a war conference "of Commissioners from all the Colonies as far Westward as Virginia" to meet in New York about November 15. Many problems had to be worked out—the readjustment of troops after Braddock's defeat and support for the Crown Point and Niagara expeditions. Shirley sent circular letters to the governors, and asked Colonel Dunbar to use his influence to persuade the Virginia and Maryland governments to bring their regiments back to their previous strength.[38]

The assemblies seemed responsive to the idea of cooperative planning for the spring campaign. Even the New Jersey Assembly, which entertained no great loyalty to Shirley because of his impeding parliamentary reimbursement to the colony several years before, called upon neighboring colonies to meet with Shirley "to agree on the further necessary Supplies and Forces for next Year that should be provided in the Winter, so that all might be at the place of rendezvous by the first of the Spring." Apparently this action was a delaying tactic as the remainder of the resolution indicates: "But as they are one of the smallest Colonies they durst not take upon them to begin a proportion to that purpose, but will most readily follow the Example of the other greater Colonies as far as their Abilities can go."[39]

As a preliminary meeting to a general conference, Shirley came in from the field at Oswego to confer with commissioners from New York, Massachusetts, Connecticut, Rhode Island, and New Hampshire at Albany on November 20, 1755. Since Johnson's army had stalled at Lake George, with supplies running low and many New Englanders already having taken off for home, it was decided to discharge Johnson's troops, except for six hundred militia from the five participating colonies for garrisoning Fort Edward and Fort William Henry. Each colony would bear a proportionate cost of maintaining the garrisons. Shirley planned to meet Governors Morris of Pennsylvania and Sharpe of Maryland in New York City after the conference, but presumably this meeting did not take place until the general conference in December.[40]

The commissioners at the Albany conference now moved to Fort William Henry to confer with Major General William Johnson, Major General Phineas Lyman (Johnson's second in command), Captain Eyre, the Chief Engineer, and Captain Glazier, the Adjutant General. Shirley did not attend, and S.G. Van Shaick and Volkert Douw substituted for Governor Hardy and Lieutenant Governor De Lancey of New York. The minutes of the Albany meeting were endorsed concerning the troop disposition at the garrisons.[41]

During December 12-13 "a grand council of war", upon Shirley's instigation, took place in New York City. Attending, besides Shirley, were the governors of New York, Maryland, Pennsylvania, and Connecticut and the various staff and field officers. Thomas Pownall and Lieutenant Governor De Lancey had sought admission into this council of war but were not invited. Governor Belcher of New Jersey was ill and could not attend; and thus Pownall, as Lieutenant Governor of New Jersey, tried to take his place, but still the council excluded him and Shirley even declined him an interview. Undoubtedly both Pownall and De Lancey owed their rebuff to Shirley, whom they were openly intriguing against. Belcher did send two assemblymen, John Stevens and John Johnston, who were accepted in an *ex officio* capacity only. As the biographer of Thomas Pownall has said: the New York Conference had the effect of "encouraging

Shirley's enemies to redouble their efforts against him. Behind the scenes Pownall, Banyar, Wraxall, De Lancey, and Daniel Claus worked steadily for Johnson, showing him the correspondence of his adversaries and painting him as an injured victim of a hateful, jealous brute."

After reading the instructions that had been given by the crown to Braddock, Shirley reported on military events and the strategic significance of the French western posts. The commissioners then adopted unanimously his plan of operations without much alteration and settled matters of rank. An army of five thousand was to attack Forts Frontenac and La Gallette and then Forts Niagara, Presque Isle, Riviere au Beuf, Detroit, and Michilimakinac; simultaneously a force of three thousand provincials would attack Fort Duquesne and a body of ten thousand militia would then proceed to Crown Point; and two thousand troops, in a feinting maneuver, would move up the Kennebec River to Quebec. The commissioners requested additional regular troops from the crown to complete the levies. Quotas were arranged for the raising of ten thousand provincials from nine colonies to be used for the Crown Point expedition, which confirmed a similar discussion on this point at the Albany conference.[42] The Earl of Loudoun's plans, however, would soon supersede those made by this conference.

While Shirley awaited the arrival of the new commander in chief, the Earl of Loudoun, he assumed the responsibility of calling a general council of war himself. Writing to Governor Morris, he proposed:

> It will be absolutely necessary for me to hold a Council of Warr at New York, consisting of Governours and Field Officers (if to be had) according to his Majesty's Instructions, before I enter upon any Operation.
>
> In my way thro Connecticut I will engage Governor Fitch, as I will Governor Hopkins likewise if I can, to be present at the Council; and as it is a matter of great Importance to his Majesty's Service, as well of Consequence to myself, I must intreat the favour of you not to fail meeting me at New York . . . .[43]

Governor Hardy of New York also urged the need for united decision among the governors.[44] But because the anti-Shirley cabal was gaining momentum and Webb and then Abercromby– and not Shirley–were interim commanders in chief until Loudoun's arrival, the initiative for convening a general congress was left to Loudoun. On July 16, 1756, however, Governor Hardy met with Abercromby and Johnson in a council of war at Albany. It was agreed that Oswego and other garrisons should be strengthened and that rangers should be raised to assist Johnson's Indians in conducting sorties against the French.[45] Loudoun landed in New York July 20 without advance announcement,[46] and one of his first aims was to hold a conference to get commitments for the war effort. More so than previous commanders, Loudoun would place greater emphasis on coordination by the political authorities.

Lord Loudoun ordered two regional conferences to take place during 1757. Since no campaign was planned for late 1756, Loudoun used the time to inventory the state of military affairs and to lay his own plans for recruiting and strategy. By December 1756 he was ready to call a conference of commissioners from the New England colonies. The conference met from January 29 to February 4, 1757. Governors Fitch, Pownall, and Hopkins headed the delegations of their colonies, and Theodore Atkinson, the secretary of New Hampshire, attended as an observer. The commissioners were soon deadlocked in discussion over an increase of quotas, largely due to Connecticut's recalcitrance, but they did agree to convey Loudoun's recommendations to their assemblies. Loudoun had expected an immediate decision to "Concert measures for our mutual defence in this time of War and great danger." Irked by the lack of a sense of urgency on the part of the New England governments, Loudoun told the commissioners to consider how their action would be viewed by the home government and "what effect it must have in Canada, when they were informed of a disunion among them."[47]

From March 15-20 Loudoun met Governor Denny of Pennsylvania and three southern governors (Sharpe, Dinwiddie, and Dobbs) at Philadelphia. Governor Lyttleton of South Carolina did not attend, and apparently Georgia was not invited. Dinwiddie brought along George Washington, who argued for southern participation in an attack on Fort Duquesne, which would be in conjunction with an assault on Canada. Loudoun vetoed this plan because he wanted the southern colonies to set up a system of defense. It was finally decided that the governors would request their assemblies to raise a large provincial force, which would cooperate with British regulars to garrison the long southern frontier. If possible, each colony would send a part of their force to South Carolina, where a French invasion from Louisiana was feared.[48]

Thomas Pownall and the Massachusetts legislature sent out invitations in December 1757 and January 1758 to the New England governors to convene a conference on military affairs. Said Secretary Andrew Oliver:

> It appeared to us, that some steps might be proper to be taken by each government for its immediate defense, both by sea and land; and

> as the interest of the colonies of New England is so nearly connected, we thought it might better be pursued by acting in concert, than by the separate, and perhaps interfering measures of each colony acting by itself.[49]

From February 2-8, five commissioners from Massachusetts and three from Connecticut met at the State House in Boston. Pownall instructed the delegates to "lay a plan for the Union of the said Colonies, which you shall judge most conducive thereto, that in case any of them are attacked either by Sea, or on the side of Canada, the Forces of all of them may Act in Conjunction, or in such manner as shall best serve to Annoy and repulse the Enemy." The two colonies decided jointly to send scouts into enemy territory. Although Pownall also wanted the commissioners to modify the quotas to a more proportionate basis and to take measures to establish stores of ammunition and a train of artillery, the commissioners did little more than to propose general principles. Negatively, they resolved that the governor of a colony could recall its forces and that the governor of the colony "in which the Forces shall be, shall have it in his Power to settle the chief Command, and where no especial appointment shall be made, the chief Command shall be in the Chief Officer of that Part of the Forces belonging to the Colony where they shall then be, unless there be an Officer of higher Rank Present belonging to the Forces of the other Colony . . . ." Rhode Island and New Hampshire were invited to come into the "contract."[50]

Pownall had not bothered to inform Loudoun of the Boston meeting of New England commissioners beforehand; and from a letter Loudoun received about the time the conference opened it was apparent he was not invited. Loudoun's only reaction from New York was to criticize the feasibility of splintered conferences, a view he made known to Secretary Pitt:

> three Provinces meeting at this Season of the Year, to make an Alteration in the Quotas of six, that have been in use to furnish their Quotas, by a rule acquiesced under so many Years; and where New York one of those Six, has never been inform'd; and the Jerseys does not appear to have been invited; and Rhode Island appears, to have refused coming to it, on the plan that has been proposed; Appears to me to be an Affair of great Consequence, which if not prevented, is likely to create disputes and Animosities among the Provinces, and will probably prevent, in a Great Measure, the Harmony that ought to be cultivated amongst them at this time, and deprive the Public, in a great Measure, of that Aid they have a right to Expect from them at this time . . . .

Loudoun refuted the idea that a governor could have a command of the army since the king had appointed a commander of all his armed forces in America;[51] he did allow, however, that subordinate field commanders should concert operations with the colonial governors.

After Loudoun's recall in early 1758, the responsibility for coordinating operations and defense fell mainly to Brigadier General John Forbes. The new commander in chief, General Abercromby, was too busy personally supervising preparations to take an army from the northern colonies to attack the French forts at Lake George. One of Loudoun's last orders had been to ask Forbes to meet with the Pennsylvania authorities in Philadelphia.[52]

At Philadelphia from mid-April to the end of June, Forbes met frequently with Governor Denny,[53] and toward the end of this period Governor Bernard of New Jersey and Governor Glen of South Carolina joined the discussions.[54] In the meantime Governor Sharpe assisted the collection of troops and supplies in person at Fort Loudoun, Shippensburgh, and Carlisle, meeting with Bouquet, Sir John St. Clair, and occasionally Washington.[55] Forbes had to spend most of his time once he went into the field with negotiations with the Indians; most of the details for the offensive against Fort Duquesne, therefore, were worked out in councils of war by Bouquet, Montgomery, St. Clair, and the various senior officers from the three participating colonies.[56]

After his victory at Louisbourg, Amherst, now the commander in chief, returned to New York by way of New England, consulting individually with Governors Pownall, Hopkins, and Fitch on military and Indian affairs.[57] Acting upon Forbes's suggestion to have all the governors together in Philadelphia during "the vacancy of their assemblys," Amherst summoned the governors of Virginia, Maryland, Pennsylvania, New Jersey, and New York for a general military and Indian conference, but the call went unheeded.[58] Actually Amherst, like Forbes, preferred unilateral consultations. But the chief reason that Amherst made no further efforts to hold an intercolonial conference was that Forbes, to whom Amherst would have entrusted much of the responsibility, died on March 11. Already a month behind Pitt's timetable, Amherst was soon off to the Lake George country to supervise the collection of a motley army of regulars, provincials, and Indians to be used against Niagara and Crown Point.

By 1760 the intercolonial military conference had fallen to disuse. Quebec had been won by royal troops without provincials. The war, for all practical purposes, was over in 1760 with the capture of Montreal. The Rangers could take care of the mop-up work. While Indian affairs would still demand intercolonial cooperation, the war emergency in the north had ceased. Other factors had also made the intercolonial military conference obsolete. Neither the crown nor the colonies viewed colonial defense any longer as a regional concern, on which basis most of the conferences had been held. Quota principles had long been determined. The crown was in the process of creating a military establishment for the colonies, which would replace the military authority of the governors, except for the governors' legislative role in appropriations. And finally, the assemblies had shown reluctance to confer plenary powers upon the governors and other commissioners at the conferences.

NOTES

[1] Simon Bradstreet to John Allyn, Aug. 23, 1689, CA, Colonial Wars, II, 17; Allyn to Bradstreet, Sep. 4, 1689, *ibid.*, 18; Proceedings of the Commissioners, – 1689, *ibid.*, 20. Plymouth commissioners – Gov. Hinckley and Maj. Walley; Conn. – Dep. Gov. James Bishop and Capt. Samuel Mason; Mass. – Thomas Danforth and Elisha Cooke.

[2] Simon Bradstreet to Governor and Council of New Plymouth, Oct. 5, 1689, *The Hinckley Papers, MHSC* , 4th Ser., V (1861), 217–18.

[3] John Walley to Thomas Hinckley, Apr. 7, 1690, *ibid.*, 233–34; Gatke, "Plans of American Colonial Union," (Ph. D. diss.), 73–75 discusses the confusion over the two calls for a congress; Jerome R. Reich, *Leisler's Rebellion: A Study of Democracy in New York, 1664–1720* (Chicago, 1953), 94. Palfrey credits Massachusetts with the original invitation. Palfrey, *Hist. of New England*, IV, 49. Actually Mass. had tried to convene a conference in Rhode Island. Leisler merely took over the responsibility for calling the congress and suggested New York City as the site.

[4] Meeting of the Commissioners, May 1, 1690, CA, Colonial Wars, II, 57; Leder, *Robert Livingston*, 71-72; Allen W. Trelease, *Indian Affairs in Colonial New York: The Seventeenth Century* (Ithaca, 1960), 303. Commissioners: Jacob Leisler and P. L. Lanoy (N.Y.); John Walley (Ply.); William Stoughton and Samuel Sewall (Mass.): William Pitkin and Nathaniel Gold (Conn.). For discussion of quotas, see Chapter 8.

[5] Peter Schuyler and Dirck Wesselsson to the Governor and Council of Conn., Aug. 26, 1690, *Winthrop Papers, MHSC*, 6th Ser., III, 13.

[6] Reich, *Leisler*, 97.

[7] The Secretary of Conn. to Governor Sloughter, June 12, 1691, *CSP*, XIII, 474.

[8] Meeting of the Pa. Council, Oct. 1, 1693, *PCR*, I, 352; Gov. Fletcher to the Committee of Trade, Oct. 9, 1693, *NYCD*, IV, 55–56; William Phips to the Lords of the Committee, Apr. 3, 1693, Parkman transcripts, MHS; Trelease, *Indian Affairs in Colonial New York*, 316; Davidson, *War Comes to Quaker Pa.*, 12–13. Davidson incorrectly says the meeting was scheduled for Philadelphia.

[9] "Minutes upon the Representation of the Assemblies of Va. and Md. lying before the Committee of Trade and Plantations," Sep. 2, 1695, Chalmers Collection (Va.), NYPL; Privy Council Instrs., Aug. 22, 1694, CA, Colonial Wars, II, 209.

[10] William Stoughton to Gov. Robert Treat, Apr. 17, 1697, CA, Colonial Wars, III, 28.

[11] *NJA*, III, 64. Commissioners: Lord Cornbury, Richard Ingoldesby, and the Governor of Connecticut.

[12] The *Boston News-Letter*, Aug. 14, 1704, in Weeks, ed., *Hist. Digest*, 118.

[13] Resolution, House of Representatives, Dec. 29, 1704, MA, Colonial, III, 105; Joseph Dudley to Fitz-John Winthrop, Dec. 4, 1704, *Winthrop Papers, MHSC*, 6th Ser., III, 273. The commissioners were: Nathaniel Byfield, James Converse, and Samuel Lynde. Wait Winthrop and Nathaniel Payne were also empowered to treat with Conn., but since only three should present the Mass. case in Conn., they did not serve.

[14] Dudley to Wait Winthrop, Mar. 25, 1709, Dudley Miscellaneous Papers, NYHS; Col. Vetch and Col. Nicholson to (? the Earl of Sunderland), June 28, 1709, *CSP*, XXIV, 403; "At a Council Meeting at Fort Anne . . .," May 23, 1709, *NJA*, XIII, 343; Waller, *Vetch*, 130–33.

[15] Journal of the Proceedings of Col. Vetch and Nicholson, June 21, 1709, PRO, CO, Vol. 9, LC.

[16] Meeting . . . , Oct. 14, 1709, PRO, CO, Vol 9, LC; Dudley, Vetch, Moody to ––, Oct. 25, 1709, *ibid.*; Gov. Saltonstall to the General Assembly, Oct. 22, 1709, CA, Colonial Wars, III, 87; Dudley to the Council of New Hampshire, Sep. 21, 1709, Nathaniel Bouton, ed., *Documents and Records relating to the Province of New-Hampshire*, 6 vols. (Manchester, 1868–72), III, 399; Waller, *Vetch*, 153–64.

[17] Waller, *Vetch*, 162.

[18] W. Hill Journal, June 27, 1711, PRO, CO, Vol. 9, LC; Proceedings of the Congress held at New London, June 21–22, 1711, *NYCD*, V, 257–61; Palfrey, *Hist. of New England*, V, 362; Samuel Smith, *The Colonial History of New Jersey* (1765), reprint (Trenton, 1890), 400.

[19] Abstract of the Journal of the Proceedings of the Governor, Council, and Assembly of Mass., June–Oct., 1711, Parkman transcripts, XXXVII, MHS.

[20] W. Hill Journal, Sep. 8, 1711 and Oct. 11, 1711, PRO, CO, Vol. 9, LC. Present at the Annapolis Royal Council of War were: General Jack Hill, Colonel Vetch, Sir Charles Hobby, Colonel Reading, Commodore Martyne, Captain Mathews, and Captain Riddell.

[21] Nov. 13, 1711, Belknap Papers, MHS. Present were Penn Townshend and Andrew Belcher (Mass. Council) and Dudley for Mass.; Gurdon Saltonstall for Conn.; Samuel Penhallow (N. H. Council) and Theodore Atkinson (N. H. Assemb.); Addington Davenport and Thomas Hutchinson (Mass. Assemb.).

[22] Morton, *Colonial Virginia*, II, 531–32. The *Pennsylvania Gazette*, Jan 21, 1729 reported the N. Y. and Pa. Governors consulting together, which may be assumed but one of a number of social calls.

[23] Law to Shirley, June 19, 1744, *Shirley Corr.*, I, 127n.; Gov. Clinton to Gov. Morris, July 23, 1744, *Papers of Lewis Morris, NJHSC,* IV (1852), 198; George A. Wood, *William Shirley (Columbia Studies . . .*, XCII [New York, 1920]), I, 197–99.

[24] See Louis E. De Forest, ed., *Louisbourg Journals*, 1745 (New York, 1932) for the unilateral siege operations of Mass.

[25] Philip Livingston and Joseph Murray to Samuel Wells, Robert Hale and Oliver Partridge, Jan 26, 1747, MA, Colonial, IV, 107; Shirley to Gov. Benning Wentworth, Dec. 28, 1747, Belknap Papers, Force transcripts, LC; George Thomas to Thomas

Penn, Apr. 26, 1746, Ettling Revolutionary Papers, (Penn Papers: Official Correspondence), IV, HSP; Clinton to Governors of Md. and Va., May 19, 1746, *Md. Archives*, XLIV, 321–22.

[26] Clinton to William Shirley, Apr. 1, 1748, MA, Colonial, IV, 116; Hammelef, "Attempts to Coordinate Defenses" (Ph. D. diss.), 59; Frothingham, *Rise of the Republic*, 119n. Commissioners were: for New York – George Clinton, Cadwallader Colden, Philip Livingston, James De Lancey, and Archibald Kennedy; for Mass. – William Shirley, Thomas Hutchinson, Andrew Oliver, and John Choate.

[27] See Chapters 1 and 7.

[28] See instructions to commissioners, CA, Colonial Wars, V, 62, May 1, 1754; Riker, "Politics Behind Braddock's Expedition," *AHR*, XIII (1908), 745. Delegates to the Albany Congress were as follows: Mass. – Samuel Wells, John Chandler, Thomas Hutchinson, Oliver Partridge, and John Worthington; N. H. – Theodore Atkinson, Richard Wibird, Meshech Weare, and Henry Sherburne, Jr.; Conn. – William Pitkin, Roger Wolcott, Jr., and Elisha Williams; R. I. – Stephen Hopkins and Martin Howard, Jr.; Md. – Benjamin Tasker and Abraham Barnes; Pa. – John Penn, Richard Peters, Isaac Norris, and Benjamin Franklin; N. Y. – James De Lancey, Joseph Murray, William Johnson, John Chambers, and William Smith. (*PCR*, VI, 57; Foster, *Stephen Hopkins*, 168–69, 226–28; *MHSC*, 3d Ser., V, 18.)

[29] "Additional Instructions for the Commissioners of this Province . . . ," June 6, 1754, MA, Colonial, IV, 471a.

[30] Gov. James Glen to Gov. Dinwiddie, Aug. 22, 1754, PRO, CO, Vol. 14, LC.

[31] Dinwiddie to the Earl of Halifax, Oct. 25, 1754, *Dinwiddie Corr.*, I, 366; Desmond Clarke, *Arthur Dobbs, 1689–1765* (Chapel Hill, 1957), 109–10; Morton, *Colonial Virginia*, II, 660–61.

[32] Alfred P. James and Charles M. Stolz, *Drums in the Forest* (Pittsburgh, 1950), 32.

[33] Council at Camp at Alexandria, Apr. 14, 1755, Loudoun Papers, Huntington Lib. (microfilm Pa. St. Archives) and Emmet Collection, #6227, NYPL; *Pennsylvania Journal*, May 1, 1755; Braddock to Sir Thomas Robinson, Apr. 19, 1755, Parkman transcripts, XLI, MHS; Gov. De Lancey to Secretary Robinson, Aug. 7, 1755, *PA*, 2nd Ser., VI, 299; Edward P. Hamilton, *The French and Indian Wars* (New York, 1962), 152; Sclesinger, "Maryland's Share in Last Intercolonial War," *Md. Hist. Mag.*, VII (1912), 250–51; Schutz, *Shirley*, 195–98. The governors present were: Shirley, Dinwiddie, De Lancey, Sharpe, R. H. Morris. Also attending: William Johnson, Admiral Keppel, lesser military officers, and others, including, William Shirley, Jr. See also William Sawtelle, "Thomas Pownall, Colonial Governor, and Some of His Activities in the American Colonies," *MHSP*, LXIII (1930), 239–40. Franklin and William Franklin accompanied the N. Y., Mass., and Pa. governors as far as Annapolis and then went to Winchester to arrange for a new postal route. Leonard W. Labaree, "Benjamin Franklin and the Defense of Pennsylvania, 1754–57," *Pennsylvania History*, XXIX (1962), 11.

[34] Arthur Pound, *Johnson of the Mohawks* (New York, 1930), 173.

[35] De Lancey to William Johnson, Apr. 16, 1755, "Expedition Against Crown Point," *Md. Hist. Mag.*, IX (1914), 251. Johnson did have a commission from Shirley and De Lancey each for what they were worth.

[36] Pound, *Johnson*, 199–200. Quote on p. 199.

[37] Council of War, Camp at Lake George, Oct. 11, 1755, PRO, CO, Vol. 17, LC; *William Johnson Papers*, II, 179. For the minutes and personnel of the council of

war, Oct. 18-20 over which Maj. Gen Phineas Lyman presided, see *Fitch Papers* (*CHSC*, XVII), I, 165–69.

38 Shirley to Col. Thomas Dunbar, Aug. 12, 1755, Emmet Collection, #6; Dinwiddie's Address to General Assembly, (Sep. 9, 1755), *Virginia Gazette*, Oct. 31, 1755; Shirley to Sharpe, Sep. 9, 1755, *Md. Archives*, XXXI, 76–77.

39 Extract of Proceedings of N. J. Assembly, n. d., Shirley Papers, MHS; Fisher, *New Jersey as a Royal Province,* 337.

40 Spencer Phips to Gov. Thomas Fitch, Nov. 4, 1755, MA, Colonial, IV, 71; Stephen Hopkins to Phips, Nov. 4, 1755, MA, Colonial, VI, 637; Hopkins to Sharpe, Nov. 6, 1755, Dreer Collection, Governors of the Colonies, HSP; Shirley to R. H. Morris, Nov. 11, 1755, William Shirley Miscellaneous Correspondence, NYPL; Sharpe to Gov. of Pa., Nov. 13, 1755, Emmet Collection, #6033, NYPL; *South Carolina Gazette*, Dec. 4, 1755; "At a Meeting held at Albany . . . ," Nov. 20, 1755, PRO, CO, Vol. 17, LC; *William Johnson Papers*, XIV, 70–71. Commissioners, in addition to Shirley were: N. Y. – Gov. Charles Hardy, James De Lancey, Daniel Horsmanden, and John Rutherford; Mass. – James Minot, John Choate, Oliver Partridge, and Samuel Levermore; Conn. – Benjamin Hall and John Hubbard. The garrisons at Ft. William Henry and Ft. Edward were to bear the proportionate contribution of troops: Mass., 185; Conn., 154; N. Y., 123; N. H., 77; and R. I., 61 – total, 600.

41 Minutes of the Council of War, Nov. 24–26, 1755, *William Johnson Papers*, III, 335–37.

42 "Minutes of a Council of War held by William Shirley," New York, Dec. 12, 1755, Shirley Misc. Corr., NYPL; *PCR*, VII, 23–29; *Fitch Papers* (*CHSC*, XVII), I, 184–92; *Md. Archives*, XXXI, 90–98; Livingston, *Review of Military Operations*, 131–136; Fisher, *N. J. as a Royal Province*, 337–38; Johnson, *Hist. of the French War*, 236; Schutz, *Pownall*, 65. Attending: Sir Charles Hardy, Horatio Sharpe, R. H. Morris, Thomas Fitch, Col. Thomas Dunbar, Col. Peter Schuyler, Maj. Charles Craven, Sir John St. Clair (Dep. QMG), Maj. James Kinneer, Maj. John Rutherford, and Shirley. All of the above signed the quota resolutions for 10,000 men, except Fitch, who had to leave before the meeting was over. Present *ex officio* were assemblymen from N. J., John Johnston and John Stevens.

43 Shirley to Gov. Morris, Apr. 18, 1756, Emmet Collection, #9180, NYPL.

44 Letter of Charles Hardy in "Proceedings of His Majesty's Council of N.J. . . . ", Mar. 9, 1756, *NJA*, 1st Ser., XVII, 7.

45 Council of War, Albany, July 16, 1756, PRO, CO, Vol. 47, LC; *Pennsylvania Gazette*, July 29, 1756. Attending: Abercromby, Sir Charles Hardy, Col. Daniel Webb, Sir William Johnson, Lt. Col. Thomas Gage, James De Lancey, Lt. Col. Francis Grant, Lt. Col. Sir John St. Clair, James Montresor.

46 *Pennsylvania Gazette*, July 29, 1756. This source disputes James High's statement that Loudoun landed in N. Y. the 23d.

47 Loudoun to Henry Fox, Feb. 8, 1757, Parkman transcripts, XLIV, MHS; Thomas Fitch to Earl of Loudoun, Jan. 31, 1757, MA, Colonial, VI, 234; Resolution of House of Rep., Feb. 2, 1757, *ibid.*, 236; *Mass. Acts and Resolves*, XVI (1909), Dec. 24, 1757, 104; Johnson, *Hist. of the French War*, 254; Instructions to the Commissioners, *Fitch Papers* (*CHSC*, XVII), I, 275–76; Loudoun to the Commissioners, Jan. 29, 1757, *ibid.*, 276–80; Commissioners to Loudoun, Jan. 31, 1757, *ibid.*, 280; *CCR*, X, Jan. 20, 1757; Pargellis, *Loudoun in North America*, 213–16. Thomas Hutchinson headed the Mass. delegation; Theodore Atkinson, Secretary of N. H., attended only as an observer; Gov. Hopkins headed the R. I.

delegation; from Conn. there were Gov. Thomas Fitch, Jonathan Trumbull, Phineas Lyman, Elihu Hall, and Eliphalet Dyer. Loudoun had asked for the following quotas of troops: Mass., 1,800; Conn., 1,400; R.I., 450; N.H., 350.

48 "Minutes of a Meeting of the Southern Governors with the Earl of Loudoun, Mar. 15–20, 1757, PRO, WO:34, Vol. 36, LC; Loudoun to Gov. Lyttleton, Apr. 24, 1757, *ibid.*; Dinwiddie to Earl of Halifax, Mar. 22, 1757, Virginia Miscellaneous Papers, Box 1, LC; Capt. Thomas Lloyd to Col. James Burd, Feb. –, 1757, Thomas Balch, ed., *Letters and Papers relating Chiefly to the Provincial History of Pennsylvania* (Philadelphia, 1855), 57; Pargellis, *Loudoun in North America*, 218–22; for the "minutes" also see, Stanilaus M. Hamilton, *Letters to Washington and Accompanying Papers*, vols. I–III (Boston, 1898–1901), II, 51. Quotas decided upon: Pa.–1,400; Md.–500; Va.–1,000; N.C.–400; S. C.–500; King's troops–1,200; total, 5,000. Also for defense of S. C.: 5 companies of regulars–500; 3 Indep. companies–200; provincial troops (S.C.)–500; N.C.–200; Va.–400; Pa.–200; total, 2,000.

49 Sec. Oliver of Mass. to Gov. Greene, Jan. 19, 1758, *RICR*, VI, 116; Pownall's Instructions to the Mass. Commissioners, Jan. 24, 1758, PRO, CO, Vol. 18, LC.

50 "Minutes of the Proceedings . . .," Feb. 2, 1758, PRO, CO, Vol 18, LC; Feb. 8, 1758, MA, VI, 258; *Fitch Papers (CHSC,* XVII), I, 322–27; Schutz, *Pownall*, 119–20. Besides Thomas Hutchinson, who presided, Mass. commissioners were: William Brattle, John Choate, John Tyne, and Benjamin Pratt. Conn. commissioners were: Ebenezer Silliman, Jonathan Trumbull, and William Wolcott.

51 Lord Loudoun to Pitt, Feb. 14, 1758, *Pitt Corr.*, I, 187.

52 Loudoun to Forbes, Apr. 13, 1758, Loudoun Papers, Huntington Lib. (microfilm Pa. State Archives, Harrisburg).

53 Sylvester Stevens *et al.*, eds., *The Papers of Henry Bouquet*, II (Harrisburg, 1951), xxxiii, 112; Forbes to Abercromby, Apr. 20, 1758, James, ed., *Forbes Writings*, 65; Forbes to Abercromby, June 7, 1758, *ibid.*, 109.

54 Gov. Francis Bernard to the Lords of Trade, July 3, 1758, *NJA*, 1st Ser., IX, 120–21. Forbes to Abercromby, June 15, 1758, James, ed., *Forbes Writings*, 113; Forbes to Bouquet, June 10, 1758, *ibid.*, 111.

55 Forbes to Stanwix, May 29, 1758, *ibid.*, 102.

56 Stevens *et al.*, *Bouquet Papers*, II, 547, 600.

57 J. C. Long, *Lord Jeffrey Amherst* (New York, 1933), 82.

58 Capt. Robert Stewart to Washington, Jan. 16, 1759, Hamilton, ed., *Letters to Washington*, III, 153; Forbes to Amherst, Jan. 26, 1759, James, ed., *Forbes Writings*, 283; Osgood, *American Colonies*, IV, 441.

CHAPTER IV

LOGISTICS

During the first three colonial wars, an obstacle to unified military action was the lack of central logistical control. Each colony outfitted and supplied its own troops, although on occasion the crown sent over arms and ammunition. A colony remote from the field of battle was often expected to contribute supplies and military stores as a substitute for troops, and much ill-feeling was generated because legislatures of the distant colonies were reluctant to contribute to the defense of a frontier not their own. In the last colonial war, a measure of coordination was achieved because of a more delineated command system and the assistance of British staff officers in the field. This chapter does not attempt to unravel the logistical support of the numerous expeditions or garrison forces in the four colonial wars, which in itself is an enormously complex topic and does not fit into the purpose or confines of this study. Rather, it is hoped that a representative treatment of the problems of supply and procurement as the colonies generally dealt with them will point to the mode and degree of colonial cooperation.

Inadequate supply spelled failure for both major expeditions of King William's War. The overland expedition was impeded by the stoppage of supplies of salted pork and biscuit from Connecticut to the colony's troops at Albany and by the failure of New York artisans to build boats for conveying the army up Lake Champlain. A French raid on Connecticut's shores at New London and the preparations for Phips's naval expedition against Quebec distracted from the New England support of the land offensive.[1] Robert Livingston, Peter Schuyler, and Stephanus Van Cortlandt put up their own money for victualling New York's troops at Albany, for which they had to wait until after the war for reimbursement.[2]

The crown's order for the colonies to send aid to the land offensive went unheeded, except for Virginia's voting £ 500 out of revenues on liquors. Governor Nicholson of Maryland responded typically: "I am very sorry that the Charge of the Warr has been so heavy upon the province of

New York; but I find that neither his Majestys honorable Councill nor the Burgesses of the House of Assembly are of Opinion that the province of New York is the safety of this."[3] The Connecticut Council complained to their agent in London that the colony had already expended considerable sums in men and supplies to help New York: "we having exhausted our own stocks in their Majesties service and by reason of blasts and other frownes of Gods Providence we are brought very low." Connecticut also pleaded the scarcity and "very deere rates" of arms, ammunition, and gunpowder, which had gone up to fifteen pounds a barrel.[4]

Several weeks of inactivity of the Phips expedition before Quebec exhausted the supplies of the New England troops. Massachusetts charged that Connecticut should have supplied the greater amount of provisions since Massachusetts and New Hampshire had provided the most men in this campaign.[5] Expected aid from England did not arrive, and when some relief came from the colonies, the provincial ship masters, who owned their own craft, were afraid to move through the mouth of the St. Charles because their ships might be destroyed in the cross-fire. For the main assault, Major Walley's men had only a half barrel of musket powder and a day's ration of one biscuit.[6] One infantryman expressed the disillusionment of his comrades: "Now indeed the want of Time the want of Ammunition and of Field pieces and Provision may be Reckoned great Obstructions to our future Attempts that we might think of. But how comes this great Scarsitie and famine upon Us."[7]

After King William's War, the four companies of two hundred regulars left in New York were on the verge of having to make the choice of starving or deserting, since the New York victuallers had given up service because of the continued delinquency in the payment of their accounts. Livingston had a common sense solution which was endorsed by Governor Bellomont: namely, have the governor's agent, Sir William Ashurst, purchase goods directly and consign them to whomever the governor saw fit. But this idea conflicted with the profit-making of London merchants, who did not want to extend credit to the Governor should he himself get into financial straits.[8]

The crown supplied a large amount of military stores for both the northern and southern campaigns during Queen Anne's War. The shortage of arms was the most grave problem; even many New England troops – colonial laws to the contrary – did not possess their own arms.[9] Relations between New Hampshire and Massachusetts were embittered with New Hampshire's charge that Massachusetts kept ordnance stores sent by the crown for the defense of the New Hampshire frontier.[10] Rhode Island and Connecticut surprisingly responded with enthusiasm in granting provisions, transport vessels, and other supplies for the Canadian expeditions. Unfortunately, however, colonial provisioners demanded ready money sterling for purchases, and wartime inflation hindered procurement. In the case of New York, stiff price regulation governed military purchases. Admiral Walker and General Hill, in preparing for the expedition against Canada, found that the previous military commissary, Colonel Andrew Belcher, had quit to enter the private capacity of contractor for supplying the New York troops. Although a new commissary was found, the Admiral had to borrow money from the New York government in order to meet the currency exchange rates.[11]

For the 1709 and 1711 expeditions Samuel Vetch was charged with superintending the overall logistics and operations. He simply adhered to the quotas alloted by the intercolony congresses, with the understanding that each colony provision its own force. Neither Maryland or Pennsylvania contributed anything, with Pennsylvania's "flat denial" a foregone conclusion even before the assembly took up the matter.[12] Virginia was more cooperative. But Lieutenant Governor Spotswood, who was ordered by the crown to buy up provisions from neighboring colonies for the Canada expedition of 1711, could only secure supplies in his own colony.[13]

With the outbreak of the war with Spain in 1739, the crown requested all the colonies except Georgia and South Carolina to assume the cost of subsistence and transportation for an intercolonial volunteer expedition to the Spanish West Indies. In anticipation of a share in the plunder, most of the colonies – including Quaker Pennsylvania – quite willingly complied. The actual expense to the colonies was not great since the British government provided clothing, tents, arms, and ammunition in addition to paying the troops.[14] A resolution of the New York assembly indicates the colonial enthusiasm:

> Resolved: That it is their Opinion, that the Success of the Expedition directed by his Majesty, against some *Spanish* Settlements in the *West-Indies,* will highly tend to the Benefit of *Great Britain,* and all its Dominions in general, as well as of this Colony in particular.[15]

New Hampshire did not provision its volunteers because a difference of opinion between the Governor and the assembly over the royal instructions had led to an impasse.[16] Former Governor William Gooch of Virginia served as quartermaster for the expedition but was excluded from the councils of war. Although the ineptness of the commander, Admiral Vernon, was a chief cause of the disaster, the disorganization of the expeditionary force, three-fourths of whom were provincials, was also a factor. As James Oglethorpe later dryly commented: "Two Battallions and a small Squadron with Mr. Vernon would at first have taken Carthagena, 4000 men after they were prepared could not do it.[17]

The Louisbourg expedition of 1745 was mainly supported by storeships from England, with initial help from the New England colonies, for which they were later reimbursed.[18] The Board of Ordnance in England was responsible for providing arms and ammunition, and the Treasury took care of victualling and transport. Each foot soldier, however, had to bring his own clothes and weapons, paid for by the colony.[19] The Duke of Newcastle ordered the governors of the New England colonies to send their men in transports to rendezvous with the British force at Louisbourg. Shirley took charge of this task. Although he had hoped for vessels from all the four colonies, "that our Transports should be divided into four Divisions, each wearing distinct colours," Shirley had to depend chiefly on Boston vessels.[20] Thirteen armed ships were furnished, of which several came from Connecticut. The Rhode Island sloop carrying ninety men arrived too late for the battle. Some artillery (including ten eighteen-pound guns), provisions, powder, clothing, and bedding came from New York, and Pennsylvania sent some provisions. But the final assault on Louisbourg had to be delayed because nine out of ten provincials had no bayonets and there was an inadequate supply of shoes. Scaling ladders proved to be ten feet too short.[21]

In February 1745 Connecticut sent Jonathan Trumbull and Elisha Williams to meet with the authorities in Boston to plan logistics. As a result, both Massachusetts and Connecticut named commissaries to contract for supplies. Although Trumbull and Williams were not authorized to purchase supplies for the army, they managed to sell powder, flints, tin kettles, measures and other items to the troops. Only the Massachusetts commissaries were allowed to purchase supplies for the British regulars.[22]

After the successful siege of Louisbourg, colonial enthusiasm for supporting a war effort waned. The colonies had a tendency to view war matériel as surplus to be disposed of as quickly as possible. Commodore Warren made an urgent appeal to the colonial governors for a new levy of men and provisions to maintain the garrison at Louisbourg,

> and I never had more occassion for your assistance than at present, in order to keep possession of a Garrison, that is the Key to all the French Settlements, upon the Continent, and of which possession every Collony will feel the good effect; therefore hope you will send with all speed your Quota of men, Arm'd & Victual'd, for at least Seven or Eight Months, to remain here for the Support of this Garrison, 'till his Majestys pleasure is known, till which time I shall continue here.[23]

The New England governments complied to the extent of stationing several hundred troops at Louisbourg, "supported in Garrison out of the Provisions raisd by the Western Governments for his Majesties Service . . . ."[24] Governor Law of Connecticut tried without success to secure a victualling contract for the regular troops for merchants of his colony.[25]

Inflation and doubts as to England's intentions towards reimbursement for the Louisbourg expedition thwarted raising of supplies for the campaign against Crown Point planned for 1746-7. The announcement that British officials would take over direct supervision of logistics[26] was not to the liking of the colonists, although Shirley did appoint William Winslow as Commissary General[27] in the hopes of controlling contract patronage as he had done with the Louisbourg expedition. Eventually, as the times looked better, Massachusetts and Connecticut voted substantial supply bills to pay for stores and provisions for the expedition against Crown Point.[28] Elsewhere, a sampling reveals a disparite reaction. The Pennsylvania legislature refused outright to vote arms and provisions, even for defense of the back country. Governor Thomas, however, tried to establish an independent fund to be at the disposal of the Governor and council.[29] The Virginia Burgesses indicated it would approve a request from the Governor for an appropriation to send arms, clothing, provisions, and accoutrements to Albany.[30] New York legislators got into a wrangle as to who should receive the colony's supplies at Albany – the captains of companies, the commander in chief, or Governor Clinton.[31] But before any of the colonies proceeded very far in arranging supplies, the Duke of Newcastle in May 1747 called off the campaign.[32]

While Virginians were jostling with the French over the possession of the Ohio Valley, Governor Dinwiddie untiringly sought supplies from neighboring colonies. He bid Governors Hamilton, Belcher, Shirley and Glen and President Matthew Rowan of the North Carolina Council to arouse their assemblies to action.[33] "It appears to me," he wrote Governor Glen of South Carolina, "more eligible in obedience to his Majesty's Commands that each Colony grant a mutual Supply, by Application to the Assemblies, without waiting to adjust the proper Quotas." But South Carolina, Pennsylvania, and New Jersey showed a complete lack of interest. To Dinwiddie, the assemblies of these colonies were "seized with a lethargic Supineness."[34] To compound his problems, arms sent from England went directly to the Governor of New York for future use in the northern theater.[35] A major cause for Washington's defeat at Great Meadows, however, Dinwiddie laid to George Croghan's dilatoriness in bringing up supplies to Fort Necessity, for which Croghan was under contract with the Virginia commissary, Major John Carlyle.[36]

In planning another offensive – awaiting Braddock's arrival – Governor Dinwiddie began assembling foodstuffs. With £ 10,000 in specie from the ministry and £ 20,000 granted by the Burgesses, Dinwiddie sent commissaries to the southern and middle colonies to contract for beef, pork, flour, and other supplies. Sir John St. Clair, the crown-appointed deputy quartermaster general, soon arrived in Virginia to take charge of securing supplies. When Braddock assumed his command he directed Pennsylvania, Virginia and Maryland "separately or conjunctively" to provide artillery, ammunition, stores, and provisions, as agreed upon at the Alexandria conference.[37] Maryland passed a supply bill only for supporting three hundred men on her western frontier.[38] Even then, Sharpe had difficulty in collecting artillery and provisions at Annapolis, and after Braddock had begun his march, leaving Maryland, the Maryland Assembly refused to vote any further appropriations.[39] Dinnwiddie provided blankets, provisions, and wagons for the Independent company from South Carolina.[40]

The precision-minded British commander constantly had insufficient logistical support." The colonies had established no magazines of provisions.[41] No wonder Braddock wrote: "The jealousy of the people, and the disunion of many colonies are such that I almost despair of succeeding."[42] After setting out on the march through a sparsely populated countryside, Braddock expected to find the twenty-five hundred horses and two hundred wagons that he had contracted for with the Virginia and Maryland governments awaiting him at Forts Frederick and Cumberland; instead there were only two hundred horses and twenty wagons.[43] Although Virginia and Maryland troops accompanied Braddock, these colonies continued to be deficient in sending supplies to the field.

Fortunately for Braddock, Benjamin Franklin and his son William stopped at Fort Frederick on the way from Winchester to Philadelphia on post office business. Franklin noted that wagons were easy to obtain in Pennsylvania, and Braddock promptly commissioned Franklin to secure one hundred fifty wagons and teams and carriage horses for £ 809 9*s*, Skilfully playing upon the greed of Pennsylvania's settled citizenry, Franklin issued a broadside stating that leasing horses and wagons would put more money into circulation and otherwise they would be impressed anyway. Franklin soon had the wagons. Franklin was also used to obtain forage, and again the threat of impressment produced results.[44]

Governor Sharpe despaired that once Braddock had taken Fort Duquesne "he will be obliged to desert the Fort . . . for want of Provisions which he cannot now expect from these Colonies."[45] Establishing a supply line was of immediate concern to Braddock. After crossing the mountains he hoped to set up a communications route to eastern Pennsylvania. It was good business for merchants to have a military road in the colony, and the Pennsylvania authorities, therefore, took the chief responsibility in building it. Governor Morris selected George Croghan, William Buchanen, John Armstrong, James Burd, and Adam Hoops as road commissioners. Since these men were also traders, they tried to run the road towards the center of the province in order to prevent its use by Virginia traders. But a delay of a month before the commisssioners assumed their duties and over two months in building the road set back Braddock's timetable drastically.[46]

Pennsylvania also accepted the task of provisioning Braddock's army in the field, although at first the assembly balked at supplying the army until it had crossed into Pennsylvania. A small supply of provisions from Virginia and Maryland was so decayed and damaged as to be of no use. Braddock reportedly said of these two colonies: "They had promised everything and performed nothing." And the Pennsylvanians "had promised nothing and had performed everything."[47] William Allen, a wealthy Philadelphia merchant, was contracted to secure provisions for Braddock, but he and his agents discovered that farmers were reluctant to travel to paymasters to get money for their produce, which entailed delay in getting provisions to the army.[48]

Simultaneously with the Braddock campaign, the New England colonies were ordered by the crown to send an army against the French at Niagara and Crown Point with each colony participating in the expedition expected to share in the cost of supplies.[49] Pennsylvania, in a rare display of neighborly good will, granted Shirley, who had the over-all command of the expedition, £ 1000 currency for provisions. But detrimental to the New England expedition, each colony insisted on retaining in its own hands the transport and maintenance of its forces.[50] Virginia and Maryland were counted upon to contribute what provisions, military stores, carriages, and horses that they could,[51] and it was expected that New York would field its militia to assist the New England force. Lieutenant Governor Spencer Phips entreated the Governors of Rhode Island, Connecticut, and New York to fulfill their share in the campaign, asserting that Massachusetts had sent and made provision for three hundred men more than had originally been pledged. "It will be unhappy indeed if the great expence we have already been at should be to no purpose for want of some addition to it," warned Phips, "but it will be much more unhappy if the lives of so many of our Country men should be lost for want of some additional strength to the Army. . ."[52] In calling a special session of the assembly, Governor Hopkins of

Rhode Island also asked for a show of patriotic unity: "Hence every Government, concerned in the present Enterprise will, I doubt not, proportion Supplies according to the Value they put upon their Religion, their Liberty, their Estates, and the Freedom of themselves and their Posterity."[53]

Initially having appointed David Rowland and Elihu Lyman as contractors for provisions, once in the field Shirley chose four new contractors: New York merchants Peter Van Burgh Livingston and Lewis Morris, Jr., William Alexander, his secretary for the Niagara expedition, and his son-in-law, John Erving, Jr. Immediately the contractors experienced difficulties. Albany merchants would not accept notes from other colonies.[54] The lure of war profiteering was greater than patriotism. For example, New York bakers raised the price of bread *2s.* per hundredweight (thus *16s. 6d.* per hundred pounds), and dried peas at Albany went from five to six and seven shillings per bushel. Alexander and his associates had the responsibility of clearing the way, building storehouse forts, supplying materials not provided by the British navy for building three ships on Lake Ontario, and furnishing provisions, bateaux, workmen, naval stores, and various miscellaneous items such as wampum and presents for the Indians. As in previous campaigns, the expedition was soon far behind schedule. Because of low water, shortage of bateauxmen and wagoners, and careless handling of supplies, so much time was used up on the way from Albany up the Mohawk to the Carrying Place that provisions were exhausted.

At Oswego, readying to attack Niagara, Shirley's army still suffered from a lack of supplies. The supply base at the Carrying Place was eighty-five miles away; the New York contractors failed to supply beef and what cattle there was to be found had to be brought in from Worcester, Massachusetts. Careless handling, rain, and other difficulties beset the supply line. Because of a shortage of laborers, Shirley had to put his troops to construction work at Oswego. The arrival of the remnant of regulars from Braddock's expedition necessitated half rations.[55] Governor Charles Hardy's efforts to impress horses and wagons were resisted by local farmers, and amidst the acute distress at Oswego, additional Massachusetts and Connecticut troops arrived without provisions.[56]

William Johnson's provincials preparing to invest Crown Point were having an even worse time of it at the encampment on Lake George. Unlike Shirley, whose expenses for the army marching on Niagara would ultimately be paid by the British government, Johnson had to rely entirely upon colonial resourses.[57] The lack of rations pushed his men to the verge of mutiny.[58]

From 1755 on, the crown established an overview of supply and transportation. Colonies were required to report inventories of ordnance and stores.[59] A new policy of fuller logistical support for the colonies was announced by the home government in March 1756. The colonies would still furnish men, pay, arms, and clothing. But all magazines of stores and provisions, however, would be supplied at the expense of the crown, which meant reimbursement for colonial outlays in provisions, subsistence, artillery stores, camp equipage, and land and water transportation. Several examples will suffice to illustrate the latitude in the colonial interpretation of this policy. Rhode Island claimed expenditures for stores and provisions remaining after troops had returned home and "several unusual unmilitary Species of provision and Stores in the said account; such as Coffee, Tea, Chocolate, Sugar, Ham, Knives, Forks, Spoons, Plates &c . . . ."[60] Needless to say, the colony's claims were not totally allowed. Massachusetts had the same laxity: "Under the Article of Artillery, they have included Tents, Drums, Colours, All Camp Necessaries, Platters, Pans, Keggs and a number of other things they have been in use of furnishing their Troops unknown in a regular Army."[61]

It seems as if fate continued to conspire against the Niagara and Crown Point expeditions. All the colonies in 1756 were expected to contribute men and matériel. But colonial rivalries hindered the war effort. For example, Virginia would not allow the Maryland or Carolina companies to be supported out of Virginia provisions.[62] All that New Jersey did for the war effort in 1756 was to cooperate in a general embargo by prohibiting exportation of provisions and military stores.[63] Quarrels between the governors and the assemblies stopped all aid from Maryland and Pennsylvania.[64].

After many months inadequate food rations and other supplies at Fort Oswego, attributed in large measure to the failings of William Alexander as coordinator[65] and the negligence of James De Lancey in the inspection of supplies delivered by New York merchant-contractors at Albany,[66] the post fell to Montcalm's force in July 1756.

When Loudoun took command he placed all blame on Shirley, and ordered a stop payment on all unpaid warrants issued by Shirley, which left the contractors with an unpaid balance of £ 14,378. Only after five years and much expense were the contractors able to collect from the British government.[67]

Though Dinwiddie planned a western expedition against Fort Duquesne in 1756, it could not come off largely because of a lack of cannon and arms. Shirley had four large cannon taken from Virginia to New York. Nor could Pennsylvania and Maryland be induced to contribute to such a scheme at this time, and North Carolina would not make any commitments beyond sending a reinforcement to "Lord Loudoun's American Regiment" and its own frontier defense.[68]

In 1757 none of the colonies were willing to go to any great lengths for the war effort. When Fort William Henry was besieged, so many dispatches from the army were sent to the New England governments unsuccessfully beseeching quick relief that messengers could hardly be found.[69] The Virginia legislature refused to supply the Independent companies ordered into South Carolina to defend the Virginia frontier.[70]

Whatever inclination the colonists might have had to cooperate in logistics was being killed with kindness from Whitehall. The home government continued the policy of supplying the provincials with arms, artillery, provisions, tents, and transportation. The colonies were expected to provide clothing and pay, with the Secretary of State to recommend to Parliament compensation for these expenses.[71] This promise had the tendency to be accepted by the colonists as a total paternalistic pledge. The chief difficulties were the same as before in the recalcitrance of the assemblies to vote the immediate funds needed for clothing and pay and the inability of the quartermaster general's department to purchase provisions and supplies on the spur of the moment.

In the preparations for the western offensive of 1758, the Virginia and Maryland assemblies did little to provide for their troops, and thus delayed their joining the regular force. For a while General Forbes had to order the Virginia and Maryland troops to stay at Winchester because of lack of supplies. There they could at least be of service "to prevent the Country people and the Cherokees that were returning home from massacring one another . . . this I hope will amuse them some time . . . ."[72] Meanwhile, Governor Dinwiddie took the Maryland Governor to task for supplying Virginia troops at Fort Loudoun with bad beef.[73] Sharpe himself informed Sir John St. Clair, the quartermaster general, that "it really is not in my Power to supply any Troops which you may have occasion to march thro this Province either with Provisions or Waggons."[74]

A priority of the Forbes expedition into western Pennsylvania was to build fortified store depots connected by a good road into the interior. Commercial rivalries led to Virginians wanting the road built via Fort Cumberland and Pennsylvanians demanding that the road be built through Raystown.[75] It was decided, however, to take the shorter route through Pennsylvania. During this time, while collecting his force and building the road, Forbes wrote Pitt that he could not maintain three months' provisions. Forbes also complained of the "villany of the Inhabitants in furnishing their worst horses," which could pull only fourteen hundred pounds instead of the two thousand contracted for. [76] As Franklin had done in 1755, Forbes threatened impressment of wagons.[77]

Of the troops collecting at camp near Raystown, in August 1758, Colonel Henry Bouquet had only words of dismay for the North Carolina contingent: they were in such "pitiable condition, and lack health, uniforms and everything. I have never seen such misery. I believe they are good only for guarding a fort." Surprisingly the Maryland troops had arrived from Fort Frederick fairly well supplied.[78] Even though Forbes tried to make prompt payment of provisions accounts,[79] some of the contractors who initially supplied troops before leaving a colony, expecting a colonial assembly to give payment until funds would be forthcoming from the crown, found themselves running up huge debits without relief.[80]

When he arrive at Raystown, Forbes found the supply situation still acute.[81] But at the last minute Pennsylvania came through as it had done in Braddock's campaign. Colonel James Burd arrived with an artillery train, and a month before the final march on Fort Duquesne, Sir John St. Clair, the Quartermaster General, having used some highhanded tactics, appeared with the much overdue wagons and provisions from the Pennsylvania contractors.[82]

For Abercromby's army at Lake George, in spite of the disastrous defeat at Ticonderoga, the New England colonies became increasingly generous in supplying provisions – largely due to the political influence of the merchant-contractors. The Connecticut Assembly permitted as much as a twelve per cent mark-up on most items and as high as fifty per cent on sugar and tobacco.[83] Sub-contractors, however, met long delays in securing payment.[84]

Colonial regiments were expected to act in conjunction with royal troops for the projected 1760 campaigns. Again the crown would furnish arms, ammunition, tents, provisions, and transportation and the colonies would provide clothing and pay of the men, which presumably would be reimbursed by the crown.[85] Amherst was instructed to take charge of the colonial commissaries. No provisions were to be sent to provincial troops except by Amherst's order. Amherst could also draw bills "for any extraordinary expences" in this service. The contractors received directions from the crown "to have constantly in store a sufficient quantity of provisions, as well for the regular National Troops, as for the Provincials."[86]

When it became evident that the war with France was over in America and that some royal troops would remain to fight the Indians, the colonists lost all interest in supporting a military establishment, although they were instructed to do so by periodic orders from Whitehall. For a while the northern colonies kept up a front of providing for logistical support.[87] For example, Pennsylvania appointed commissioners to procure and purchase new clothing for men already in service for the projected campaign at a commission not exceeding 2½% – expense of clothing to be deducted out of pay due to each soldier.[88] The southern colonies had less heart. Maryland afforded a typical case. Although Maryland was entreated to "Continue most Chearfully to Co-operate with, and Second to the utmost, the large Expence and Extraordinary Succours, Supplied by the Kingdom of Great Britain for their preservation and future Security," Governor Sharpe informed Amherst that, having granted supplies previously "by no other motive than Fear (our Frontiers being then laid waste and depopulated by the Savages)," Maryland could not be expected to contribute to troop support.[89] By the end of 1763 the Pennsylvania Assembly went on record refusing to consider support for provincial or royal troops,[90] and the New Yorkers were objecting to the disproportionate burden assessed the colony for frontier defense.[91] As peace set in, the colonies wanted no part of a general military establishment.

The Seven Years War had brought about royal control over logistics. The colonies, however, were allowed to set up their own commissary systems to assist the quartermaster service. But defects were twofold: the authority of royal commanders to compel colonial cooperation was limited (for example, they could impress supplies only in the theater of war); and there was the misunderstanding, particularly in the southern colonies, over who should be responsible for requisitioning supplies – the governors and their legislatures or the regular army commanders. The creation of the office of commander in chief, which subordinated the military powers of the governors,[92] did not help matters. The governors at least knew what concessions had to be made to their assemblies.

NOTES

1 Dunn, *Puritans and Yankees* 291–92; Osgood, *American Colonies*, 86–87.

2 Leder, *Robert Livingston*, 81–82, 91–101, 108.

3 Gov. Andros to Sec. Shrewsbury, June 4, 1695, Bancroft transcripts, NYPL; Assembly Proceedings, Oct. 16, 1694, *Md. Archives*, XIX, 97; Answer to Gov. of N.Y. Letter, Oct. 19, 1695, *ibid.*, XX, 334.

4 Council of Conn. to Fitz-John Winthrop, Oct. 19, 1694, Winthrop Papers, *MHSC*, 6th Ser., III, 20–21.

[5] Simon Bradstreet to Governor and Council of Conn., Oct. 30, 1691, CA, Colonial Wars, II, 154.

[6] "Major Walley's Journal in the Expedition against Canada in 1690," in Thomas Hutchinson, *The History of the Colony and Province of Massachusetts Bay*, ed. Lawrence S. Mayo, I (Cambridge, 1936), 459–67; Francis Parkman, *Count Frontenac and New France under Louis XIV* (Boston, 1903), 287–88.

[7] "Sir William Phips's Expedition to Canada: The Narrative of John Wise," with letters to Phips, ed. Samuel A. Green, *MHSP*, 2d Ser., XV (1902), 296, 306.

[8] "Memorial of the Agent for N. Y. to the Council of Trade and Plantations," Dec. 29, 1698, *CSP*, XV, 592; Lawrence H. Leder, "Dam'me Don't Stir a Man: Trial of the N. Y. Mutineers in 1700," *The New York Historical Society Quarterly*, XLII (1958), 263; Leder, *Robert Livingston*, 81–82, 91, 101–8, 135–36.

[9] J. Colleton *et al.* to Sir Nathaniel Johnson, Mar. 22, 1704, A. S. Salley, Jr., ed., *Commissions and Instructions from the Lords Proprietors of Carolina to Public Officials of South Carolina, 1685–1715* (Columbia, S. C., 1916), 185–86; Hanna, "New England Military Institutions" (Ph. D. diss.), 30. For Queen Anne's War, the crown supplied £ 10,000 of military stores and expected repayment from the colonies. Board of Ordnance to Lord Carteret, Apr. 17, 1722, *CSP*, XXXIII, 44.

[10] Council of Trade and Plantations to the Queen, Nov. 8, 1708, *CSP*, XXIV, 138.

[11] Waller, *Vetch*, 212.

[12] James Logan to William Penn, May 12, 1709, Deborah Logan, ed., *Correspondence between William Penn and James Logan, 1700–50*, 2 vols. (Philadelphia, 1870–72), II, 346.

[13] Spotswood to Council of Trade, Jul. 25, 1711, Brock, ed., *Spotswood Corr.*, I, 90; Spotswood to Lords of the Treasury, July 28, 1711, *ibid.*, 99.

[14] Excerpt from *Pennsylvania Gazette*, Aug. 7, 1740, *FP*, II, 288; Hanna, "New England Military Institutions" (Ph. D. diss.), 130–31; Osgood, *American Colonies*, III, 497–501.

[15] Proceedings of Assembly of N. Y., June 30, 1740, *The American Magazine* (Philadelphia, 1741), 67.

[16] Osgood, *American Colonies*, III, 222.

[17] Gen. Oglethorpe to the Trustees, Feb. 12, 1743, "Letters from Oglethorpe to the Trustees," *GHSC*, III (1873), 143.

[18] *FP*, III, 155n. The Privy Council on Jan. 15, 1747 approved the requests for reimbursement.

[19] *CCR*, Feb. 26, 1745, IX, 83–84; Weaver, *Trumbull*, 35.

[20] William Shirley to Benning Wentworth, Mar. 2, 1745, *Shirley Corr.*, I, 190–93.

[21] Andrew Oliver to William Pepperrell, Feb. 26, 1745, Belknap Papers, MHS; Warren to Duke of Newcastle, Nov. 23, 1745, PRO, CO, Vol. 44, LC; De Forest, *Louisbourg Journals* (8th Journal, anon.), 110; Johnson, *Hist. of the French War*, 156; Chapin, *Privateering in King George's War*, 113; F. E. Whitton, *Wolfe and North America* (Boston, 1929), 112–13.

[22] Shirley to Roger Wolcott, Mar. 8, 1745, *Shirley Corr.*, I, 193; Weaver, *Trumbull*, 35–36; Schutz, *Shirley*, 94. Commissaries for Conn.: Colonels Thomas Welles, Hezekiah Huntington, and Gurdon Saltonstall; Captains Theophilus Nikolas and John Hubbard – later in the year also Andrew Burr, John Fowler, and Jabez

Hamlin. Commissaries for Mass.: Charles Apthorp, Thomas Hancock, John Osborn, Nathaniel Sparhawk, William Shirley, Jr., John Shirley, and John Erving, Jr.

[23] Commodore Peter Warren to Lewis Morris, June 24, 1745, *Papers of Lewis Morris, NJHSC,* IV (1852), 254.

[24] Jonathan Law to Spencer Phips, Aug. 21, 1745, *Law Papers (CHSC,* XIII), II, 35.

[25] Jonathan Law to Peter Warren, Apr. 8, 1746, *ibid.*, 201.

[26] Wynne, *General History* (1770), I, 513.

[27] William Shirley to the Duke of Newcastle, Nov. 6, 1745, *Shirley Corr.*, I, 288.

[28] *Mass. Acts and Resolves*, XIV (1907), 120; John Ledyard to Jonathan Law, June 13, 1746, *Law Papers (CHSC,* XIII), II, 233.

[29] George Thomas to Thomas Penn, Apr. 26, 1746, Ettling Revolution Papers (Penn Papers: Official Correspondence), IV, HSP.

[30] *JHB–Va.* (1742–47), July 11, 1746, 226.

[31] Alice M. Keys, *Cadwallader Colden: A Representative Eighteenth Century Official*, reprint ed. (New York, 1967), 149.

[32] Duke of Newcastle to William Shirley, May 30, 1749, *Shirley Corr.*, I, 386–89.

[33] Dinwiddie's letters to Govs. Hamilton, Belcher, Shirley, Glen, Matthew Rowan (Pres. N. C. Council), Mar. 1–5, 1754, *Dinwiddie Corr.*, I, 85–91.

[34] Lords of Trade to Gov. Belcher, July 5, 1754, *NJA*, 1st Ser., VIII, 294; Dinwiddie to Gov. Glen, Aug. 5, 1754, William L. McDowell, ed., *Colonial Records of South Carolina: Documents relating to Indian Affairs, 1750–1754* (Columbia, S. C., 1958), 528; Dinwiddie to Horace Walpole, Oct. 25, 1754, *Dinwiddie Corr.*, I, 371; Dinwiddie to James Abercromby, Nov. 16, 1754, *ibid.*, 409.

[35] Belcher to Gov. Shirley, Dec. 21, 1753, Belcher Letter Book, MHS.

[36] Nicholas B. Wainwright, *George Croghan: Wilderness Diplomat* (Chapel Hill, 1959), 62–64; John A. Caruso, *The Appalachian Frontier* (Indianapolis, 1959), 52.

[37] St. Clair to Gov. Morris, Jan. 14, 1755, Gratz Collection, Colonial Wars, HSP; Braddock to Gov. Morris, Mar. 22, 1755, *ibid.*; Nichols, "Braddock" (Ph. D. diss.), 185.

[38] Newton D. Mereness, *Maryland as a Proprietary Province* (New York, 1901), 313.

[39] Gov. Sharpe to Gov. Hopkins, July 15, 1755, Miscellaneous Boundary Collection, 1749–60, MHS; Sharpe to Braddock, July 9, 1755, in Edgar, *Sharpe*, 54.

[40] Dinwiddie to Major Carlysle, May 7, 1754, William Hardin, ed., "James Mackay, with his correspondence," *Ga. Historical Quarterly*, I (1917), 77-98. Dinwiddie sent 400 small arms to Braddock, 500 to N. J., and 800 to N. Y., which he said depleted the Virginia magazine. Dinwiddie to Sharpe, June 2, 1755, Emmet Collection #13444, NYPL.

[41] Daniel Dulany, "Military and Political Affairs in the Middle Colonies (1755)," *PMHB*, III (1879), 13–14.

[42] Braddock to Sir Thomas Robinson, Mar. 18, 1755, quoted in Koontz, *Dinwiddie*, 322.

[43] Braddock to Sir Thomas Robinson, June 5, 1755, Parkman transcripts, MHS; Thayer, *Growth of Pa. Democracy*, 39.

[44] Whitfield J. Bell and Leonard W. Labaree, "Franklin and the 'Wagon Affair,' 1755," *Proceedings of the American Philosophical Society*, CI (1957), 551–58; Leonard W. Labaree, "Benjamin Franklin and the Defense of Pennsylvania, 1754–57,"

Pennsylvania History, XXIX (1962), 12; also Bennett J. Nolan, *General Benjamin Franklin* (Philadelphia, 1956), *passim*.

[45] Sharpe to Calvert, July 5, 1755, in Edgar, *Sharpe*, 52.

[46] Lily Lee Nixon, *James Burd: Frontier Defender, 1726–93* (Philadelphia, 1941), 22–24; Wainwright, *Croghan*, 80–82.

[47] *FP*, VI, 66n.

[48] Nixon, *Burd*, 22–23.

[49] *The New-York Mercury*, June 30, 1755; Arnold, *Hist. of R. I.*, II, 189.

[50] Gov. Shirley's Agreement with Rutherford and Lyman, CA, Colonial Wars, V, 163; Bradley, *Fight with French for North America*, 148.

[51] Shirley to Sharpe, Aug. 13, 1755, Dreer Collection (Governors of the Colonies), HSP.

[52] Lt. Gov. Phips to the Governors of R. I., Conn., and N. Y., July 30, 1755, MA, Colonial, VI, 613.

[53] Stephen Hopkins to Spencer Phips, Sep. 5, 1755, *ibid.*, 631.

[54] Sachs, "Interurban Correspondents," *New York History*, XXXVI (1955), 330.

[55] Theodore Thayer, "The Army Contractors for the Niagara Campaign, 1755–56," *WMQ*, 3d Ser., XIV (1957), 31–46.

[56] Gov. Charles Hardy to Sir Thomas Robinson, Nov. 27, 1755, PRO, CO, Vol. 17, LC; Pargellis, *Loudoun in North America*, 163.

[57] Pound, *Johnson*, 185.

[58] William Johnson to Shirley, Nov. 9, 1755, *William Johnson Papers*, II, 284.

[59] John Pownall to Gov. and Company of Conn., Sep. 19, 1755, Privy Council Orders, 1743–75, CHS; H. Fox to the Gov. and Co. of R. I., Mar. 13, 1756, *RICR*, V, 520.

[60] "Case of the Colony of Rhode Island respecting the Repayment of Sundry Disbursements on accounts of the Troops raised there by order of the Crown in 1756," Chalmers Collection (R. I.), NYPL.

[61] Loudoun to Pitt, May 3, 1757, *Pitt Corr.*, I, 57.

[62] Washington to Adam Stephen, Nov. 18, 1755 (typescript), Adam Stephen Papers, LC.

[63] Fisher, *New Jersey as a Royal Province*, 341. Troops at Albany were not assembled until June and were not furnished with necessary supplies for marching until August. Thomas F. Gordon, *The History of Pennsylvania . . . to . . . 1776* (Philadelphia, 1829), 317.

[64] Clarke, *Dobbs*, 134. Pennsylvania attended merely to clearing up accounts of the Braddock expedition. *PCR*, Jan. 30, 1756, VII, 10.

[65] See Pargellis, *Loudoun in North America*, 147–60, for a detailed account of logistical problems at Fort Oswego.

[66] Schutz, *Shirley*, 241–42.

[67] Thayer, "The Army Contractors for the Niagara Campaign," *WMQ*, 3d Ser., XIV (1957), 32–46.

[68] Dinwiddie to Henry Fox, May 10, 1756, PRO, CO, Vol. 17, LC; Washington to John Robinson, Nov. 9, 1756, Fitzpatrick, ed., *Washington Writings* I, 502; Clarke, *Dobbs*, 135. Loudoun had a new contract for victualling the army drawn up in England with the firm of Baker and Kilby, thus replacing Morris and Livingston. Osgood, *American Colonies*, IV, 383. For an example of confusion of one victualler, Edward Croston, who had unpaid accounts because of the duplication of

provincial-crown authority and an existing over-supply of regular troops during 1758–59, see *PA*, 8th Ser., VI (1935), 5181–82.

69 C. F. Adams, ed., *The Works of John Adams*, II (Boston, 1850), 34.

70 Lords of Trade to Sec. William Pitt, Jan. 21, 1757, Bancroft transcripts (Colonial Documents, 1748–64), NYPL; Dinwiddie to Pitt, May 14, 1757, *Pitt Corr.*, I, 65.

71 Extract of letter of Loudoun to [Pa. Gov.?], Aug. 20, 1756, Ettling Revolution Papers, HSP; Pitt to Gov. and Co. of R. I., Feb. 4, 1757, *Pitt Corr.*, I, 4; Pitt to Governors of Mass. Bay, N. H., N. Y., Conn., R. I., N. J., Dec. 30, 1757, *ibid.*, 138–39; Pitt to Governors of Pa., Md., Va., N. C., S. C., Dec. 9, 1758, *ibid.*, 419; Fitzpatrick, ed., *Washington Writings*, I, 209–10n.

72 *Pennsylvania Gazette*, Apr. 13, 1758; Sharpe to William Sharpe, May 27, 1758, *Md. Archives*, IX, 188; Forbes to Stanwix, May 28, 1758, James, ed., *Forbes Writings*, 102; James *et al., Drums in the Forest*, 45.

73 Dinwiddie to Sharpe, June 28, 1757, *Md. Archives*, IX, 32.

74 Sharpe to St. Clair, May 29, 1758, *ibid.*, 191; Branch, "Bouquet," *PMHB*, LXII (1938), 46. Because St. Clair got the quartermaster accounts so entangled, Bouquet, for all practical purposes, took over as Quartermaster General.

75 Forbes to Bouquet, July 23, 1758, in Hugh Cleland, ed., *George Washington in the Ohio Valley* (Pittsburgh, 1955), 175; Nixon, *Burd*, 48.

76 Forbes to Pitt, Sep. 6, 1758, Cleland, *ibid.*, 198. For the building of Forbes Road, see Niles Anderson, "The General Chooses a Road: The Forbes Campaign of 1758 to Capture Fort Duquesne," *Western Pa. Hist. Mag.*, XLII (1959), 109–38, 241–58, 383–401.

77 Forbes to Denny, Sep. 9, 1758, James, ed., *Forbes Writings*, 206; Stephens *et al., Papers of Henry Bouquet*, II, 297.

78 Bouquet to Forbes, Aug. 3, 1758, Stephens *et al., Bouquet Papers*, II, 313.

79 Forbes to Bouquet, June 19, 1758, *ibid.*, 112.

80 Sharpe to Pitt, Aug. 27, 1758, *Pitt Corr.*, I, 331.

81 Forbes to Bouquet, Sep. 17, 1758, Cleland, *Washington and the Ohio Valley*, 200.

82 Forbes to Abercromby, Oct. 24, 1758, James, ed., *Forbes Writings*, 244; Nellie Norkus, "Virginia's Role in the Capture of Fort Duquesne," *Western Pa. Hist. Mag.*, XLV (1962), 291–308.

83 Weaver, *Trumbull*, 83.

84 Thomas Fitch to Amherst, Mar. 3, 1759, PRO, WO:34, XXVIII, LC.

85 Pitt to Governors in North America (Mass., N. H., Conn., R. I., N. Y., N. J.), Jan. 7, 1760, *NYCD*, VII, 421.: Pitt to Gov. and Co. of Conn., Jan. 7, 1760, Trumbull Papers, CSL.

86 Pitt to Gen. Amherst, Jan. 7, 1760, *Pitt Corr.*, II, 240.

87 Sharpe to Calvert, Apr. 9, 1761, *Md. Archives*, IX, 496.

88 "An Act . . . 1759," Apr. 21, 1760, *The Statutes at Large of Pennsylvania*, VI (1896), 21.

89 Amherst to Sharpe, Feb. 21, 1760, *Md. Archives*, IX, 564–66; Sharpe to Amherst, Apr. 10, 1760, *ibid.*, 393. Va. voted £26, 298.17.8 for clothing, provisions, and recruiting for its military force. *JHB–Va.* (1758–61), Feb. 27, 1759, 69.

90 Letter of George Bryan, Mar. 21, 1764, quoted in Burton Konkle, *George Bryan and the Constitution of Pennsylvania, 1731–91* (Philadelphia, 1922), 46.

[91] Smith to Gates, Nov. 22, 1763, Gates Papers, NYHS.

[92] Hanna, "New England Military Institutions," (Ph. D. diss.), 175. The governor still had to submit regular inventories of all military stores in his colony and account for their disposition. Also, of course, the governor was the commander in chief of the militia and responsible for maintaining forts of his colony.

CHAPTER V

FINANCES

Several problems impeded cooperation of the colonies in financial assistance. The colonists themselves would not establish a common fund, and if they had done so, no intercolonial taxing agency existed to compel contributions. Colonial legislatures, in appropriating money, gave priority to the immediate needs of a colony's defense, which often excluded financial aid to the theater of war at the frontier of another colony. Some colonies resorted to the inveterate practice of large paper emission, which depreciated so rapidly that the money was often refused in the purchase of supplies in neighboring colonies. Furthermore, the requisition system, hardly more than guidelines set by both the crown and the colonies where colonies were expected to meet assigned quotas, had no means of enforcement. Legislatures frequently rebuffed a pledge of the governor or commissioners in order to wrest financial powers from the governor. The assemblies insisted not only on the right to vote appropriations but to control executive functions over their expenditure. The governors saw their position as a linchpin in the American empire and hence had broader views of imperial defense policies; whereas the assemblies were bent upon winning autonomy.[1] Again, as in the previous chapter, a representative cross section of the intercolonial response to a general war effort will be taken rather than to give a graphic study of the war finances of each colony.

During the first colonial war the colonies raised and supported their own troops, though, as we have seen, some supplies were sent over by the crown. The first bills of credit as money in history were issued in Massachusetts to pay for the Phips attack on Quebec. Rhode Island sent £300 instead of men for this expedition.[2] For the most part, after 1690, the colonial assemblies reneged on the cost to maintain their quotas of troops. In revolution-torn New York, Jacob Leisler wrote that "we find the people very slack in bringing up money; they will not convene us an Assembly to levy the same, though our writs were long ago issued to the various counties for the purpose."[3] For the abortive land expedition against Canada, New York had to depend for the maintenance of its troops upon the credit advanced by Albany merchants.[4]

In answer to Governor Fletcher's plea of 1693 for aid from neighboring colonies to defend the New York frontier, he got no response at all from Connecticut, Rhode Island, and Pennsylvania; East Jersey sent no men but voted £ 248. Virginia decided to send £ 600; the bills of exchange sent by Maryland were of little value.[5] As the war had now reached a lull, the colonies avoided any real commitment.

The attitude seemed to be to let the mother country take the full responsibility. The position of the Virginia House of Burgesses in 1695 was typical: "the Low circumstances of the Country would not admit of any greater fund or assistance then five hundred pounds: the inhabitants not being able to pay larger taxes then are annually imposed for the defence of the frontier of this Country." There was not enough revenue to pay the "contingent charges" of government, "much less that of the assistance commanded; nor is there any probability of its being better supplied during the war, the number of our merchant-ships and trade being much lessened . . . .the dependance of this country on New York is not so immediate as has been presumably represented to Their Majesties, so as to require such supplies nor our assistance of such service . . . ."[6] Pennsylvania did not renew its £ 300 grant of 1696, which Governor Fletcher of New York had spent on Indian affairs so as not to offend the Quaker conscience, because of the "infancy" and poverty of the colony.[7]

Although the crown continued to require intercolonial support of frontier defense in New York, by the time of Queen Anne's War, all but Connecticut had given up any pretext of cooperation.[8] Virginia and Maryland took the position that only in time of emergency was their assistance required. As Governor Blakiston of Maryland informed the Virginia Governor: "I find your Assembly stil sitting I should be glad to heare they give a ready complyance to the paying the money his Majesty has required for *New York* for if it should not be done in *Virginia* I doubt it will make our Assembly here boggle for they are glad to take hold of any Example when it is to raise their money."[9]

When Queen Anne's War began, only Massachusetts showed any sense of responsibility and any regularity in voting funds for intercolonial military purposes. For the six years before 1709 Massachusetts spent £30,000 per annum but bad feeling had developed because New York had "sat easy," having the advantage of the King's Independent companies, and maintained a "criminal neutrality with the Indians."[10] Before 1709 several unilateral offensive actions characterized the extent the colonists cared to go in raising money for fighting the war, and these were in the nature of border sorties, chiefly to hold the Indians in check. Benjamin Church's fifth and last expedition against the Indians in 1704 was financed out of the Massachusetts bills of credit, and Colonel James Moore's campaigns into Spanish Florida in 1702 and 1704 led to South Carolina's first paper emission.[11]

The colonial assemblies had been reluctant to participate in a general war effort because they anticipated assistance in troops, supplies, and money from the crown. Moreover, the assemblies had discovered the power of the purse in withholding moneys from the governors. Robert Quary, the agent for the Board of Trade in America, understood the source of the trouble:

> I cannot see how it is possible for any Governor to serve the interest of the Crown that must depend upon the precarious humors of the people for a subsistence. They will never part with their money unless they have an equivalent or something more valuable. It lays the Governor under the temptation of making sometimes a very disadvantageous bargain. A Governor ought to have his support as well as dependence immediately from the Crown, though at the same time the fund ought to come from the People, but by such ways and means as ought first to settle it in the Crown.[12]

With the Board of Trade's acceptance of Samuel Vetch's scheme for a joint sea and land campaign against Canada, employing British regulars and provincials from the northern colonies, the assemblies responded by voting substantial sums. The three New England colonies spent a total of £ 46,011 12 *s.* 6*d.*[13] in preparing for the abortive 1709 sea expedition, and in 1710 voted similar revenue for another offensive.[14] Connecticut spent £ 20,000 and New York £ 18,000 in vain for the 1709 fiasco,[15] only to be duped into new appropriations by promised British aid and the actual arrival of the British fleet in 1711. In spite of Quaker opposition, New Jersey came up with £ 3000 in 1709;[16] in 1710 the assembly voted £ 5,000 to be obtained through issue of bills of credit to support two hundred men in the field,[17] and in 1711, prompted by Governor Hunter, a similar amount was to be raised from 12,500 ounces of plate equal to £ 5,000 currency.[18] Except for a meager offering of £500 for the services of the crown, which Governor Gookin refused as an insult, and occassionally allowing for the sending of provisions, the Pennsylvania assembly did not aid financially the war effort. Quaker principles and resentment that Virginia and Maryland had not been required to contribute to the planned operations accounted for Pennsylvania's obstinacy.[19]

Two legacies of Queen Anne's War in the field of finance in particular challenged the royal prerogative. The colonial legislatures were insisting upon, as in the case of New York, the right to appoint "all the Officers of the revenue to the utter exclusion of all the Crown Officers" and to control the salaries of all colony officials, including the Governor's.[20] Despite orders from the crown to the contrary, the colonies continued to emit paper currency. Massachusetts regularly issued bills of credit, and in 1721 floated a £ 50,000 issue to fund the existing debt going back to the war and to meet current government expenses.[21] New Jersey did the same in 1733 with a £ 40,000 emission.[22] Other colonies were also discovering the easy road to public financing.

After the war Great Britian maintained small garrisions in New York and South Carolina, while the colonies made only niggardly preparations for frontier defense against the Indians. Later the South Carolina garrison was moved to the new colony of Georgia. The average amount appropriated by Parliament to support the several Independent companies in these garrisons averaged annually about £ 13,000. These troops, mostly old disabled veterans, literally vanished out in the boondocks. In 1748 the Georgia garrison was abandoned.[23]

With the beginning of the Spanish War in 1738, Governor Oglethorpe asked for aid of other colonies since Georgia had only three hundred men capable of bearing arms. Several colonies pledged money or men for the defense of the Georgia frontier, but none made good their promises.[24] Starting in 1739 the crown made heavy demands on the colonies for men and money; not until half way through King George's War, however, did the colonies do much more than deliberate on the requisitions.[25] In 1740, Oglethorpe went to Charles Town, where he successfully enlisted support for an expedition against Florida. The assembly voted £ 40,000 "Carolina money" to pay for the colony's troops to accompany Oglethorpe, and eventually the expenses ran to £ 70,000 currency. So disgusted with Oglethorpe's failure to take St. Augustine, the assembly refused to cooperate with any further invasion plans.[26]

The struggle between the governors and assemblies over the powers of the purse reached new proportions during King George's War. Governors fought unsuccessfully for the right to amend in council military bills. Governor Clinton of New York found that to secure assembly backing for New York's share in the war he had to agree to the assembly's right to pass annual support bills and to designate specific appropriations.[27] A resolution of the South Carolina assembly best sums up the constitutional controversy in that colony as well as elsewhere:

> It is an undoubted Principle in the English Constitution that the Commons in Consequence of their being Representatives of the People have an indisputable Right of laying Taxes and granting Money to the King; and that the Lords have no other Power than to pass or reject the Bill without Alteration or Amendment: It is with equal Surprize and Concern that we are acquainted that his Majesty's Council in this Province insist on a Privilege of altering and amending Bills framed by the Commons for granting Aids and Supplies to his Majesty; which we humbly apprehend is inconsistent with the Rights of the People we represent, and the Privileges of this House and is claiming a Power which no Instruction can warrant, or Usage in this Province can justify and which no Law whatsoever countenances or confirms . . . .we hope, for the Sake of Posterity that neither the present or any future Assembly will weakly betray, or give up the Birthrights and Inheritances which the People who send them derive from the Laws and fundamental Constitution of their Mother Country.[28]

For the Louisbourg expedition, Massachusetts, Connecticut, and New Hampshire contributed substantially in money for the support of their troops. Massachusetts issued £ 50,000 in bills of credit, as distinct from legal tender currency which the crown had prohibited. No aid was forthcoming from New York although cannon and money had been promised; Rhode Island sent only a sloop and crew.[29] Surprisingly, Pennsylvania in 1745 granted £ 4000 for the King's use in the purchase of bread, beef, pork, flour, wheat, "and other grain."[30] Although the New Jersey assembly voted £ 40,000 to aid the Louisbourg expedition, most of this money was put to other use;[31] £ 2000 was also voted to help maintain the fortress on Cape Breton Island, but on the condition that the trustees of the fund be accountable only to the legislature and that the money be taken from the regular allocation for support of the government.[32]

Encouraged by the announcement that Parliament had decided to reimburse the expenses of the colonies in the Louisbourg expedition, the colonies as far south as Virginia endorsed plans for intercolonial expeditions against Montreal and Quebec, which would also employ regular troops. Provincial troops would be paid by the crown, while the colonies were to furnish provisions and transport, for which they would later be reimbursed. Of the New England colonies, Connecticut most enthusiastically voted two supply bills totalling £ 600,000; unfortunately, however, merchants of the colony preferred to await the direct payment from the crown.[33] New Jersey issued £ 10,000 in bills of credit to pay for the raising of five companies of one hundred men each, and later passed two additional bills of £ 850 and £ 1000 each.[34] Pennsylvania responded with a meager £ 5000 in bills of credit over Governor Thomas's objections that the new issue should be secured in excise or loan office receipts.[35] Governor Clinton of New York could not get the assembly to act; therefore, he had to issue bills of exchange, for which he could become personally liable, on the treasury and the paymaster general.[36]

Pay of provincial troops was frequently held up in anticipation of immediate settlement of accounts with the crown, which did much to dampen morale. The wheels of bureaucracy turned slowly. Even when Parliament voted to pay directly provincial troops and other expenses, the money was held up by the Lords of the Treasury in order to certify accounts.[37] Moreover, the large paper emissions depreciated the value of pay for the troops. For example, Massachusetts in 1746 offered £ 30 in bills of credit plus a blanket and bed for each enlistee, but the value in sterling was only £ 4.[38] Most of the Massachusetts paper emission, however, was used to buy presents for Indians rather than pay for the troops.[39] Desertion was rife because of troops not being paid and sometimes soldiers deserted after they received pay.[40] At the end of the war all the New England troops were in pay arrears. The Connecticut assembly in 1748 refused to enact further paper emission, although expenses still had to be met for two hundred troops on the Massachusetts frontier, three companies in New York, and eighty men on the Connecticut coast.[41] Discharging the troops presented a problem. Governor Clinton simply drew up drafts on the crown as pay indentures.[42] Governor Shirley recommended two ways to pay the troops upon disbandment: (1) bills of credit to be voted by the assembly; and (2) borrowing from merchants "upon publick bills" until the crown provided funds.[43] As for paying for purely local defense, three colonies – Massachusetts, New York, and Pennsylvania – experimented during the war with lotteries.[44]

William Bollan, agent for Massachusetts, finally succeeded in obtaining the promised Parliamentary reimbursement for New England troops in the siege and garrisoning of Louisbourg. In 1749 £ 183,649 arrived in the form of 653,000 ounces of silver and ten tons of copper in Boston. Massachusetts received most of it, but some of the money went to the other three New England colonies. Parliament intended the reimbursement to have the effect of reforming the currency by allowing the redemption of paper currency in specie. This view was soon justified when in Massachusetts the value of paper currency jumped to only one-fifth less the value of specie.[45] No small factor in Massachusetts' receiving the lion's share of the reimbursement money was the appointment of the Massachusetts Governor along with Admiral Knowles to audit all accounts submitted by the colonies.[46] Of the £ 54,273 *7s. 6d.* put in for by Connecticut, £ 28,863 *19s. 1d.* was awarded.[47] Governor Shirley also supervised the auditing for the partial reimbursement by the crown for the colonial preparations of 1746-8, which stirred up some ill-will. For example, Shirley reduced or eliminated many of the claims of New Jersey on grounds that certain items had been for domestic use or were not reimbursable; only £ 2,231 of £ 5,302 was allowed. Governor Belcher of New Jersey was so piqued by this interference that he proclaimed New Jersey would hereafter refuse "to toot other people's fiddles where they must assist in Rozining the Strings without proper and decent notice."[48]

In 1753 the Earl of Holdernesse ordered each of the colonies to have their assemblies convene to devise a means of cooperation for financing defense measures against French aggression in the west. The colonies should contribute to a "Common Fund" to be administered by crown officials and "to be employed provisionally for the General Service of North America." In 1755 Braddock received the dubious appointment as the sole executor of such a fund.[49] Governor Dinwiddie proposed that Parliament should levy a poll tax of half a crown on all the colonies to be applied to a fund for a particular expedition. The Board of Trade tentatively favored this scheme but the idea of taxing the colonies directly was not otherwise well received.[50] It was hoped that the Albany conference would establish a common fund; and, indeed, if the Plan of Union had gone into effect, a "General Treasury" would have been effected, supported by general taxation.

The annual expense of the British military forces in America for many years amounted to £ 80,000, with about £ 13,000 of this amount spent on the several Independent companies in the colonies.[51] With an all-out Anglo-French struggle for North America impending, military expenses in America could be expected to skyrocket. A common fund of the colonies would be the best means to insure colonial cooperation in sharing part of the financial burden. As William Alexander of New York put it: "Without a general constitution for warlike operations, we can neither plan or execute. We have a common interest, and must have a common council; *one head* and *one purse."*[52] Braddock urged the governors "to constitute one common Stock of the Money granted in the Several Colonies to Serve as a provisional Fund for the general Service of the Expedition, and that it might be Subject to my Orders." But he was not very optimistic. "I almost despair of their complying with it, from the jealousy of the people, and the Disunion of the Several Colonies, as well among themselves as one with another . . ."[53] The colonies, however, preferred to rely on the old requistion system, in which they could at will decide how much they should comply with quotas and could control the expenditures.

The Maryland assembly set the pace in 1754 by voting £ 6000 for colonial use but nothing for a common fund.[54] Virginia allocated £ 10,000 in the same year but set up a joint committee of both houses to supervise expenditures, which was controlled, as a similar committee in 1746 had been, by the lower house.[55] Governor Dinwiddie asked for another £ 20,000, which the Burgesses refused to consent to unless he rescinded the pistole fee. The Governor had to prorogue the legislature on two occasions, still without getting the grant.[56] Dinwiddie disgruntedly reported the impasse to Sir Thomas Robinson: "Thus, Sir, our Enemies increase in Powers and Numbers, whilst my Hands are restrained for want of Money, and consequently Men to strengthen and support His Majesty's Troops."[57]

For Dinwiddie's planned western offensive in 1754, Governor Dobbs of North Carolina raised a body of militia with promise of pay for each man of three shillings a day, but when they marched northward the pay was reduced to eight pence; the troops mutinied, and were disbanded.[58] Governor Hamilton of Pennsylvania refused to consent to a £ 15,000 grant to assist Virginia because he disagreed with the legislature over the life of the bills of credit.[59] After Washington's defeat, Dinwiddie found that the funds of the colony were depleted and the troops were without adequate equipment. He, therefore, appealed to the home government for aid, which, with an alacrity uncharacteristic of Whitehall, arrived in November 1754 in the form of 2,000 stands of arms, £ 10,000 specie, and £ 10,000 credit. Meanwhile, the pistole fee controversy had subsided between the governor and the assembly, and the Burgesses finally passed the £ 20,000 aid bill.[60] Thus Virginia was ready for another western expedition.

Braddock's fear of the colonies not meeting their share in contributing to a western campaign was soon justified. New York voted £ 1000 for Braddock's expedition but stipulated that the sum had to be used for transportation and subsistence of the two Independent companies to be sent to Virginia.[61] Pennsylvania gave £ 15,000 "for the king's use" in the Braddock campaign, and at the end of the year granted £ 60,000 "for the Defence of the Countrey." Most of this money, however, was spent on building forts on the Pennsylvania frontier rather than as actual aid to the army.[62] The Quaker assembly, which had sought to raise the revenue by taxing proprietary lands, yielded when Franklin worked out a compromise, avoiding the taxes and exempting Quakers from military service. A donation of £ 5000 by the proprietors for the war effort also eased the situation.[63]

With insufficient support, the Crown Point and Niagara expeditions of 1755 came to naught. As William Johnson had correctly presaged in May 1755: "I dread Confusion, want of Money, and that my hands will be too much tied up. Provincial Quotas will I foresee occasion an argumentative war, and I dread will retard if not destroy our Success."[64] At the camp at Lake George, New York troops were in a mutinous condition because of lack of pay.[65] New Jersey would not appropriate money for troops serving outside the colony other than her own; but small funds were voted to complete the New Jersey contingent of Captain Peter Schuyler's regiment in 1755 and 1756.[66]

Elsewhere, in the South, the Virginia Council refused to send a "trifling" £ 1000 to South Carolina for defense as ordered by the Privy Council to be appropriated from the tobacco export duties.[67] Dinwiddie, however, did extend £ 6000 of the Parliamentary granted credit, but would not send more aid because he felt that South Carolina should have the primary responsibility for its own defense.[68] Dinwiddie intended the money to be used as gifts and in building a fort for the protection of loyal Indians, who, in turn, would send a band of warriors to aid Braddock's expedition; but Braddock had to get along without the Indian assistance. Before February 1756, all that Maryland, which was plagued by the same proprietor-assembly problems as Pennsylvania, contributed was £ 6000 for its small force of garrison troops and a company of sixty men, who accompanied Braddock.[69]

Thus, in the opening round of the French and Indian War, the colonies showed little inclination to finance war operations outside the realm of their immediate concern. As one observer wrote: "since notwithstanding the present common Danger, no two Governments can agree upon any Measures, nor has any one Government separately, except the Massachusetts-Bay, acted with any Degree of Vigour."[70] Even then, instead of a new taxation, Massachusetts fell back on the £ 20,000 grant from the home government, which had been received when Virginia had been given the £ 10,000 mentioned earlier, bills of credit (the issue of £ 40,000 during 1753-4 being the only one during the war), bills of exchange, and lotteries.[71] The situation at the end of 1755 looked hopeless to Dinwiddie. He called for tight control by the home government, but confessed

> . . . how to reduce them to obedience to His Majestys Orders, and to their own Preservation, I know not, unless a British Parliament take it in hand, by oblidging each Colony to supply a proper Quota of Men, Money &c And then without some Regulars from Home, with some proper General and Field Officers, I dread the Consequence.[72]

The Board of Trade held a hearing on the colonial contribution to the Fort Duquesne, Crown Point, and Niagara campaigns of 1755. In addition to the cost by the crown to maintain the New England soldiers in the garrisons at Nova Scotia, the Board estimated the total colonial expense for the three western offensives at £ 170,000, and recommended that Parliament grant the colonies £ 120,000 to serve as "an Encouragement to exert themselves for the future in their mutual and common Defence."[73] Parliament finally voted £ 115,000 reimbursement for the New England colonies, New York, and New Jersey.[74] After protests from Virginia and North Carolina for being excluded, Parliament in 1757 granted these colonies £ 50,000. Because of their negligence, Pennsylvania and Maryland did not come under the reimbursement.[75] Only the American commander in chief could certify the accounts of the individual colonies, and Generals Shirley and Loudoun especially came under fire from the governors and assemblies for their dilatoriness in presenting the colonial claims.[76]

The delay in receiving the Parliamentary reimbursement hampered military preparations for 1756. The colonies were only willing to subsist barely their own troops already in the field. Thus, for example, New York voted £ 40,000 for its force in the Crown Point expedition.[77] By September, Connecticut claimed the colony was too exhausted financially and could only supply one thousand men to Loudoun's army, after having issued £ 62,000 bills of credit and having borrowed £ 10,000 from Governor Shirley.[78] Pennsylvania, as before, was out of funds. The New England colonies, awaiting the Parliamentary reimbursement to redeem as much of their paper currency as possible, were forced in 1756 and 1757 into further emissions to subsist their troops in the western army.[79]

For 1757 Loudoun announced that the colonies were expected to contribute to a general fund "to be issued and applied for such Articles of a general Concern as come properly under the general Service." To the colonial mind this meant a continuation of support of their own troops in the field, which, including "levy money," the colonists expected would come under eventual reimbursement. For certain priorities, such as defense of the South Carolina frontier, Loudoun said he would advance some money from "the General Service fund" to be used as "levy money."[80]

New York and the New England colonies voted no more money than they had to in order to sustain their troops posed at Lake Champlain for a Canadian offensive and at the frontier garrisons. Only Pennsylvania provided substantial financial assistance in 1757. With the provincial troops on the verge of mutiny, pressure from Loudoun, and a report that the enemy planned to attack Fort Augusta on the Susquehanna, Governor

Denny assented to an act to raise £ 100,000, even though it violated his instructions by giving the assembly control over expenditures.[81] The southern colonies responded negatively. Maryland reduced its frontier force to only three hundred men and restrained any troops from leaving the colony except in the pay of the crown. As before, Maryland's recalcitrance was due chiefly to disputes between the assembly and the proprietor and because the colony had been left out of the Parliamentary reimbursement for 1755.[82] The Virginia assembly managed at least to vote a scanty £ 8000. Dinwiddie wrote Sharpe that Maryland's lack of cooperation made it difficult to secure aid in his colony:

> it appears to me very inconsistent and unmannerly in Your Assembly to make any Hesitation, or to dispute his Lordships Power and more so when so solemnly concerted and agreed to at the Meeting of the Governors with his Lordship [Loudoun]; no Doubt if they persist in their ill-natured Opposition, some Method probably may be found out to make them repent of the Folly, indeed their parsemonius *[sic]* Behavior at this Time of imminent Danger has occasioned me much Trouble with the Assembly of this Dominion.[83]

Appropriations in North Carolina and South Carolina, as before, were directed chiefly towards defense measures against the Indians.

For the military operations of 1758, colonial financial cooperation followed the same lines as in the two previous years. The lure of future reimbursement accounted to a large degree for the northern colonies keeping men in the field. In Maryland, Governor Sharpe vetoed a bill to raise one thousand men and £ 45,000 to pay them because it proposed to tax proprietary estates. The few troops maintained in provincial pay at Forts Cumberland and Frederick, raised in October 1757, had to be disbanded in April 1758 because of pay arrears. The promises of Forbes and Loudoun for reimbursement fell on the deaf ears of the Maryland assembly.[84] Forbes expressed his utter disgust to Governor Sharpe: "I must Confess that your Assemblys breaking up without Concurring in any way with His Majesty's Demands, is such a Piece of Presumption that Deserves a much Severer Chastisement, than I shall pretend to think of."[85] Pennsylvania applied the appropriation of £ 100,000 voted the previous year towards raising hopefully 2,700 men. General Forbes, under orders of General Abercromby, spent much time guiding the course of assistance in Pennsylvania and settling disputes between the Governor and the legislature.[86] Most of the money raised in 1758 in Pennsylvania went for the Forbes compaign.[87]

Of the northern colonies, Massachusetts made the greater exertion in 1758. The Bay Colony pledged credit for one-half million sterling.

Undoubtedly, the reimbursement of £ 27,380.19.11¼ for expenses in 1756 explains much of the colony's enthusiasm.[88]

From 1759 to 1763 Parliament annually granted large remuneration to the colonies for military services. Each year Pitt, as Secretary of State, and his successor, Lord Egremont, sent circular letters to the governors requesting troops and promising to recommend to Parliament reimbursement of expenses.[89] The colonies were reluctant to spend any more money on their own, and contributed to the war effort only so mcuh as they could expect reimbursement. The problem was the requisition system. The British ministry missed an opportunity to work out some form of taxation on the colonies when they were in most dire need of help. The Albany Plan to administer a common fund for the general service coupled with direct taxation would have been the best solution, and, had this been presented as a *sine qua non* of British policy in 1755-56, the colonists might have been prevailed upon to accept a colonial directed tax union for military purposes, at least as a wartime expedient. The chief deterrent to order and responsibility in colonial war financing was the failure of the British government to have a definite policy – everything was makeshift from year to year – and the colonies could plea good intentions but obstacles to their participation, such as currency problems, constitutional controversy, or remoteness from the front.

Even Massachusetts, which had been as cooperative as any colony in intercolonial military operations, by 1759 had lost heart. As Governor Pownall informed Pitt:

> Altho' from my certain knowledge of the impossibility of the Governments raising money for the Bounty Billeting and pay of any Number of Men, from the impracticability of borrowing the Cash (all that cou'd be Spared out of Trade being already borrow'd of the Money'd men) I cou'd not presume to give you any hopes of the Province again exerting itself this Year unless reinstated into a Condition of doing so by the Receipt of Compensation.[90]

This was the same attitude of North Carolina. In December 1758 the colony had presented an unpaid bill to the new general, Amherst, for aid given to the intercolonial war effort since 1753, totalling £ 67,706.[91] Rhode Island quarreled over part of that colony's reimbursement being readjusted in favor of Pennsylvania.[92]

In the last years of the war, the colonies argued that they had exhausted their financial resources. As the Connecticut Governor complained: "The Government has no more Resources, for Payment of the Troops but by the use of public credit . . ."[93] In 1759 New Jersey elaborately pleaded the same excuse that the colony already had raised "great sums" for the "extraordinary purposes of the War," which since 1757 amounted to £ 140,000 proclamation money, and a new emission recently voted could not "carry us thro' the next campaign." Besides, the provincial debt exceeded £ 200,000, a "large sume for so small a community, that has little or no foreign trade."[94] The Pennsylvania Governor, James Hamilton, persisted in vetoing money bills on grounds that they were inconsistent with crown and proprietary instructions.[95] Governor Sharpe summed up the futility of attempting to raise money and men under the requisition system in 1762:

> I did till about three weeks ago entertain hopes that I should never more be laid under the necessity of applying to the Assembly of this Province for either Men or Money but I was it seems a little too sanguine in my Wishes, the Earl of Egremont and the Commander in Chief of His Majestys Forces on this Continent have once more demanded from us as large a Number of Men as can be raised in this Government so next Monday the Assembly and I are to begin to play again the old Game.[96]

To the colonial mind, rumors that after the war Great Britain intended to maintain ten regiments of provincials in the pay of the colonies in addition to fifteen regiments of regulars in the pay of Great Britain,[97] must have seemed unrealistic indeed. The announcement of the abandonment of reimbursement was in itself a signal for the colonies to refrain from cooperating in meeting their requisitions, which, in turn, would justify an imperial military system in the colonies.

For their part in the Seven Years War, the colonists spent a total of £ 2,515,038.[98] The total Parliamentary reimbursement, as free gifts or as compensation for supplies and pay, amounted to £ 1,072,784.[99] By a report of the Board of Trade in 1765 the total unpaid debt in the colonies was estimated at £ 760,435,[100] which was not excessive considering the length of the war and the broad field of operations and defense (the insufficiency of colonial support notwithstanding). But it must be kept in mind that the war deficit had been accompanied by increased prosperity and a broadening of the tax base in the colonies.

Nevertheless, a lack of realism had characterized colonial war finance. The colonies looked after their own selfish interests and put constitutional gains above general security. Overlapping emissions of bills of credit and exchange and planning anticipatory of reimbursement had jeopardized the fiscal stability of the colonies. In some future war, a central agency based on the common interest, with powers of direct taxation, would have to be found. If the British government expected to continue a military establishment for frontier defense, it could not depend upon the colonies to fix a permanent revenue.

NOTES

[1] See Evarts B. Greene, *The Provincial Governor in the English Colonies of North America*, reprint ed. (New York, 1966), 117–24; Greene, (J. P.), *Quest for Power*, 51–168.

[2] Arnold, *Hist. of R. I.* I, 520.

[3] Jacob Leisler to the Bishop of Salisbury, Mar. 31, 1690, *CSP*, XIII, 243.

[4] Leder, *Robert Livingston*, 62–81.

[5] *CSP*, XIV, xvii.

[6] R. Wormeley to Duke of Shrewsbury, June 10, 1695; PRO, CO, Vol. 1307, LC; Sec. of Va. to Lords of Trade and Plantations, June 10, 1695, *CSP*, XIV, 499.

[7] Proud, *History of Pennsylvania*, 415–16.

[8] Gov. and Gen. Assembly of Conn. to Gov. of N. Y., May 13, 1703, R. C. Winthrop Collection, CSL. In 1703, Conn. granted £ 450 towards erecting a fort at Albany.

[9] *JHB–Va.* (1695–1702), Sep. 24, 1701, 307.

[10] Dudley to Wait Winthrop and Mr. President Leverett, Mar. 25, 1709, Saltonstall Papers, MHS; Kimball, *Dudley*, 124–25; William T. Morgan, "The Five Nations and Queen Anne," *MVHR*, XIII (1927), 185.

[11] Sirmans, *South Carolina*, 84-87, 109; Greene, *Quest for Power*, 109–10.

[12] Col. Robert Quary to the Lords of Trade, June 16, 1703, *NYCD*, IV, 1047.

[13] Dudley, Nicholson, Vetch, and Capt. Moody to [? the Earl of Sutherland], Oct. 24, 1709, *CSP*, XXIV, 493. Mass. – £ 30,811 12 *s.* 10 *d.* and £ 5000 "before the forces can be disbanded;" N. H. – £ 3500; R. I. – £ 6700.

[14] Osgood, *American Colonies*, I, 436.

[15] Waller, *Vetch*, 164.

[16] Col. Nicholson and Col. Vetch to [? the Earl of Sutherland], June 28, 1709, *CSP*, XXIV, 405.

[17] Kemmerer, "Struggle for Self-Government in Colonial N.J." (Ph. D. diss.), 199.

[18] Smith, *Hist. of New Jersey* (1765), 399–400; Edwin P. Tanner, *The Province of New Jersey, 1664–1738* (*Columbia Studies*. . ., XXX [New York, 1908], 576–79.

[19] Waller, *Vetch*, 138, 216.

[20] H. Walpole to the Lords Commissioners of the Treasury, Apr. 26, 1722, *CSP*, XXXIII, 45.

[21] Council of Trade and Plantations to the King, Sep. 8, 1721, *CSP*, XXXII, 415.

[22] Lewis Morris to the Council of Trade and Plantations, Oct. 4, 1733, *CSP* XL, 205.

[23] Beer, *British Colonial Policy*, 11-13.

[24] Reese, *Colonial Georgia*, 75-76.

[25] For the heavy demands upon Maryland, see Charles A. Barker, *The Background of the Revolution in Maryland* (*Yale Historical Publications*, XXXVIII [New Haven, 1940]), 201-2.

[26] Alexander Hewatt, *An Historical Account of the Rise and Progress of the Colonies of South Carolina and Georgia* (1779), reprint ed. (Spartanburg, S. C., 1962), II, 76; Sirmans, *South Carolina*, 211-12.

[27] Katz, *Newcastle's New York*, 184.

[28] *JCHA–S.C.*, Answer to Message of His Majesty's Council, Apr. 12, 1739, I, 699.

[29] Downey, *Louisbourg*, 57.

[30] Sidney G. Fisher, *Pennsylvania: Colony and Commonwealth* (Philadelphia, 1897), 95; see Franklin's "Plain Truth," (1747), *FP*, III, 195.

[31] Gov. Morris to Lt. Gov. Phips, Sep. 2, 1745, *Papers of Lewis Morris, NJHSC*, IV (1852), 267.

[32] Fisher, *New Jersey as a Royal Province*, 325.

[33] John Ledyard to Jonathan Law, June 13, 1746, *Law Papers* (*CHSC*, XIII), II, 232–33.

[34] Fisher, *New Jersey as a Royal Province*, 325–29.

[35] Keith, *Pennsylvania Chronicles*, II, 880–81.

[36] Katz, *Newcastle's New York*, 215.

[37] Eliakim Palmer to Jonathan Law, Apr. 10, 1748 and Mar. 4, 1749, Colonial Agents Letters, CHS; Thomas Hubbard to Jonathan Trumbull, Mar. 7, 1748, Trumbull Papers, CHS.

[38] Shirley to Duke of Newcastle, May 31, 1746, Parkman transcripts, XXXVIII, MHS.

[39] Shirley to George Thomas, June 1, 1747, Emmet Collection, #4570, NYPL.

[40] Gov. Clinton to the Duke of Newcastle, May 11, 1747, *NYCD*, VI, 341; S. G. Drake, Chronicles of the Indians, Sep. 10, 1747, NYPL.

[41] Jonathan Law to Shirley, June 14, 1748, MA, Colonial, IV, 29.

[42] Gov. Clinton to the Duke of Newcastle, Nov. 9, 1747, *NYCD*, VI, 409.

[43] Shirley to Belcher, Oct. 29, 1747, Sedgwick Papers, MHS.

[44] John Swift to John White, Apr. 12, 1748, Balch, ed., *Letters and Papers . . . Pennsylvania*, 16; John S. Ezell, *Fortune's Merry Wheel: The Lottery in America* (Cambridge, 1960), 32-33.

[45] Hunt, "Sir William Pepperrell," in *Lives of American Merchants*, II, 143.

[46] Schutz, *Shirley*, 126.

[47] Eliakim Palmer to Jonathan Law, Nov. 18, 1747, *Law Papers* (*CHSC*, XV), III, 460; Benjamin Avery to Jonathan Law, Aug. 6, 1750, *ibid.*, 471.

[48] Quoted in Fisher, *New Jersey as a Royal Province*, 325–29.

[49] High, "Horatio Sharpe" (Ph. D. diss), 101.

[50] Kate Holback, *Chatham's Colonial Policy: A Study in the Fiscal and Economic Implications of the Colonial Policy of the Elder Pitt* (New York, 1917), 172. Braddock pressed for the colonies contributing to a common fund, after the crown had recommended this policy to the colonies, and he hoped the colonies would name a treasurer to handle the fund. Message of R. H. Morris, Mar. 18, 1755, *PA*, 8th Ser., V (1931), 3859.

[51] Paul Carr, "The Defense of the Frontier, 1760–1755" (unpubl. Ph. D. diss., State University of Iowa, 1932), 23.

[52] Livingston, *Review of the Military Operations in North-America, passim; The New-York Mercury*, May 13, 1754 expressed the belief that "our Enemies have the very great Advantage of being under one Direction, with one council, and one Purse." This issue also carried Franklin's cartoon "Join or Die" published earlier in Pa.

[53] Braddock to Sir Thomas Robinson, Mar. 18, 1755, PRO, CO, Vol 46, LC; Braddock to Gov. Morris, Mar. 10, 1755, Emmet Collection, # 3778, NYPL.

54 High,"Horatio Sharpe"(Ph. D. diss.), 101.

55 Dinwiddie to Matthew Rowan, Mar. 23, 1754, *Dinwiddie Corr.*, I, 122; James M. Leake, *The Virginia Committee System and the American Revolution* (*JHUS*, XXXV [Baltimore, 1917]), 47.

56 *NCCR*, V, xvi; Connell, *Savage Years*, 43.

57 Dinwiddie to Sir Thomas Robinson, June 18, 1754, *Dinwiddie Corr.*, I, 204.

58 Connell, *Savage Years*, 43.

59 Thayer, *Growth of Democracy in Pa.*, 29.

60 Hayes Baker–Crothers, *Virginia and the French and Indian War* (Chicago, 1928), 48–54.

61 James De Lancey to Gov. Hamilton, Apr. 19, 1754, Emmet Collection, #1748, NYPL.

62 Gov. Dobbs to Gov. Morris, Dec. 18, 1755, Gratz Collection (Colonial Governors), HSP; *Pennsylvania Gazette*, Nov. 27, 1755; Fitzpatrick, ed., *Washington Writings*, I, 258n.; Davidson, *War Comes to Quaker Pa.*, 5.

63 See John J. Zimmerman, "Benjamin Franklin and the Quakers, 1755–56," *WMQ*, 3d Ser., XVIII (1960), 302–7.

64 William Johnson to Robert Orme, May 19, 1755, *William Johnson Papers*, I, 522. Upon hearing that the Conn. Legislature had voted a reinforcement for Johnson of 2000 men, the New York Assembly did the same in the fall of 1755, and increased real and personal property taxes to pay for the anticipated troops. *The Colonial Laws of New York*, III (Albany, 1894), Sep. 11, 1755, 1131–39.

65 William Johnson to James De Lancey, Sep. 4, 1755, *William Johnson Papers*, II, 6.

66 Fisher, *New Jersey as a Royal Province*, 337–40. Because of lack of additional funds, N. J. could not pay its meager force.

67 Philip A. Bruce, *History of Virginia*, I (New York, 1924), 368.

68 Dinwiddie to Sir Thomas Robinson, Nov. 24, 1755, PRO, CO, Vol. 17, LC; Baker–Crothers, *Virginia and the French and Indian War*, 63–64.

69 Black, *Maryland's Attitude in the Struggle for Canada* (*JHUS*, 10th Ser., VII [Baltimore, 1892]), 25.

70 William Clarke, *Observations on the Late and Present Conduct of the French with Regard to their Encroachments upon the British Colonies in North America together with Remarks on the Importance of these Colonies to Great Britain* (Boston, 1755), 30.

71 William Douglass, *A Summary, Historical and Political of the First Planting, Progressive Improvements and Present State of the British Settlements in North-America*, 2 vols. (Boston, 1755), I, 535; Charles H. J. Douglas, *The Financial History of Massachusetts* (*Columbia University Studies* . . ., I [New York 1892]), 103, 133–34.

72 Dinwiddie to Earl of Halifax, Nov. 15, 1755, Virginia Miscellaneous Papers, Box 1, LC.

73 Lords of Trade to Secretary Fox, Jan. 16, 1756, *NYCD*, VII, 1–2; Beer, *British Colonial Policy*, 53 and 53n. The Board of Trade's estimate for the three expeditions was as follows:

N. Y.	£ 18,900	R. I.	£ 8,000	
N. J.	6,900	Va.	22,000	
N. H.	9,000	N. C.	8,000	
Mass.	60,000	Pa.	3,800	
Conn.	29,000	Md.	4,500	Total–£ 170,100.

[74] Beer, *British Colonial Policy*, 54 and 54n.; Johnson, *Hist. of the French War* 238; Norreys J. O'Conor, *A Servant of the Crown in England and in North America, 1756–61* (New York, 1938), 36. The grant was to be divided as follows: Mass. – £54,000; N.H. – 8,000; Conn. – 26,000; R. I. – 7,000; N. Y. – 15,000; and N. J. – 5,000. Total – £ 115,000.

[75] Beer, *British Colonial Policy*, 54–55.

[76] James Abercromby to Maj. Gen. Abercromby, Mar. 12, 1758, James Abercromby Letter Book, Va. State Lib.; Lord Loudoun to Pitt, Apr. 25, 1757, *Pitt Corr.*, I, 45.

[77] When passed by both houses the Assembly grant of £ 40,000 was raised to £52,000, with the usual restricting clause attached, as in this case, that the 1315 officers and men to be supported by this grant "are to be employed in Conjunction with the Neighbouring Colonys in Reducing the French Fort at Crown Point . . . ." *The Colonial Laws of New York*, IV, Apr. 1, 1756, 68; New York Assembly, Jan. 28, 1756, New York Records, Ebenezer Hazard Collection, LC.

[78] Thomas Fitch to Henry Fox, Apr. 16, 1756, PRO, CO, Vol. 17, LC; Fitch to Earl of Loudoun, Sep. 20, 1756, *ibid.*, Vol. 47.

[79] William H. Fry, *New Hampshire as a Royal Province* (*Columbia University Studies . . .*, XXIX [New York, 1908]), 404–7 The Pa. Governor refused his assent to a bill granting £ 40,000 to "the King's use" because it taxed the Proprietary estates, "Message of the House of Rep. to the Gov.," July 22, 1756, *PA*, 8th Ser., V, 4284.

[80] Sep. 22, 1756, Loudoun Papers, Huntington Lib. (microfilm, Pa. State Archives, Harrisburg); Clarence J. Attig, William Henry Lyttleton:" A Study in Colonial Administration," (unpubl, Ph. D. diss.), University of Nebraska, 1958, 87.

[81] A Message from the Governor to the Assembly, Mar. 22, 1757, *PA*, 1st Ser., III, 98; Nicholas B. Wainwright, "Governor William Denny in Pennsylvania," *PMHB*, LXXXI (1957), 179–81; Ralph L. Ketcham, "Conscience, War, and Politics in Pennsylvania, 1755–57," *WMQ*, 3d Ser., XX (1963), 434–35.

[82] Black, *Maryland's Attitude in the Struggle for Canada*, 62-63.

[83] Dinwiddie to Gov. Sharpe, June 14, 1757, *Md. Archives*, IX, 24–25.

[84] Gov. Sharpe to William Sharpe, July 13, 1759, *ibid.*, 353; Sharpe to Amherst, 10 Apr., 1760, *ibid.*, 393; "Queries Addressed to a Friend of Lord Baltimore," Sep. 19, 1758, in Verner W. Crane, *Benjamin Franklin's Letters to the Press, 1758–1775* (Chapel Hill, 1950), 3.

[85] Forbes to Sharpe, May 25, 1758, *Md. Archives* IX, 188.

[86] Forbes to Gov. Denny, Apr. 28, 1758, Gratz Collection (Colonial Wars), HSP; Forbes to Pitt, May 1, 1758, James, ed., *Forbes Writings*, 76; Wainwright, "Governor Denny," *PMHB*, LXXXI (1957), 187–90. For views of the Penn-legislative controversy over taxing proprietary estates, see H. Trevor Colbourn, "A Pennsylvanian Farmer at the Court of King George: John Dickinson's Letters, 1754–56," *PMHB*, LXXXVI (1962), 419ff.

[87] Thayer, *Growth of Democracy in Pa.*, 67. Pa. troops got extra hazardous duty pay when stationed at the extremity of the frontier. John W. Jordan, ed., "Journal of James Kenny, 1761–63," *PMHB*, XXXVII (1913), 400.

[88] Gov. Pownall to Pitt, Dec. 8, 1758, *Pitt Corr.*, I, 413.

[89] Beer, *British Colonial Policy*, 56–57 and 57n.

1759 – £ 200,000
1760 – £ 200,000
1761 – £ 200,000
1762 – £ 133,000
1763 – £ 133,000

[90] Gov. Pownall to Pitt, Mar. 16, 1759, *Pitt Corr.*, II, 70–71.

[91] Gov. Dobbs to Amherst, Dec. 16, 1758, PRO, CO, Vol. 54, LC. The sums were primarily spent for troops sent to Virginia (1754–55), New York (1756), South Carolina (1757), the Ohio country (1758); building and maintenance of forts were also included in the estimate.

[92] Gov. Hopkins to Gov. Hamilton, Sep. 20, 1763, *PA*, 1st Ser., IV, 121.

[93] Thomas Fitch to Amherst, May 28, 1762, PRO, WO:34, XXVIII, LC.

[94] Gov. Bernard to Pitt, Mar. 20, 1759, *Pitt Corr.*, II, 75–76.

[95] Thayer, *Growth of Democracy in Pa.*, 75.

[96] Sharpe to Sir John St. Clair, Mar. 13, 1762, *Md. Archives*, XIV, 32.

[97] *The New-London Summary*, Mar. 4, 1763.

[98] Lawrence H. Gipson, "Connecticut Taxation and Parliamentary Aid Preceding the Revolutionary War," *AHR*, XXXVI (1931), 722.

[99] Gipson, *British Empire*, X, 50. For a colony–by–colony summary of the accrued war debts, reimbursement, and liquidation, see chapters 2 and 3, *ibid.*

[100] Gipson, "Connecticut Taxation," *AHR*, XXXVI (1931), 722.

CHAPTER VI

MANPOWER

The northern colonies had become accustomed to work out in conference proportionate quotas for intercolonial participation in military operations. This had been the practice of the New England Confederation, and with the outbreak of the French War in 1689 the New England colonies and New York hastened to put a combined army into the field. At first, conditions were so disheveled because of the recent overthrow of the Dominion of New England that confusion ensued in the determination to secure a pooling of the troops. By correspondence of Jacob Leisler and the New England governors and the abortive revived meeting of the Confederation in the fall of 1689, the northern colonies seemed to agree in principle on a quota system.[1] But a regional cooperative war effort between New England and New York would not fully materialize.

After the attack on Schenectady, Robert Livingston, who journeyed to New England to secure help for the defense of New York, was able to get an immediate commitment of two companies of troops – 124 men – from Connecticut to reinforce Albany, but he had no success with Massachusetts.[2] The delegates at the New York City conference of May 1690 pledged a total of 855 troops for an overland attack upon Montreal.[3] The New England contingent that showed up at Albany to assist a New York force fell slightly short of the quotas; troops promised by Maryland did not arrive. Lack of provisions, squabbles over command, small pox, and the failure of Indians to accompany the army (fifteen hundred had been expected) led to abandonment of the expedition.[4] Sizeable New England forces, consisting almost entirely of Massachusetts and Plymouth troops unsuccessfully assaulted Quebec and took Acadia (to be lost the next year) with virtually no help from other colonies.[5] The doughty old Indian fighter, Major Benjamin Church, with three hundred Massachusetts and Plymouth troops swept through abondoned Indian villages on the Maine frontier during 1690-1[6] to be followed in 1692 by Governor Phips, with four hundred fifty New Englanders, on a fort building mission into the Indian country.[7]

Outside New England and New York there was little sense of duty to assist those colonies threatened by the French and Indians. Thus, the Virginia Council expressed relief in being isolated from the threat: "It having pleased Almighty God of his infinite Goodness and mercy to keep this their Majestys Dominion in peace, when all the Neighboring Colonies have been in great disturbance and Dangers . . . ."[8]

In 1692 the crown began the practice of ordering the governors of certain colonies to fix war quotas. Governor Fletcher of New York, as the commander in chief, could require reasonable assistance from the Governors of New England, Pennsylvania, Virginia, and Maryland. In practice, Fletcher had absolutely no success in obtaining troop commitments from neighboring colonies.[9]

Two years later, the crown ordered the ten colonies to furnish each a quota of men, totaling 1,358, for the protection of the New York frontier. In this instance, none of the colonies were willing to obey the royal order to assist New York.[10] A cooperative venture of New England troops and the British fleet, however, was planned against Quebec in 1694, but because of the long delay in the appearance of the fleet from the West Indies no preparations were actually made.[11] Fletcher's authority over the Connecticut militia during an emergency was admitted by Connecticut to extend only over a quota of the colony's troops "to be drawne out and commanded onely in proportion with the forces to be drawne out of the other Collonyes"[12] – a precedent which Connecticut firmly held to under the general command of Bellomont and Dudley a few years later.

Unilateral military action against the Indians characterized the last year of the war. In 1696 Benjamin Church led his second eastern expedition of five hundred men to Penobscot and Chignecto at the head of the Bay of Fundy, where he again plundered and burned Indian towns.[13] In the following year Massachusetts had the assistance of "the Helpers of the War" from Connecticut, to borrow Cotton Mather's phrase, in Captain John Whiting's expedition against the Saco Indians.[14] In the same situation as New York, Massachusetts sought help from the crown, "humbly praying That your Majesty would be graciously pleased to order that your Majestys several Governments within these Teritorys may be jointly concerned in the prosecution of the War, and Supporting the Charge thereof."[15] Although the home government in 1696 re-assigned quotas (the same as in 1694),[16] the individual colonies were more concerned with their own affairs than to aid their neighbors. Governor Andrew Hamilton of East Jersey objected to "the exemption or noncomplyance of the nighboring Colonies, nor wil this ever be remedyed unlesse the support of the frontiers reaches all North America; as it is the remoter Colonies are soe many asylums".[17]

At the beginning of Queen Anne's War, the British government set up the same quotas for the northern colonies used in the previous war, to be at the disposition of Governor Dudley.[18] But New England agents in London used their influence to prevent granting complete powers to Dudley to federalize the militia.[19] The Massachusetts Governor, and commander in chief, was unable to obtain assistance from either Rhode Island or Connecticut for the campaigns he planned in 1703 and 1704. He asked for one hundred and fifty men "between them" but received nothing.[20] A local committee of war at Hartford petitioned the Connecticut Governor "to take off those calumnies our neighbors one way and the other have laid on us".[21] Nor would Rhode Island send any troops from its quota to the defense of New York "by reason this Collony is a frontier to the sea, and none of H. M. Provinces in America [is] more exposed to the danger and assaults of the common enemy, to which we have not as yet received H. M. commands."[22]

In the spring of 1706 Dudley applied to the assemblies of both his provinces of Massachusetts and New Hampshire and to Connecticut and Rhode Island for one thousand men for an expedition against Port Royal. Connecticut declined, but the other three colonies offered assistance.[23] Meanwhile, New York was putting its forces in readiness. "Country Militia" and city militia along with seven hundred New Jersey troops mustered in New York City on July 4, 1706, making a total muster of four or five thousand men.[24] In the following year, a New England force, aided by several British naval units, attacked Port Royal. Massachusetts furnished most of the one thousand troops; Rhode Island supplied only eighty men and New Hampshire, two companies. Petty jealousies, inexperience of leaders and militia, and lack of heavy guns impeded the attack. After an ambush and skirmishes, without even starting siege operations, the force returned to Boston. Governor Dudley would not let the troops land until they went back again to assault the fortress. Colonel Wainwright took over the command from the ailing Colonel John March, and led the troops back to go through the pretense of an eleven-day siege.[25] Samuel Sewall lamented that if there had been twelve hundred "good men from N. Britain" the siege would have carried; he did not have much faith in any future attempt by provincials to take Acadia.[26]

Thus the colonies during the first seven years of Queen Anne's War displayed slight interest either in cooperative action or fully prosecuting the war. The only colony with any enthusiasm, Massachusetts, had only participated in a haphazard fashion. New York looked after its own defense. In the south, Colonel James Moore, with a small South Carolina force, twice recklessly invaded Spanish Florida.[27]

But in 1709, the home government, accepting Samuel Vetch's plan for a dual attack on Canada, assigned quotas to all the northern colonies. Massachusetts, New Hampshire, and Rhode Island were expected to raise twelve hundred men for the sea offensive; and Connecticut, New York, New Jersey, and Pennsylvania should furnish sixteen hundred troops against Montreal. With "Christians and Indians togather" each force would number two thousand.[28] Quaker pacificism and provincialism, however, obstructed Pennsylvania's cooperation. As James Logan lamented: "Under the present Constitution, they can enact no law for arming of men, nor raise money" for military purposes.[29]

But when all was ready for the two-pronged attack on Canada, the captains of the British frigates decided against proceeding to Quebec because of the lateness of the season and lack of orders; intelligence also arrived that the expected military stores had been sent to Portugal instead of the colonies. Throughout most of the summer of 1709, Nicholson, in command of the land expedition, waited in the woods off Lake Champlain with fifteen hundred men, only to return to Albany when he learned of the failure of the eastern operations.[30] Disease had wrought havoc to his troops.[31]

For 1710, the British ministry resolved upon a single expedition against Port Royal, with Nicholson in command. Four regiments of New Englanders, aided by a regiment of royal marines, made up the fighting force of two thousand men. Port Royal fell easily. Next, the Secretary of State, Viscount Bolingbroke, and the new Tory ministry planned to offset Marlborough's European victories by renewing the dual attack on Canada. British navy units, with seven regiments of veterans from the European war and a battalion of marines would join provincials in an attack upon Quebec. New England and New York raised two regiments of fifteen hundred men under Colonels Samuel Vetch and Shadrach Walton. When the expeditionary force set sail it consisted of sixty-eight vessels and 6,500 men. The fleet never reached Quebec – eight ships foundered off a small island during a fog and 884 men drowned, which forced Admiral Hovenden Walker to turn back. Meanwhile, with most of the 1,340 troops requisitioned from New York, the Jerseys, and Connecticut (Pennsylvania did not contribute any men towards its quotas), General Nicholson marched against Montreal. When news of the eastern fiasco, however, reached Nicholson at Wood Creek he had no choice but to disband his troops.[32] Having made a fair effort in raising troops for the intercolonial venture, the colonists were embittered at being denied a prize so ripe for the plucking as Canada.

Significantly, the colonists had responded to definite projects planned by the authorities in England; they had not done so when the impetus for bringing the war to the enemy was colonial-inspired. As long as they received some material assistance – in naval units, regular troops, or supplies – the colonists were willing to allow the direction of the war and the determination of troop quotas to be set by the home government. Despite the confusion in British policy and the inability to enforce rigid observance of troop requisitions,[33] Queen Anne's War did demonstrate a willingness of intercolony military cooperation under imperial control.

The lure of adventure lifted the colonies out of boredom in 1740, when the crown appealed to all the colonies, except Georgia and South Carolina, to furnish troops for an expedition against the Spanish West Indies. The colonies whole-heartedly cooperated. Maryland raised three regiments.[34] Pennsylvania raised its first levies ever for an intercolonial cause – seven companies of troops were sent "to the great Concern and Amazement of some who had persuaded themselves, that the Expedition was chimerical; and to the Pleasure and Satisfaction of all that had the Wellfare and Honour of the British Nation at Heart." Governor Thomas tried to get the assembly to vote a bounty in order to prevent indentured servants from enlisting, but without success.[35] New York and Connecticut responded enthusiastically with troops. Rhode Island sent two companies, and Massachusetts furnished five hundred men.

Two companies of North Carolina troops, originally intended to join Oglethorpe's expedition against St. Augustine, were sent on to Jamaica when the Florida expedition failed.[36] Virginia, Maryland, Massachusetts, and Rhode Island gave bounties, and all participants hoped to share in the plunder.[37]

Virginia used the opportunity to get rid of undesirable persons. The county courts were directed to impress any who were not freeholders or indentured servants. So successful was this policy that it was continued, and Governor Gooch could write in 1746 that there had been for three years past "a succession of recruiting officers from Georgia, Jamaica and South Carolina who carried away all the idle fellows out of a country settled only by planters".[38]

In all there were thirty-six hundred men in the American regiment, divided into four battalions. The British failed to capture their two objectives, Carthagena (near the Isthmus) and Santiago de Cuba, largely because many of the American troops had been incapacitated from tropical sickness. Governor Gooch returned wounded and disease-ridden. Most of the provincial troops did not return; for example, only fifty of the

Massachusetts contingent of five hundred came back. One estimate set the total number of British and American dead at eight thousand.[39] A lasting significance of the expedition was the bad feeling for the first time over discrimination in rank between regulars and provincials.[40] Because so many of the provincial soldiers had been deemed riff-raff probably explains in large part why the colonists treated the huge loss with so much equanimity. A humorous item circulating in the colonial papers in 1750 attests to an ability to consider even the worst of events with levity:

> We hear from the *Raritons*, in *New Jersey*, that within about six Weeks past, three Women in those Parts, have been deliver'd of eight children, all alive and well. *As those Parts yielded a good Number of Soldiers sent to* Carthagena, *they seem to be in great Forwardness to replenish their Loss.*[41]

Governor Oglethorpe raised a regiment of provincials (from Georgia, North Carolina, South Carolina, and Virginia) in 1740 to attack Florida. In addition to the four hundred provincials he had the assistance of several companies of regulars and the use of nine small naval vessels from the British fleet. But Oglethorpe lost the element of surprise, and the Spaniards evacuated the city of St. Augustine. The harbor was too shallow for the English ships. Other factors contributed to the failure of the expedition: Spanish reinforcements; the Carolinian troops taking sick; approaching hurricanes; and a shortage of provisions.[42] For the overland invasion of Florida in 1742, neither the Carolina troops nor British regulars from Jamaica joined the expedition as Oglethorpe had hoped for. South Carolina's main reason for participating in the first expedition had been to root out a sanctuary on the southern border for escaped slaves. Two Negro insurrections and an epidemic of small pox dampened any further military zeal in South Carolina.[43]

Soon after learning of the declaration of war, Governor Shirley in 1744 sent reinforcements to Annapolis in Nova Scotia. These troops arrived in time to fend off an Indian attack and a siege by a French force from Louisbourg.[44] For an attack upon Louisbourg in 1745, all the colonies as far south as Pennsylvania were invited to participate, but only the New England colonies and New York accepted. In all, 4,270 troops were raised for the expedition: Massachusetts, 3,300; Connecticut, 516; and New Hampshire, 454. Rhode Island managed to furnish only one armed vessel with a crew of ninety men, although an additional one hundred fifty men arrived too late to join in the siege.[45] New York, in spite of an initial interest, did nothing. Daniel Horsmanden, a member of the Council, nevertheless made an eloquent appeal to his fellow countrymen to participate in the Louisbourg expedition:

> The Destruction of Canada, being Allowed by every Englishman, to be as necessary for the welfare of his Majesty's Plantations in North America as was the Destruction of Carthage for the Weal of Rome; Every step towards an Event, so important to his Majesty, and his Dominions, ought to be pursued with all imaginable ardour, especially as the English are in Possession of Cape Breton the key by Sea.[46]

After the victory, fourteen hundred New England troops stayed on to garrison the fortress, but the colonies, other than Massachusetts, were not willing to continue sending reinforcements. Until British troops relieved the provincial force at the garrison in the spring of 1746, eight hundred ninety New Englanders had died, mostly of disease.[47]

In April 1746, royal instructions went to the colonies calling for a dual offensive against Quebec and Crown Point. The Newcastle-Bedford plan to employ both regular and provincial troops, as against the Warren-Shirley proposal to rely mainly on a colonial force, had been accepted by the ministry.[48] The colonists were to raise as many troops as they could and the king would furnish arms, pay, and clothing. Some four thousand soldiers were expected from New England to attack Quebec, and twenty-eight hundred from the middle colonies, Maryland, and Virginia were to take Crown Point. A thousand regulars, "Gibralter troops," were to be dispatched to Louisbourg to rendezvous with the New England force, whereupon the combined army under Lieutenant General St. Clair would proceed under convoy of the British fleet to Quebec.[49] Delays in recruiting resulted because of the harvest season and the refusal of some colonial officers to serve until they had received their commissions. Shirley could announce, however, in the fall that three thousand troops had been raised for the land expedition and that 1000-1200 troops were ready in New England. But it was now too late in the year for the Quebec offensive, and Shirley, as the commander in chief of the New England provincials, ordered his troops to join the Crown Point offensive,[50] except for the New Hampshire troops sent to scout and erect fortifications along the northern frontier[51] and a detachment moved to Annapolis.[52]

Shirley had over-estimated the willingness of the colonies to cooperate for the land expedition. He had relied upon the enthusiastic reports in New York and the initial reaction elsewhere, but he had not taken into account the reluctance of colonies to deploy troops from their own borders. Assembling the Crown Point army was also beset with other troubles.

Lieutenant Governor Gooch of Virginia refused to accept his commission as commander, and Shirley named Samuel Waldo to take his place.[53] Confusion over rank and pay lowered morale, and governors had to order out their troops before commissions from the crown arrived for the officers.[54] Although New Jersey deployed troops to the northern army, the legislature revolted against providing the full quota of troops because it felt the need for a new consultation among the colonies and because New Jersey had not been given "any of the common Priviledges or Management in the said Expedition."[55] General Schuyler's paying in full the New Jersey troops serving in New York aroused resentment among the unpaid New York troops. Governor Clinton objected to New York levies being in service and training longer than troops of other colonies and receiving the same pay.[56]

The Duke of Newcastle cancelled the campaign for 1747. Any further war effort in America would have to be the total responsibility of the colonies. Shirley tried to organize a new campaign. But, with intercolonial rivalry in the service and no prospect of aid from the mother country, the colonists had no heart for continuing the war. The New Jersey legislature spoke for the general dissatisfaction in 1748. Since the colony had already cooperated allegedly "beyond their Abilities, for His Majesty's Service" they "are therefore of Opinion, that any Applications from the Governments concerned in the Propos'd Expedition with respect to the Royal Instructions, so far as the same shall concern this Colony, may and ought to be looked upon inconsistent with that Liberty and Freedom they have hitherto enjoyed."[57]

From his own past experiences, in early 1754 Governor Shirley realistically gauged the problem of the troop requisition system. He thought the old quotas going back to the reign of William III should be revised and the new quotas should be enforced by the crown: "it shall be determined by his Majesty what is each Colonys just Quota of Men or Money, which it shall raise or contribute in the common cause, when any one or more of them shall be invaded, or harrass'd by the French or Indians whether in a time of open declared Warr or not, and they shall be obliged in some Effectual manner (as his Majesty shall think most proper) to conform to that determination. . ." Shirley observed that the habit of the colonies to bicker over quotas could not easily be erased; their wrangling would continue to be "an Obstacle to the carrying into Execution any general Plan for cementing an Union among his Majesty's Subjects upon this Continent, for the Defence of His Majesty's Territories committed to their Trust."[58]

In the next war, Dinwiddie's plan to attack the French on the Ohio was predicated upon the assumption that he could raise an army of 1010 men from the militia of Virginia, Maryland, and North Carolina and from royal Independent companies from South Carolina and New York.[59] But everything seemed to go wrong with the intercolonial cooperation. Dinwiddie tried to heal differences over rank by distributing command among the participants.[60] At first, the Carolina commander refused to serve under the provincial commander, George Washington. Some Virginia troops refused to march beyond the colony's boundaries. North Carolina, although putting about four hundred men on the march, came up too slowly, and the Independent companies of New York and South Carolina were also late in reaching the theater of operations. Dinwiddie placed a large share of the blame for Washington's defeat upon these troops not arriving in time. The Independent companies were under the control of the War Department in London, but consisted mainly of provincials and were independent of colonial administration.[61] Since Pennsylvania stood to gain most by a defeat of the French at Fort Duquesne, it was expected that the colony would add troops to Dinwiddie's force; but none were sent.[62]

Although all the colonies were ordered to cooperate in war against the French, the home government placed too much confidence on the Albany Congress' ability to set up military operations. Except for some discussion on quotas, that body did nothing to establish new guidelines for intercolonial contributions to a war effort.[63]

Washington's defeat, however, did have shock value in demonstrating the danger of French engulfment of the frontier to both the colonies and to Whitehall. In taking responsibility for an offensive in America, the crown ordered two regiments of foot to Virginia, commanded by Sir Peter Halket and Colonel Dunbar. The regiments were to be augmented by from five to seven hundred each in Virginia. Shirley and Pepperrell were ordered to raise immediately two regiments of one thousand men each.[64] The grand strategy for 1755 called for simultaneous expeditions to Crown Point (including the reinforcement of the Oswego garrison), Nova Scotia, and Fort Duquesne.

The reduction of Crown Point was to be undertaken by provincial troops alone raised in the northern colonies to the number of about forty-four hundred, as agreed upon at the Alexandria conference in April 1755. Colonel William Johnson was named to this command. Pepperrell with two companies and two Independent companies from New York was to reinforce the Oswego garrison.[65] The New England colonies filled their quotas and then some.[66] New York passed an act to raise 1,715 men "to be employed in conjunction with the Neighboring Colonies" for the reduction of Crown Point, more than double the colony's quota.[67] Quaker Pennsylvania did not officially participate, but a large number of volunteers were enlisted within the colony's borders.[68] Johnson assembled some forty-five hundred troops before Crown Point – a greater number of Indians turned up than had been expected. For the reinforcement of Oswego, Shirley and Pepperrell met at the Carrying Place to join their forces of eight hundred men plus Colonel Schuyler's regiment of five hundred Jersey troops.[69]

Governor Hopkins of Rhode Island attested to the zeal of the New England colonies. Writing General Johnson, he said if there were not enough troops "to over match the Enemy" that Johnson should "let it be known in New England as soon as possible for men enough are here yet left, ready and willing if the Cause so require, speedily and very greatly to increase your Number."[70] However, as the last of the New England troops from Connecticut, "all on Horseback and in high spirits, " were about to leave, the Governor countermanded their orders, on grounds that he thought the colony "already too much drained of its Inhabitants to leave it entirely naked."[71] But most of the last contingent from the New England colonies of two thousand men made their march to aid Johnson.[72]

For the expedition to Nova Scotia, Shirley worked in concert with Governor Lawrence, raising two thousand levies to "prevent the Accadians from rising, and to repel any Attempt of the French for making Themselves Master of the Peninsula."[73]

Braddock had about two thousand troops for his western campaign. Originally a force of twenty-four hundred was planned: two British regiments; two New York Independent companies; and provincial troops from Virginia, Maryland, and North Carolina.[74] In all, eight hundred provincials accompanied Braddock's army.[75] Virginia again had to reach into the bottom of the barrel, drafting those not gainfully employed between the ages of twenty-one and fifty and exempting freeholders and indentured servants.[76]

After Braddock's defeat, Colonel Dunbar stationed about two hundred fifty provincials at frontier posts, but many of these deserted, and eventually only about one hundred militia from Braddock's campaign were left in service, mainly at Fort Cumberland.[77] So demoralized had the provincial service become in Virginia, that the Reverend James Maury wrote in June 1756 that the Governor had filled up the old companies

> raised last Fall, with raw, needy and tyrannical Scots, several of them mere boys, dragged from behind the counters of the factors here; that

> regiment from an exceeding good one has degenerated into the most insignificant and corrupt corps perhaps upon earth; such as one scarce any of our countrymen think it consistent with their honor or virtue to intermingle or have any connection with . . . .[78]

Shirley's and Johnson's troops also were decimated by sickness and desertion. Shirley estimated in September 1755, of the three regiments and the Independent company fit for duty there were less than fourteen hundred, and since four hundred of these were needed for garrison duty, this left only about one thousand effectives.[79] The New England troops, in the fall months, were engaged in the construction of Fort William Henry on Lake George and in garrisoning Fort Edward. In November, most of the provincials were discharged.[80]

While Shirley was arranging preparations for another offensive in the spring of 1756, a royal circular letter informed the governors of a new plan of operations and that the Earl of Loudoun would be the next commander in chief. The colonial legislatures were to raise as many men as possible, to serve only in North America and, upon discharge at the end of the war, to receive two hundred acres of land.[81] With Shirley's recall, Major General Abercromby officially took over as commander in chief on June 25 at Albany until Loudoun's arrival. Abercromby's force consisted principally of the forty-fourth, forty-eighth, fiftieth, and fifty-first regiments, four Independent companies, the New Jersey regiment, four North Carolina companies, the Highland regiments, and the remnant provincials of the previous Crown Point expedition.[82] Before he returned to England, Shirley had managed to raise three thousand new levies in New England, under Major General John Winslow, and he sent this force to Albany to join in the expedition against Crown Point. Considering the population of New England in 1756 at nearly a half million, such a troop commitment was meager indeed. Had it not been for the blockade of French ports and the campaign in Germany, France could have placed ten men in the field for every British regular or provincial.[83] Abercromby continued Shirley's plan of moving the New England army to a siege of Crown Point. But Winslow's force made "so many Stops" that by September 22 they had proceeded no further than Fort William Henry. The new commander in chief, Loudoun, fearing a French invasion, cautiously ordered all provincial troops at Fort William Henry and the New York and New Hampshire troops at Albany to stay put. Morale among the troops was so low that desertion was rife; "no less than forty went off at once . . . ."[84]

Finding the number of provincials in the field inadequate for an offensive, Loudoun called upon the colonies for additional levies. After personally dealing with the New England governments, he finally secured commitments from the assemblies for four thousand troops, although the four assemblies kept appropriations at a bare minimum.[85] Massachusetts and Connecticut filled their quotas, and New Hampshire sent one regiment to the Hudson; Rhode Island did not send any troops at all. Of two other colonies to send troops, New York responded satisfactorily, and New Jersey filled half its quota[86] The massacre at Fort William Henry in August and the feverish dispatches from General Webb at Fort Edward calling for help, however, aroused the northern colonies to further effort.[87]

From the governors of Pennsylvania and three southern colonies, Loudoun exacted commitments to raise three thousand and eight hundred troops, most of whom would be used to assist twelve hundred regulars in garrisoning the frontier from Georgia to Pennsylvania. Maryland was to raise five hundred troops to supplement the two hundred fifty already at Forts Frederick and Cumberland; but the Maryland Assembly scaled down the new levies to three hundred, which were then stationed at the forts of the colony and placed outside any royal jurisdiction.[88] The Virginia assembly voted for a regiment of twelve hundred men and three companies of rangers of one hundred each, with a draft of one out of forty, freeholders excepted, "and to take up all Vagrants or such as have no visible Method for getting their Living." Virginia, placing its safety above that of other colonies, took no action to augment Washington's regiment serving outside the colony – thus not fulfilling its quota.[89] The poorer colonies of Georgia and North Carolina did nothing; South Carolina, plagued by money troubles, only raised half its quota. Colonel Henry Bouquet, who was sent to command the southern frontier force, must have been relieved that no enemy appeared.[90]

With the combination of a war fever running high, Pitt's continually prodding the governors and his commander in chief, and the promised Parliamentary reimbursement, there would be little difficulty in obtaining large levies of troops in the colonies for the campaigns of 1758. Fifty-one thousand troops were required, about one-half to be furnished by the colonies. Attacks would be made upon Crown Point – the wedge for a land invasion of Canada; Louisbourg – the key to Quebec; and Fort Duquesne – the gateway to the Ohio Valley. In circular letters sent to governors of all the colonies on December 30, 1757, the southern colonies (including Pennsylvania) were asked to enlist five thousand men and the northern colonies twenty thousand.[91] Loudoun, however, not desiring to dampen enthusiasm for volunteering, refused to raise previous quotas of individual colonies to meet this demand; he told Pownall that he "could not agree to make any Alteration, in the only rule that had been universally followed and acquiesced under . . . ."[92] Troops raised in the northern colonies were to be used by Abercromby, and those from the southern colonies by Forbes for the attack on Fort Duquesne. New England supplied the four companies of rangers for Amherst at Louisbourg.[93]

For Abercromby's expedition against Crown Point in 1758 the northern colonies voted 17,480 men, about two hundred fifty short of the requisition, with about 16,300 actually entering service. All these colonies paid "Levy Money" and subsistence to their troops; none paid for clothing except New York and the Jerseys..[94] Although some of the Massachusetts troops had to be impressed by drafts from the militia regiments, public support for the war ran high, as is indicated in Pownall's report to Pitt: "The People in general seem to be well spirited to enlist: An Union of the Strength of the Colonies is what they have professed earnestly to desire: And nothing will discourage me unless it be the backwardness and want of like Zeal in the other Governments."[95] John Reading, President of the New Jersey Assembly, was gratified with the enthusiasm of enlistments. He said his colony could not condone the draft as it would be "Unconstitutional and not strictly in the Power of the Legislature of this Coloney in the Case of Offensive War," but there were sufficient volunteers. "Every American must be warmed with the generous and kind Efforts of his Majesty to succour them and 'tis their duty effectually to second them and of this the Inhabitants of this Coloney are fully Convinc'd."[96] However, delays in arrival of troops were exasperating. Early in July the army was to move down Lake George. But the disastrous assault upon the breastworks at Fort Ticonderoga, defended by Montcalm's force half the size of the British-American force of fifteen thousand, put an end to any immediate advance.[97]

Meanwhile, in late summer 1758, Colonel John Bradstreet, with three thousand of Abercromby's provincials, took Oswego and Fort Frontenac.

Planning for the Forbes campaign included the use of a battalion of Highlanders and a detachment of Royal Americans to join with the provincial levies.[98] The Royal Americans were to be recruited in the colonies under officers bearing royal commissions. Most of the volunteers for the Royal Americans were Pennsylvania Germans and other non-English speaking inhabitants of the colonies.[99] General Abercromby raised the provincial quota to six thousand when he temporarily succeeded Loudoun.[100]

In Philadelphia, Forbes and his quartermaster general, John St. Clair, kept in close touch with the governors on the progress of recruitment.[101]

Forbes assembled his forces in early July at Fort Cumberland and Raystown (now Bedford, Pennsylvania): 1,260 Highlanders under Montgomery, 363 Royal Americans under Bouquet, 1,400 of the two Virginia regiments under Washington, 2,500 Pennsylvania militia, 270 Maryland militia, and 180 from various provincial attachments. In all, there were 1,623 regulars and 4,350 provincials.[102] Three Independent companies were retained in South Carolina as protection against the Indians;[103] the three companies of foot and two of rangers, raised in South Carolina, far short of the seven hundred asked for by Pitt, were also needed for Indian defense of the colony. Forbes put the provincials to work building a new road, repairing Braddock's road, and erecting forts and storehouses.[104]

Eventually Forbes's army met the French and Indians: eleven hundred of the enemy were repulsed at the post at Loyalhanna on October 12 with only nominal losses.[105] When Forbes formally took possession of Fort Duquesne, on November 25, he left about six hundred provincials, evenly divided among Virginians, Marylanders, and Pennsylvanians.[106]

The grand strategy for 1759 called for assaults on Montreal via Ticonderoga and Quebec. Instructions to the governors and the new commander, Sir Jeffrey Amherst, went out in December 1758 to raise men according to the requisitions of the year before. Amherst, however, in circular letters to the governors, asked for greater contributions than the previous year. Somewhat unrealistically he ordered seventeen thousand provincials to be employed for the attack on Montreal, to be assisted by about twelve thousand regulars. The Quebec attack would be accomplished by royal troops alone. Amherst decided to postpone the Montreal campaign until spring and returned the army to Crown Point, where provincial troops, on the verge of mutiny, were furloughed, and the regulars made winter quarters in Albany and New York.[107]

The success of Forbes in taking Fort Duquesne stimulated pride in being British-American and encouraged enlistments. "The Smiles of Providence on his Majesty's Arms in America, have put a new face on things here," wrote Jonathan Trumbull, and

> with the almighty submission and humble dependence on him for his Divine Blessing, we hope Our Troublesome Neighbours at Canada will be Subdued, and Truly Such an Acquisition must be greatly advantageous to the Nation as well as to us, who are in America – Indeed this is but a New Country, our great Business is clearing, Subduing, and Fencing the Lands, and unable to bear heavy Taxes, yet our People have with great Alacrity exerted themselves, even beyond Their Abilities."[108]

Next year, having re-collected an army of over eleven thousand men, Amherst invested Ticonderoga which fell easily because Montcalm had failed to reinforce the fort. Half of Amherst's troops were provincials. Ten days later he occupied Crown Point, after the French forces had withdrawn.[109] On October 11, 1759, Amherst, with one thousand regulars plus rangers and sailors and "a few Draughts from the Provincials," left Crown Point for St. John's.[110] Meanwhile, twenty-five hundred Massachusetts troops served in garrison duty at Louisbourg and Nova Scotia, thus relieving regulars for Wolfe's Quebec expedition.[111]

Although colonial levies had fallen off slightly in 1759, the colonists were, nevertheless, expected to furnish the same quotas for 1760 as they had previously. A rumor of peace with France and a weariness of the colonies' going through the same motions each year raising troops had led to delays in getting troops to Amherst at Crown Point. The commander in chief complained that "The Sloth of the Colonies in raising their Troops, and sending them to their Rendez-vous, made it impracticable for me to move the Troops on, so soon as I could have wished, and all I could do, was sending Partys to the other Ends of the Lake Champlain, keeping the Enemy in a constant Alarm. . . ." To encourage enlistments, officers as high as colonels could serve in the same rank they held in the militia. As before, the crown furnished all the men with arms, ammunition, tents, and provisions and promised to reimburse the colonies for levying, clothing, and paying the men. Amherst did not count on levies from the Carolinas, where Indians rampaged on the frontier; he even ordered some of his "light Infantry" to New York to be in readiness to move to aid the southern colonies. Buoyed by the victory at Quebec, the colonies gave Amherst a fair return of troops – 15,862 – by the fall of 1760.[112]

After the surrender of Montreal and with Canada virtually subdued, the colonies were still asked to provide troops much on the same basis as before. Military considerations now dealt chiefly with the occupation of Canada and Detroit, the Cherokee War, and preparations for a campaign in the West Indies – especially the expedition to Martinque under General Monckton, the newly appointed Governor of New York, who sailed with twelve thousand men, part of whom were provincials.[113] In 1761, the colonies supplied merely 8,796 troops. Lord Egremont had sent circular letters requiring the same number of troops to be raised from the colonies as in the past year. He also rebuked the southern colonies for failure to fill their quotas, as Pitt had done in 1760. But as it became apparent there was little need to keep a large army in the field, Amherst, in November, dismissed most of the provincials, keeping only those necessary for garrison duty during the winter. But many of these soldiers deserted before discharge.[114]

Again in 1762 roughly the same number of troops were requisitioned, this time for service in the Caribbean and to attack remaining French outposts in North America. The colonies were also ordered to recruit for the royal regiments "with all convenient Expedition, to their full Complement of Effectives . . . seeing the impracticability how this Country is drained by the great Number of Men furnished for the various Services in all Parts of the World." Amherst required four thousand recruits from the colonies to fill the royal regiments, assigning quotas to all the colonies. He dispatched four thousand troops to aid in the attack on Havana; provincials from New Jersey (222), Rhode Island (217) New York (567), and Connecticut (912) served in this successful expedition.[115] New Jersey was the most outspoken opponent to the new requisitions, echoing a traditional objection of most of the colonies, namely the unconstitutionality of sending troops to serve in a regular establishment outside the colony. The New Jersey legislature, however, did augment its volunteer regiment to serve with Amherst. The commander in chief wrote that he was much concerned with the "Behaviour" of the New Jersey assembly, "as I fear it may have a Bad Effect on the other Provinces, which have not yet come to any resolution of His Majesty's Requisitions; and the colonys are too Apt to take Example from one another . . . ."[116]

Another order of business for 1762 was to take St. John's on the Richelieu River, which was accomplished by Amherst with a mixed force of regulars and provincials – the provincials were "no ways inferior" to the regulars "in driving the french from the severall out posts which they endeavoured to maintain," at least according to Governor Bernard's observation.[117] Commanding at Crown Point in October 1762, Amherst sent most provincials home during the winter as he had done the year before.[118] He knew the difficulties of keeping a large force of colonial troops intact during periods of inaction. Governor Arthur Dobbs of North Carolina, writing to Amherst, briefly touched upon an underlying contradiction in the military stance: "it will be necessary to have some British Force to Keep Down the rising Spirit of Independency – and don't doubt but the Assembly will allow the Garrison's Provisions, as allow'd in the other Colonies."[119]

Most of the provincials remaining in service at Halifax and Crown Point were dismissed in the spring of 1763.[120] There were rumors that regular units would be stationed in South Carolina, but other colonies would for the time being be expected to maintain their own frontier defenses.[121] Before Amherst left for England he requested troops from the colonies to be used for fighting the Indians, and his successor, General Gage, would do the same – the last requisitions to be placed on the colonies.[122]

A motley colonial force, collected under the requisition system, had largely served its purpose – but more as a defensive barrier rather than as an offensive army. Had the French resources of manpower to draw upon, the fight for North America might well have been a different story. But, as a hypothetical case could be made for the potential American military strength during the American Revolution, so it may be conjectured that had the French threat been more formidable the colonists would have rallied with far greater troop commitments. As it was, the crown had to rely chiefly on the more cooperative colonies of Massachusetts, Connecticut, and New York.[123] The requisition system was confusing, wasteful, and suitable only for short-term, limited operations; it could not prevail over a colony placing priority on its own safety or withholding support on constitutional grounds. The long struggle with France would have been won more quickly with a completely royalized army.

NOTES

[1] Simon Bradstreet to Robert Treat, Oct. 5, 1689, CA, Colonial Wars, II, 22; Jacob Leisler to Gov. Robert Treat, Apr. 19, 1690, *ibid.*, 56; Reich, *Leisler's Rebellion*, 95.

[2] Robert Livingston to Sir Edmund Andros, Apr. 14, 1690, *NYCD*, III, 708.

[3] "At a meeting of commissioners . . .," May 1, 1690, CA, Colonial Wars, II, 57. Quotas: N.Y. – 400; Mass. – 160; Ply. – 60; Conn. – 135; Md. – 200. Total – 855.

[4] See above chapters for further details; also George A. Cook, *John Wise* (New York, 1952), 61–62; Reich, *Leisler's Rebellion*, 103–5.

[5] According to his own account of the Acadia expedition in 1690, Phips had 7 ships and 700 men; for the attack on Quebec, he had 30 ships and 2,300 men. "Sir William Phips' account of his expedition against Acadia and Quebec," Apr. 21, 1691, *CSP*, XIII, 415.

[6] Samuel Drake, *The Border Wars of New England* (New York, 1897), 66–67.

[7] Douglass, *A Summary Historical* (1755), I, 555.

[8] H. R. McIlwaine, ed., *Legislative Journals of the Council of Colonial Virginia*, 3 vols. (Richmond, 1918–19), I, 136.

[9] Order in Council (to Gov. of Pa.), Oct. 11, 1692, *PA*, 8th Ser., I, 129; *CSP*, xvii–xx; also see Chapter 5.

[10] Privy Council Instructions, Aug. 22, 1694, CA, Colonial Wars, II, 209; Arthur H. Buffington, "The Policy of Albany and English Westward Expansion," *MVHR*, VIII

(1922), 348–49. The quotas requested of the colonies were as follows:

Mass.	– 350	E. N. J.	– 60	
N. H.	– 40	W. N. J.	– 60	
R. I.	– 48	Pa.	– 80	
Conn.	– 120	Md.	– 160	
N. Y.	– 200	Va.	– 240	total – 1358

Va. and Md. sent £ 900 to aid N. Y.; E. N. J. sent money and men for the Albany garrison. Trealease, *Indian Affairs in Colonial New York*, 315.

11 Palfrey, *Hist. of New England*, IV, 145.

12 The Queen to the Governor of N. Y., June 21, 1694, *CSP*, XIV, 299; Fitz-John Winthrop to the Lords Commissioners of Trade (1695?), *Winthrop Papers, MHSC*, 6th Ser., III, 24.

13 Johnson, *Hist. of the French War*, 119–20.

14 Cotton Mather, *Decennium Luctuosum . . . Remarkable Occurrences in the Long War . . . with the Indian Savages*, in Charles H. Lincoln, ed., *Narratives of the Indian Wars*, 1675–99 (*Original Narratives Series* [New York, 1913]), 269.

15 "Draught of a Humble Representation and Address to the King," Sep. 24, 1696, *Mass. Acts and Resolves*, III (1878), 123.

16 Lords of Trade to Proprietors of E. and W. New Jersey, Feb. 9, 1697, *NJA*, 1st Ser., II, 134–35.

17 Gov. Andrew Hamilton to Gov. Fletcher, June 26, 1696, *ibid.*, 113–14.

18 James T. Adams, *Revolutionary New England, 1691–1776* (Boston, 1923), 66.

19 Minutes of Council in Assembly of New Hampshire, May 28, 1702, *CSP* XX, 355; Kimball, *Dudley*, 144.

20 Kimball, *Dudley*, 144.

21 The Committee of War [Hartford] to Fitz-John Winthrop, July 3, 1704, *Winthrop Papers, MHSC*, 6th Ser., III, 235–36.

22 Reply of the Governor and Company of R. I., Feb. 1, 1706, *CSP*, XXIII, 34.

23 Jeremy Belknap, *The History of New-Hampshire*, 3 vols. (Boston, 1812), I, 273

24 *Boston News Letter*, July 8, 1706, in Weeks, ed., *Hist. Digest*, 354.

25 Kimball, *Dudley* 121–22; Fry, *New Hampshire as a Royal Province*, 503; Johnson, *Hist. of the French War*, 131. For on-the-spot impressions of the attack, see Col. Winthrop Hilton to Gov. Dudley, July 16, 1707, Belknap Papers, MHS.

26 "Samuel Sewall Letter Book," Apr. 26, 1708, *MHSC*, 6th Ser., I, 367.

27 The surprise attack in 1702 consisted of 400 troops under Col. Moore, in laying siege of St. Augustine, and 100 men under Col. Daniel overland to St. John's River. "Statements made in the Introduction to the Report of General Oglethorpe," B. R. Carroll, ed., *Historical Collections of South Carolina*, 2 vols. (New York, 1836), II, 351–52.

28 Instructions to Captains Mathews, *et al.*, – 1709, PRO, CO, Vol. 9, LC; Journal of the proceedings of Francis Nicholson and Samuel Vetch, June 29, 1709, Parkman Transcripts, XXXVI, MHS; Drake, *Border Wars*, 251–53. New York had already voted to bolster its troops for the projected Canada expedition by 487 men. *The Colonial Laws of New York*, June 7, 1709, I (1894), 659.

Sea expedition quotas:		and expedition quotas:	
N.H.	– 100	N.Y.	– 800
R. I.	– 200	Pa.	– 150
Mass.	– 900	N. J.	– 300
total	– 1200	Conn.	– 350
		total	– 1600

[29] James Logan to William Penn, May 11, 1709, Logan, ed., *Penn-Logan Corrs,.*, II, 344, Thayer, *Growth of Pa. Democracy*, 10.

[30] Fry, *New Hampshire as a Royal Province*, 203; Kimball, *Dudley*, 125; Bird, *Navies in the Mountains*, 39. Nicholson's army actually consisted of about 800 N. Y. troops; Pa., 150; N. J., 200; and Conn., 100–300.

[31] Connecticut lost 80–90 men by disease, more than from among all the other troops together. Gurdon Saltonstall to Lords Commissioners of the Privy Council, Nov. 21, 1710, Parkman transcripts, XXXVI, MHS.

[32] Fry, *New Hampshire as a Royal Province*, 505–6; Smith, *History of New Jersey*, 400; Davidson, *War Comes to Quaker Pa.*, 18; Kemmerer, "The Struggle for Self-Government in Colonial New Jersey," (Ph. D. diss.), 198–99. Quotas had been levied at the New London conference as follows: 1000 total from Mass., R. I., and N. H. for the attack on Quebec; for the overland expedition – N. Y., 600; Conn., 300; E. Jersey, 100; W. Jersey, 100; and Pa., 240. Proceedings of the Congress held at New London, June 21–22, 1711, *NYCD*, V, 257–61.

[33] For the negative influence of Queen Anne's War on British-American solidarity, see G. M. Waller, "New York's Role in Queen Anne's War, 1702–13," *New York History*, XXXIII (1952), 44–52.

[34] Clayton C. Hall, *The Lords Baltimore and the Maryland Palatinate* (Baltimore, 1902), 161.

[35] Gov. Thomas's Speech to the Assembly, July 2, 1740, Columbia University Special Collections; *South-Carolina Gazette*, Oct. 9, 1740; *Pa. Gazette* Abstract, Sep. 18,1740, *FP*, II, 289; Osgood, *American Colonies*, III, 498.

[36] Samuel A. Ashe, *History of North Carolina*, I (Greensboro, 1908), 261.

[37] Osgood, *American Colonies*, III, 498. For details of the colonial participation in the expedition to Carthagena and the effect upon a separateness of American identity, see Albert Harkness, Jr., "Americanism and Jenkins' Ear," *MVHR*, XXXVII (1950), 61–90.

[38] Quoted in Morton, *Colonial Virginia*, II, 527.

[39] Extract from *The Boston Weekly News-Letter*, July 2, 1741, *NJA*, 1st Ser., XII (1895), 96–97.

[40] Douglass, *A Summary Historical* (1755), I, 554; Osgood, *American Colonies*, III, 499–500.

[41] Extract from *The Boston Evening Post*, Dec. 17, 1750, *NJA*, 1st Ser., XII (1895), 695.

[42] Carroll, ed., *Historical Collections of South Carolina*, I, 335, 339; E. Merton Coulter, *Georgia: A Short History* (Chapel Hill, 1947), 45–46. With the reinforcement of the South Carolina regiment under Col. Alexander van der Dussen at St. John's, Oglethorpe had about 800 men. "A Ranger's Report of Travels with General Oglethorpe, 1739–42," in Newton D. Mereness, ed., *Travels in the American Colonies* (New York, 1961), 226–28.

43 E. Merton Coulter, ed., *The Journal of William Stephens, 1741–43*, 2 vols. (Athens, Ga., 1958), Nov. 9, 1742, II, 136; Carroll, ed., *Hist. Colls. of S. C.*, I, 366; Thomas Gamble, "Colonel William Bull: His Part in the Founding of Savannah," *Ga. Hist. Quarterly*, XVII (1933), 119; Reese, *Colonial Georgia*, 78–79; Osgood, *American Colonies*, III, 502–6.

44 *FP*, III, 55n.

45 De Forest, ed., *Louisbourg Journals, 1745*, 8th journal, 110 and 110n. Frederick Huidekoper, "The Sieges of Louisbourg in 1745 and 1758," *Some Important Colonial Military Operations* (Washington, D. C., 1914), 4–5; Fry, *New Hampshire as a Royal Province*, 507–8. An officer sent from Boston to recruit in the southern colonies had to return because his vessel ran ashore. William Bryan to William Pepperrell, Mar. 3, 1745, Pepperrell Papers, MHS.

46 Daniel Horsmanden Papers, n. d. [1745], NYHS.

47 Shirley to the Duke of Newcastle, May 10, 1746, Parkman transcripts, XXXVIII, MHS.

48 Buffington, "The Canada Expedition of 1746," *AHR*, XLV (1940), 569–70.

49 William Pepperrell to the Duke of Newcastle, May 21, 1746, PRO, CO, Vol. 44, LC; Newcastle to Gooch, Apr. 9, 1746, *ibid.*, Vol. 45; Pepperrell to Shirley, Apr. 30, 1746, Pepperrell Papers, MHS; Message to the Gov. of Mass. from the House of Representatives, July 16, 1746, MA transcripts, NYPL; *Journal of the Legislative Council of New-York*, 2 vols. (Albany, 1861), II, 927, June 6, 1746; Proclamation of Gov. Thomas Bladen, June 7, 1746, *Md. Archives*, XXVIII, 359-60; Wynne, *General History* (1770), I, 513; Wood, *Shirley*, 330. For the Quebec campaign, Mass. was to furnish 20 companies; N. H., 2; R. I., 3; Conn., 10; total 35 companies. For operations against Crown Point, the colonies would contribute 29 companies: Va., 2; Md., 3; Pa., 4; the Jerseys, 5; N. Y., 15.

50 Shirley to Benning Wentworth, Nov. 12, 1746, Belknap Papers, XXXIX, MHS; Shirley to Duke of Newcastle, July 28, 1746 and Sep. 19, 1746, Parkman transcripts, MHS.

51 Wentworth to Duke of Newcastle, June 7, 1747, PRO, CO, Vol. 15, LC.

52 Shirley to the Duke of Newcastle, June 8, 1747, Parkman transcripts, XXXIX, MHS.

53 Schutz, *Shirley*, 115.

54 E. g., Order of Gov. Thomas Bladen, July 8, 1746, *Md. Archives* XXVIII, 362–63.

55 *Pennsylvania Journal*, Mar. 1, 1748 (Resolution of the N. J. House, Jan. 23, 1747).

56 Extract of Gov. Clinton's letter to Gov. Shirley, Dec. 7, 1747, PRO, CO, Vol. 45, LC; Osgood, *American Colonies*, IV, 184–85.

57 *Pennsylvania Journal*, Mar. 1, 1748.

58 Shirley to the Earl of Holderness, Jan. 7, 1754, *Shirley Corr.*, I, 28; see Koontz, *Dinwiddie*, 262–72.

59 Dinwiddie to Gov. Hamilton, July 31, 1754, Virginia Miscellaneous Papers, LC. Breakdown of forces expected:

South Carolina Indep. Co.	– 100
New York Indep. Co.	– 160
Virginia Regiment	– 300
North Carolina troops	– 350
Maryland troops	– 100

[60] Dinwiddie to Matthew Rowan, Mar. 23, 1754, *Dinwiddie Corr.*, I, 122; Dinwiddie to Sharpe, June 20, 1754, in Hardin, ed., "Mackay," *Ga. Hist. Quarterly*, I (1917), 91–92. Order of command as follows: Col. James Innes, commander in chief; Col. Washington, 2d in command; Capt. Clark (N. Y.) 3d in command, to take over Dinwiddie's command as Lt. Col.; Capt. McKay (S. C.), 4th in command. Dinwiddie had expected 1000 troops from Pa., as Gov. Hamilton had also hoped for.

[61] Dinwiddie to Lords of Trade, June 18, 1754, *Dinwiddie Corr.*, I, 206; Dinwiddie to Sir Thomas Robinson, June 18, 1754, *ibid.*, 204; Dinwiddie to Earl of Albemarle, July 24, 1754, *ibid.*, 247; Dinwiddie to Gov. De Lancey, July 31, 1754, *ibid.*; Robert C. Alberts, *The Most Extraordinary Adventures of Major Robert Stobo* (Boston, 1965), 37; Bradley, *Fight for France in North America*, 69; Koontz, *Dinwiddie*, 244; James, *Drums in the Forest*, 32.

[62] Shirley to Wentworth, Mar. 18, 1754, Belknap Papers (Force transcripts), I, LC; Lords of Trade to Gov. Shirley, July 5, 1754, Bancroft transcripts (Colonial Documents), NYPL; Thomas Robinson to Lt. Gov. of Pa., July 5, 1754, Ettling Revolution Papers, U. S. MSS, HSP.

[63] Resolution of N. Y. General Assembly, Mar. 27, 1755, Ebenezer Hazard Coll., N. Y. Records, LC. Quotas for N. Y. and Mass. were 800 and 1400, resp.

[64] Thomas Robinson to Governor and Company of Conn., Oct. 25, 1754, Trumbull Papers, CSL.

[65] Braddock to Sir Thomas Robinson, Apr. 19, 1755, Parkman transcripts, XL, MHS.

[66] Resolution of the Conn. Assembly, May, 1755, CA, Colonial Wars, V, 119; Shirley to William Johnson, May 31, 1755, *William Johnson Papers*, I, 522–23; Benning Wentworth to William Johnson, June 17, 1755, *ibid.*, 606; Hall, "Chatham's Colonial Policy," *AHR*, V (1900), 663. Quotas for the Crown Point expedition arranged at Alexandria:

N. Y.	– 800
Conn.	– 1000
Mass.	– 1500
R. I.	– 400
N. H.	– 500
total	– 4200

Also 200 Indians were to be employed; N. J., not assigned a quota, contributed troops.

[67] *Journal of the Legislative Council of New-York*, Apr. 1, 1756, II, 1255.

[68] Address to the General Assembly, Feb. 13, 1756, *PCR*, VII, 37.

[69] Extract of a letter from Richard Peters, Sec. of Pa., July 17, 1755, PRO, CO, Vol. 16, LC; Shirley to Gov. Hopkins, June 9, 1755, Shirley Miscellaneous Correspondence, NYPL. In June 1755, Shirley marched through R. I. and Conn. to Albany, collecting troops on the way.

[70] Stephen Hopkins to Major General Johnson, Sep. 24, 1755, Emmet Collection, #2320, NYPL.

[71] *Pennsylvania Gazette*, Sep. 25, 1755.

[72] Lt. Gov. Spencer Phips to Maj. Gen. Johnson, Sep. 26, 1755, Gratz Collection (Colonial Governors), HSP.

[73] Shirley to Sir Thomas Robinson, Jan. 24, 1755, Parkman transcripts, XL, MHS.

[74] Shirley to Robinson, June 20, 1755, *ibid.*, XLI, MHS.

[75] Hall, "Chatham's Colonial Policy," *AHR*, V (1900), 662.

[76] *Virginia Gazette*, Nov. 7, 1754.

[77] Dinwiddie to the Lords of Trade, Sep. 6, 1755, Bancroft transcripts (Colonial Documents), NYPL.

[78] Rev. James Maury to John Fontaine, June 15, 1756, *ibid.*, (Virginia Papers), NYPL.

[79] Shirley to Sharpe, Camp at Oswego, Sep. 9, 1755, "Letters Relating to the French and Indians," *Md. Hist. Mag.*, IV (1909), 346.

[80] Weaver, *Trumbull*, 73.

[81] Fisher, *New Jersey as a Royal Province*, 339–40.

[82] [Livingston], *Review of Military Operations, MHSC*, 1st Ser., VII (1801), 150.

[83] Extract of letter of Shirley to Maj. Gen. Winslow, July 26, 1756, PRO, CO, Vol. 47, LC; Chauncey W. Ford, ed., *Broadsides, Ballads &c Printed in Massachusetts, 1639–1800* (Check List), *MHSC*, LXXV (1922), Aug. 23, 1756, 147; Robert Rogers, *Reminiscences of the French War containing Rogers' Expedition . . . as published in London in 1765* (Concord, N. H., 1831), 24; Hall, "Chatham's Colonial Policy," *AHR* V (1900), 662. Mass. alone had agreed originally to raise 3500 troops for the Crown Point expedition.

[84] Enclosure to Loudoun's letter of Aug. 19, 1756, PRO, CO, Vol. 47, LC; Shirley to Henry Fox, Sep. 16, 1756, *ibid.*, Vol. 46, LC; *New Hampshire Gazette*, Oct. 7, 1756; Loudoun to Cumberland, Oct. 3, 1756, Pargellis, *Military Affairs*, 239.

[85] Loudoun to Henry Fox, Feb. 8, 1757, Parkman transcripts, XLIV, MHS; "Military Letters of Captain Joseph Shippen of the Provincial Service, 1756–58," May 30, 1757, *PMHB* (1912), 426. Quotas Loudoun requested: Mass. – 1800; Conn. – 1400; R. I. – 450; N. H. – 350. Later, in Philadelphia, Loudoun ordered a general press, whereby he obtained 100 men.

[86] Gov. Fitch to Pitt, Mar. 16, 1757, *Pitt Corr.*, I, 26; Benning Wentworth to Gen. Abercromby, Apr. 13, 1758, PRO, WO:34, XXIV, LC; Fry, *New Hampshire as a Royal Province*, 514.; Fisher, *New Jersey as a Royal Province*, 161. New Hampshire complained that the colony had already supplied rangers and had to resort to impressment to fill the quota of 800. Connecticut, in voting for 5000 troops, however, stipulated that if other colonies "should fail in exerting themselves . . . . or any other occurence shall happen to prevent the army from proceeding, this Assembly desire his Honour the Governor, with the advice of the Council," to recall the troops sent from Connecticut. (*CCR*, XI, Mar. 24, 1758, 106–7.)

[87] Sharpe to Baltimore, Sep. 5, 1757, *Md. Archives*, IX, 79; Fry, *N. H. as a Royal Province*, 515–17. Eighty of 200 N. H. men were killed or captured by the Indians.

[88] High, "Loudoun and Sharpe," *Md. Hist. Mag.*, XLV (1950), 19, 24–25; Gov. Lyttleton to Pitt, July 12, 1757, *Pitt Corr.*, I, 86; Sharpe to William Sharpe, June 1, 1757, *Md. Archives*, IX, 11–12; Beer, *British Colonial Policy*, 59.

[89] Dinwiddie to Sharpe, June 14, 1757, *Md. Archives*, IX, 25; John Kirpatrick to Washington, June 19, 1757, Hamilton, ed., *Letters to Washington*, II, 113; Baker-Crothers, *Virginia and the French and Indian War*, 122–23; Beer, *British Colonial Policy*, 59.

[90] Loudoun to John Pitt, Mar. 10, 1757, Parkman transcripts, XLIV, MHS; E. Douglas Branch, "Henry Bouquet: Professional Soldier," *PMHB*, LXII (1938), 44.

[91] Pitt to Gov. of N. H., Dec. 30, 1757, Bouton, ed., *N. H. Provincial Papers* VI, 656; Basil Williams, *The Life of William Pitt,* reprint ed. (New York, 1966), 365; Beer, *British Colonial Policy,* 59–61, 59n. Specific quotas requested:

	regulars	provincials
1) Louisbourg exp. under Amherst	14,215	600 rangers
2) Crown Pt. exp. under Abercromby	9,447	20,000
3) Duquesne exp. under Forbes	1,880	5,000
total –	25,542	25,600

[92] Loudoun to Pitt, Feb. 14, 1758, *Pitt Corr.*, I, 187.

[93] Rogers, *Reminiscences* (1765), 49. As an example of the manpower resources in Mass., Gov. Pownall reported that the colony had 32 regiments on the alarm list – 45,764 men in all, of which 37,446 "are bound by law to train in the field. (Pownall to the Lords of Trade, Jan. –, 1758, Bancroft transcripts [Colonial Documents], NYPL.)

[94] "Return of men raised by the Colonies of North America . . . under command of General Abercrombie," 1758, Thomas Penn's Letters, Bancroft transcripts, NYPL; Committee Report, S/ Ebenezer Silliman, Mar. 1758, CA, Colonial Wars, VII, 147; Thomas Fitch to Gen. Abercromby, Mar. 17, 1758, PRO, WO:34, XXVIII, LC; *The Colonial Laws of New York*, Mar. 7, 1758, IV (1894), 215.

Numbers voted by assembly		in service	time in service
Mass.	– 7,000	6,500	5 months
Conn.	– 5,000	4,550	5 months
N. H.	– 800	740	5 months
R. I.	– 1,000	960	5 months
Jerseys	– 1,000	1,000	5 months
N. Y.	– 2,680	2,557	5 months
total	– 17,480	16,307	

[95] Gov. Pownall to Pitt, Mar. 23, 1758, *Pitt Corr.*, I, 213; Gen. Abercromby to Pitt, Apr. 28, 1758, *ibid.*, 226. Pownall thought N. Y. should contribute on a 4 to 7 ratio with that of Mass., according to the Albany Conference of 1754, which quota ratio N. Y. had recognized.

[96] John Reading to Gen. Abercromby, Apr. 28, 1758, PRO, WO:34, XXXI, LC.

[97] Alden, *General Gage in America*, 45; Fry, *N. H. as a Royal Province*, 518–19.

[98] Beer, *British Colonial Policy*, 60n.

[99] Sipe, *Indian Wars*, 388.

[100] *Pennsylvania Gazette*, Apr. 13, 1758; Fitzpatrick, ed., *Washington Writings* I, 210n.

[101] E.g., John St. Clair to Sharpe, Apr. 24, 1758, Dreer Collection (Officers Serving in Amer. Before the Rev.), HSP.

[102] Huidekoper, "Struggle Between the French and English . . .," in *Some Important Colonial Military Operations*, 33; Williams, *Pitt*, 375; Rev. Cyrus Cort, *Colonel Henry Bouquet and his Campaigns, 1763–64* (Lancaster, 1883), 11; Thayer, *Growth of Democracy in Pa.*, 67; Mary C. Darlington, ed., *History of Colonel Bouquet and the Western Frontiers of Pennsylvania, 1747–64* (Pittsburgh, 1920), 88.

Thayer, Darlington, and Fitzpatrick (*Wash. Writings*, I, 210n.) give the higher estimate of Forbes' army. A lower estimate is found in "Provincial Troops under the command of Brig. Gen. Forbes," n. d., Thomas Penn Letters, Bancroft transcripts, NYPL: Pa., 2727; Va., 1868; Md., 227; N. C., 127 – total, 4949. A further breakdown of the troops in Forbes's army is as follows:

Name of Corps	Field Officers	Co. Officers	Total trps
Royal Americans, 1st	1	12	363
Bn, Div. of Highland, or 62nd Rgt	3	37	998
Division of 62nd Rgt	3	12	269
1st Va. Rgt	3	32	782
2nd Va. Rgt	3	35	702
3d N. C. Companies	1	10	141
4th Md. Companies	1	15	270
1st Bn, Pa.	3	41	755
2nd Bn, Pa.	3	40	666
3d Bn, Pa.	3	46	771
Three Lower Counties (Del.)	3	46	263
			total – 5980

Troops in frontier detachments and on detail on road communications not included in above. (Sipe, *Ind. Wars*, 387).

103 Forbes to Pitt, May 1, 1758, James, ed., *Forbes Writings*, 76; John R. Alden, *John Stuart and the Southern Colonial Frontier* (Ann Arbor, 1944), 65–73.

104 See Stephens *et al.*, *Vouquer Papers*, II, Introd. and pp. 152–592 for day-to-day activities of Forbes's army.

105 *Pennsylvania Gazette*, Oct. 26, 1758. Twelve were killed, 18 wounded, 31 missing.

106 Forbes to Gov. Denny, Nov. 26, 1758, *NYCD*, X, 114; Sharpe to Calvert, Nov. 28, 1758, *Md. Archives*, IX, 305. The Md. Assembly insisted, however, that the colony's troops be sent to Fort Frederick.

107 Pitt to Governors of R. I., Mass. Bay, N. H., Conn., N. Y., and N. J., Dec. 9, 1758, *RICR* VI (1861), 179; Amherst to Gov. of R. I., Dec. 13, 1758, *ibid.*, 180; Extract of letter of Amherst to Gov. Pownall, Feb. 12, 1759, PRO, CO, Vol. 54, LC; Circular Letter of Amherst to the northern governors, Feb. 16, 1759, *ibid.*; Thomas Fitch to Gen. Amherst, Jan 8, 1759, PRO, WO:34, XXVIII, LC; James Robertson to Earl of Morton, Dec. 19, 1758, Pargellis, ed., *Military Affairs*, 429; Fry, *N. H. as a Royal Province*, 518; Alberts, *Stobo*, 268.

108 Jonathan Trumbull to Messrs. Lane and Booth, Feb. 20, 1759; Thomas Fitch to Amherst, Mar. 30, 1759, PRO, WO:34, XXVIII, LC; Pitt to Gov. of N. H., Feb. 5, 1759 Belknap Papers (Force Transcripts), LC. Conn. enthusiastically voted 3600 troops. The New England colonies were to supply sailors and workmen as Rear Admiral Saunders, commander in chief of all His Majesty's ships employed in North America, might require. New York conducted a recruiting campaign for volunteers, between the ages of 19 and 28 and 5'8" tall; arms, clothing, accoutrements would be furnished; and pay per week for the duration of a two year enlistment varied from that of a matross gunner at 9*s.* 6*d.* per week to that of Sergeant at 19*s.* 8*d.* See advertisement in *The New-York Mercury*, Feb. 19, 1759.

109 Sharpe to Baltimore, Apr. 19, 1759, *Md. Archives*, IX, 337; Alden, *General Gage in America*, 48-49. When Amherst arrived at Fort Edward to take field

command, his total force amounted to 11,533 men (5,279 of which were provincials. Hugh Hastings, ed., *Orderly Book and Journal of Major John Hawks on the Ticonderoga-Crown Point Campaign under General Amherst, 1759–60* (New York, 1911), x–xi.

[110] N. Whiting to Jonathan Trumbull, Oct., 12, 1759, Trumbull, Sr. Papers, CHS; Benjamin Pomroy to his wife, Oct. 10, 1759, Benj. Pomroy Miscellaneous Papers, NYHS.

[111] Mayo. ed., Hutchinson's *Hist. of Mass.*, III, 57. Mass. had also voted 6,500 troops to serve with Amherst, plus another 300 to serve as "pioneers" to be used by Wolfe upon application.

[112] Amherst to Pitt, June 21, 1760, *Pitt Corr.*, II, 305; Pitt to governors of Mass., N. H., Conn., R. I., N. Y., and N. J., Dec. 17, 1760, *ibid.*, 366–67; Amherst to Pitt, Oct. 18, 1760, *ibid.* 343; Pitt to Gov. and Company of R. I., Jan. 7, 1760, *RICR*, VI, 234–45; Beer, *British Colonial Policy*, 64–65 and 65n.

Number of troops voted		Number raised
N. H.	800	796
Mass.	5,500	4,964
R. I.	1,000	952
Conn.	5,000	3,397
N. Y.	2,680	2,468
N. J.	1,000	935
Pa.	2,700	1,350
Md.	–	–
Va.	1,000	1,000
N. C.	500	–
S. C.	–	–
total –	20,180	15,862

[113] O'Conor, *A Servant of the Crown*, 159–60.

[114] Amherst to Pitt, Nov. 27, 1761, PRO, CO, Vol. 61, LC; Amherst to Col. Bradstreet, Oct. 28, 1761, Emmet Collection, #1778, NYPL; "Return of the Troops Furnished . . . 1761," MA, Colonial, VI, 270; Jordan, ed., "Journal of James Kenny, 1761–63," *PMHB*, XXXVII (1913), 28; Arnold, *Hist. of R. I.*, II, 233.

troops voted (1761)		actually raised and in field	remaining during the winter
N. H.	534	438	51
Mass.	3,220	2,637	591
R. I.	666	395	64
Conn.	2,300	2,000	323
N. Y.	1,787	1,547	173
N. J.	600	554	64
Pa.	–	–	–
Md.	–	–	–
Va.	1,000	1,000	–
N. C.	500	225	–
S. C.	–	–	–
total –	10,607	8,796	

For these and other statistics on the state of provincial troops, 1759–63, compare J. Clarence Webster, ed., *The Journal of Jeffrey Amherst, 1758–63* (Chicago, 1931),

Tables A–F, pp. 326–32. The discrepancy between Long's figures and those cited in this chapter is largely due to Long's crediting N. C. and S. C. with a greater contribution.

[115] Earl of Egremont to Gov. and Co. of Conn., Dec. 12, 1761, Trumbull Papers, CSL; Amherst to Earl of Egremont, May 12, 1762, PRO, CO, Vol. 62, LC; Colden to Amherst, May 20, 1762, PRO, CO, WO:34, Vol 29, LC; *Pennsylvania Journal*, Mar. 25, 1762; Webster, *Amherst Journal*, Feb. 19, 1762, 279; Beer, *British Colonial Policy*, 67–68.

[116] Amherst to Gov. Hardy, Mar. 13, 1762, PRO, WO:34, XXXI, LC; Order of the General Assembly of N. J., Mar. 9, 1762, *NJA*, 1st Ser., XXIV, 26–27.

[117] *Pennsylvania Gazette,* Sep. 16, 1762; Gov. Bernard to Lord Barrington, Oct. 20, 1762, Channing *et al*, ed., *Bernard-Barrington Corr.*, 62–64.

[118] Amherst to Colonel Whiting, Oct. 24, 1762, Amherst Miscellaneous Manuscripts, NYHS.

[119] Arthur Dobbs to Amherst, Dec. 4, 1762, PRO, WO:34, XXXV, LC.

[120] Amherst to Gov. Bernard, May 8, 1763, *ibid.*, XXVII, LC.

[121] Capt. John Brown to Gates, Mar. 12, 1763, Horatio Gates Papers, Box 1, NYHS; Amherst to Bouquet, Sep. 7, 1763, (microfilm), Amherst Papers, CL.

[122] Amherst to Col. Bradstreet, Nov. 1, 1763, Sir Jeffrey Amherst Letters (transcriptions of W. B. Sprague Collection, Albany), LC; Gage to Halifax, Dec. 9, 1763, Clarence E. Carter, ed., *The Correspondence of General Thomas Gage . . ., 1763–75*, I (New Haven, 1931), 3–4. See Chapter 9.

[123] Mass., N. Y., and Conn., with one-third of the population, furnished seven-tenths of the troops. Beer, *British Colonial Policy*, 70–71.

CHAPTER VII

NORTHERN INDIANS

Ambivalence marked intercolony relations in Indian affairs. The expansion of the frontier and the colonial wars brought attention to the need for generalization of Indian relations, and at the same time aggravated colonial rivalries. Colonial Indian policy had as its chief objectives the cession of land, military aid from the Indians or at least neutrality in wartime, and regulation of the fur trade. Each colony claimed an exclusive jurisdiction over its own Indians, which even the imperialization at mid-century could not change. But the Indians themselves forced considerations of Indian relations as a federal problem; inter-tribe raiding parties, the Indian boundary, and the fur trade, which knew no single colony limitations, in spite of the spheres of interest staked out by individual colonies. To hold the loyalty of the redskins, it was necessary to present an image of strength and a united front. When separate or competing policies threatened to obstruct the general interest, the colonists turned to intercolonial Indian conferences, but is is significant that they did so under the shadow of war clouds.

At the outbreak of the first French and Indian War, New England and New York followed conflicting paths. New York tried to enlist the Iroquois against the French on its frontier, whereas the New England colonies sought to involve the Five Nations against the eastern Indians in Maine. The point of controversy were the Maquas (Caughnawagas),[1] who raided the New England frontier, while at the same time proffered friendship to the Five Nations and New York.

In September 1689, commissioners from Massachusetts, Plymouth, and Connecticut met with the Iroquois at Albany "to renew the Friendship with the Five Nations,[2] and to engage them against the Eastern Indians," but the Iroquois refused because they had no quarrel with the eastern Indians and had no desire "to increase the Number of their Enemies." Furthermore, the "People of Albany likewise have always been averse to engage our Indians in a War with the Eastern Indians, lest it should change the Seat of the War, and bring it to their own Doors." The Iroquois reiterated their position of 1684 that if the English expected aid from them, they must receive troops to help guard their most exposed areas against French invasion. These views of the Iroquois were abetted by the Albany Convention, which continued to meet with the Indians after the New England delegates had gone home.[3]

The Governor of New York was entrusted by the crown with the responsibility for maintaining the Iroquois alliance. When Henry Sloughter arrived in New York, March 1691, he brought with him £ 100 for Indian presents.[4] During Sloughter's administration he treated Iroquois affairs as a New York problem, but he did not hesitate in 1691, when it appeared the Maquas were defecting to the French, to write the New England colonies and Virginia for military aid.[5] Sloughter managed to persuade the Iroquois to send a war party out to harass the enemy.[6] But Massachusetts-New York relations were again strained over the Maqua question; while Sloughter negotiated with the Maquas at Albany, a band of these Indians attacked Wells on the Maine frontier, and Massachusetts also considered that the New York government should show good faith by contributing to building a fort at Pemaquid "or elsewhere in the County of Cornwall."[7]

Working against active Iroquois participation in the war was the disunity of the colonies. The Iroquois felt that the assistance of New York alone was not enough. With a bit of native common sense, the Indians could see that Governor Fletcher's promise of the royal favor and backing of all the colonies from New England to Virginia[8] were only empty words. As an Onondaga sachem queried the New York Governor at an Albany conference in May 1694:

> The only Reason . . . of our sending to make Peace with the French, is the low Condition to which we are reduced, while none of our Neighbours send us the least Assistance, so that the whole Burthen of the War lyes on us alone. Our Brethren of New-England, Connecticut, Pensilvania, Maryland and Virginia, of their own accord thrust their Arms into our Chain; but since the War began we have received no Assistance from them . . . .
>
> Brother Cayenguirago, speak from your Heart, are you resolved to prosecute the War vigorously against the French, and are your Neighbours of Virginia, Maryland, Pensilvania, Connecticut and New-England, resolved to assist us? If it be so, we assure you, notwithstanding any Treaty hitherto entered into, we will prosecute the War as hotly as ever. But if our Neighbours will not assist, we must make Peace, and we submit it to your Consideration, by giving this great Belt fifteen deep.[9]

On August 15-17, 1694, Governor Fletcher held a conference with the Iroquois and Maquas at Albany, with Andrew Hamilton of the Jerseys and agents from Massachusetts, Connecticut, and the New York Council also attending. Each colony brought a contingent of troops to impress the Indians. Although the Iroquois had already made peace with the French, the purpose of the meeting was to "confirm the ancient friendship" and to renew the loyalty of the Indians "to the Crown of England." The New England commissioners' "desire that the Indians be checked for not condoleing the Blood shed lately in New England" was not approved because "it cannot be safe to make any particular Treaty in Behalfe of New England lest it expose and put a mark upon other Provinces." The commissioners did approve the raising of troops from the various colonies for frontier defense, of which five hundred was considered "the least number requisite." Indian presents brought by the commissioners were doled out in the name of the crown and all the colonies so as to avert bad feeling of the Indians towards those colonies which had not attended or sent gifts.[10]

Fletcher's personal domination of the Indian conference did not contribute to his intention of generalizing northern Indian affairs. The New England colonies suspected the New York Governor's views on Indian affairs to be too closely connected with his desire to exercise wartime military authority over the northern colonies. Fletcher's sending to the governors a copy of the Indian treaty coupled with request for men and money according to the quotas fixed by the crown did not alleviate this impression.[11] As Governor of Pennsylvania as well as New York and commander in chief of the Connecticut militia, with powers to require troop quotas from most of the colonies, Fletcher discovered that efforts to exercise this authority "forced the colonies to co-operate, not militarily against the French but politically in opposition to Fletcher himself."[12]

Lord Bellomont, as Governor of Massachusetts and New York, fully saw the need for cooperation of other colonial governors in trading with the "far Indians" and the significance of the Iroquois as the only barrier between the French in Canada and New York, Maryland, and Virginia.[13] But Bellomont's tenure was too short and his attention too diverted by bitter political factionalism for his being able to develop any intercolonial Indian policy. Meanwhile, in New York, Robert Livingston was serving as the colony's Secretary of Indian Affairs under a patent from William III. His duties included the keeping of records of Indian commissioners and assisting at Indian conferences. Livingston had a variegated career: he was dismissed by Fletcher, reinstated by Bellomont, and again dismissed by Cornbury. But his patent was renewed under Queen Anne.[14]

The inaction of the crown during Queen Anne's War in failing to strengthen the Iroquois alliance and frontier defense may be partially explained by the expectation of annulling the independent charters. Even the New York agent, Robert Quary, was arguing for such a means of accomplishing colonial unity,[15] and proceedings had already begun to this effect. The Board of Trade had also reported that the colonies "are so disunited in those distinct interests" that hardly anything could be expected of them in military and Indian affairs.[16]

During the war, the Iroquois insisted upon neutrality with both the French and the colonists. The Albany traders, afraid of disrupting their profits, saw to it that New York adopted also a *de facto* neutrality, much to the consternation of New England, where the eastern natives ravaged the frontier. In 1704, Governor Dudley and Winthrop both urged the New York Indians to make war on the French. Cornbury, preferring to stand by his own and the Albany traders' interests, refused to permit the Indians to aid the New Englanders or even to open the war on the New York frontiers[17] – in view of the lack of colonial military aid in the past, the Iroquois would not have done so anyway.

In September 1707, Cornbury met with the Indians at Albany. The several Iroquois sachems present complained that "the People of Virginia Maryland and Pensilvania do not come and renew the Covenant Chain." Cornbury replied that he had previously come to Albany and had renewed the covenant on behalf of the other colonies. Cornbury promised to make inquiries and report to the Indians at the next meeting. At the meeting of the New York commissioners with the Iroquois at Albany in 1708 the Indians re-confirmed their neutrality.[18]

The New England colonies persisted in applying to New York to prompt the Iroquois into war against the French. At a conference with the Five Nations in 1710, Governor Hunter reiterated Cornbury's position by refusing to enlist the Indians in the war. Hunter informed the New England governments that New York could not risk a counterattack for which the colony was unprepared.[19]

The Treaty of Utrecht recognized Iroquois neutrality, whereby the Indians were free to trade with whom they chose, but the question of sovereignty over the Five Nations was left to future determination.[20]

A point of contention between New York and the southern colonies after the war was the Iroquois' committing hostilities against Indians allied with the southern colonies. The French traders were considered to have abetted these raids, and in turn southern Indians attacked French traders. In 1715 Colonel Caleb Heathcote advised Governor Hunter

> whether it would not be very proper with as little losse of time as may be, for your Excellency to desire a meeting or congresse at some convenient place, of all or as many of the Governours on this Continent as can with conveniency come and attend it . . . . for as every part of North America is struck at, so all our interests are the same . . . .[21]

Governor Spotswood dispatched Captain Christopher Smith in early 1717 to Albany to reclaim prisoners taken by the Five Nations. Smith did not have success in meeting with the Indians or with New York and Pennsylvania commissioners. At Philadephia, Smith found Governor Keith agreeable to the idea of the colonies putting a united front to the Iroquois but unwilling himself to take any action. Upon Smith's return to Virginia, Governor Spotswood sent Keith a scathing message:

> Now your Commissioners are either afraid or unwilling to urge upon those People their late Violences committed against the Southern Governments, to remonstrate to them their many Infractions of their Treaties and Promises, or to take the least notice of the Plunder and Captives . . . .[22]

Hunter called for Virginia deputies to attend an Albany conference with the Indians,[23] and the ubiquitous Virginia governor, who had already traveled 5,026 miles in six years by his own reckoning in exploration and Indian affairs, went himself. Spotswood had hoped that the governors of Maryland, Pennsylvania, and New York would attend the conference and "concert" action against the Iroquois. But Governor Hunter could not get away because his assembly was in session, and Governor Hart of Maryland took ill. Nevertheless, Spotswood went with Keith and James Logan from Philadelphia to New York to confer with Hunter. A "get tough" policy was agreed upon, and "certain Preliminaries" were drawn up for future negotiation with the Indians: particularly, to draw a line at the Potomac and the Blue Ridge, with the Iroquois and their tributaries to stay westward and the Virginia Indians to keep east of the line.[24]

When William Burnet replaced Hunter as Governor of New York he took a greater interest in colonial unity in Indian affairs. One of his first actions was to order commissioners Myndert, Peter Schuyler, and Robert Livingston, Jr. to the Seneca country "to impress upon them a proper Sense of their Duty to his Majesty and their Connexion with this Government to prevent their making War upon any Indians in Alliance with the adjacent Colonies or such as may be inclined to come and Trade at Albany . . . ." While still feeling his way during his first year in office. Burnet met with the Iroquois at Albany. In the later judgment of Peter

Wraxall, Burnet missed the opportunity to take advantage of the "present happy disposition" of the Indians to conclude a positive treaty of alliance, although Burnet on this occasion did renew the covenant chain. Wraxall thought that Burnet had made "that Capitol Error of most Colony Governors" by treating with the Indians unilaterally.[25] But this is a responsibility that bore heavily on the crown for the system of separate executives in the colonies. Indeed each governor was urged to use his "utmost endeavours" to prevent traders, English and French, from exploiting the Indians. To this end the governors individually could enter into treaties and alliances with the Indians and build forts and garrisons, although they were expected to be in communication on such matters with each other.[26]

In May–June 1721, Governor Keith of Pennsylvania met with Spotswood in Virginia, where they held several conferences on Indian affairs. The Virginia Indians agreed to respect the Potomac-Blue Ridge line.[27] Meanwhile, James Logan got the same assurances from the Conestoga Indians of Pennsylvania.[28]

All that was now left was to have the Iroquois agree to the Indian boundary line. For this purpose Burnet called an intercolonial conference at Albany, which met in September 1722, with Governors Burnet of New York, Spotswood of Virginia, and Keith and four commissioners of Pennsylvania attending. The Iroquois agreed not to make raids southward, but they insisted on the freedom of travel. The murder of Seneca Indians by the Conestogas was forgiven by the Iroquois. A sore point of the conference was a law that had been passed by Virginia that any Indian of the Five Nations found south of the Potomac or east of the Blue Ridge without a passport from some governor would be put to death or transported beyond the seas, and any southern Indian going in the opposite direction could be put to death by anyone. The conference did agree unrealistically that passports could be issued to no more than ten Indians at a time to pass beyond the barriers.[29]

When the eastern Indians went on the rampage in 1723, Massachusetts requested New York to employ the Iroquois against the hostile Indians. The Five Nations sent deputies to Boston to consider this proposal in the summer of 1724, but negotiations broke up because the Iroquois wanted the Boston authorities to arrange a peace meeting with the eastern Indians and then the Iroquois would act as "Sureties for the Eastern Indians." The Iroquois position, however, was interpreted as meaning they would take up the hatchet against the eastern Indians if they refused mediation. To secure the Iroquois support, Boston commissioners met with Iroquois chiefs and

New York agents at Albany in September 1724, but the Iroquois were adamant in their refusal to send aid. Eventually in 1725, commissioners and the lieutenant governors of Massachusetts and New Hampshire made peace with the eastern Indians at Falmouth, which proved to be long lasting.[30] Joint Indian commissioners from Massachusetts and New Hampshire continued to look after the peace with the eastern Indians.[31]

In the 1730's marauding Iroquois were stirring up trouble again in the Catawba and Cherokee country, and French-allied Indians plundered frontier settlements. A total lack of cooperation among the colonies in Indian affairs characterized this period. A proposal by New York authorities to send Iroquois chiefs to Virginia came to naught; and as Peter Wraxall commented on the individual colonies pursuing a policy of merely giving gifts to the Indians that it "appears to me to be only reconcilable to Dutch Generosity and Patriotism."[32]

Pennsylvania solved its problems with the Iroquois by purchasing their claims to all lands east of the Susquehanna in 1736 and west of that river in 1742.[33] But Iroquois hunting parties still ventured into the southern frontier. After repeated altercations, including in 1743 a skirmish between Iroquois and Virginians in which several on both sides were killed, Governor Gooch of Virginia notified Governor Thomas of Pennsylvania that Virginia would accept Pennsylvania's mediation in their dispute with the Six Nations. The Great Council at Onondaga accepted the offer and a conference was arranged for the spring next year at Harris Ferry (Harrisburg). Later it was decided to move the conference to Lancaster. A circular letter from the crown, ordering the governors to control the growing restlessness of the Iroquois, was a factor in calling the conference.

The Lancaster conference lasted from June 22 to July 4. Commissioners represented Pennsylvania, Maryland, and Virginia. Canassatego, the chief negotiator for the Iroquois, opened the affair in the crowded court room by singing a song to the Virginia, Maryland, and Pennsylvania delegations. Fortunately the dominating figure was Conrad Weiser, the official interpreter of the three colonies, who was held in high esteem by both parties. After mutual harangues and threats by both sides over trespass of the Indian boundary line of 1721, the conference settled down to particulars. The Iroquois agreed to release their western Virginia lands for £ 200 in goods and £ 200 in gold and an open road to the Catawba country. They also granted to Maryland the lands above the uppermost fork of the Potomac for £ 300, which agreement Shikellimy, the Oneida chief and vicegerent over the tributary Shawnee and Delawares, would not sign. The Indians agreed to maintain the old alliance with the colonists and to prevent any attack by the French on English settlements. The greater significance of the Lancaster Treaty was that it retained the friendship of an ally capable of serving as a barrier to the French expansion in the Ohio Valley. Virginia, however, interpreted the treaty as a release by the Iroquois of all claims to Virginia territory, a matter which had to be corrected by the Treaty of Fort Stanwix of 1768.[34] Governor Glen of South Carolina, in appraising the Lancaster Treaty several years later, feared that the English might forfeit the loyalty of the Catawbas: "I hope we shall not suffer them to be drawn from our Interest by the Promises of other Provinces or frightened from their present Settlements by the Threats of their Enemies."[35]

Also to secure Iroquois neutrality in the north, Massachusetts, Connecticut, and New York commissioners met with the Iroquois first at Robert Livingston's home and then at City Hall in Albany from June 8-11, 1744. A promise of neutrality on the part of the Iroquois was all that was obtained. Massachusetts attempted to have the pledge include tribes in Canada as well. It seems that the conference was intended to be a preliminary session to a larger meeting in the future.[36]

Delegates from New York, Connecticut, Massachusetts, and Pennsylvania attended a conference at Albany from October 5-14, 1745. The New Jersey assembly refused to act on Governor Clinton's invitation because the colony had no interest in Indian affairs except to aid a neighboring colony in offensive war. The southern colonies expressed no interest in an intercolonial Indian conference at this time, although Clinton had warned the Maryland Governor of "the Wavering disposition of the Indians and the fatal Consequences which may arise to all the Colonies in General in Case they should be withdrawn from their Fidelity and Dependance upon the British Interest: Whereupon there seems to be an absolute Necessity for the Colonies uniting their Endeavours at all Events to secure the Indians effectually in Our Interest at this Critical Conjuncture . . . ."[37] Probably from exaggerated reports of the Iroquois to the French commander at Fort Frederick, the French mistakenly thought the Albany conference was attended by commissioners of all the colonies as far south as South Carolina. Although the conference was not productive, the colonial press reported that the Iroquois "readily renew'd their ancient Covenant with the several Governments that treated with them by their Delegates" and were "ready to take up the Hatchet against the *French* and *Indian* Enemy" as soon as ordered by the Governor of New York. The commissioners pledged mutual aid in case of attack and to contribute to "any well concerted scheme for the annoyance of the common Enemy . . . ."[38]

New York and Pennsylvania commissioners met at Albany in July 1746 to treat with the Iroquois, but Governor Clinton divided the Iroquois by demanding their aid against the French.[39] Shortly afterwards, Massachusetts commissioners joined the negotiations between New York and the Iroquois at Albany, but again an impasse was reached.[40] Clinton wrote the governors of Massachusetts, Connecticut, and the southern colonies to help bear the expense of the presents for the Indians arranged at these conferences.[41]

It became clear that the preparations of the colonies for offensive operations during King George's War had effect upon the Iroquois. Governor Clinton had correctly surmised that including the Indians in the military campaigns would attach them to the British cause and at the same time provide a means of demonstrating to them the power and unity of the colonies.[42] This policy bore some fruit at the Albany conference of July 23-27, attended by New York and Massachusetts commissioners, officers of the Independent company, and 1,450 Indians. The Iroquois agreed not to send a delegation to Canada and to keep warriors in readiness to aid the English.[43] However, much opportunity was lost in the two governors' discussing means to keep their assemblies in check. Governor Shirley after the conference went to New York City to consult further on the constitutional questions. At least one intangible result of the Albany conference was the friendship between Shirley and Colden, the New York Lieutenant Governor.[44]

Clinton renewed his efforts to get other colonial governors "to concert a general comprehensive Plan, to unite together in one Band of Friendship all the Indians upon the Continent," but he elicited little response. The main obstacle to colonial unity in Indian affairs was Pennsylvania, whose governor and assembly took for granted the Iroquois loyalty and considered the Ohio country outside the boundaries of Pennsylvania. Besides Pennsylvania was engaged in a running controversy over western lands with Connecticut. Clinton, however, found the most sympathetic ear for coordination of Indian policy in Governor Glen, who was more interested in the Catawba alliance than in the Iroquois.[45] In writing to Glen in September 1750 Clinton urged correspondence among the governors relating to Indian affairs. He advised:

> As nothing can be more for his Majestys Service, and for the welfare and safety of his Provinces upon this Continent than an union of Councils amongst the several Governours, upon Indian affairs . . . . I should think it might be of great use, if besides the particular knowledge of Indian Affairs which every Governour is supposed to have within his own district, he had also a general Sketch of them in other Governments . . . .[46]

In a circular letter of December 18, 1750 to all the governors on the continent, Clinton invited the governors to a congress at Albany to meet with the Six Nations the next June. He proposed that the commissioners draw up "a state of Indian Affairs to be laid before His Majesty" and also possibly a representation to the Governor General of Canada.[47] Clinton repeated his invitation in April when he invited specifically Governors Wentworth, Phips, Hamilton, Glen, Johnson, Ogle, Belcher, Wolcott, and the "President of Virginia."[48] Discussion over the proper meeting place – Glen favored a site in Virginia – and the dilatoriness of the assemblies to take action (and most did not) delayed the convening of the conference. Most of the assemblies probably balked because Clinton had requested that each colony provide presents for the Indians at the conference.[49] By June, nevertheless, Clinton announced that governors of all the colonies, except Virginia which had not yet replied, approved an intercolonial Indian congress.[50]

In the meantime the French-inspired Iroquois-Catawba war alarmed the southern colonies. Thomas Lee, the acting Governor of Virginia, and Governor Glen of South Carolina laid the groundwork for a peace treaty to be held at Fredericksburg in the summer of 1751, and Governor Hamilton of Pennsylvania also agreed to attend. But the props were knocked from under this conference when Clinton proceeded to arrange his conference for the same time and the Iroquois refused to go to Fredericksburg.[51]

When the Albany congress convened on July 6, 1751, four colonies were represented: New York, Massachusetts, Connecticut, and South Carolina. William Bull and six Catawba Indians (perennial enemies of the Iroquois) represented South Carolina. Also attending were the mayor and corporation of Albany and several officers of the Independent companies in New York. The meeting opened with the usual ornate amenities and a pledge "to renew the Covenant Chain, to cleanse away all Rust, to brighten it, and strengthen it so that it may forever endure . . . ." Nothing decisive emerged from the conference. Clinton perhaps suggested the most unusual proposal of sending missionaries to the Six Nations, which, however, was not well received by the colonial emissaries since this program would require funds.[52] For the conference, Colden had written a "state" of Indian affairs, pleading for fair treatment of the Indians, which in itself, as the biographer of Colden asserts, was testimony to William Johnson's overthrow of the Albany cabal.[53]

If the Albany conference of 1751 did not accomplish any great improvement in Indian affairs, it did generate a broader intercolony interest. And, for the first time, South Carolina was represented in a northern Indian conference – a generality that would help pave the way for the Albany congress of 1754.

Virginia still had not settled its differences with the Iroquois, and now with land speculators active in the Ohio Valley, the western tribes had to be reckoned with. Dinwiddie hoped to enlist the Pennsylvania Governor in a mutual Indian policy. Almost too humbly, he wrote Governor Hamilton:

> Permit me to express my real Wishes for a frequent Correspondence between Us, to promote and forward any incident that probably may tend to the Advancement of His Majesty's Interest, or the welfare of these Provinces. Whenever anything may occur wherein I can be of service, be persuaded Sir, you may freely command me.

Dinwiddie went on to declare that he would send a delegation for a treaty to be held at Logstown and would also present gifts to the Six Nations at that time.[54]

At Logstown, eighteen miles below the confluence of the Allegheny and Monongahela, Pennsylvania and Virginia commissioners sat down on June 1, 1752 to work out differences with the Delawares, Shawnees, and Mingoes over claims to the Ohio Valley, where the Ohio Company of Virginia wanted to bring settlers. War clouds hung over the conference. Already the French-led Indians had taken the Twightwee (Miami) town of Pickawillany on the upper Great Miami River, which may be regarded as the beginning of the French and Indian War, and the French were ready to descend in force into the Ohio Valley. The Twightwees had appealed to Pennsylvania and Virginia for aid, and both colonies raised money for their relief.[55] The Six Nations were also invited to the conference, but refused to attend on grounds that "it is not our custom to meet to treat of affairs in the woods and weeds" and that if they were wanted at a conference it would have to be held at Albany with the Governor of New York present. About all that came out of the conference was a promise from some of the Indians not to molest any settlements on the southeast side of the Ohio. The Treaty was never approved by a council of the Six Nations.[56]

Virginians and Pennsylvanians jumped to the conclusion that the Treaty of Logstown opened the way for western fur trade and land speculation, for which it was hardly a mandate.[57] "As it was, the Treaty of Logstown was a bastard treaty," says Lois Mulkearn, a "conference without official sanction and therefore without legal standing with the Six Nations."[58]

Indians from the Six Nations met with a Virginia delegation and various Ohio Company associates and Pennsylvania Indian traders at Winchester in the fall of 1753. After a week of frivolities, a treaty was signed, which did not settle any real differences. Thereupon the Indians went to Carlisle to meet with Richard Peters, Benjamin Franklin, and Isaac Norris, commissioners appointed by Governor Hamilton of Pennsylvania. William Fairfax, who had presided over the Winchester conference, had sent a letter via George Croghan notifying Hamilton of the Indians' views. The Carlisle conference ended October 4, accomplishing only a renewal of friendship. The Half King declared that if the governors of Pennsylvania and Virginia "will join hands and be as one," then "we, the Six Nations, will be the third brother." Neither treaty was satisfactory, to the English point of view, since the Iroquois refused to surrender lands along the Ohio.[59]

Piecemeal negotiation with the Indians was totally insufficient in face of the stepped-up activity of the French along the frontier. But there would be little room for improvement while Indian policy continued to be broadly determined by officials in London and implemented individually by the royal governors. Such a decentralized system was inadequate both to meet French intrigues among the Indians and the intercolonial friction over Indian trade and lands.

Events of King George's War, however, had paved the way for centralization. Governor Clinton of New York had diverted Indian affairs in New York from the Albany commissioners and appointed William Johnson in charge of diplomacy with the Iroquois. Johnson was "Colonel of the Warriours of the Six Nations" from 1746 to 1751. Because of lack of assembly support Johnson resigned in 1751, but his work received high praise from both Clinton and Shirley, who jointly recommended to the Board of Trade the appointment of an imperial Indian commissioner.[60]

Archibald Kennedy in his pamphlet urging confederation in 1751 recommended Indian affairs be put

> under the direction of one single person of capacity and integrity, of his majesty's appointment, during good behaviour, with a handsome allowance, in the nature of a Superintendent of Indian affairs, with full powers to do summary justice upon all occasions.[61]

Cadwallader Colden made a detailed proposal for an Indian superintendency similar to Kennedy's.[62] Lord Halifax had a scheme before the Board of Trade to establish two commissary-generals in two districts to conduct treaty and trade relations and to dispense Indian presents. Government factories should be set up at posts along the frontier. Since the Board of Trade already favored sending out a military commander for the colonies, Halifax argued that he should also be given charge of Indian affairs. Under this plan the colonies would maintain frontier posts, provide for Indian presents, and pay the salaries of the commander in chief and the commissaries.[63]

The idea of some unified agency to treat with the Indians was popular among the colonial governors. In fact, the need to coordinate Indian policy was the primary reason for the general participation in the Albany Congress. Even Jonathan Belcher, who, as Governor of New Jersey, had never shown much interest in Indian affairs, indicated that

> the Alliance and Friendship of the six Nations and their Dependance on the Crown of Great Britain must by every thinking Man be looked upon as the greatest Security the Settlers on the Northern Boundary of this Province can have to prevent the Incursions of those Nations of Indians . . . .[64]

Shirley viewed an intercolonial Indian conference with optimism:

> Such an Union of Councils, besides the happy Effect it will probably have upon the Indians of the Six Nations, may lay a Foundation for a general one among all his Majesty's Colonies, for the mutual Support and Defence against the present dangerous Enterprizes of the *French* on every Side of them.[65]

With rumors of French troops being moved to America and the continued failure to secure pledges of aid from the Iroquois and even the possibility of their defection, the Board of Trade called for an intercolonial conference at Albany with the Six Nations. At the Albany Congress of 1754, Thomas Pownall stated that the Iroquois were now at a stage where they were forming into a nation and therefore some "stateholder," who should be a man of great influence, should be appointed by the crown over the Iroquois. Pownall's paper was later forwarded to London with the proceedings of the Congress. Johnson also argued the importance of Indian aid in a war with France.[66] The Indian phase of the Albany Congress lasted June 18–29. The Indians were pleased with the presents they received but demanded more effort of the English in establishing forts along the frontier as the price for their assistance against the French. A treaty was signed, mutually renewing the ancient friendship and for the first time recognizing the independence of the Iroquois.[67]

Although the Albany Plan was rejected or simply not acted upon by the colonies, there was some expectation that the Plan would be imposed by Great Britain. Thus Charles Thomson of Pennsylvania wrote concerning news of deliberation on the Plan in England:

> 'tis thought will soon be brought to bear, an event much to be desired, since it effectually will secure us from the insults of our haughty aspiring neighbors, the French, and make our security independent of the fickle humor of our Indian allies.[68]

Colden thought, whether or not the Albany Plan went into effect, there should be a singularity of command in military and Indian affairs, with a "Captain General or General Officer" to have in addition to the supreme military command "the sole management of all affairs with the Indians and of regulating the trade with them, with the Consent of the Council."[69]

About the same time that the Board of Trade named Braddock commander in chief in America it also decided to create the office of Indian superintendent and selected Johnson. Theoretically, the superintendent was the sole agent of the crown. But after Johnson's appointment, colonial governors continued to vie for control of Indian affairs. Sir Charles Hardy of New York and Shirley both thought that they should be the primary determinators of Indian policy affecting their colonies. A conflict over military authority developed between Shirley, as commander in chief, and Johnson, who held a commission as major general from Braddock. Shirley issued a new commission to Johnson, omitting the words "Sole Superintendent" of the Braddock commission. Johnson, however, considered the commission given him by Braddock according to royal instructions still in force. Shirley complained to the home government that Johnson interfered with his efforts to secure military aid from the Iroquois and other Indians, that Johnson followed the directions of Governor Hardy (particularly in giving French prisoners to the Iroquois), and that he refused to cooperate with Shirley's negotiations with the Indians. Eventually Shirley acknowledged Johnson's commission, and in the meantime the Board of Trade, as a result of Johnson's petitioning, gave him a new commission.[70] Shirley and the other governors finally acquiesced in returning to the crown moneys advanced for Indian affairs to constitute a common fund for Johnson's use.[71]

In 1756, Governor Robert Hunter Morris of Pennsylvania declared war on the Delaware and Shawnee Indians without consulting Johnson, who had started peace negotiations between the Six Nations and these tribes. Informing Shirley of Morris's precipitous action, Johnson wrote:

> These hostile measures which Governor Morris has entered into, is throwing all our schemes into confusion, and must materially give the Six Nations such impressions, and the French such advantages to work against us, *that I tremble for the consequences.* I think without consulting your excellency, without the concurrence of the other neighboring provinces, without my receiving previous notice of it, this is a very unadvised and unaccountable proceeding of Governor Morris.

Shirley, in this instance, took Johnson's side, and tried to obtain a reversal of the order. Morris would not withdraw the declaration but amended it to include only those "implacable and obstinate enemies, and not against any that now are or hereafter may be disposed to hearken to the Six Nations in our favor."[72] Two conferences at Easton with the Delawares, with Morris in July and with his successor, William Denny, in October and November, were inconclusive, with the Indians charging the proprietors with land fraud. Denny's meeting with the Indians had been authorized by Johnson, but the new commander in chief, Lord Loudoun, insisted that Indian diplomacy was strictly the province of Johnson.[73]

Loudoun also disapproved of Denny's holding a treaty at Bethlehem with the East Branch of the Susquehanna Indians (Delawares).

> I must here answer in general and once for all; That His Majesty having entirely taken out of the Hands of the Governments and Governors all Right to treat with, confer, or make War or Peace with the five Nations or any of their Allies or Dependents.

Loudoun considered Johnson the sole Indian agent "under my Direction," and warned of any further meddling by the governors independently in Indian affairs.

> I do hereby for the future forbid you [Denny] or your Government from conferring or treating with these Indians in any Shape or on any Account whatever, and I do direct that whatever Business in that Branch of His Majesty's Service shall arise to your Government or Province you do refer it and put it into the Hands of his Majesty's Sole Agent, who will according to the Powers with which he is invested, negotiate and settle such Matters in the Way his Majesty has directed.[74]

The western tribes were still detached from an English alliance. Johnson ordered his deputy, George Croghan to join with Governor Denny of Pennsylvania to treat with the Indians, which led to the two treaties of Easton, 1757 and 1758. The official delegates to the Easton conference of July 15–August 2, 1757 were Denny and six members of the Council, Speaker Isaac Norris and six provincial commissioners, and Governor Bernard of New Jersey, who had also previously declared war against the Delaware Indians and their allies. A Quaker faction at the meeting convinced the Indians of their rightful claims and nothing was accomplished, except the usual pledge of peace.[75] In August 1758 Denny accepted Bernard's invitation for a meeting in Burlington. Three members of the Pennsylvania Council attended and six from the New Jersey Council. This session appears to have served as a preliminary discussion for the Indian conference at Easton, October 8–26, 1758. The fourth Indian council at Easton again dealt with land claims, principally along the

Susquehanna River, and securing the neutrality of the Ohio Indians. Attending were some five hundred Indians from the Senecas and Cayugas of the Six Nations and Delawares, Conoys, Wapings, Tuteloes, Minisinks, and Nanticokes. Representing the colonial interests were Governor Denny and members of the provincial assembly and council, Governor Bernard and commissioners for Indian affairs in New Jersey, Croghan, Conrad Weiser, and a delegation of Philadelphia Quakers. General Forbes's victory influenced the Indians in changing their position. All Indian grievances in Pennsylvania, except a 1737 purchase which had been referred to the crown, were settled, and the Indians reaffirmed peace. Lands west of the Alleghenies purchased by the Penns in 1754 were deeded back to the Six Nations. Although Johnson personally had no hand in the negotiations, this immensely successful treaty vindicated the northern Indian superintendency.[76]

Although Amherst, as commander in chief, took charge of Indian affairs for the Ohio country, he had the tendency to scorn and underrate the Indians,[77] and he ignored the growing restlessness of the western tribes because he was too busy planning military operations. Forbes, shortly before his death in 1759, beseeched Amherst to call an Indian conference with the governors of Virginia, Maryland, Pennsylvania, New Jersey, and New York. Without such a meeting "the Indian affairs to the Northward and westward must necessarily fall into the greatest confusion, and The Indians themselves tho now well Disposed to us and easily secured fall again under the French Direction."[78] Amherst, in New York, hesitated, waiting instructions for the campaign, but on February 11, 1759 he wrote Governor Fauquier of Virginia to be prepared to attend an Indian conference. Fauquier said he could not leave the colony because he would have to prorogue the legislature, but he did favor a meeting of the governors after the campaign and cooperative regulation of the Indians.[79] Meanwhile, Pennsylvania held a treaty with the Mingoes over exchange of prisoners in July 1759 and promised that the King of England would protect the Indians in all their rights.[80]

Because of the pressure of his war duties, Amherst did not turn his attention again to Indian negotiations until late summer 1761, when he ordered Johnson to hold a treaty with the western Indians.[81] Johnson met with representatives of thirteen tribes (including Iroquois) at Detroit in September 1761. The Indians agreed to surrender prisoners, to set up a western confederacy, and to abide by Johnson's trade regulations.[82] But the western tribes would soon find English rule a threat to their very existence, and the council fires on the Ohio would send this treaty up in smoke.

Those prerogative servants most attuned to the realities of Indian affairs recognized the need for more stringent regulation by the crown. Colden and Johnson had frequently spoken for more uniform control of Indian affairs. Both agreed that traders should be closely regulated, and both advocated an imperial establishment similar to Archibald Kennedy's recommendations of 1751 and the later Board of Trade plan of 1764.[83] Henry McCulloh, member of the North Carolina Council, ascertained that there were three priorities in 1761: (1) to determine boundaries with the Indians; (2) "To form a System in Indian Affairs, in regulating the Trade carried on with them; in which, particular Care ought to be taken to have all the colonies act upon one system . . . ;" (3) to regulate collecting and "accompting for the Revenues in America," including the regulation of currency, if it were necessary to raise funds to defray the expenses of Indian affairs.[84] But to bring order into Indian affairs would not be an easy task. As William Smith said, writing to Gates in 1763 on the Indian troubles in the Ohio country: "Tis an old saying that the Devil is easier raised than laid."[85]

The expulsion of the French from the Ohio Valley, with fertile lands and the lucrative fur trade beckoning, excited the pioneer spirit. The home government would have to find means of checking a persistent expansion and at the same time guaranteeing lands west of the Alleghenies to the Indians, as pledged by the Treaty of Easton of 1758 and other treaties.

The problem of maintaining an Indian boundary line was manifold. The individual colonies could not be expected to unite in measures to provide troops on a common frontier, protect reservation lands, and regulate the fur trade in the interests of the crown – all of which were contrary to the colonial disposition.

Thus the state of Indian affairs at the end of the French and Indian war posed a challenge to imperial authority. Here was the opportunity – as well as the necessity – to combine imperial control of military affairs, interior trade, and expansion into one system. But a unitary-imperial regulation of the frontier as attempted after 1763 would stir constitutional qualms among the colonists and require a vast outlay in personnel and money; without proper planning, enforcement would be futile. Introducing an element of federalism in western policy would have been the sensible solution.

NOTES

[1] The Maquas were prosyletized Iroquois re-settled on the St. Lawrence near Montreal.

[2] Refers to the first regional intercolonial Indian Conference at Albany in 1684, in which Va., Md., and Mass. were represented.

[3] Cadwallader Colden, *The History of the Five Indian Nations of Canada* (1747), 2 vols. (New York, 1922), I, 119-26. The New England commisioners were: Col. John Pynchon, Maj. John Savage, and Capt. Jonathan Bull.

[4] See Trelease, *Indian Affairs in Colonial New York,* 329, *passim.*

[5] H. Sloughter to Gov. Treat, May 31, 1691, CA, Colonial Wars, II, 132.

[6] "Propositions Made by the Maquas Sachems to Governor Sloughter," June 4, 1691, *CSP,* XIII, 469. Leder, *Robert Livingston,* 61.

[7] The Governor of Mass. to Governor Sloughter, June 18, 1691, *CSP,* XIII, 475.

[8] Wraxall, *Abridgement of N.Y. Indian Records,* ed. McIlwain, Feb. 25, 1693, 19.

[9] Colden, *Five Indian Nations,* May 4, 1694, I, 214–15; Frothingham, *Rise of the Republic,* 118n.

[10] Phips to Gov. and Council of Conn., July 19, 1694, MA, Colonial, II, 219a; William Stoughton to Gov. and Council of Conn., July 23, 1694, *ibid.*, 221; Trelease, *Indian Affairs in Colonial New York*, 317; N.Y. Council meeting held at Albany, Aug. 13–20, 1694, "New York and the New Hampshire Grants," *NYHSC,* II (1869), 408–17; *CSP,* XIV, xxii–xxiv. Mass. commissioners–Col. John Pynchon and Samuel Sewall; Conn. commisioners–Col. John Allyn, Penn Townshend, and Capt. Caleb Stanley; N.Y. Council commisioners–Col. Stephen van Cortlandt, Col. Nicholas Bayard, Col. William Smith, Maj. Peter Schuyler, and Chidley Brooke.

[11] E.g., the Virginia Council, after having the treaty and the "New Scheme of Assistance" read, refused to send any aid to the defense of the New York frontier. *EJCC–VA.*, Oct. 23, 1964, I, 320.

[12] James S. Leamon, "Governor Fletcher's Recall," *WMQ*, 3d Ser., XX (1963), 527–28.

[13] See Friedelbaum, "Lord Bellomont" (Ph. D. diss.), Chapter 6; Wraxall, *Abridgement of N.Y. Indian Records*, ed. McIlwain, lxii–iii.

[14] Wraxall, *ibid.*, Aug. 28, 1695, 27; Lawrence H. Leder, ed., *The Livingston Indian Records, 1666–1723* (Gettysburg, Pa., 1956), 8.

[15] Col. Quary to the Council of Trade and Plantations, Mar. 26, 1702, *CSP*, XX, 176–77.

[16] *NYCD*, IV, 227, 445.

[17] Kimball, *Dudley*, 101, 103n.

[18] Wraxall, *Abridgement of N.Y. Indian Records*, ed. McIlwain, Sep. 29, 1707 and Aug. 2, 1708, pp. 51 and 58.

[19] Richard L. Beyer,"Robert Hunter, Royal Governor of New York"(unpubl. MA Thesis, Iowa University, 1927), 88.

[20] Wraxall, *Abridgement of N.Y. Indian Records*, ed. McIlwain, xiv.

[21] Col. Caleb Heathcote to Gov. Hunter, July 8, 1715, in Fox, *Heathcote*, 165.

[22] Spotswood to Keith, – 1717, *PCR*, III, 77–80; "Journal of the Lieutenant Governor's (Spotswood) Travels and Expeditions Undertaken for the Public Service of Virginia," *WMQ*, 2nd Ser., III (1923), 40–45; *EJCC–Va.*, Aug. 13, 1717, III, 450.

[23] Gov. Hunter to the Council of Trade and Plantations, July –, 1717, *CSP*, XXIX, 863; Bruce, *Hist. of Va.*, I, 128.

[24] Robert Livingston, Jr. to Robert Livingston, June 13, 1717, Leder, *Livingston Indian Records*, 222; "At a Council at Philadelphia," Sep. 28–Oct. 30, 1717, *PCR*, IV, 19–20; "Spotswood's Journal," *WMQ*, 2nd Ser., III (1923), 45; Spotswood to the Lords of Trade, Feb. 27, 1718, *Spotswood Corr.*, II, 261–62; Leonidas Dodson, "Alexander Spotswood, Governor of Virginia" (unpubl. Ph. D. Diss, University of Iowa, 1927 [pub. 1932], 345, 348–49; Frederick B. Tolles, *James Logan and the Culture of Provincial America* (Boston, 1957), 105.

[25] Wraxall, *Abridgement of N.Y. Indian Records*, ed. McIlwain, –Sep. 1721, 137–38.

[26] "State of the British Plantations in America . . . Representation of the Lords Commissioners for Trade and Plantations," Sep. 8, 1721, *NYCD*, V, 626–27.

[27] *PCR*, June 3, 1721, III, lll; *ibid.*, Dec. 1, 1733, 569–70; Tolles, *Logan*, 109. Another instance of the Pa. Governor visiting Virginia was Gov. Patrick Gordon's conference with Lt. Gov. Gooch in 1733 concerning enforcement of the acts of trade and navigation.

[28] Tolles, *Logan*, 109–11.

[29] Gov. Burnet to Lords of Trade, Nov. 21, 1721, *NYCD*, V, 655; *JHB–Va.* (1727–40), July 6, 1730, 105; Dobson,"Spotswood"(Ph. D. diss.), 267; Keith, *Pa. Chronicles*, II, 612–17; Frothingham, *Rise of the Republic*, 119n. Pa. commissioners, in addition to Keith, were: Isaac Norris, John Hill, John French, and Andrew Hamilton.

[30] Wraxall, *Abridgement of N.Y. Indian Records*, ed. McIlwain, May 31, 1723 and Sept. 19, 1724, 147–49 and 155.

[31] Gov. Belcher to Capt. Coram, Nov. 27, 1736 and Jan 13, 1737, Belcher Letter Book, MHS. Belcher served as one of these commissioners.

[32] Wraxall, *Abridgement of N.Y. Indian Records*, ed. McIlwain, Feb. 14, 1730, Aug. 25, 1738, and 1740–41, pp. 177–78, 211, and 221; John T. Lanning, "American Participation in the War of Jenkins' Ear," *Ga. Hist. Quarterly*, XI (1927), 139.

[33] Charles A. Hanna, *The Wilderness Trail*, 2 vols. (New York, 1911), II, 316.

[34] Commissioners of Indian Affairs to Lt. Gov. Clarke, May 30, 1743, *NYCD*, VI, 240; Joseph S. Walton, *Conrad Weiser and the Indian Policy of Colonial Pennsylvania* (Philadelphia, 1900), 93–122; Sipe, *Indian Wars of Pa.*, 121–22, 125; Morton, *Colonial Va.*, II, 533; William Brewster, *The Pennsylvania and New York Frontier* (Philadelphia, 1954), 20–24. 252 Iroquois attended. Commissioners for Va.–Thomas Lee, Col. William Beverly, and William Black; Pa.–Gov. Thomas and William Peters; Md.–Edmund Jennings, Philip Thomas, and Witham Marshe.

[35] James Glen's Address to the Assembly, Mar. 13, 1746, *JCHA–SC*, VI, 132.

[36] "Journal of the Commisioners . . .," Jacob Wendell Papers, June 8, 1744, MHS; Bouton, ed., *New Hampshire Provincial Documents*, June 7, 1744, Council held at Portsmouth, V, 99–100. N.H. apparently did not consider the appointment of commissioners until too late. Attending, Mass. commissioners–Stoddard and Wendell; Conn.–Wolcott and Stanley; N.Y.–De Lancey, Murray, and Horsmanden. In October, Shirley issued a Declaration of War against the Cape–Sable and St. John's Indians and forbade any "friendliness" with them. *American Weekly Mercury*, Nov. 15, 1744.

[37] Clinton to Gov. Bladen, Jan. 27, 1745, *Md. Archives*, XXVIII, 353.

[38] "Heads to be observed at a Conference," Oct. 14. 1745, Horsmanden Papers, NYHS; *Boston Evening Post*, Oct. 28, 1745; Messrs. de Beauhanois and Hocquart to Count de Maurepas, Sep. 12, 1745, *NYCD*, X, 18; Minutes of the Council at Albany, Oct. 5–14, 1745, *ibid.*, VI, 289–305; Sipe, *Indian Wars of Pa.*, 129; Fisher, *N.J. as a Royal Province*, 330–31. Representing Mass. were John Stoddard, Jacob Wendell, Samuel Wells, and Thomas Hutchinson; for Pennsylvania, Thomas Lawrence, Isaac Norris, and John Kinsey.

[39] "Proceedings . . . expedition to Canada," July 16, 1746, MA transcripts, NYPL; Davidson, *War Comes to Quaker Pa.*, 82–83. Commissioners for Pa.–John Kinsey, Thomas Lawrence, and Richard Peters. Conrad Weiser accompanied the commissioners along with George Croghan, who assisted Weiser as interpreter.

[40] For R.I. refusing any participation in the conferences or sharing in contributing supplies to the Iroquois, see Arnold, *Hist. of R.I.*, II, 168; Copies of Speeches of Clinton and the Indians, Aug. 19, 1746, *CP*, III, 247–49. Commissioners for N.Y.–Clinton, Colden, Philip Livingston, and John Rutherford; for Mass.–Samuel Wells and Jacob Wendell. The Mayor and Corporation of Albany also attended.

[41] *Virginia Gazette*, Aug. 14, 1746.

[42] Gov. Clinton's Speech to the Gen. Assembly, June 21, 1748, *Journal of the Leg. Council of New York*, II, 1017–18.

[43] Aug. 11, 1748, S.G. Drake, Chronicle of the Indians, NYPL; Dillon, *Oddities of Colonial Legislation*, 307; Frothingham, *Rise of the Republic*, 119n. Pa. negotiated the first English treaty with the Miami Indians at Lancaster in 1748. Commissioners at the Albany conference of July 23–27, 1746 were: for N.Y.–Gov. George Clinton, Cadwallader Colden, Philip Livingston, James De Lancey, and Archibald Kennedy; for Mass.–Gov. William Shirley, Thomas Hutchinson, Andrew Oliver, and John Choate.

[44] Keys, *Colden*, 206–7; Burns, *Controversies . . . Royal Governors*, 338–39.

[45] Gov. Clinton to Gov. Glen, Dec. 18, 1750, *NYCD*, VI, 605; Thomas Penn to James Hamilton, Dec. 25, 1750, Bancroft transcripts (Thomas Penn Letters), NYPL; Nichols, "The Braddock Expedition" (Ph. D. diss.), 10. Thomas Penn did support unilateral action of the colonies to maintain the Iroquois alliance.

[46] Glen to Clinton, Sep. 25, 1750, Clinton-Glen Correspondence (microfilm), CL.

[47] Clinton: A Circular Letter Inviting the Several Governors . . . (copy), Dec. 18, 1750, *ibid.*

[48] Circular Letter . . ., Apr. 13, 1751, *ibid.*

[49] Gov. Glen to Gov. Clinton, May 21, 1751, *NYCD*, VI, 708–10; William Bull to Gov. Glen, June 7, 1751, William McDowell, ed., *Colonial Records of South Carolina: Documents relating to Indian Affairs, May 21, 1750–Aug. 7, 1754* (Columbia, S.C., 1958), 33–34. Gov. Belcher of N.J. refused to attend and the N.J. Assembly declared that it would not consent to any Indian treaties. See Fisher, *N.J. as a Royal Provinces*, 331.

[50] Gov. Clinton to the Lords of Trade, June 13, 1751, *NYCD*, VI, 703.

[51] Lois Mulkearn, "Why the Indian Treaty of Logstown, 1752," *VMHB*, LIX (1951), 7–10.

[52] "Journal of the Commissioners. . .," June 25–July 12, 1751, Jacob Wendell Papers, MHS; "Meeting of Gov. Clinton and Commissioner Bull with the Six Nations and the Catawba Indians," July 6, 1751, McDowell, ed., *Documents relating to Indian Affairs* (S.C.), 138. Commisioners for Mass.–Jacob Wendell, Joseph Dwight, Oliver Partridge; for Conn.–William Pitkin and John Chester; for N.Y.–Gov. Clinton,

Cadwallader Colden, James Alexander, James De Lancey, and Edward Holland; for S.C.–Gov. William Bull.

53 Keys, *Colden*, 251ff.

54 Dinwiddie to Gov. Hamilton, Dec. 18, 1751, *Dinwiddie Corr.*, I, 15.

55 Dinwiddie to Gov. Glen, Nov. 8, 1752, McDowell, ed., *Documents relating to Indian Affairs* (S.C.), 360; Morton, *Colonial Virginia*, II, 616–17. Pennsylvania's gratuities for a single year to the Indians amounted to £ 8000. The Assembly demanded the Proprietors bear a greater share.

56 Sylvester Stevens and Donald H. Kent, eds., *Wilderness Chronicles of Northwestern Pennsylvania* (Harrisburg, 1941), 30–31; Sipe, *Indian Wars of Pa.*, 140; Dillon, *Oddities of Colonial Legislation*, 310; Morton, *Colonial Virginia*, II, 614–17. Va. commissioners–Joshua Fry, Lunsford Lomax, and James Patton; Pa.–George Croghan; Andrew Montour acted as interpreter. Among Pa. traders and Va. Company representatives at the Logstown Treaty were Christopher Gist and William Trent.

57 But William Brewster in *The Pa. and New York Frontier*, p. 28, calls the Logstown Treaty a "great success" because the Indians pledged loyalty to the English. Brewster does not take into account that the Iroquois were not a party to the Treaty; nor were the western Indians fully represented, and the Treaty was vague.

58 Mulkearn, "Why Logstown," *VMHB*, LIX (1951), 20.

59 Stuart E. Brown, Jr., *Virginia Baron: The Story of Thomas 6th Lord Halifax* (Berryville, Va., 1965), 126–28; Hanna, *The Wilderness Trail*, I, 371–72; Wainwright, *Croghan*, 54–56. Among those attending the Winchester conference were: William Fairfax, George Fairfax, Andrew Montour, Col. James Wood, Capt. William Gilpin, William Cocks, Capt. Bryan Martin, George Croghan, Capt. William Trent, Christopher Gist, and Maj. John Carlyle.

60 Mary F. Carter, "James Glen: Governor of Colonial South Carolina" (unpubl. Ph. D. diss., University of California, Los Angeles, 1951), 30; John R. Alden, "The Albany Congress and the Creation of the Indian Superintendencies," *MVHR*, XXVII (1940), 193–96.

61 Kennedy, *The Importance of Gaining and Preserving the Friendship of the Indians* . . . (1752), 15.

62 See Colden to Clinton, Aug. 8, 1751, *CP*, IV, 271–87.

63 For a full discussion of the factors leading up to Johnson's appointment–the influence of the Albany Congress, the Peter Wraxall manuscript, Johnson's own efforts, etc.–see Alden, "The Albany Congress and . . . Indian Superintendencies," *MVHR*, XXVII (1940), 193–212. The decision to name a Superintendent of Indian Affairs for the southern colonies was also reached at this time.

64 Gov. Belcher to the General Assembly, Apr. 29, 1754, Belcher Letter Book, MHS.

65 Gov. Shirley's Speech to the General Court, *The Boston Evening Post*, Apr. 19, 1754.

66 Alden, "The Albany Congress and . . . Indian Superintendencies," *MVHR*, XXVII (1940), 193–212.

67 Livingston, *Review of Military Operations* (1757), 76–77; Sipe, *Indian Wars of Pa.*, 173.

68 Charles Thomson to Joseph Shippen, Jr., Jan 31, 1755, Balch, ed., *Letters and Papers . . . Pa.*, 32–33.

[69] Colden to Halifax, Aug. 3, 1754, Pargellis, ed., *Military Affairs in North America*, 21.

[70] Clinton to Johnson, – 1755, *William Johnson Papers*, I, 115; Alden, "The Albany Congress and . . . Indian Superintendencies," *MVHR*, XXVII (1940), 209–10.

[71] Braddock to Sir Thomas Robinson, Mar. 18, 1755, Parkman transcripts, XL, MHS; Johnson to Braddock – 1755, *William Johnson Papers*, I, 513; Shirley to Johnson, Dec. 10, 1755, *Shirley Corr.*, II, 338–40; Shirley to Sir Thomas Robinson, Jan. 22, 1756, *ibid.*, 355–64.

[72] Johnson to Shirley, Apr. 24, 1756 and Richard Peters to Shirley, May 6, 1756, quoted in William Stone, *The Life and Times of Sir William Johnson, Baronet*, 2 vols. (Albany, 1865), II, 11.

[73] Theodore Thayer, *Israel Pemberton, King of the Quakers* (Philadelphia, 1943), 107–12, 123–31.

[74] Loudoun to Gov. Denny, Sep. 22, 1756, Loudoun Papers, Huntington Library (Microfilm Pa. State Archives). A similar retort to Denny is found in Loudoun to Denny, Apr. 1. 1758, *ibid.*

[75] Wainwright, "Gov. Denny," *PMHB*, LXXXI (1957), 185; Gordon, *Hist. of Pa. to 1776*, 359; Wainwright, *Croghan*, 128–33; Brewster, *Pa. and N.Y. Frontier*, 105; Thayer, *Israel Pemberton*, 140–46.

[76] Jordan D. Fiore, "Francis Bernard" (unpubl. Ph. D. diss., Boston University, 1950), 41–42; Gov. Francis Bernard to Gov. Denny, Aug. 10, 1758, Gratz Collection (Colonial Governors), HSP; James De Lancey to Abercromby, Aug. 30, 1758, PRO, WO:34, XXIX, LC; Forbes to Pitt, Sep. 6, 1758, Cleland, ed., *Washington and the Ohio Valley*, 197; Charles Thomson to Franklin, Dec. 10, 1758, *FP*, VIII, 200–211; Sipe, *Indian Wars of Pa.*, 373–77; Wainwright, *Croghan*, 146–50. Gov. Sharpe was somewhat envious over Pennsylvania's promptness in appropriating funds for treaties. Sharpe to William Sharpe, July 6, 1757, *Md. Archives*, IX, 45.

[77] Wainwright, *Croghan*, 196.

[78] Forbes to Amherst, Jan. 28, 1759, James, ed., *Forbes Writings*, 286.

[79] Fauquier to Board of Trade, Aug. 29, 1761, Bancroft transcripts (Virginia Papers), NYPL; Norkus, "Francis Fauquier," (Ph. D. diss.), 80–81.

[80] Jordan, "Journal of James Kenny," *PMHB*, XXXVII (1913), July 9, 1759, 428.

[81] Amherst to Johnson, Aug. 18, 1761, Emmet Collection, #8814, NYPL.

[82] Wainwright, *Croghan*, 182–83; Stone, *Johnson* II, 141–54.

[83] Siegfried Rolland, "Cadwallader Colden" (unpubl. Ph. D. diss., University of Wisconsin, 1952), 393. See above and Chapter 1 for Kennedy's views.

[84] Henry McCulloh, *Miscellaneous Representation relative to Our Concerns in America* (1761), in *Some Eighteenth Century Tracts concerning North Carolina*, ed. William K. Boyd (Raleigh, 1927), 152.

[85] William Smith to Gates, Nov. 22, 1763, Gates Papers, I, 140, NYHS.

CHAPTER VIII

SOUTHERN INDIANS

Each of the southern colonies had individual trade connections with the Indians, which gave them Indian allies. But the intercolonial rivalry over the fur trade was a more disrupting factor in Indian relations than among the northern colonies, where New England, New York, and Pennsylvania had separate emporiums.

By the end of the seventeenth century, the Indians along the Maryland and Virginia border had either moved further to the frontier or had been placated with reservation lands. Eventually Virginia's interest in Indian affairs would gravitate toward the northern Indians – the Iroquois jaunting down along the Allegheny barrier and the western tribes in possession of the Ohio country.

Many small tribes, who were inclined to consider neighboring Indians as enemies, dotted the inland Tidewater and Piedmont of the Carolinas and Georgia, and thus it was easy for the colonies to play the game of divide and conquer. Gradually, trade and settlement pushed to the domain of the larger Five Civilized Tribes (later so-called), two of which were of special concern to the colonists of the eighteenth century – the Cherokees and Creeks. These tribes, as did the Iroquois in the north, served as a buffer between the English settlements and the French and Spaniards. Yet their neutrality hung in a delicate balance even though the French and Spaniards had little military power in the south and west. A congress of the Chickasaws and Choctaws convened in 1703 by the French at Mobile caused alarm.[1] If the Cherokees and Creeks should also be driven to a protective sphere at Mobile then the security of the colonies would be in peril.

One early problem in intercolony Indian affairs was the location of tributary tribes. No antagonism developed between Virginia and Maryland on this question as the Potomac conveniently divided jurisdiction; and the Governor of Maryland kept the Virginia Governor informed of the situation among the Maryland tributary Indians.[2] But Virginia and North Carolina claimed overlapping jurisdiction over frontier Indians. Both colonies required tribute from the Meherrin tribe along the disputed boundary. These Indians perferred dependence upon Virgina, and, by virtue of the "Treaty of Peace made at Middle plantation" in 1677, the Virginia Council in 1713 ordered the Meherrins not to "obey any such summons without the License of the Governor of this Colony first obtained for so doing."[3]

On the other hand, there were instances of cooperation, as when Virginia and North Carolina supported South Carolina's appeal to restrain several free Negro traders from encouraging the Windaws to take captives from a South Carolina tribe, the Wawees.[4] To prevent tributary tribes from being involved in colonial boundary disputes, Governor Spotswood of Virgina insisted, as in the case of the Meherrins, that Indians living within several colonies should be regarded as having an extra-territorial status, under the administration of the crown.[5]

Virginia traders boldly entered the Carolina back country to trade with the Cherokee and Catawba and brought their furs and skins down the rivers to Savannah Town and Charles Town. The authorities at Charles Town decided to erase this competition by engrossing the Indian trade within the colony's bounds. Pack horses were prohibited from coming into the colony in 1701, and two years later, export duties of three pence were placed on deer-skins – an added hardship to the Virginia traders who also had to pay Virginia customs. In 1707 South Carolina passed an ordinance that all traders had to secure a license in Charles Town and to pay an annual fee of £8, posting a bond of £ 400. This meant on the average, annually, Virginia trading groups held about one out of seven licenses granted by the South Carolina commissioners for Indian trade. In 1708 the Charles Town government levied a prohibitive tax on all Virginia goods coming into the colony. Acting upon complaints from Virginia, the Privy Council in 1709 ordered South Carolina to refrain from levying duties upon Virginia goods, but South Carolina ingored this order and renewed the law. By the time the king-in-council disallowed the South Carolina impost, seizures of goods of non-licensed Virginia traders had the desired effect of creating a South Carolina monopoly on the Indian trade within its borders.[6]

After the Tuscarora War, Governor Spotswood of Virginia feared that unscrupulous traders would again touch off another Indian war. The expense of frontier commerce made it difficult for individual enterprise. Only a few Virginians still attempted to trade along the Carolina frontier.[7] But there were trade possibilities closer to home that had not yet been fully exploited. In 1714 the Virginia assembly established the Virginia Indian Company as a public stock company of about twenty wealthy planters to have sole control of the local Indian trade for twenty years. Spotswood saw in the Company a corporation that would have multiple responsibilities: to supervise trade, to carry out Indian policy, to serve as an agency to educate and Christianize the Indians, and to promote the building of forts and roads on the frontier. All tributary Indians of Virginia were required to trade at Christianna on the Meherrin River. Thus Spotswood hoped to set up a "good Barrier" against "the Incursions of any forreign Indians, and also keep in awe our other Tributarys." But Spotswood was soon in for a disappointment; the Act was disallowed because of its monopolistic features.[8]

Meanwhile, everywhere on the southern frontier trade had quieted down because of the decline of profits. The high duties and low prices of skins and furs in England discouraged the fur trade. Spotswood warned the home government that if it did not find means to stimulate the fur trade, the Cherokees would possibly defect to the French.[9] In the 1720's French, Carolinian, Virginian, Pennsylvanian traders moved into the Ohio Valley, but the Carolinians soon retired because of the vast distance involved and the competition.[10]

Since Charles Town provided the natural center for the Indian trade along the whole Carolina frontier, North Carolina, under the same proprietary control as South Carolina until 1721, made little effort to contest the South Carolina hegemony over the Indian trade before that date.[11] But a sharp rivalry existed between South Carolina and Georgia. Licensing acts in both colonies recognized the desirability of uniformity in Indian trade regulations – such as the South Carolina Act of 1711, which stated: "all persons that trade in the same place and trade ought to be under the same regulations, prohibitions and restrictions. . . ."[12] But instead of developing a cooperative policy of licensing traders, each colony sought uniformity through maintaining exclusive jurisdictions over their traders. In 1737, however, a legal opinion from the crown declared that a license for trading with the Indians was not meant to exclude traders from other colonies.[13]

Trade relations with the Indians increasingly became interwound with the problem of keeping peace between whites and Indians and among the Indians themselves. Trade was interrupted in the Yamassee War and during disturbances among the Creeks and Cherokees from 1724 to 1730.[14] Each colony, however, preferred unilateral handling of Indian affairs.[15] But because of the continued precariousness of the Indian situation, the intercolonial trade rivalry, and the sparseness of settlement in the back country, there was need for imperial control of the Indian frontier. Such intervention would not come about until dictated by military and mercantilist considerations.

An unusual bit of Indian diplomacy occurred in 1730 when Sir Alexander Cuming, who had come to South Carolina on business, suddenly turned up at the Lower Towns of the Cherokee country, and announced he would hold a conference with the various Cherokee tribes. At the subsequent meeting in April, Cuming conferred upon Chief Moytoy the title of Cherokee Emperor, and the Cherokees pledged allegiance to the crown. Cuming took six of the chiefs back to England. Curiously, the Board of Trade itself – not unlike the United States Senate at the Treaty of New York in 1790 – negotiated a treaty with the visiting chiefs, which was signed by the Indians at Cuming's house. The treaty provided for the exclusive trade rights of the English, the right of the English to build forts in Cherokee territory, and that an Englishman killing a Cherokee and vice versa would be tried with equal justice under English law. Although this treaty had no legality, with the Indian deputies being unauthorized to hold a treaty, it did dramatize friendship and that colonial Indian policy was backed by a powerful sovereign.[16]

Meanwhile, the Virginia–South Carolina–Georgia trade rivalries were again proving troublesome. To regain control of the Cherokee trade at the expense of the Virginians, Governor Robert Johnson of South Carolina built forts to hold the Catawbas (enemies of the Cherokees) in check and abetted a war between the Tuscaroras and the Catawbas. When brought to task for this policy by the Board of Trade, Johnson explained that only skirmishes among the Indians had taken place and they had heeded his warning not to attack white men. He amplified on this strategem of his Indian policy: "It is always the maxim of our Government upon the Continent to promote war between Indians of different Nations with whom we Trade and are at peace with ourselves, for in that consists our safety, being at War with one another prevents their uniting against us."[17]

After its founding in 1735 on the Savannah River, Augusta became the center of the Creek trade. Most of the traders were South Carolinians, who took out licenses from their own government rather than from Georgia.[18] Oglethorpe kept an agent at New Windsor to search for rum coming from South Carolina and he deployed militia in the Indian country to seize goods of traders licensed only by South Carolina.[19] But there were signs indicating an awareness of common interest. Both colonies in the 1730's jointly planned defense of the frontier and appealed to the crown for assistance.[20] When the Spanish War broke out, South Carolina permitted Georgia to appoint an agent for the Cherokees to prevent their defection to the Spaniards, and Governor Bull of South Carolina agreed to suppress the rum traffic.[21] In 1740 it appeared that Carolina and Georgia traders went about "without interrupting each other."[22]

Throughout the forties it was necessary for Virginia and the Carolinas to subsidize the Catawbas heavily to keep them as a counterbalance against threats of other Indians.[23]

From December 1743, when he arrived, until his retirement as Governor of South Carolina in 1756, James Glen assumed the responsibility for conducting southern Indian affairs for the crown. Glen believed that the French were the real enemy and therefore he sought to unite all the tribes into an English alliance. Glen made peace between the Creeks and Cherokees, secured help of Governor Clinton of New York to make peace between the Catawbas and the Six Nations, and impressed upon the Board of Trade the importance of the southwest Indians – the Catawbas and Chickasaws.

In 1746, Glen toured the South Carolina border, settling disputes among the Catawbas, Cherokees, Creeks, and Chickasaws. From the Cherokees and Creeks, he received pledges to resist the French advancement. Although Glen was himself extensively involved in the Indian trade, his firm policies brought a relative security to the Indian frontier. In 1748, the South Carolina Governor obtained reimbursement in the form of a £3000 annual grant from the Board of Trade for Indian presents. A joint commission from South Carolina and Georgia was to administer these gifts, but, with Oglethorpe objecting to South Carolina determining the distribution, Georgia offered little cooperation. The main problem was that the money was to be distributed by the "Governor, Council and Assembly" of South Carolina "in conjunction" with a single representative appointed by the trustees of Georgia. Later in the year the crown scaled down the grant to £1500 at the same time sending three Independent companies over to defend the South Carolina frontier.[24] The Board of Trade took Glen to task for not punctually delivering Indian gifts.[25]

As noted earlier, Glen was unable to attend the intercolonial Indian conference at Albany in 1751 called by Governor Clinton, but he did send an emissary, William Bull, who was accompanied by Catawba chiefs. Glen proposed that the main point on the agenda should be removing "all the Obstacles to a Peace, in reconciling all the Differences, and cementing together in a close Union the Northward and Southward Indians." Furthermore, he hoped "that any Representation concerning Indian Affairs might be laid before His Majesty as the united Sense of New York, Carolina and New England, the Center and the two Extremes of the

Continent will not fail of having its due weight."[26] Specifically, Glen wanted Clinton to order the Iroquois to refrain from attacking the Catawbas and Creeks, "who are equally the Friends of the English and the Children of the same Great King," or "we shall be under a necessity of revenging their Quarrel."[27] Bull had an interview with Governor Clinton on May 30, when the South Carolina commissioner was simply informed that the conference was being delayed because delegates from other colonies and the Iroquois had not yet shown up and the New York assembly had not voted money for presents.[28] Bull, however, stayed in Albany for the prefunctory conference in July.[29]

Glen found a competitor in Indian affairs in Governor Dinwiddie. Both men favored cooperative action in Indian affairs, but Dinwiddie thought mainly in terms of obtaining Indian allies against the French in the Ohio Valley, while Glen felt the other colonies should follow his lead in smoothing out problems of trade with the Indians. Dinwiddie wanted Glen to use force to bring the warring Creeks and Cherokees to terms with each other.[30] Dinwiddie, who had been ordered by the Secretary of State, Thomas Robinson, to use part of a military grant of £10,000 to erect a fort among the Overhill Cherokees, desired only a token fort (costing £1000), while Glen hoped to use about £7000 of these funds to construct a strong fort.[31]

Glen accused Dinwiddie of abetting Virginia traders in supplying rum to the Indians, which Carolina traders were prohibited from doing. He also charged that South Carolina Indians were being enticed into Virginia by means of presents. Actually, Dinwiddie has resisted a bid from the Overhill Cherokees to open trade because of the South Carolina embargo on Indian trade during the Cherokee-Creek War; but it was true that he had given a Cherokee delegation presents to ease the rebuff. Dinwiddie did acknowledge that the Cherokee trade was within South Carolina's sphere of action.[32]

When Dinwiddie called for an intercolonial conference with Indian chiefs at Winchester in 1754, Glen refused to attend and advised the Cherokees and Creeks, whom he considered under his jurisdiction, to do likewise. Dinwiddie protested to the Lords of Trade and blamed Glen for preventing Indians from aiding the Virginia expedition to the Ohio Valley.[33] Glen's policy was to put a general peace with all the Indians above use of Indian bands in military operations, which he thought would jeopardize the unsteady truce among the southern tribes. "Our great security," wrote Glen, "is the friendship of the *Indian* Nations, which I therefore study to cultivate with the greatest care; and as I find the *French* spare no pains in stirring up strife, that by constant wars they may weaken one another, I endeavour to heal and reconcile all their differences."[34] Glen proposed a general conference, with at least six colonies participating, to meet in Virginia sometime after the Albany Congress to treat with the southern Indians and the Iroquois as a whole. "We are greatly allarmed at the present Proceedings to the Northward," he said, and "we think that a small spark may kindle a great Fire, and are afraid that if the Flame bursts out, all the Water in the Ohio will not be able to extinguish it, but that it may soon spread and light up a general Conflagration. . . ."[35]

Dinwiddie believed Glen's holding back Cherokee and Catawba warriors was a factor contributing to Braddock's defeat; this additional strength and the Indians' "Method of bush fighting" would have made for victory.[36] The defeat earned contempt for British arms by the Indians and endangered the whole system of Indian alliances. A prominent Charles Town merchant saw the situation much the same as Dinwiddie:

> Our Ministry would do well to prosecute a War in America with Americans. Only they are not frightened out of their wits at the sight of Indians which by our Accounts was the case with your English Veterans. We wish they had staid at home as the advantage the Enemy have gain'd by their shamefull behaviour will put us to ten times the inconveniency in this part of the World. . . . it is much to be feared we shall loose our Interest with most of the Indians on the Continent which would extremely embarass us and half ruin our Colonys, particularly this to support a War against them.[37]

Rather than to rely upon the South Carolina Governor, Dinwiddie, in December 1755, sent his own commissioners to the Cherokees to secure their aid.[38] A major factor in Glen's recall in 1756 may be attributed to Dinwiddie's complaint and the reaction in England to Braddock's defeat. Glen's somewhat pompous successor, William Henry Lyttleton, saw to it that the Virginians in 1756 had an auxiliary force of eighty Cherokees to accompany Major Andrew Lewis's rangers against the Shawnee towns on the Ohio. In 1758, a Cherokee force served in Forbes's expedition. On both occasions, the Cherokees returned home disgruntled because they had been treated as inferior troops.[39] During the campaign of 1758, General Forbes complained the Cherokees were unmanageable and "grow extreamly licentious." The efforts of Governor Sharpe of Maryland, Bouquet, and Sir John St. Clair quieted them temporarily,[40] as did the diplomacy of ex-Governor James Glen of South Carolina who journeyed to Pennsylvania for this purpose.[41]

Following the appointment of a military commander for America in 1755, the Board of Trade took the advice of Thomas Pownall, George

Clinton, William Shirley, Archibald Kennedy, and others by naming two superintendents of Indian affairs. The southern superintendency went to Edmund Atkin, a Charles Town merchant in the Indian trade, who had submitted to the Board of Trade a "Plan for Imperial Indian Control."

Atkin's "Plan" had called for two Indian superintendents, a system of forts to be built by British engineers, and an Indian service to include missionaries, rangers, secretaries, gunsmiths, interpreters, and commissioners. The colonies should provide part of the revenue needed in Indian relations, to be raised by a poll tax on every British male subject, a duty on wines and rum, and post office revenue. Atkin explained the need for immediate re-structuring of Indian affairs:

> The Importance of Indians is now generally known and understood. Doubt remains not, that the prosperity of our Colonies on the Continent, will stand or fall with our Interest and favour among them. While they are our Friends, they are the Cheapest and strongest Barrier for the Protection of our Settlements. . . .[42]

With the creation of the two Indian departments, however, further generalization of the administration of Indian affairs lagged. Although Shirley ordered a treaty with the southern Indians in 1756 and asked Pennsylvania, Virginia, and Maryland to send commissioners and the governors of the two Carolinas "to assist at the Treaty and appoint the place where it is to be held," nothing came out of this proposal.[43]

Holding his commission from the crown, the new Indian superintendent for the southern colonies had broad powers over Indian affairs. Atkin's official title was "Superintendent of the Affairs of Our faithful Allies the several Nations inhabiting the Frontiers of Our Colonies of Virginia, North and South Carolina, and Georgia and their Confederates." Because Atkin's ability was doubted, Henry Fox, then the Secretary of State, privately gave Lord Loudoun powers to replace Atkin if he did not prove energetic enough.[44] Primarily, the superintendent conducted political relations with the Indians; but increasingly the staking out of Indian boundaries took up much of his time. The superintendent had authority over the distribution of presents, but the governors often secured the supplies and gave them out independently, the sums for which were then taken out of the royal grants for Indian gifts.[45]

To what extent were the superintendents under the jurisdiction of the commander in chief? John Richard Alden disputes Clarence E. Carter's assertion that the Indian superintendents played a subordinate role to the military commanders. Carter's thesis is based mainly upon Braddock's issuing Johnson his commission and Loudoun's holding authority over the southern department. But, after 1756, the year of Atkin's appointment, military commanders no longer could appoint Indian superintendents. Thus the power was a temporary expedient lasting for a year. Alden sums up the relation with the commander in chief: "Obviously the superintendents were always required to render obedience to the commands of the ranking general in America in regard to political relations with the Indians, *provided those commands did not conflict with instructions received by the Indian agents from the Board of Trade and the secretaries of state.*"

Until 1768 the military commander could decide on the amount of funds spent by the Indian departments, but the actual outlays were determined in England. Both Johnson and Atkin considered themselves directly responsible to officials in England; in 1763, the northern and southern superintendents were instructed to report to the Board of Trade. The commanders in chief did not interfere with the superintendents in Indian affairs, although Loudoun and Amherst tried to instigate a retrenchment in disbursements. General Gage kept a closer eye on Indian affairs than did his predecessors – especially in the regulation of the Indian trade.[46]

Atkin had to face a good deal of competition from the governors. Though theoretically the governors' powers in Indian affairs were limited to intra-colony concerns, the governors continued to operate in a broader sphere in negotiating peace treaties, disbursing colonial funds, regulating the Indian trade, and maintaining order in the Indian country. Governor Dinwiddie was the most cooperative in turning over funds, mostly provided by the crown, to the Indian superintendent. But Dinwiddie also submitted most of his colony's expenses in Indian affairs to Atkin because the other colonies would not help, and he refused to acknowledge Atkin's authority over the Indian trade. Pennsylvania and Maryland persistently refused Atkin's call for financial assistance and also would not let Atkin give out presents to the Cherokees passing through the two colonies.[47] Atkin objected to the colonies giving bounties for Indian scalps (particularly to the Cherokees taking Chickasaw scalps), which led to "pernicious consequences" since the Cherokees had the "art of making four scalps out of one man killed." Such provincial meddling, Atkin felt, conflicted with the "general interest of the colonies."[48]

Lack of money impeded Atkin's work. The Maryland assembly refused to vote funds, and Governor Sharpe wrote Atkin that if he wanted money for victualling the Indians he should apply to the British ministry. Sharpe felt that instructions from home would be necessary to prevent a colony from passing an act relating to Indian affairs that conflicted with Atkin's plans.[49] Another factor undermining Atkin's efforts was that the Earl of Loudoun avoided giving Atkin financial aid. Loudoun believed that the southern tribes were not of military value against the French as were the northern tribes.[50]

At Winchester in the summer of 1757, assisted by Christopher Gist, Atkin conducted lengthy negotiations with the Cherokee, Catawba, and other tribes. Atkin, however, quarreled with Johnson's assistant, George Croghan, at the meeting. Croghan thought the colonies independently could give out Indian gifts and had himself given presents to the Cherokees who had entered the northern district, contrary to Atkin's policy that the southern superintendent had exclusive jurisdiction over the southern Indians.[51]

In 1758 Atkin traveled into the Creek country, where he had no success in making a treaty but did effect some conciliation. Next he journeyed to the Choctaws, who agreed by treaty to make peace with the Chickasaws in return for trade.[52] Atkin's task was more difficult than in the north because there was no organized confederacy of the Indians and his commission, unlike Johnson's, had omitted "sole" agent. The superintendent's courage and skill among the Creeks and other wavering Indians, in spite of his being badly wounded from an attempted assassination, did pay dividends in detaching these Indians from joining the Cherokees in their war against the English in 1760-1.

What had seemed as undue neglect of Cherokee affairs and too much emphasis on the other tribes was probably the best policy after all. Atkin left much of the Cherokee negotiations to Governor Lyttleton of South Carolina, who had deferred to Atkin's authority in Indian affairs. During the Cherokee War, Atkin advised the South Carolina Council on military preparations and accompanied the colony's army into the field.[53]

Although Atkin's recommendations of the fur trade probably influenced the later decision of complete imperial regulation, he did not concern himself much with the smoothing out the differences among the colonies over the fur trade. Georgia and South Carolina continued to seek control of their spheres of interest through licensing traders, while Virginia left the Cherokee trade open.[54] South Carolina in 1761, as a war measure, prohibited the exportation of "Provisions, and of all Goods, and Ammunition necessary for the Indian Trade." Although many persons objected to this Act on constitutional grounds since it "restrained the Exportation, and consequently the Consumption of British Commodities," South Carolinians reportedly "universally acquiesced in it."[55] Governor Thomas Boone did not re-open the South Carolina trade with the Cherokees until June 1762, when they surrendered their captives. Boone favored that all colonies trading with the Cherokees should establish public monopolies, which South Carolina did in May 1762.[56]

Royal instructions in 1761 prohibited the governors or any other official from giving any land to the Indians; no license for purchasing land was to be issued except through clearance from the Board of Trade. The governors were ordered to prosecute anyone illegally holding land.[57]

After the French and Indian War, the Indian threat loomed even larger. With the French and Spanish thrust in the wilderness now gone, there would be greater temptation for settlers to move into the lands along the Indian barrier. Rumors were being spread among the Creeks that, with the French having been expelled, English settlers would soon descend upon their lands.[58] With Pontiac's conspiracy brewing in the north, there was a real possibility of a general conflagration of the whole western frontier.

Lord Egremont, Secretary of State for the Southern Department, although underestimating the Indian problem in the Ohio country, realized the need to take positive action to keep the southern tribes in check. Thus, in March 1763, he ordered the new superintendent, John Stuart, and the governors of Virginia, North Carolina, South Carolina, and Georgia to hold a treaty with all the major southern tribes (Catawbas, Cherokees, Creeks, Chickasaws, and Choctaws). The congress at Fort Augusta lasted from November 5–10. Seven to eight hundred Indians attended; also present were Governors Wright of Georgia, Boone of South Carolina, Dobbs of North Carolina, and Fauquier of Virginia. Some Indians came from as far away as six hundred miles. The treaty, signed on November 10, reaffirmed a variety of past pledges, granted the king's clemency to the Indians, and extended the Creek boundary westward. Provisions were also made for return of slaves and punishment of murderers, Indian and white. After the congress Stuart wrote the Earl of Egremont that there was still need to place trade on "a general, safe, equitable footing" and that he did not expect the individual colonies to do this.[59] The congress had not dealt with a southern boundary line with the Creeks, which would be a source of misunderstanding in future Creek-English relations.[60]

Hardly was the ink dry on the treaty than the Upper Creeks murdered several traders and soon thereafter fourteen other whites. Stuart demanded the Indians execute the culprits, and at the same time apprised the southern governors of the situation and asked military officials at Pensacola for assistance if it should be necessary. Stuart, however, favored the exhaustion of negotiations before interdicting the Creek trade – a policy which Governors Wright and Boone proposed. The two governors eventually agreed to Stuart's policy. General Gage, who had his hands full with Pontiac's Indians, also backed Stuart. By 1764, the Creek crisis eased, but the problems of the Indian boundary and trade regulation were now more delicate than before because the Creeks no longer had a bargaining position between the Spaniards and the English.[61]

Already in early 1763, the two secretaries of state, Egremont and Halifax, were beginning to formulate policies for the administration of the west, which would call for a comprehensive regulation of Indian affairs and establishment of a frontier perimeter. The colonists conceded to the necessity of imperial control over Indian affairs, but they would not accept what they considered tantamount to foreign interference with their birthright to the resources of the land.

NOTES

[1] Gerald Forbes, "The International Conflict for the Lands of the Creek Confederacy," *Chronicles of Oklahoma*, XIV (1936), 483.

[2] *EJCC–Va.*, Sep. 4, 1700, II, 104.

[3] *Ibid.*, Apr. 24, 1703, II, 315; *ibid.*, Oct. 16, 1713, III, 352.

[4] *Ibid.*, Mar. 3, 1704, II, 351; *ibid.*, Aug. 9, 1704, II, 381–82.

[5] Spotswood to the Council of Trade, Oct. 24, 1710, *Spotswood Corr.*, I, 25.

[6] Council of Trade and Plantations to the Queen, Dec. 19, 1702, *CSP*, XXVII, 112–13; Meeting of July 9, 1712, A.S. Salley, ed., *Journal of the Commissioners of the Indian Trade of South Carolina*, Sep. 20, 1710–Apr. 12, 1715 (Columbia, S.C., 1926), 42; Allen, "Travel and Communication in the Early Colonial Period" (PH. D. diss.), 253; Robinson W. Stitt, "Virginia and the Cherokees: Indian Policy from Spotswood to Dinwiddie," in Darrett B. Rutman, ed., *The Old Dominion: Essays for Thomas Perkins Abernethy* (Charlottesville, 1964), 26–30; Verner Crane, *The Southern Frontier, 1670–1732* (Ann Arbor, 1929), 154–56; Morton, *Colonial Virginia*, II, 437–38.

[7] Gov. Spotswood to Board of Trade, July 26, 1712, *NCCR*, I, 863.

[8] Spotswood to the Lords Commissioners of Trade, Feb. 16, 1716 and May 9, 1716, *Spotswood Corr.*, II, 141 and 149; Morton, *Colonial Virginia*, II, 436. This Act was omitted in Hening, *Va. Statutes at Large*. See Murray Lawson, ed., "An Act for the Better Regulation of the Indian Trade," 1714, *VMHB*, LV (1947), 329–32.

[9] Spotswood to the Board of Trade, Feb. 1, 1720, *Spotswood Corr.*, II, 331.

[10] W. Neil Franklin, "Pennsylvania–Virginia Rivalry for the Indian Trade of the Ohio Valley," *MVHR*, XX (1934), 464–65.

[11] Hugh T. Lefler, *History of North Carolina*, I (New York, 1956), 74.

[12] "An Act to oblige those Traders that come from Virginia . . .," June 28, 1711, *The Statutes at Large of South Carolina*, II (1837), 357.

[13] W. Roy Smith, *South Carolina as a Royal Province, 1719–76* (New York, 1903), 218–19.

[14] Col. John Herbert to Eleazer Wiggan, Jan. 31, 1727, A.S. Salley, ed., *Journal of Colonel John Herbert*, Oct. 17, 1727–Mar. 19, 1728 (Columbia, S.C., 1936), 22–23.

[15] Thus in 1721 South Carolina concluded a treaty with the Cherokees and made Colonel George Chicken supervisor of the Indian trade. John P. Brown, "Eastern Cherokee Chiefs" *The Chronicles of Oklahoma*, XVI (1938), 4.

[16] Board of Trade Journal, Sep. 7, 1730, *NCCR*, III, 129; Hewatt, *An Historical Account* (1779), II, 3–10; Chapman J. Milling, *Red Carolinians* (Chapel Hill, 1940), 275–77; Carroll, *Historical Collections*, I, 281–83; Brown, "Cherokee Chiefs," *Chronicles of Okla.*, 5–7.

[17] Richard P. Sherman, *Robert Johnson: Proprietary and Royal Governor of South Carolina* (Columbia, S.C., 1966), 96–98, quote on p. 98.

[18] Gipson, *British Empire*, IV, 37–38. Compare Clarence Attig, "William Henry Lyttleton: A Study in Colonial Administration" (unpubl. Ph. D. diss., University of Nebraska, 1958), 109.

[19] Thomas Causton to Col. Broughton, July 1, 1736, *JCHA-SC*, I, 88; Gen. Oglethorpe to Lord –, July 26, 1736, *Oglethorpe Letters, GHSC*, III (1873); Patrick Tailfer *et al.*, *A True and Historical Narrative of the Colony of Georgia in America, 1741* (*American Colonial Tracts*, I [Rochester, 1897]), 31.

[20] Governor and Council to His Majesty and Commons, Apr. 9, 1734, Carroll, *Historical Collections*, I, 303, 307; James R. McCain, "The Executive in Proprietary Georgia, 1732–52" (unpubl. Ph. D. diss., Columbia University, 1914), 32. Oglethorpe had been granted powers by the Trustees to keep peace with the Indians.

[21] Gen. Oglethorpe to the Trustees, Oct. 11, 1739, *Oglethorpe Letters, GHSC*, III (1873), 84.

[22] *GCR*, May 4, 1740, V, 345.

[23] See Norman W. Caldwell, "The Southern Frontier During King George's War," *The Journal of Southern History*, VII (1941), 37–54.

[24] Gov. Glen to the Duke of Bedford, Oct. 10, 1748, Bancroft transcripts (Colonial Documents), NYPL; *GCR*, May 24, 1748, I, 515; Carter, "James Glen" (Ph. D. diss.), 31, 126; McCain, "The Executive in Proprietary Ga." (Ph. D. diss.), 50; Milling, ed., *Colonial South Carolina: Two Contemporary Descriptions*, xii–iii.

[25] Wilbur R. Jacobs, *Wilderness Politics and Indian Gifts: The Northern Colonial Frontier, 1748–63* (Lincoln, Nebraska, 1966), 44n.

[26] Gov. Glen to Gov. Clinton, May 24, 1751, McDowell, ed., *Docs. relating to Indian Affairs* (S.C.), 84–86.

[27] Glen to Clinton, July 7, 1750, Clinton-Glen Corr., (microfilm), LC.

[28] William Bull to Gov. Glen, June 7, 1751, McDowell, ed., *Docs. relating to Indian Affairs* (S.C.), 33–34.

[29] See Chapter 7.

[30] Dinwiddie to Gov. James Hamilton, May 21, 1753, Emmet Collection, #1752, NYPL.

[31] See Chapters 9 and 10; Dinwiddie to Gov. Glen, Feb. 8, 1755, *Dinwiddie Corr.*, I, 484–87; Attig, "William Henry Lyttleton" (Ph. D. diss.), 25, 34.

[32] David H. Corkran, *The Cherokee Frontier: Conflict and Survival, 1740–62* (Norman, 1962), chapters 3 and 4.

[33] Letter of Capt. Stobo, June 28, 1754, *Memoirs of Robert Stobo of the Virginia Regiment* (Pittsburgh, 1854), 87; Carter, "James Glen" (Ph. D. diss.), 81–84, Only six or seven Catawbas and Cherokees showed up for the battle at Great Meadows.

[34] Gov. Glen to Gov. Dinwiddie, June 21, 1753, *JHB–Va.* (1752–58), 518.

[35] Gov. James Glen to –, Aug. 15, 1754, PRO, CO, Vol. 14, LC. Glen thought the governors from six colonies (N. and S.C., Va., Md., Pa., and N.Y.) should attend the conference.

[36] Dinwiddie to Gov. Glen, July 28,1755, *Dinwiddie Corr.*, II, 125; Carter, "James Glen" (Ph. D. diss.) . 84–85.

[37] Henry Laurens to James Cowles, Aug. 20, 1755, Philip M. Hamer, ed., *The Papers of Henry Laurens* (Columbia, S.C., 1968), I, 321.

[38] Gov. Arthur Dobbs to Gov. Morris, Dec. 18, 1755, Gratz Collection (Colonial Governors), HSP.

[39] Dinwiddie to Henry Fox, Mar. 20, 1756 and May 24, 1756, *Dinwiddie Corr.*, II, 372–73 and 412–16.

[40] Forbes to Stanwix, May 29, 1756, James, ed., *Forbes Writings*, 102.

[41] Stevens *et al.*, eds., *Bouquet Papers*, June 16, 1758, II, 103.

[42] Wilbur R. Jacobs, ed., *Indians of the Southern Colonial Frontier: The Edmond [Edmund] Atkin Report and Plan of 1755* (Columbia, S.C., 1954), vii, 3; Gov. Dobbs to the Board of Trade, Nov. 26, 1755, *NCCR*, V, 478–79; Wilbur R. Jacobs, "Edmund Atkin's Plan for Imperial Indian Control," *Journal of Southern History*, XIX (1953), 313–18; Attig,"William Henry Lyttleton"(Ph. D. diss.), 112; Corkran, *Cherokee Frontier*, 148. Gov. Dobbs had recommended the appointment of six or eight imperial Indian agents to supervise the fur trade, to be paid out of the "Surplus" raised by the colonies for maintaining frontier posts. Lyttleton proposed a system of "Residentary Agents" in each of the major Indian nations.

[43] William Trent to Washington, Jan. 21, 1756, Hamilton, ed., *Letters to Washington*, I, 191. The Md. Assembly voted to send two commissioners and £ 300 for Indian presents. (*Md. Archives*, Assembly Papers, Mar. 3, 1756, LII, 316.) Atkin consulted with Johnson and Loudoun in late 1756 and early 1757. He also attended the military conference in Philadelphia in March 1757, with governors of Pa., Md., Va., and N.C. attending. Except for discussion on future Indian treaties and the role of Indians in southern defense, this conference dealt with military operations. See Chapter 5 and Wainwright, *Croghan*, 121–22.

[44] Alden, "The Albany Congress and . . . the Indian Superintendencies," *MVHR*, XXVII (1940), 210; Jacobs, ed., *Atkin's Indian Report*, xxii.

[45] John R. Alden, *John Stuart and the Southern Colonial Frontier* (Ann Arbor, 1944), 140–41; Louis De Vorsey, Jr., *The Indian Boundary in the Southern Colonies, 1763–75* (Chapel Hill, 1966), 13.

[46] Alden, *John Stuart*, 142–49; Jacobs, *Indian Gifts*, 42; Carter, "The Significance of the Military Office in Amer.," *AHR*, XXVIII (1923), 475–88.

[47] Jacobs, ed., *Atkin's Indian Report*, xxiv–vi; Alden, *John Stuart*, 72, 74; Smith, *South Carolina as a Royal Province*, 84ff.

[48] Extract of a letter of Atkin to Gov. Sharpe, June 30, 1757, Dillon, *Oddities of Colonial Legislation*, 319.

[49] Sharpe to Atkin, July 29, 1757, *Md. Archives*, IX, 60.

[50] Jacobs, ed., *Atkin's Indian Report*, xxix.

[51] *Ibid.;* xxiii; Jacobs, "Atkin's Plan for Imperial Indian Control," *Journal of Southern History*, XIX (1953), 311; Wainwright, *Croghan*, 126.

[52] Reese, *Colonial Georgia*, 116–17.

[53] Jacobs, ed., *Atkin's Indian Report*, xxvii–xxix; Corkran, *Cherokee Frontier*, 166–77. Atkin's title was somewhat embellished in a S.C. newspaper: "Edmund Atkin, Esq. His Britannic majesty king GEORGE'S agent for, and superintendent of the affairs of his allies, the several nations of Indians inhabiting the frontier of Virginia, North and South Carolina, and Georgia, and their confederates." *South Carolina Gazette*, Apr. 7, 1760.

[54] Abbot, *Royal Governors of Ga.*, 91.

[55] Lt. Gov. William Bull to Pitt, Feb. 18, 1761, *Pitt Corr.*, II, 395.

[56] Alden, *John Stuart*, 177–79.

[57] "Additional Instructions for Gov. and Capt. Gen. Thomas Boone of South Carolina," Sep. 9, 1761, *Providence Gazette*, July 23, 1763. The Instructions were sent to all the colonial governors.

[58] Mowat, "The Southern Brigade," *Journal of Southern History*, X (1944), 60; Alden, *John Stuart* 180.

[59] Gov. Thomas Boone to Earl of Egremont, June 1, 1763, Bancroft transcripts (England and America), NYPL; *Providence Gazette*, Nov. 12, 1763 and Dec. 31, 1763; Norkus,"Francis Fauquier" (Ph. D. diss.), 308; Carr, "Defense of the Frontier" (Ph. D. diss.), 102; Abbot, *Royal Governors of Ga.*, 93; Flippin, *Royal Government in Ga.*, 133–34; Alden, *John Stuart*, 176–85. Egremont arranged for £ 4000–£ 5000 in presents to be given by the congress to the Indians. Except for Gov. Wright, the governors preferred Dorchester, S.C. as the site for the congress, but the Creeks refused.

[60] See De Vorsey, *The Indian Boundary,* chapter 8, for the problems of the East Florida–Creek boundary line.

[61] Alden, *John Stuart*, 186–91.

CHAPTER IX

INDIAN WARS

If territorial aggression arouses pride in country for the aggressor, it equally stirs nativism in the defender. For this reason the red man would suddenly turn and fight in defense of his territorial prerogative, but also because of his pronative pride he could not effect an intertribal front against the English. Since Indian hostility would break out at a specific point, it was incumbent upon the colony immediately threatened to stamp out the resistance. A neighboring colony would give aid only in proportion to the danger of the spread of the contagion. The jealousies of the colonies over Indian policy affected cooperation for mutual defense and offense against the Indians.

Four bush wars – three insurgencies of southern tribes and a full-scale, determined belligerency of the western Indians – demonstrated the need for an intercolonial or imperial frontier force.[1]

If the colonial authorities had cared to read the signs of over a decade, they could have surmised a mounting tension among the Tuscaroras. Swiss and Palatine settlers steadily encroached upon the Indian hunting lands along the Neuse and Pamlico Rivers. Cheating the Indians in trade and luring young braves, on the pretext of giving them an education, for sale into bondage added fuel to the fire.

On the eve of the Tuscarora War, Governor Spotswood attempted to secure a defensive stance of Virginia, Maryland, and the Carolinas in order to provide mutual aid if a colony were attacked.[2] As a royal governor, Spotswood considered it his duty to look after the protection of the frontier in the neighboring proprietaries.[3] To coordinate military preparations, Spotswood met with commissioners from North Carolina in July 1711, April 1712, and with the Governor of North Carolina in December 1712.[4]

Autumn of 1711 was an apropos time for the Indians to strike. A drought left the settlers ill-provisioned, and the colony was in the midst of civil dissension between the Thomas Cary and Edward Hyde factions, sometimes known as 'Cary's Rebellion.' At dawn on September 22, 1711 numerous small bands of Tuscaroras simultaneously swept down on the settlements on the Roanoke, Neuse, and Chowan Rivers. One hundred and thirty settlers were killed and thirty taken captive, and homes, crops, and livestock were destroyed in this sudden vent of fury. The newly arrived Palatines and Swiss at New Bern, on the Neuse, braced themselves during the winter for an expected attack. Governor Hyde of North Carolina immediately applied to Virginia and South Carolina for assistance.[5]

Spotswood offered to send troops to aid North Carolina if North Carolina would provision them, which was not done. He applied to the home government for arms and ammunition, in which the Virginia militia were "wholly destitute," and he could "not conceal from Your Lordships the incapacity of this Country for an Offensive or Defensive War." Spotswood prohibited all trade of Virginia with the hostile Indians.[6] Meanwhile, he met with Tuscarora emissaries, who disclaimed tribal responsibility for the massacre. In December, Spotswood and Tom Blount, the Tuscarora chief, signed a treaty at Williamsburg, whereby English captives were to be surrendered and each Indian town would give up two Indian children as hostages to be educated by Virginia. The Indians showed little inclination to abide by this treaty, and it was soon evident that they were merely waiting out the winter before striking again.[7]

South Carolina had to come to the rescue of North Carolina, where the government was still so rent by factionalism that it could not take measures for the safety of its own inhabitants. The South Carolina assembly voted £ 4000 for the war, and Governor Charles Craven sent a small band of militia under Colonel John ("Tuscarora Jack") Barnwell, who were joined by several hundred Cherokees, Creeks, Catawbas, and Yamassees.[8] At the end of January 1712 they attacked Tuscarora towns, but Barnwell was too ill-equipped to continue to press the Indians, and the scant provisions supplied by North Carolina had run out.[9] He "clapt up a peace with the Indians upon very unwarrantable conditions," according to the infuriated Spotswood, who had wanted to work out with the North Carolina Governor terms for a solid peace with the Indians.[10] Furthermore, Barnwell's expedition had cut the ground from under Spotswood's own Indian policy:

> when I had by a solemn treaty made in the presence of our Assembly, engaged the upper towns of the Tuscaroras to joine in cutting off those concerned in the massacre, and had communicated the same to the Governour of North Carolina. That Government instead of concurring with me, in stipulations that provided solely for their succour, and the relief of their captives: rather chose to denounce war against all the towns in general and without waiting to see whether

> those upper towns would perform any of their engagments, they imediately fell upon those very people who (how little soever they designed to execute their promises) hereupon argued that we had violated ours.[11]

If he could not get Virginia to give any aid to North Carolina, Spotswood did prevail upon his fellow Virginians to show compassion "for the poor people that have been plundered by the heathen." The Virginia assembly voted £ 1000 and nine hundred yards of "course clothing" for the suffering settlers. This was accomplished in spite of the fact that

> I am the only person of this Government that ever proposes giving any assistance to North Carolina in its distresses, and must alone furnish the arguments to obtain the Council's concurrence, or to procure any supplys from the Burgesses: besides that whatever I undertake in behalf of that distracted country, I am forced to push on with a great deal of trouble and expence to myself. On the other hand there reigns such stupidity and dissent in the Government of North Carolina, that it can neither concert any measures, nor perform any engagements for it's own security.[12]

With renewed hostilities in the fall of 1712, North Carolina again appealed to Virginia and South Carolina for assistance.[13] Because of rumored aid to the Tuscaroras by the Iroquois, the war now threatened Virginia's security. Spotswood called for active participation by Virginia and he issued an impassioned plea to the Burgesses, which fell on deaf ears:

> Under these Deplorable Circumstances your nearest Neighbours your Brother Christians and your Fellow Subjects Send hither for Succour Imploring you by all the Ties of Christianity and all the Ties of Humanity to help to Stop the Desolation of their Country And Save their Wretched familys from the merciless fury of the Heathen.[14]

Colonel James Moore, son of the former governor of South Carolina by the same name, marched into the Tuscarora country in January 1713 with a force of thirty-three whites and over eight hundred Indians. Snowfall delayed the attack. Finally, in March, after a bloody siege of an Indian fort, those Tuscaroras that were not captured and sold into slavery fled into Virginia north of the Roanoke River. The refugees, abetted by Iroquois warriors, continued to harass frontier settlements until checked by a body of Virginia tributary Indians under Colonel Robert Hix. By the resulting treaty, the Tuscaroras agreed to become tributaries of Virginia and promised to deliver up hostages and to surrender to North Carolina those responsible for murder.[15] Soon the Tuscaroras moved to New York to join the Iroquois confederacy.

The loyalty of the Yamassees had long been taken for granted. Living between Port Royal and the lower Savannah River, this tribe had been a buffer against the Spaniards in Florida and had served English interests in trade. The irony was that the Yamassees had just helped the English defeat the Tuscaroras, and now found themselves in the same vise. They were cheated and plied with rum by traders, and some of them were now being enslaved by the whites.

In the spring of 1715 the Yamassees rose in rebellion, joined by some warriors from the Congarees, Catawbas, Cherokees, Creeks, and lesser tribes – thus posing the possibility of a generalized Indian war. The Yamassees attacked Port Royal and Saint Bartholomew, with Apalachis and Muscoghees in the war party. Meanwhile, traders were murdered in the Cherokee and Choctaw villages; only the Chickasaws kept entirely aloof.[16]

South Carolina geared for the war emergency. Martial law was declared. Agents were sent to Virginia and England to seek help. Bills of credit were issued, which brought the public debt to £ 80,000. The province had only about twelve hundred able-bodied men, and many of these, as had been the case of North Carolina during the Tuscarora War, were leaving the colony to avoid military duty. If the Indians should go unpunished it was possible that the French from Mobile might join forces with them. Governor Craven proclaimed an embargo on all ships to prevent emigration from the colony, and he seized arms and ammunition.[17]

Responding to a request made by commissioners in person from South Carolina, Governor Spotswood sent powder and muskets from the Jamestown magazine and allowed Captain Arthur Middleton to raise about one hundred fifty troops in Virginia. North Carolina provided eighty provincials and sixty Indians. Spotswood not so magnanimously demanded from South Carolina an able-bodied woman for every man sent from Virginia to stay in Virginia until the men returned – though this was nonsense, Spotswood was probably serious. Governor Craven increased the pay of his Virginia troops by £ 4 per month.[18]

Spotswood dispatched letters to the governors of Maryland, Pennsylvania, and New York requesting aid for South Carolina and that they be on their guard against a spread of the war. To the Maryland governor he warned of a potential conspiracy among the Iroquois:

> And as I am certainly informed, that there has been a more than ordinary intercourse between the Southern and Northern Indians for some time past, and that the Southern Indians under pretence of making war upon the Seniquors and other Northern Indians furnished themselves with great Quantityes of Ammunition and Armes which

they have now turned against the people of South Carolina, I am very apprehensive there may be the same Treacherous designe on foot amongst the Northern Indians, Wherefore I think it Concerns all these Governments to be upon their Guard and to have a watchfull Eye upon the Indians in their Neighbourhood . . . .[19]

Spotswood had already written the British authorities in June for an additional supply of munitions, especially a part of those stored in New England and New York after the Canadian expedition. He also petitioned for a royal bounty out of the deficiency of quit rents to be used in "opposing the Common Enemys" of both Virginia and Carolina.[20] One of Spotswood's frontier schemes, designed to shorten the war, did not fare very well: namely, resettling some of the lesser tribes who were suspected of aiding the Yamassees from the frontier into the North Carolina interior, which naturally that colony vetoed as a wild idea.[21]

After Governor Craven's successful march through the Yamassee towns and a Virginia force having dispersed Indians threatening Charles Town from the south, the Indian allies of the Yamasees began to defect. Colonel Maurice Moore, with a display of force and having the good luck that Creeks had recently killed several Cherokee chiefs, signed a treaty with the Overhill Cherokees, who then joined with Moore's force to pursue maurading Creeks. Soon the Creeks themselves withdrew from aiding the Yamassees, and other tribes followed their example. Thus, without Indian allies, the Yamassees fled to the protection of the Spanish fort at St. Augustine, from where for the next decade they would conduct sorties along the southern border of South Carolina. Lands in South Carolina vacated by the Yamassees were set aside for white settlers.[22]

Threat of Indian war did not cease with the defeat of the Yamassees. Iroquois raiding parties against southern Indians imperiled the security of the Virginia frontier – hence Spotswood's efforts in 1717–8 to concert Indian policy with northern governors and the Albany conference of 1722,[23] which had a temporary restraining effect on the Iroquois.

One of the results of the Yamassee War was the hastening of royalization of South Carolina. The proprietors were blamed for not providing for military protection of the colony. An anonymous tract of the time underlined the insufficiency of proprietary rule:

for it is very naturall to think, that if they [proprietors] could not send Forces to assist them, it would be as difficult to correct them, and also (as they hoped) to put them in the same Circumstances with His Majesty's other Colonies in America, who they found, had proper Assistance from the Crown. As there was therefore neither Fear, nor Love, nor Interest to support this Government, how could it long subsist?[24]

The Proprietors earned further enmity by repealing provincial laws that had opened Yamassee lands for settlement and by taxing profits from the Indian trade. They also refused to assist the colony in paying off the large war debt. Thus the rebellion of 1719 – instigated by a political faction of recent settlers outside of Charles Town – was easily accomplished, and the crown soon took over the reins of government. Both the first royal governor, Francis Nicholson, and his successor, Arthur Middleton, were able to renew alliances with the Cherokees and Creeks.[25]

In the 1730's, French expansion in the southwest was checked by the Natchez war against the French and their Choctaw allies.[26] But the Spanish stronghold at St. Augustine still provided a center for influence over the lower Creeks. In 1736, Oglethorpe complained to the Trustees that South Carolina neglected to aid Georgia in preparing defenses against the Indians and Spaniards, because "the People of Carolina desire to have entirely destroyed and united to theirs" the Georgia defense system, "that they may have the benefit of the improvements here and the liberty of oppressing both the Indians and the English Poor as they do their own."[27]

The southern Indian frontier was relatively quiet during the 1740's, although during King George's War the French sent agents to stir up the southern tribes against the English. The Cherokee alliance was threatened by several of the Overhill towns making peace with the French, and most of the Cherokees, until 1746, allowed Iroquois and Shawnees to use their villages as bases in their war with the Catawbas. Fortunately for the southern colonies, the French were still trying to rid Louisiana of remnant Chickasaws, who had earlier joined with the Natchez.[28]

In 1750 Governor Glen proposed to send troops to assist the Choctaws, who had turned against their French ally, and to give arms and ammunition to other Indians to encourage their joining with the Choctaws. The Council voted down both requests but consented to send presents to the Choctaws. By the end of 1750, however, the Choctaws were reconciled to the French.[29]

Georgia maintained friendly relations with the Creeks by continuing the policy of the Trustees in giving out presents – subsidized by the crown to the amount of £ 1500 a year, building up the Creek trade, and outlawing private purchasing of Creek lands. This wooing of the Creeks conflicted with the Cherokee-oriented policies of South Carolina, whose Governor in 1749 had pledged aid to the Cherokees in the event a Cherokee-Creek war flared up–which it did from 1750–2. But, unable to secure the backing of Georgia, Governor Glen refused to honor his commitment to the Cherokees, which proved to be a major factor in alienating them.[30]

In 1755, Dinwiddie of Virginia and Glen of South Carolina competed for the loyalty of the Overhill Cherokees by each building a fort for the Indians within a few miles of each other on the Little Tennessee River. Supposedly, the fort building was in return for Indian aid to the northern campaigns aginst the French, but both governors had an eye open to the Carolina fur trade. Such duplication of policy confused the loyalty of the Indians.[31]

In April 1759 the Cherokee Indian War began when a war band attacked North Carolina settlers along the Yadkin and Catawba Rivers. The Cherokees had many accumulated grievances, which included encroachments upon their land, soldiers from Fort Prince George violating squaws while the warriers were away, and the government having cut off supplies and ammunition.[32]

Soldiers straying away from Fort Loudoun were captured by the Indians. William Henry Lyttleton, who had replaced Glen as Governor of South Carolina in 1756, convened the assembly, which dispatched messengers to General Stanwix and the governors of Virginia and Georgia. Fortunately, the troops under Captain John Stuart at Fort Loudoun had enough supplies and ammunition to wait out a siege.[33]

Lyttleton audaciously journeyed into the Indian country to treat with the chiefs of the Lower Towns and the Overhills to prevent their joining the hostiles. Not receiving commitments to his liking in this effort at Indian diplomacy, Lyttleton, upon his return to Charles Town, decided to awe the Indians with a show of force. On October 26, he marched fourteen hundred volunteers from Charles Town to Fort Prince George, on the Keowee in the heart of the Lower Cherokee country. Lyttleton had to hurry because enlistments expired January 1. The army moved to a rendezvous on the Congarees, where Lyttleton expected to join forces with troops from North Carolina.

Meanwhile, the Governor of Georgia took precautions for his colony "by putting the Militia in readiness" and repairing Fort Augusta near the Cherokee country. The Virginia legislature held an emergency session and recommended that the remaining work on Fort Loudoun be completed and three hundred men be raised to protect the back settlements.

Governor Dobbs of North Carolina ordered Colonel Hugh Waddell to raise three regiments in addition to the two companies already in service – this force was to link up with Lyttleton's army. Most of the North Carolinians, however, refused to serve beyond the colony's boundaries. With only a small band, Waddell arrived too late in the Indian country to aid Lyttleton.[34]

Trying again to allay any further hostilities by using diplomacy, Lyttleton met with Attakullakulla (second chief of the Overhills, also known as Little Carpenter) on December 18 and warned the Indians that if hostilities continued they could expect to fight a combined force of the colonies:

> You know well the strength of our province, and that one-third part of it is sufficient to destroy your nation. Besides, the white people in all the provinces are brothers, and linked together; we come not alone against you because we have suffered, for the Virginians and North Carolinians are prepared to march against you, unless satisfaction be given me. My brother the governor of Georgia will also prevent any ammunition from coming to you.[35]

Scarcely had the South Carolina Governor left the Cherokee country than the Indians fell upon Fort Prince George; failing to take the garrison, they massacred some forty traders and settlers nearby. Communication with Fort Loudoun was cut off. Georgia ordered militia to Augusta, and Lieutenant Shaw and Ensign Lachlan McIntosh took a detachment of Independent troops to the Presidio and Fort Moore.[36] Major General John Stanwix at Fort Pitt released his eight hundred Virginia troops to return to Virginia.[37]

Before surrendering his office to the new Governor, William Bull, Lyttleton appealed for aid to Amherst. Colonel Archibald Montgomery with 1,200 crack troops of the first and seventy-seventh regiments were sent immediately to Charles Town, though Amherst kept transports at Charles Town ready to bring the troops back. Planning a three-pronged attack against the Indians, Lyttleton called for assistance from the governors of Virginia and North Carolina.[38]

Governors Dobbs, Bull, and Fauquier agreed to concert operations against the Cherokees. Montgomery, reinforced with three hundred fifty South Carolinians, was to march to the Lower Towns, while Virginians and North Carolinians were to go through the Overhill towns with provisions for Fort Loudoun. Although the South Carolina Governor neglected to provide transportation for Montgomery's force, the British Colonel covered as much as sixty miles a day and surprised the Lower Towns. After giving battle and fearing an ambush, he returned to Charles Town. Bull, however, accused Montgomery of having needlessly inflamed the situation.

Promises exceeded performance on the part of South Carolina's neighbors. Governor Ellis of Georgia, more concerned with a possible Creek outbreak, used the colony's rangers to patrol the Creek frontier; but he did try to incite the Creeks to war against the Cherokees by offering bounties for scalps.[39] Governor Bull's high hopes that "measures may be concerted to act with more Energy by timing our Motions, or uniting our power, with the Troops of his Majesty and our Neighbours"[40] were also in for disappointment from Virginia and North Carolina.

Although Virginia sent one thousand of fourteen hundred troops then in service of the colony to relieve Fort Loudoun,[41] the troops did not arrive in time. On August 8, 1760 the fort was evacuated; whereupon the Indians fell upon the fleeing provincials, killing Captain Raymond Demere and twenty-nine others and capturing the rest.[42] The Virginia relief force had been delayed because the commander, William Byrd, could not get sufficient arms and supplies and he had slowed his march to construct posts at twenty-five mile intervals all the way to the Holston River–even building a fort in the middle of the river. Furthermore, Byrd considered his mission primarily to make peace. North Carolina did not send aid at this time because Governor Dobbs vetoed an appropriations bill on grounds that it called for emission of paper money.[43]

The Cherokees had decided to make no commitments to Governor Bull of South Carolina, who had also sent out peace feelers, until they had negotiated with Byrd. The Virginia commander met with Attakullakulla, who promised that he could hold the other Cherokee chiefs from hostile actions until March. Byrd had no authority to conduct diplomacy, but he had confidence that personally negotiating through Attakullakulla would end the war.[44]

But small war parties continued hostilities, and Governor Bull, therefore, decided to renew operations. In October, he ordered Major William Thomson with 268 rangers to supply Fort Prince George, which succeeded without incident. South Carolina officers in the meantime tried to enlist troops not only in South Carolina but also in North Carolina. Bull urgently asked Amherst for help.[45] Governor Fauquier of Virginia wrote the home governmennt:

> If this war grows serious it will be impossible for the Carolinas to defend themselves without assistance from Mr. Amherst–I dare say this Colony will do all in their power; their interest is at stake; but I am of opinion, the security and safety of part of his Majestys Colonies, cannot be procured by Provincial Troops only.[46]

Bull again hoped to arouse North Carolina to participation. Writing to Governor Dobbs, he said

> I make not the least doubt that a proper direction of the force of our Several Provinces, we may have it in our power by carrying the War into the Enemies Country to give them Such a Stroke, as will Secure

> us from any Molestation from them hereafter. The consequence of their making any further progress in this province, and the Calamities that must from thence be derived to our Neighbours, are too Obvious to Stand in need of being discanted upon.[47]

The North Carolina assembly passed a bill for sending five hundred troops to aid South Carolina and Virginia, but this time Governor Dobbs vetoed the bill because of a rider giving the assembly the right to name the agent in London.[48] Not until summer 1761 were these troops finally raised in North Carolina.

Again Bull applied to General Amherst to send regulars to aid South Carolina troops against the Lower and Middle Cherokee towns and a detachment from Fort Pitt to assist a Virginia and North Carolina force to attack the Overhills. Bull consulted with the other governors and they agreed to joining militia with regular troops. Fauquier somewhat over-spiritedly ordered the Virginia regiment of one thousand men "federalized," to be under the command of Amherst in order to act in conjunction with regular and militia troops in South Carolina "lest any clashing of orders might obstruct the good of the whole."[49]

At first Amherst refused to send additional troops, but, when news of the fall of Fort Loudoun reached him, he dispatched about two thousand regulars to South Carolina, to be placed under Colonel James Grant, who already commanded the few regulars in South Carolina. The South Carolinians added a new regiment, and Chickasaws and Catawbas were also enlisted. Early in May 1761 the whole force proceeded to Fort Prince George, and then, taking the same trail as Montgomery the year before, on to Ninety-Six.

North Carolina raised a force of nearly five hundred, which did not set out until August 1761, and never did join the Virginians as intended.[50] Virginia voted £ 32,000 for an expedition against the Cherokees, and Byrd was again given the command. Enlistments fell short of the one-thousand-man levy, and the colony appealed to Amherst for assistance. When this was refused, and even though Byrd was asking for seven hundred additional men, the House of Burgesses ordered Byrd to march to the Indian country. In July, at Samuel Stalnaker's plantation, he had only six hundred men and inadequate supplies.[51]

Fortunately, an anti-war faction grew among the Cherokees. The Creeks had been kept out of the war by presents liberally given out by Governors Bull of South Carolinia and Wright of Georgia. Colonel Grant, who had felt that the Cherokee War was largely a figment of the imagination of South Carolina, soon negotiated a peace treaty. Colonel

Adam Stephen, who had replaced Byrd at the head of the Virginia troops, advanced as far as the Long Island on the Holston and made a separate peace with Old Hop, head chief of the Overhills at their capitol town of Chota, which may be regarded as ending the Cherokee War.[52]

Along the Ohio frontier, hostilities from the western tribes and some of the Iroquois had become so widespread in early summer 1763–with every post west of Fort Pitt, except Forts Ligonier and Detroit, having fallen to the Indians, and Forts Pitt, Ligonier, and Detroit under siege–that Amherst sent out a punitive expedition under Colonel Henry Bouquet. Bouquet's force consisted of less than five hundred men–Highlanders, Royal Americans, and Rangers. In several skirmishes, culminating at Bushy Run, Bouquet routed the Indians.[53]

Amherst received instructions from the President of the Board of Trade, the Earl of Halifax, "to call upon the colonies . . . to contribute to the general Defence of the Country, and Annoyance of the Indians, by raising and employing such Numbers of Provincial Troops, or Militia, as You shall find requisite." Halifax had long been an advocate of using as many provincial troops as possible in military operations. Letters were also sent to the governors of the New England colonies, New York, New Jersey, Pennsylvania, and the two Carolinas to cooperate with any requisitions from Amherst.[54] In November, before turning his command over to Gage, Amherst levied quotas upon New York and New Jersey, fourteen and six hundred men respectively. This corps would be joined with regulars to attack the Indians by way of Niagara. For an expedition against the Indians on the Ohio, he asked for one thousand men from Pennsylvania and five hundred from Virginia.[55]

Virginia was the only colony to attempt meeting the requisitions immediately. New York and New Jersey both made it a condition of acceptance that the New England colonies also participate. Initially Pennsylvania enacted a law to raise seven hundred men "to be divided, stationed and employed in protecting the Frontiers, within the purchased Parts of the Province, during the Time of Harvest," which the colony considered according to the "Purpose specified in the General's Requisition." Amherst sent a regular officer to command these troops, but the colony refused this arrangement and would not let the militia accompany the regular troops into the Indian country.[56] But this was generally conceded to be too strict an interpretation of Amherst's requisition, and the assembly soon passed a military aid bill for the one thousand men requested. Governor John Penn of Pennsylvania, however, objected to a rider levying a tax on proprietary land, and refused to sign the bill. Not until after much further bickering and mounting public pressure was the bill signed into law the next year, May 30, 1764.[57] Pennsylvania levies did not join Bouquet's army until July 1764, long after the battle at Bushy Run.

Some four hundred Virginia militia under Colonel Adam Stephen assisted Bouquet, and, in addition, "this publick spirited Colony" sent "a body of the like number of men under the command of Colonel Lewis for the defence and protection of their South West frontiers," wrote General Amherst. "What a contrast this makes the conduct of the Pennsylvanians and Virginians, highly to the honor of the latter, but places the former in the most despicable light imaginable."[58]

Meanwhile, all the Independent companies in the northern colonies had been disbanded and two battalions of the Royal Americans had been sent home. When Bouquet set out from Carlisle on August 5 on his second expedition he had only the partly filled 42d and 60th regiments of the king's troops, about two hundred Virginia volunteers, a few of the two hundred friendly Indians he had expected, and most of the one-thousand-man Pennsylvania contingent.[59] Bouquet had counted on a large force of Virginia militia, but because about seven hundred militia were already in service for defense of the Virginia frontier, only the volunteers arrived.[60] Amherst had agreed that the militia of Virginia could not be ordered out of the colony except for volunteers.[61] The Governor of Pennsylvania cooperated by issuing press warrants for teams to carry supplies and munitions, and the western counties of Pennsylvania raised volunteer troops for their own defense, which released regular soldiers on garrison duty for service on the frontier.[62] A conflict in authority occurred when William Johnson, the Indian superintendent, wrote Colonel Adam Stephen, who commanded the Virginia volunteers, to use his force to attack the Shawnee towns on the Ohio.[63]

By the time Bouquet reached Fort Loudoun on August 13 his Pennsylvania troops had dwindled to seven hundred because of desertion. Bouquet, therefore, applied for reinforcements to the Governor of Pennsylvania, who sent additional troops. Once "beyond the settled parts of Pennsylvania," Bouquet asked Governor Fauquier of Virginia to send aid, and some of Virginia's frontier militia soon joined with Bouquet's force—after all, the army was now operating on part of Virginia's frontier. Bouquet spent several weeks at Fort Pitt and then set out into the Indian country, with his total force now numbering 1500 men. Eventually he reached the Muskinghum River, where he concluded peace and exchanged prisoners.[64]

Colonel John Bradstreet, accompanied by Sir William Johnson, led a force of two thousand–militia from New Jersey, New York, and Connecticut, regulars, and Indians[65] – to re-occupy the northern posts that had fallen to the Indians. Massachusetts, New Hampshire, and Rhode Island had ignored the request for troops for Bradstreet's army. The expected Indian opposition melted away as it had before Bouquet's advancing army.[66]

Pontiac's War greatly embarrassed the English ministry, pointing out the lack of defense preparations, and popular resentment in England demanded attention to this subject.[67] It was a war without glory and should not have happened: instead of "decisive Battles" and "Colours and Cannon," there were only "woodland Skirmishes" and "Trophies" of "stinking scalps," and it was a war "conducted by a spirit of Murder rather than of brave and generous offence."[68]

Coming as it did upon the heels of the Cherokee uprising, Pontiac's War forced strategic considerations upon the British government. Occupation of Florida would be regarded as essential to the protection of the Ohio and Mississippi valley as would be the northern posts.[69] The frontier would be viewed in its totality–hence the Proclamation of 1763. The Indian wars demonstrated the need for general protection by the crown of the frontier and coordinated Indian relations and land policy. The wars had also proved the reluctance of one colony to fight the battles of another and that effective action required the substantial employment of a regular force.

NOTES

[1] Excluding the intermittent border strife along the eastern Massachusetts frontier during King William's and Queen Anne's War.

[2] Spotswood to the Secretary of State, Feb. 8, 1711, *Spotswood Corr.*, I, 146.

[3] Morton, *Colonial Virginia*, II, 428.

[4] "Spotswood's Journal," *WMQ*, 2nd Ser., III (1923), 40–41.

[5] John H. Wheeler, *Historical Sketches of North Carolina*, reprint ed. (Baltimore, 1964), I, 37; Edward McCrady, *The History of South Carolina Under the Proprietary Government*, 1670–1719 (New York, 1901), 417–18; Alonzo T. Dill, "Eighteenth Century New Bern: A History of the Town and Craven County, 1700–1800, Part III, Rebellion and Indian Warfare," *NCHR*, XXII (1945), 295–310; Beth G. Crabtree, *North Carolina Governors, 1585–1958* (Raleigh, 1958), 27; Milling, *Red Carolinians*, 117.

[6] Spotswood to Council of Trade, Oct. 15, 1711, *Spotswood Corr.*, I, 117.

[7] Milling, *Red Carolinians*, 118; Morton, *Colonial Virginia*, II, 430.

[8] Hewatt, *An Historical Account* (1779), I, 202; Ashe, *Hist. of North Carolina*, I, 186–87; Carroll, *Historical Collections*, I, 179–80; William J. Rivers, *A Sketch of the History of South Carolina to the Close of the Proprietary Government by the Revolution of 1719* (Charleston, 1856), 253. Accompanying Barnwell were 218 Cherokees under Captains Harford and Turston; 79 Creeks under Capt. Hastings; and 41 Catawbas under Capt. Pierce.

[9] John Barnwell to Governor of S.C., Apr. 20, 1712, "Journal of John Barnwell," *VMHB*, VI (1899), 50; Spotswood to Lord Dartmouth, May 8, 1712, *Spotswood Corr.*, I, 147; Dodson, "Spotswood" (Ph. D. diss.), 335. Virginia had apparently furnished 400 "buckskins worth of ammunition."

[10] Spotswood to the Council of Trade, May 8, 1712, *Spotswood Corr.*, I, 148–50.

[11] Spotswood to the Council of Trade and Plantations, July 26, 1712, *CSP*, XXVII, 17.

[12] *JHB–Va.* (1712–26), Nov. 15, 1712, p. 27; Spotswood to the Council of Trade and Plantations, Feb. 11, 1713, *CSP*, XXVII, 133.

[13] Spotswood to the Lord Proprietors, Feb. 11, 1713, *NCCR*, II, 14; McCrady, *South Carolina*, 525.

[14] Address of the Governor, Nov. 3, 1712 *JHB–Va.* (1712–26), 26–27.

[15] Message of the Governor, Dec. 7, 1713, *ibid.*, 68; Mr. Rainsford to the Secretary, Feb. 17, 1713, *NCCR*, II, 16; James H. Rand, *The Indians of North Carolina and Their Relations with the Settlers (James Sprunt Hist. Pubs.*, XII [Chapel Hill, 1913]), 30; Morton, *Colonial Virginia*, II, 431. Originally the S.C. force was estimated at 1100. Not all Tuscaroras rebelled. Tom Blount and his tribesmen were assigned the task of punishing those Indians who had joined the warring Tuscaroras–Corres, Mattamuskeets, and Catechines.

[16] Milling, *Red Carolinians*, 104, 119; Hewatt, *An Historical Account* (1779), I, 218–19; McCrady, *South Carolina*, 53738.

[17] "Memorial from Mr. Beresford Representing the Present State of South Carolina," June 23, 1716, *NCCR*, II, 229–30; Board of Trade Journal, May 10, 1717, *ibid.*, 280–81; Carroll, *Historical Collections*, II, 145. Boone and Beresford, agents for Carolina, asked the King to supply 600 men: 200 to be disbanded in 12 months, 200 in 18, and 200 in 24 months.

[18] Francis Le Jau to John Chamberlain, Aug. 22, 1715, Frank Klingberg, ed., *The Carolina Chronicle of Dr. Francis Le Jau, 1706–17 (Univ. of Calif. Pubs. in History*, LIII [Berkeley, 1956]), 161: Philip A. Bruce, *The Virginia Plutarch* (Chapel Hill, 1929), I, 128; McCrady, *South Carolina*, 545; Morton, *Colonial Virginia*, II, 438.

[19] Spotswood to the Governor of Maryland, May 27, 1715, *Md. Archives*, XXV, 310. Gov. Hunter of N.Y. claimed to have "prevailed with our Indians to interpose in the Carolina war" and that they have sent several parties out to "view (the) Indian enemys and discover their situation and the passages." Hunter to Council of Trade and Plantations, July (?), 1717, *CSP*, 363.

[20] Spotswood to Lords Commissioners of Trade, June 4, 1715, *Spotswood Corr.*, II, 115; Spotswood to the Lords of Treasury, July 15, 1715, *ibid.*, 117.

[21] Council Journal, Aug. 4, 1716, *NCCR*, II, 242–43.

[22] Assembly of S.C. to Messrs. Boone and Beresford, Mar. 15, 1716, *CSP*, XXIX, 50; Le Jau to the Secretary, Apr. 25, 1716, Klingberg, ed., *Carolina Chronicle* 177; Morton, *Colonial Virginia*, II, 438; Sirmans, *South Carolina*, 111–15; Crane, *Southern Frontier*, 167, 174; Milling, *Red Carolinians*, 148. After the Cherokees allied themselves with the English, their raids on Creek and Yamassee towns hastened the end of the war.

[23] See Chapter 7.

[24] *A Narrative of the Proceedings of the People of South Carolina in the Year 1719* (London, 1776), ed. Carroll, *Historical Collections*, II, 161.

[25] John Fiske, *Old Virginia and Her Neighbours* (Boston, 1897), II, 228. For French and Spanish military measures to deter English expansion, see William B. Griffin, "Spanish Pensacola, 1700–63," *Florida Historical Quarterly*, XXXVII (1959), 243; also "Tobias Firch's Journal to the Creeks" (1725), in Mereness, ed., *Travels*, 204.

[26] Dillon, *Oddities of Colonial Legislation*, 301.

[27] Gen. Oglethorpe to the Trustees, July 1, 1736, *Oglethorpe Letters, GHSC*, III, 37.

[28] Caldwell, "The Southern Frontier During King George's War," *Journal of Southern History*. VII (1941), 39; Sirmans, *South Carolina*, 264–67. For Glen's efforts to save the Choctaw alliance, see *ibid*. [Sirmans], 267–69, 278, 282–84, 288.

[29] Caldwell, *ibid.*, 50–54.

[30] Flippin, *Royal Government in Ga.*, 133–40; Sirmans, *South Carolina*, 288.

[31] Dinwiddie to Pitt, June 18, 1757, *Dinwiddie Corr.*, II, 641–42; Philip M. Hamer, "Anglo-French Rivalry in the Cherokee Country, 1754–57," *NCHR*, II (1925), 314–22; Morton, *Colonial Virginia*, II, 660, 683; Alden, *John Stuart*, 47. For the best discussion on the complicated Cherokee diplomacy, see Corkran, *The Cherokee Frontier*, chapters 5–9.

[32] Philip M. Hamer, "Fort Loudoun in the Cherokee War," *NCHR*, II (1925), 442–458.

[33] M. De Filipis, trans. and ed., "An Italian Account of Cherokee Uprisings at Fort Loudoun and Fort Prince George, 1760–61," *NCHR*, XX (1943), 250. This account contains a number of inaccuracies.

[34] Gov. Lyttleton to Lords of Trade, Oct. 23, 1759, Bancroft transcripts (Colonial Documents), NYPL; Henry Ellis to Amherst, Nov. 2, 1759, PRO, WO:34, XXXIV, LC; *Pennsylvania Journal*, Nov. 29, 1759 (concerning Va. Gov.'s speech, Nov. 2, 1759); Gov. Dobbs to Pitt, Jan. 21, 1760, *ibid.*, 245–46.

[35] Gov. Lyttleton's conference with Attakullakulla, Dec. 18, 1759, Carroll, *Historical Collections*, I, 448.

[36] De Filipis, "Italian Account," *NCHR*, XX (1943), 253–54; Brown, "Cherokee Chiefs," *Chronicles of Okla.*, XVI (1938), 12; Alden, *John Stuart,* 101–6.

[37] Stanwix to Pitt, Mar. 17, 1760, Parkman transcripts, MHS.

[38] "A Short Description of the Province of South Carolina ... written ... 1763" (London, 1770), in Carroll, ed., *Historical Collections*, II, 528; Hamer "Fort Loudoun," *NCHR*, II (1925), 451; Brown, "Cherokee Chiefs," *Chronicles of Okla.*, XVI (1938), 12.

[39] "A Short Description," *ibid.*, 528; Hewatt, *An Historical Account* (1779), II, 229; Hamer, "Ft. Loudoun," *NCCR*, II (1925), 453; Norkus, "Francis Fauquier" (Ph. D. diss.), 155–56; Alden, *John Stuart*, 107–9.

[40] William Bull to Amherst, Aug. 15, 1760, PRO, WO:34, XXXV, LC. Creek murders of South Carolina traders in the spring of 1760 led to the threat of "an immediate general Indian War from the Creeks and probably the Choctaws . . .," so spoke the Governor of North Carolina, upon being alerted by Governor Bull; "these Southern Provinces" would be caught "between two fires"–therefore the Governor asked the Assembly "to put this Province in a state of defence and to support our Southern Neighbours . . . ." Governor's Speech to Council and Lower House of Assembly, Apr. 24, 1760, *NCCR*, V, 439.

[41] Lt. Gov. Fauquier to Pitt, Apr. 11, 1761, *Pitt Corr.*, II, 416.

[42] Hamer, "Ft. Loudoun," *NCHR*, II (1925), 451–58; Brown, "Cherokee Chiefs," *Chronicles of Okla.*, XVI (1938), 12.

[43] Alden, *John Stuart*, 115.

[44] *Ibid.*, 119–22.

[45] *Ibid* ., 123; Brown, "Cherokee Chiefs," *Chronicles of Okla.*, XVI (1938), 15.

[46] Gov. Fauquier to the Lords of Trade, Sep. 17, 1760, Bancroft transcripts (Virginia Papers), NYPL.

[47] Gov. Bull to Gov. Dobbs, Sep. 21, *NCCR*, VI, 314.

[48] Ashe, *Hist. of N.C.*, I, 301.

[49] Fauquier to the Board of Trade, May 12, 1761, *JHB–Va.* (1758–61), 294–95.

[50] Fauquier to the Board of Trade, Sep. 27, 1761, *ibid.*, 297–98.

[51] *South Carolina Gazette*, June 27, 1761; Capt. Robert Steward to Washington, Apr. 6, 1761, Hamilton, ed., *Letters to Washington*, III, 211; Alden, *John Stuart*, 123–26; Brown, "Cherokee Chiefs," *Chronicles of Okla.*, XVI (1938), 15–16; Ezekial Sanford, *History of the United States before the Revolution* (Philadelphia, 1819), 176–77.

[52] Alden, *John Stuart*, 127ff; Milling, *Red Carolinians*, 306.

[53] See Howard H. Peckham, *Pontiac and the Indian Uprising* (Chicago, revised ed., 1961), 210–13 and Francis Parkman, *The Conspiracy of Pontiac and the Indian War after the Conquest of Canada*, 2 vols. (Boston, 1898–99), II, 33 and chapter 20. For the siege of Fort Pitt by the Indians and Bouquet's relief of the garrison with his little army of 560 regulars, see Slick, *William Trent*, chapter 9.

[54] A copy of this circular letter is to Earl of Halifax to Governor and Company of Conn., Oct. 19, 1763, Trumbull Papers, CSL.

[55] Halifax to Amherst, Oct. 19, 1763, Clarence E. Carter, ed., *The Correspondence of General Thomas Gage with the Secretaries of State and with the War Office and the Treasury*, 1763–75, 2 vols. (*Yale Historical Publications*, XI–XII [New Haven, 1931–32]), II, 3–4; Amherst to Gage, Nov. 17, 1763, *ibid.*, 211–12.

[56] Votes of the Assembly, Mar. 3, 1764, *PA*, 8th Ser., VII (1935), 5560–65.

[57] John R. Dunbar, ed., *The Paxton Papers* (The Hague, Neth., 1957), 19.

[58] Sir Jeffrey Amherst to Sir William Johnson, Aug. 27, 1763, *NYCD*, VII, 546.

[59] *South Carolina Gazette*, June 18, 1763; John R. Alden, *General Gage in America* (Baton Rouge, 1948), 94; Sidney G. Fisher, *Pennsylvania: Colony and Commonwealth* (Philadelphia, 1897), 25.

60 [William Smith?.] *An Historical Account of the Expedition Against the Ohio Indians under the Command of Henry Bouquet . . . to which are annexed Military Papers* (London, 1766), (reprint Cincinnati, Ohio, 1868), 32–33.

61 Amherst to Mr. President Blair, Oct. 5, 1763, PRO, WO:34, XXXVII, LC.

62 Arthur D. Graeff, "The Relations between the Pennsylvania Germans and the British Authorities," *Pa. German Society Proceedings*, XLVII (Norristown, Pa., 1939), 184–85.

63 Amherst to Sir William Johnson, Sep. 10, 1763, *William Johnson Papers*, IV, 201.

64 Smith, *An Hist. Account . . . Bouquet*, 33–39.

65 Besides 728 Indians from the Six Nations and other tribes, Bradstreet's force consisted of the following:

17th Regiment	– 243
55th Regiment	– 98
N.Y. Regiment	– 344
N.J. Regiment	– 209
Conn. Regiment	– 219
Battoe men	– 74
Carpenters	– 9
total	1196;

and including Indians, 1924. "Papers Relating to the Expeditions of Colonel Bradstreet and Colonel Bouquet in Ohio, A.D., 1764," *Western Reserve and Northern Ohio Historical Society,* Tract No. 13 (Feb., 1873), 2.

66 Alden, *General Gage*, 96ff.

67 *Providence Gazette*. Oct. 22, 1763.

68 Smith to Gates, Nov. 22, 1763, Gates Papers, NYHS.

69 Alden, *John Stuart*, 194; see C.N. Howard, "The Military Occupation of British West Florida, 1763," *Florida Historical Quarterly*, XVII (1939), 181–99.

CHAPTER X

FRONTIER PERIMETER

In the seventeenth century there was little conception of an outer frontier line. It is true that there were bitter confrontations with local Indian tribes resisting the concentrated expansion of the coastal settlements, but the hinterland was merely the unknown, the "Devil's Den." Towards the end of the century, first Virginia and then the northern colonies began to establish military posts to mark the further advance of the frontier in order to protect traders and settlers. In the eighteenth century, as the colonies became aware of mutual problems of trade and defense, they looked more and more to the frontier as a whole entity and an imperial concern.

Governor Thomas Dongan of New York in the 1680's planned to establish a chain of forts through the Iroquois country from Albany to the Great Lakes primarily to secure trade with the western tribes.[1] With the French invasion of New York in 1689, the value of maintaining a frontier watch was realized. Captain Abram Schuyler set up an outpost at Crown Point, and Captain John Schuyler led a roving band of New York militia and some Mohawks to reconnoiter and harass the enemy in the northern reaches of the colony.[2]

Some cooperation among the New England colonies was achieved during King William's War in the joint garrisoning of frontier posts. Massachusetts and New Hampshire pooled resources on the eastern frontier. Since New Hampshire wound up with practically all of the responsibility for manning the garrisions, the colony used this excuse to limit participation in the expeditions against Canada. Massachusetts and Connecticut used friendly Indians "as a flying army to scout upon the heads of the out Towns and Plantations."[3] In 1694, acting Governor William Stoughton of Massachusetts requested Connecticut to relieve the garrison at Deerfield "by posting 40 to 50 fresh men" for a period of six months at Massachusetts's expense.[4]

There was no sense of common concern over the protection of the further western frontiers in the north. Complained Governor Andrew

Hamilton of East Jersey that efforts for mutual protection went unheeded: "the exemption or noncomplyance of the neighboring Colonies" will never "be remedyed unlesse the support of the frontiers reaches all North America; as it is the remoter Colonies are soe many asylums."[5]

The need to have a defensive barrier along the frontier gave impetus to the idea of interior colonization. For this reason the crown encouraged immigration, especially from 1684 to 1732 in promoting the creation of a southern population barrier against the French and Spaniards. One would-be promoter of immigrant frontier settlement was Dr. Daniel Coxe (Sr.), physician and Jersey proprietor. Coxe unsuccessfully attempted to interest the Lords of Trade in granting him a large tract in western Virginia, Pennsylvania, and New York stretching to the "South Seas." Coxe did manage to acquire the old Heath patent of 1629 to the area between 31° and 36° with the expectation of settling a French Protestant colony west of Apalache Bay. But an expedition that Coxe sent out was turned back by the French at the mouth of the Mississippi. Coxe's hopes to set up a gigantic joint stock company were disappointed. The Attorney General upheld only a small part of Coxe's claim.[6]

The idea of setting up a sort of frontier march system, as used in early Europe, occurred to several prominent colonists. In 1699, Colonel Andrew Hamilton, Governor of New Jersey, proposed that a large royal force could be maintained on the frontier by giving the soldiers forty to fifty acre lots and placing a poll tax of 15 *s.* upon every freeman, a sixteen years or older. He thought the colonies would rather pay then provide the troops.[7]

Although neglecting to repair the frontier defenses and even to muster the militia during his administration,[8] Lord Bellomont suggested the sending of missionaries among the Indians to counteract the "sinister artifices" of the Jesuits[9] and that the Mohawk Valley should be settled in order to develop the production of tar, pitch, rosin, ship-timber, hemp, and iron. Bellomont also thought that British veterans could be stationed along the border to work in the forest industries. After Bellomont's death, Caleb Heathcote became the leading exponent in New York for expansion of the frontier. Heathcote thought the colonial militia on a rotating basis could be employed in the forest industries, while at the same time receiving military discipline. Two hundred men should be kept free to mount guard while the rest were put to work. Needless to say that Heathcote's idea anticipated later plans of universal military service and the moral equivalents of war suggested by William James and Randolph Bourne. In 1705, Heathcote joined with sixteen other partners as a group of "undertakers" sponsored by Connecticut for a monoply in producing naval stores for that colony. This plan apparently immediately fizzled out.[10]

In 1701, Robert Livingston presented the Board of Trade with ideas for a frontier defense barrier. He felt that the royal troops in New York at that time (two companies of sixty men each) were ill-prepared to defend the colony's frontier. The soldiers were discontented because their remuneration was 30-40% less than in England due to the difference in value between New York money and the pound sterling. Furthermore, troops trained in European wars could not grasp frontier fighting conditions. But there was a way to shape British regulars into a frontier guard. They should simply be set up as frontier farmers. Two hundred troops should be sent to New York every two years and after brief service be discharged and given land. Soon these soldier-settlers would adapt to the ways of the woods. In addition Livingston suggested fort-building on an intercolonial basis, which could best be done through the establishment of three-super colonies (North, Middle, South).[11]

Queen Anne's War brought about a greater consciousness of the need for a general defense along the frontier but elicited an almost nil response in cooperative action. Repeatedly Governor Dudley and the Massachusetts General Court wrote New York to seek aid against the French and Indians along the eastern border, but because of the Iroquois neutrality, New Yorkers were unwilling to make the plight of the New England colonies their own. Thus the French were free to concentrate their attacks on the eastern frontier of Maine, New Hampshire, and Massachusetts. The Iroquois allowed hostile Indians to send war parties through their territory and supplied them with arms and ammunition.

Even though British policy was to have the colonies establish frontier posts, Massachusetts refused to erect posts outside the colony's jurisdiction. Governor Dudley, however, did organize a snowshoe brigade, ready to march to a remote trouble spot, at twenty-four hours notice, and he sent scouting parties to the eastern frontier. When the western frontier of Massachusetts was invaded in 1703, with the massacre of fifty inhabitants at Deerfield, troops were stationed in the exposed settlements and small squads were sent to search for the Indian raiding parties. Massachusetts, however, would vote no appropriations to keep up New Hampshire forts, although several of these forts were repaired under direction of royal engineers and garrisoned at the expense of

Massachusetts.[12] The Bay Colony sent a committee to inspect the Pemaquid fort in 1701, and the commissioners in their report reflected the general colonial attitude that the colony should rebuild the fort but that the crown should garrison it.[13]

During 1704 and 1705 an alarm spread about every two months that a large force of French and Indians would invade New England. Snowshoemen with twenty days subsistence patrolled the frontier over two hundred miles distant. But the French invasion never materialized.[14] The neutrality of the Iroquois, who were concerned with protecting their role as middlemen in the fur trade, prevented the English from building forts into the north-western interior. But, by 1709, the Iroquois interest was beginning to shift to the English. New York sent five sachems of the Five Nations to England to help plead the colonial cause for imperial aid in defending the New York frontier.[15] Wait Winthrop, in 1709, optimistically expected the colonies would combine efforts to defend their exposed borders.

> It is the Current opinion of every body with us, and we believe of our Neighbour Colonys, and we can't but persuade our Selves of your Lordships too; that it is a necessary and most reasonable Expectation, that all her Majesties Governments lying so contiguous should combine to yeild mutual succors and Assistance each to other, and by an united force opposed the power of the Common Enemy.[16]

The Board of Trade took a dim view of the lack of preparedness and cooperation for frontier defense in the proprietary colonies. Chief among the complaints was

> That they do not in general take any due care for their own defence and security against an enemy, either in building forts or providing their inhabitants with sufficient arms and ammunition, in case they should be attacked, which is every day more and more to be apprehended, considering how the French power increases in those parts. . . .[17]

Towards the end of Queen Anne's War, Governor Spotswood of Virginia proposed that the southern frontier be secured with settlements of tributary Indians. In 1708 the Saponi had been placed on the Meherrin River to serve as a defense against the Tuscaroras; soon other tribes joined the Saponi. According to Spotswood's plan each of three groups of Indians would be located on separate reservations with Englishmen living among them to teach their children and to encourage trade. The Tuscaroras were to be settled along the Rappahannock, the

Saponi above the fork of the James, and the Appomattox, Nottoways, and Meherrins along the Meherrin River. Each group were to have a hunting ground nearby. In 1714, chiefs of the Tuscaroras, the Saponi, and the Nottoways agreed to Spotswood's plan, but soon the Tuscaroras made peace with North Carolina and returned to that colony, only to raise the tomahawk once again. Spotswood moved the Saponi south of the Meherrin, where Fort Christianna was built, and the Nottoways to the north side of the Meherrin. The Virginia Governor also began a settlement of German-Swiss immigrants at Germanna on the frontier at the Rappahannock.[18]

Massachusetts viewed its frontier as a safety valve for excess population. At the end of Queen Anne's War, it was the first colony to adopt the old Roman policy of granting lands to veterans. In the 1720's, the Bay Colony tried to round up surplus population in Boston for settlement in Maine. The New England colonies were experiencing a population boom, and the resulting immigration to the outlying areas served to stabilize a barrier against the Indians. During the years 1713-40, all of New Hampshire was settled, the Connecticut population doubled, and Massachusetts could boast one hundred thirty new towns.[19] One significant result of the population growth was that New Hampshire could now stand on her own instead of seeking aid from Massachusetts for frontier defense.[20]

After Queen Anne's War several colonial leaders addressed the crown to set up a system of control over frontier defense and trade. Governor William Keith of Pennsylvania in 1719 proposed a western trade union under the auspices of the crown:

> . . . every Colony would find a Solid and certain advantage by a Union amongst them, according to their situation, Power and Ability to advance their Trading Settlements westward upon the Lakes and adjacent Rivers, where these vast Nations of Indians would soon perceive by Our united Intent, Power, and Traffick that we were far preferable to Our Rivals, the French, and in every Way much fitter to be chosen for their friends and Allies. . . . This Trade cannot be managed to any purpose without the mutual assistance and concurrence of all the English Colonies. But from the different Constitutions and particular Interest of these Colonies, such a Regulation is not to be obtained without the Authority of Great Britain.[21]

About the only response of the Board of Trade was to send a letter to the governors of Pennsylvania and the southern colonies asking that they call a conference to solve their rivalries over the fur trade. But the governors could not agree.[22]

Galfridus Gray came up with the most comprehensive plan for frontier regulation during this period. He simply proposed that a "path" be cut through the woods "on the Back of all his Majesties Colonys from the head of the Bay de Chaloner, which Runes up about 90 Miles into Nova Scotia out of St. Laurance River. . . to. . .westernmost Bounds of S. Car. which is 1050 Miles." One thousand blockhouses should be erected on this path, four to twenty-four miles distance from each other. Gray somewhat humorously pointed out that his plan did not envisage a "China Wall or Roman earth Wall in England," but merely a path. Such a line would be a barrier, boundary, and "communication." This, he said, would be the "only Method which can make his Majesties Subjects on the Continent of America Safe in their Lives and fortunes. . . ." The specific advantages that Gray saw in this path through the woods were: (1) it would prevent Indians from going beyond boundaries on pretense of trade and would keep them "from Straggling Down Among the English to breed Private Quarrels which in time past have Ended in Publick Wars; (2) the Indian trade could support the maintenance of the line; (3) with only 200% instead of 1000% interest, trade would gain greater satisfaction among the Indians and increase four times American manufactures; and (4) the safety afforded by the line would raise the value of crown lands.[23] Gray thus anticipated the famous Proclamation line of 1763.

In the 1730's Governor Robert Johnson of South Carolina proposed that four forts be built, one hundred miles apart, along the boundary of South Carolina, with the home government supplying additional troops to the one Independent company sent over during Nicholson's administration to man the posts.[24] Governor Belcher of Massachusetts in 1731 had the idea of a frontier ranger corps.

> And while as a Fruit of his Majesty's great Wisdom and steady Government, we are in a perfect Peace and Tranquility with all the World around us, would it not be wise and prudent to be gaining the Knowledge of our own Country? I mean to imploy a Number of capable, active Men (at a good Encouragement from the Government) to Traverse the Wilderness, and make themselves well acquainted with the more remote and distant Parts of the Province, as well as to lay out and make more Commodious Roads on the whole Length of the Frontiers.[25]

Although the initiative in the formulation of British western policy was being undertaken by the colonists themselves, it was expected that the crown should assume responsibility for fortifying the frontier.[26] The colonists were willing to subscribe to an imperial entity of frontier defense but showed little inclination to make it an intercolonial one. Except in wartime, any action taken to police the frontier turned out to be unilateral. For example, Governor Thomas of Pennsylvania, not receiving any reply from Maryland and Virginia to his offer for cooperation, took it upon himself to remove German settlers from the Juniata Valley in 1740.[27] During King George's War, Governors Clinton (New York) and Morris (New Jersey) pledged mutual assistance if either colony should be invaded by the French,[28] but the suggestion for a defensive entente bore no practical result other than the military operations in New York. Governor Shirley of Massachusetts attempted to have Connecticut contribute garrision troops "for the Protection of Our Settlements that are a Frontier to that Colony," but apparently Connecticut did not agree.[29] In 1746, the New York Council voted that £ 13,000 be appropriated to build blockhouses in the "line of Communication" continuing from the New England defenses.[30]

In the south during King George's War the lack of military success spurred interest in securing greater royal protection of the frontier.[31] Although some Virginia and South Carolina troops joined Oglethorpe's invasion of Florida in 1740, Georgia officers visiting Virginia and South Carolina in 1743 had trouble getting recruits to come to the defense of Georgia's frontier.[32]

At the end of King George's War, American population was bursting at the seams. Everywhere pioneers were filling the back country.[33] Eager settlers were waiting to jump beyond the Appalachian frontier. Visionaries, such as Franklin, thought families should be allowed to swarm into the Ohio country. Franklin realized that Great Britain must provide for American expansion: "how careful should she be to secure Room enough, since on the Room depends so much the Increase of her People?"[34] As Paul Connor says, Franklin "was a claustrophobe in fear of American suffocation." Franklin, however, stood for unity and coordination in the advance to the west. To Franklin, the Albany Plan of Union was more than a defense scheme; it would provide a means for an orderly distribution of lands and supervision of purchases from the Indians.[35]

By mid-century Americans viewed the frontier as a natural and limitless depository for surplus population. Hitherto, the concept of the frontier was mainly territorial, respecting Indian claims; now it was to be considered an open land as far as settlers cared to go, making little pretense regarding Indian rights. This attitude was reinforced by the Treaty of Lancaster in 1744 by which the Iroquois gave Virginia,

Maryland, and Pennsylvania the right to land "as far as it was then Peopled, or hereafter should be Peopled." It is true that these lands lay primarily in the Ohio Valley outside the Iroquois territorial claims. This clause was reaffirmed by the Treaty of Logstown in 1752, even though it was of doubtful validity from both the imperial and Indian viewpoints. Political considerations would come later. Not the least significance of these treaties is that they paved the way for a rush of speculation in the huge public domain. Entry into the Ohio country, challenging the French and western Indians alike, would require the maintenance of a western military establishment, which the colonies would ill-regard at public expense.[36]

The speculative craze in the late 1740's and 1750's strained imperial-colonial relations. Competing policies over chartering land companies put the colonies and the home government at cross purposes. The history of the Ohio Company and other land speculative companies is better told elsewhere. Suffice it to say, the British government, from the start of the French and Indian War, assumed an increased responsibility over regulating western settlement. The first step in a generalized western land policy was set forth in an order of the king-in-council of July 18, 1754, which granted to all future settlers in the west remission of quitrents for ten years and limited speculation by prohibiting the taking up of any tract larger than one thousand acres. This policy had largely been in response to a petition from the Virginia assembly protesting the royal grant to the Ohio Company; Virginia was already following a policy of opening her western lands to poorer settlers and exempting actual settlers from quitrents for fifteen years.[37] Besides insisting on a more democratic base for western land policy,[38] the crown ordered unauthorized land companies to remove settlers from lands not ceded by the Indians.[39]

On the eve of the French and Indian War the colonists became acutely aware of the need for a north-south defense perimeter, since all colonies were vulnerable in varying degrees to French or Indian attack. To the English point of view, the French fort building in the Ohio Valley violated the Treaty of Utrecht, which had given the English the right to build forts in the Iroquois country.[40] But the French had nevertheless established their line of defense; either the English must accept it or destroy it, at the same time setting up a defense line themselves. Especially French forts in upper New York drove home the challenge. Secretary Willard of the Massachusetts General Court sharply saw the crisis:

> Crown Point is the Carthage of New England and New York, and unless it be demolished, will be a constant scourge to them in times of war, being a place of retreat and shelter for the enemy, after their depredations upon the English frontiers, and besides this in time of peace, the situation of it so near the Indians has a great tendency to draw such of them as are wavering to the French interest.[41]

Again it was one thing to know what should be done and another to bring it about through cooperative action. Petty jealousies among the colonies prevented any general scheme of fort building on the western frontier. New York considered the French on the Ohio a Pennsylvania matter as Pennsylvania had regarded the French at Crown Point the problem of other colonies.[42] Pennsylvania, by 1756, however, had erected a chain of forts that ran diagonally from the north of Easton on the eastern border southwestward into Cumberland County near Maryland. As evident from their location these forts were intended only for defense.[43] Because of the dispute with Virginia over claims to the Ohio Valley, the Pennsylvania proprietors banned the building by Virginia of any fort along the Ohio – which was challenged by Virginia's erecting Fort Necessity.[44] Elsewhere in the north, New Hampshire refused to bear any expense for building a fort on the Connecticut River because the colony had its own frontier to defend.[45] New York in 1754 unsuccessfully sought cooperation from Connecticut to build forts in the Indian country.[46] In New Jersey, the border towns petitioned Governor Belcher for protection against the Indians. Belcher recommended to the assembly the building of blockhouses on the Delaware River to be maintained by a frontier force of 300-400 men. About all that was done, however, was to keep about one hundred fifty men on the frontier; two assemblymen were also sent to New York to confer with Shirley concerning frontier defense.[47]

The crown ordered Virginia to build forts sixty miles apart in the Ohio country. But, Virginia first attended to immediate defense by erecting a cordon of forts; by 1756 there were eighty-one posts, poorly garrisoned, extending from Great Cape Capon in Hampshire County to South Fork of the Mayo River in Halifax County.[48]

At the start of the French and Indian War, the whole thinking in the colonies concerning military affairs, with the exception of bold views of such men as Governors Shirley, Dinwiddie, and Hardy, was to maintain a defense line along the international zones of friction rather than aggression. In the early confrontation only Shirley argued for expulsion of the French from Canada. Even the objective of Braddock's expedition was simply to recover territory.[49] Frontier defense dominated the military views of the Albany commissioners in 1754. Thomas Pownall went so far as to propose setting up a solid wall against French encroachment: (1) blockhouses and forts at regular intervals at the furthermost reach of the frontier, which would cut off communication between Louisiana and Canada; and (2) "border colonies" in western New York, the Iroquois country, and at the forks of the Ohio. Free land, exempt from quitrents, would attract settlers to the barrier regions. The pioneers would unite for their own defense, and thus they would serve as a "cover army" for the regular British troops.[50] James De Lancey at the Albany Congress suggested that the commissioners direct a comprehensive system of fort building in the west, but "they seemed so fully persuaded of the Backwardness of the several Assemblies to come into joint and vigorous Measures, that they were unwilling to enter upon the Consideration of these Matters," and thus shifted the burden of responsibility to a colonial union "enforced by Act of Parliament."[51]

If the Albany Plan were adopted, Franklin saw the rapid increase of population west of the Alleghenies under the auspices of a colonial union. Western settlement continuing exclusively under the authority of individual colonies would proceed only "inch by inch." But "if the colonies were united under one governor general and grand council, agreeable to the Albany Plan, they might easily, by their joint force, establish one or more new colonies, whenever they should judge it necessary or advantageous to the interest of the whole." Franklin advocated the chartering of joint stock companies made up of the settlers themselves. Two western colonies could be founded as far west as the Scioto River and between the Ohio and Lake Erie. A fort should be located at each settlement. Such a colony barrier, Franklin thought, would have definite advantages:

> 1. They would be a great security to the frontiers of our other colonies; by preventing the incursions of the French and French Indians of Canada, on the back parts of Pennsylvania, Maryland, Virginia, and the Carolinas; and the frontiers of such new colonies would be much more easily defended, than those of the colonies last mentioned now can be, as will appear hereafter.
>
> 2. The dreaded junction of the French settlements in Canada, with those of Louisiana would be prevented.
>
> 3. In case of a war, it would be easy, from those new colonies, to annoy Louisiana by going down the Ohio and Mississippi; and the southern part of Canada by sailing over the lakes; and thereby confine the French within narrower limits.
>
> 4. [Friendship with the western Indians would be secured.]

> 5. The settlement of all the intermediate lands, between the present frontiers of our colonies on one side, and the lakes and Mississippi on the other; would be facilitated and speedily executed, to the great increase of Englishmen, English trade, and English power.[52]

The French success in the west and Indian raids during 1754 led settlers to flee in panic from the frontier, and convinced the ministry in England to send over regular troops.[53] The stratagem for 1755 was to be bold defensive action. The war was to be carried to the French in the west and in Nova Scotia, and the colonies were expected to build forts at close intervals. Shirley thought it indispensable to victory to construct a strong fort near the French at Niagara and at Crown Point. To this effect he sent commissioners to other colonies, who were successful in enlisting support. Shirley also called for using regulars in garrision duty, thus freeing provincials for offensive operations.[54] Governor Glen of South Carolina endorsed Shirley's ideas.[55]

Military defeat in 1754–5 taught the colonists the need for establishing a stable frontier perimeter. One anonymous author put it aptly: "If therefore we would secure our *American* dominions against the French, we must *out-fort* as well as *out-settle* them."[56] Franklin was sent by Pennsylvania authorities to build a line of forts in the northwestern part of the colony,[57] and Virginia's program for a chain of forts was already underway. Lewis Evans pinpointed the problem of establishing a frontier barrier. He believed that five thousand families had been ready to leave the Carolinas, Virginia, Maryland, Pennsylvania, New Jersey, and Connecticut to settle on the Ohio had it not been for Braddock's defeat and had land been granted. The main drawback, Evans felt, was that no land was available for settlers "And without Settlers, our Nation is not capable of defending large extended Frontiers."[58]

Southerners took the view that the real danger of French aggression was on their frontiers. A petition from merchants trading with Virginia and Maryland called attention to the precariousness of the southern colonies. The lack of defenses "both by Sea and by Land" and the large number of slaves and "domestic enemies" hindered the colonies' ability to resist a "French military force from their Mississippi and mobile settlements" and their "barbarous Allies."[59] Governor James Glen of South Carolina wanted forts built through the Cherokee country to the upper Mississippi in order to cut off Canada from Louisiana. Forts should also be located at the other extreme: at the confluence of the Ohio and Mississippi, between Tennessee and the Ohio River, and between the Ohio and Wabash Rivers. Glen hoped the crown as well as the colonies of New York, South Carolina, Maryland, Virginia, and Pennsylvania would contribute to the maintenance of these forts. If the northwestern frontier had been regarded as the primary theater of the war, Glen might have had his way.[60] Governor Dobbs of North Carolina suggested that a system of western forts be manned by "all the convicted Felons and Vagabonds transported to the Colonies," with guards placed over them at night.[61]

Governor Sharpe in the summer of 1756 built a fort on the Potomac River, about fifteen miles above Conogochieg, and Virginia militia of "seven of the most contiguous Counties" garrisoned Fort Loudoun near Winchester. Both colonies maintained Fort Cumberland.[62] Maryland provided, according to a requisition from Lord Loudoun, five hundred men for the "Immediate Defence of the Province" and in emergency to cooperate with the forces of other colonies operating on the Maryland frontier; but the colony would not send troops to garrison forts outside its borders. When the Forbes expedition in 1758 made Maryland's frontier safe, the colony lost all interest in frontier garrisons.[63] Sharpe deprecated the fact that a "Defensive War is the utmost any of our Assemblies will think of or provide."[64] It was wistful thinking on the part of the young Washington who had declared earlier: "I wish sincerely the three Colonies [including Pennsylvania] cou'd be brought to act in conjunction as our frontiers are so contiguous."[65] Both Virginia and Maryland, however, did contribute a few troops to Colonel John Stanwix's advanced guard in western Pennsylvania during 1757–8.[66]

A chief objective in the military posture for 1758 was to keep up a strong frontier defense line. Governor Pownall of Massachusetts had scouts on the northeastern frontier, patrolling the two hundred miles along the Penobscot and Kennebec River country.[67] Colonel Bouquet supervised the building of posts from Carlisle to the Ohio.[68] Forbes, in charge of the western army, expected that English mastery of the Ohio Valley would give security to the rest of the frontier and pave the way for invasion of Canada.[69] But he was dismayed over the negligence of Virginia, Maryland, and Pennsylvania in providing troops during the winter "for the protection of their frontiers and garrisioning the posts and footing we have got so nigh the Enemy;" there were too few regulars to perform in this capacity.[70] Instructions from England directed Forbes to restore Fort Duquesne or erect another in its place and the Governors of Virginia, Maryland, and Pennsylvania to offer assistance, otherwise failure to do so would "reflect the greatest Blame on their

Conduct."[71] Fortunately the French withdrew from the Ohio Valley in 1758 and, by the end of 1759, from the posts in New York and Niagara. New York troops were used to help repair the works at Niagara and Oswego, but the New York assembly provided for their subsistence only on a month-by-month basis.[72]

Meanwhile, Amherst, instructed by the home government to finish a defense line in the west between the forts on the Ohio and Fort Niagara "without retarding the Main Object" of attacking Canada,[73] dispatched Brigadier General Monckton from Fort Pitt to garrison the posts at Detroit, Michillimakinac, and elsewhere. In order to man these posts, British regulars were withdrawn from the frontiers of Pennsylvania, Virginia, and South Carolina. The colonies offered no assistance. With the conquest of Canada, Pennsylvania refused to provide levies for frontier garrisons outside the colony because it was felt that the victory now released enough British troops for this duty; Virginia and South Carolina withdrew their few troops from Monckton's garrison army because they were needed in the Cherokee War.[74]

But, from 1760-3, several of the colonies assisted in the frontier defense. Several hundred Virginia militia, under Colonels Adam Stephen and Andrew Lewis, and about five hundred British regulars roamed the frontier and occupied abandoned forts.[75] Amherst hoped Virginia troops would annoy the enemy should they return in the west and thereby prevent their joining in strength in Canada.[76] In 1761 Amherst sent two companies of New York militia to western forts.[77]

In 1763 the crown employed the idea of a "flying army" to protect the frontier; regulars were used rather than provincials, thus indicating a further imperialization of the frontier. Colonel Bouquet, at the head of a small force of Highlanders, Royal Americans, rangers from Lancaster and Cumberland counties, and assorted woodsmen,[78] not only was to keep the Indians in check but to catch the various banditti along the Pennsylvania, New Jersey, and Virginia frontiers, who were boldly plundering supplies going to Fort Pitt.[79] One remedy that Bouquet tried was to issue a proclamation on October 30, 1761 forbidding settlement west of the mountains of anyone without permission from the governor of his province – disobedience would lead to a trial by court martial.[80] The effect of the new guarded frontier upon the Indians was best expressed in the discomfiture of an Indian chief attending a conference at Easton in August 1761:

> When we look towards you, General Johnson, the Governor of Virginia and Brother Onas [Governor of Pennsylvania] we esteem you all as one; how comes it then that you do not speak all alike? We,

> your Brethren of the seven Nations, are penned up like Hogs; there are Forts all around us, and therefore We are apprehensive that Death is coming upon us.[81]

With the English now in control of the west, what was to be done in maintaining a frontier barrier? In December 1761 colonial governors were ordered not to grant any lands in Indian territory.[82] Proposals for mass settlement of immigrants beyond the frontier would be discouraged.[83] The creation of an imperial public domain by the Proclamation of 1763 coincided with the new policy to bring greater uniformity in colonial government east of the Alleghenies.[84] A line was drawn beyond which settlers could not go – except as the crown saw fit to move the barrier.

There were many who saw the prosperity and loyalty of the colonies linked to opening the doors of expansion. Franklin humorously warned that expansion was inevitable unless colonial midwives were to "stifle" the birth of every third or fourth child.[85] An anonymous publication in Edinburgh (1763) presented a more reasoned argument:

> So that, however valuable these our Colonies are (and that they are of great value, is certain) yet they may be made infinitely more so to *Britain* as a trading nation, conjoined with, and by a proper improvement of our new acquisition. For, if the Settlements here proposed were made, our old Colonies would see it their interest, to extend their Plantations, each as far as the *Forks.* This they would be encouraged to do, from the motives of gain, safety, undisturbed possession, the prospect of improving their lands at pleasure and to the best purposes, with the convenience of Navigation, whether for Export or Import, by the rivers that run from the *Apalachian* mountains into the *Ohio,* by the *Ohio* itself, and the *Mississippi.* Thus the old Colonies and the new one proposed, might be joined before many years to their unspeakable mutual help and interest.[86]

The colonists expected the British government to inaugurate a bold policy for the west – but also to recognize colonial rights and the need for expansion. Policy came in the form of sweeping edicts, with little thought to the realities of the colonial situation or to means of implementation. No wonder the colonists felt a sense of disillusionment, as voiced by William Smith: "The British affairs must now become so complicated and extensive, as to suffer immediately by Inattention – We in these Dispersions of that vast Empire grow sickly, and want aid from the prime source of political Influence."[87]

From the struggle for empire for nearly a century the colonists inadvertently evolved the conception of the frontier as a total entity, which they were ill-prepared to treat with, but which they could entrust to royal administration. The colonists, however, faced the reality of the pulling force of the frontier; the authorities at Whitehall did not – hence the stumbling block for imperial control of the west. Unmindful of the demographic aspects, British policy would be determined by mercantilist and military considerations. The colonists, on the other hand, would not regard the frontier as a fixed line or barrier constraining unorderly expansion but as a promised land, stretching from sea to sea, due the posterity of British Americans.

NOTES

[1] Buffington, "The Policy of Albany," *MVHR*, VIII (1922), 344–45.

[2] Bird, *Navies in the Mountains*, 36–37.

[3] By order of Simon Bradstreet, July 17, 1789, CA, Colonial Wars, II, 10.

[4] William Stoughton to Governor and Council of Conn., Dec. 12, 1694, *ibid.*, 243. New Hampshire petitioned the crown for funds, 200 troops, a "fourth rate man of war" to cruise off the eastern shores, and that Mass. be compelled to turn over ordnance stores for the protection of the eastern frontier. (Council of Trade and Plantations to the Queen, Nov. 8, 1708, *CSP*, XXIV, 138–39.)

[5] See Gov. Andrew Hamilton to Gov. Fletcher, June 26, 1696, *NJA*, 1st Ser., II, 114.

[6] Verner W. Crane, "Projects for Colonization in the South, 1684–1732," *MVHR*, XII (1926), 25–26. An effect of the colonial wars was Great Britain's encouraging of acquisition of lands on easy terms for immigrants to the southern frontier. (Sellers, *Charleston Business*, 110–11.)

[7] "Col. Hamilton's scheme for the Maintenance of Soldiers," Feb. 14, 1699, *NYCD*, IV, 679–80.

[8] *CSP*, XX, xviii.

[9] *CSP*, XVII, xxviii.

[10] Fox, *Heathcote*, 144–45.

[11] Leder, *Robert Livingston,* 164–66; see Chapter 1 and Livingston to the Board of Trade, May 13, 1701, *NYCD*, IV, 870–75.

[12] *Campbell's Newsletter*, June 1, 1703, in Weeks, ed., *Hist. Digest*, 45; Dillon, *Oddities of Colonial Legislation*, 295; Kimball, *Dudley*, 102–4.

[13] *CSP*, XX, xxiii.

[14] *The Boston News–Letter*, June 19, 1704 and Feb. 26, 1705, in Weeks, ed., *Hist. Digest*, 93 and 169, resp.

[15] Wraxall, *Abridgement of N.Y. Indian Records*, ed. McIlwain, xlv; Morgan, "The Five Nations," *MVHR*, XIII (1927), 177–79.

[16] Memorial of Wait Winthrop and John Leverett to Gov. Lovelace of N.Y., June 27, 1709, New York Colony Manuscripts (Letters of Governors), NYPL.

[17] Report of the Board of Trade on Proprietary Governments, Mar. 26, 1701, Jensen, ed., *English Historical Documents*, IV, 251.

[18] Spotswood to the Council of Trade and Plantations, Nov. 16, 1713, *CSP*, XXVII, 250–51; Morton, *Colonial Virginia*, II, 432–34; 436–37.

[19] Clifford K. Shipton, "The New England Frontier," *NEQ*, X (1937), 29.

[20] "To Lords of . . . Privy Council," Oct. 17, 1739, Barrett Wendell Papers on Relations between Mass. and N.H., MHS.

[21] Gov. Keith to the Board of Trade, Feb. 16, 1719, quoted in Phillips, *The Fur Trade*, I, 384–85.

[22] *Ibid.*, 386, 389. See Crane, "Projects for Colonization," *MVHR*, XII (1926), 30–31. The Board of Trade advocated the building of a string of forts on the southern frontier, which the S.C. agent, John Barnwell, had originally proposed; the scheme, however, did not meet the approval of the crown.

[23] Galfridus Gray to Lords of Trade, Jan. 26, 1725, *NJA*, 1st Ser., V, 107–9.

[24] Memorial of Gov. Robert Johnson of S.C., n.d. (between 1730–34), Bancroft transcripts (American Colonies), NYPL.

[25] Gov. Belcher's Speech to the Gen. Assembly, Boston, *Pennsylvania Gazette*, Feb. 10, 1731.

[26] E.g., Address of the Council to the Governor, Nov. 17, 1734, Horsmanden Papers, NYHS.

[27] Sipe, *Indian Wars of Pa.*, 121.

[28] Gov. Clinton to Gov. Morris, May 28, 1744 and Morris to Clinton, May 31, 1744, *Papers of Lewis Morris, NJHSC*, IV (1852), 188–89. R.I. during King George's War assumed more responsibility than usual, and, among various defense measures, erected seven "Watch and Ward Houses" to protect the coasts. *Pennsylvania Gazette*, Apr. 10, 1746.

[29] Shirley to John Stoddard, May 12, 1746, Shirley Papers, MHS.

[30] *Journal of the Legislative Council of N.Y.*, May 1, 1746, II, 924.

[31] Address of the Commons House of Assembly to Gov. Bull, *South Carolina Gazette*, July 18, 1740.

[32] Amos A. Ettinger, *James Edward Oglethorpe* (Oxford, 1936), 243; *South Carolina Gazette*, Apr. 14, 1743.

[33] For the policy of granting lands to veterans on the New England frontier, see Rising Lake Morrow, *Connecticut Influences in Western Massachusetts and Vermont (Tercentary Commission of the State of Conn.*, LVIII [New Haven, 1936]), 9–19.

[34] "OBSERVATIONS concerning the Increase of Mankind . . .," *FP*, IV, 233.

[35] Conner, *Poor Richard's Politics*, 93–95; Gerald Stourzh, *Benjamin Franklin and American Foreign Policy* (Chicago, 1954), 54.

[36] For the opening of the West to land speculators and the role of an Indian agent extraordinary and a member of the Ohio Company, see Howard Lewin, "A Frontier Diplomat: Andrew Montour," *Pennsylvania History*, XXXIII (1966), 153–186.

[37] Thomas L. Montgomery, *Report of the Commission to Locate the Site of the Frontier Forts of Pennsylvania*, 2 vols. (Harrisburg, 1916), II, 162; Morton, *Colonial Virginia*, II, 618–19.

[38] For comment on the Virginia–Pennsylvania rivalry and imperial policy, 1761–3, see Alfred P. James, *The Ohio Company: Its Inner History* (Pittsburgh, 1959), 118; Kenneth P. Bailey, *The Ohio Company of Virginia and the Westward Movement, 1748–92* (Glendale, Calif., 1939), 71, 82; Sewell E. Slick, *William Trent and the West* (Harrisburg, 1947), 25.

[39] E.g., the Susquehannah Company. See Julian P. Boyd, ed., *The Susquehannah Company Papers*, reprint ed. (Ithaca, 1962), I, xlii and II, xxxv.

[40] "Halifax's Observations on Robinson's Proposal," in Theodore C. Pease, ed., *Anglo–French Boundary Disputes in the West*, 1749–63, *IHSC*, XXVII *(French Series*, II [Springfield, 1936]), 111–13.

[41] Sec. Willard for the Gen. Ct. to Gov. Shirley, Dec. 28, 1752, Bancroft transcripts (Massachusetts Papers – Letters of Shirley and Willard), NYPL.

[42] Davidson, *War Comes to Quaker Pa.*, 106.

[43] See William A. Hunter, *Forts on the Pennsylvania Frontier, 1753–58* (Harrisburg, 1960), chapter 5.

[44] Neville B. Craig, *Lecture upon the Controversy between Pennsylvania and Virginia about the Boundary Line* (Pittsburgh, 1843), 6. Gov. Hamilton removed 200,000 acres along the Ohio for Pennsylvania troops.

[45] Gov. Benning Wentworth to Gov. Shirley, Mar. 22, 1752, Pepperrell Papers, MHS; "The Humble Address of the Council and Assembly," Dec. 11, 1754, Bouton, ed., *N.H. Provincial Papers*, VI, 324.

[46] "By Order of the General Assembly . . .," Apr. 17, 1754, New York Colony MSS (photostat), NYPL; James De Lancey to Gov. Wolcott, Apr. 22, 1754, Trumbull Papers, CSL.

[47] Fisher, *New Jersey as a Royal Province*, 337–38, 347.

[48] Koontz, *The Virginia Frontier, 1754–63*, 98–100. See also Appendix A, *ibid*: Dinwiddie to Earl of Halifax, Apr. 27, 1754, *Dinwiddie Corr.*, I, 135.

[49] Julian S. Corbett, *England in the Seven Years' War*, 2 vols. (New York, 1907), I, 24–27.

[50] Phillips, *Fur Trade*, I, 529; Schutz, *Pownall*, 41–48; Sawtelle, "Pownall and Some of His Activities," *MHSP*, LXIII (1930), 248.

[51] James De Lancey's Speech to the General Assembly, Aug. 20, 1754, *Journal of the Legislative Council of N.Y.*, II, 1162.

[52] "A Plan for Settling Two Western Colonies" (1754?), *FP*, V, 456–63.

[53] Newcastle to Albemarle, Sep. 5, 1754, *Anglo–French Boundary Disputes, IHSC*, XXVII (1936), 51; Darlington, ed., *Hist. of Col. Bouquet*, 88.

[54] Message from Gov. R.H. Morris to the Assembly, Mar. 22, 1755, PRO, CO, Vol. 15, LC; Shirley to Sir Thomas Robinson, Feb. 18, 1755, Parkman transcripts, XL, MHS.

[55] Shirley to Thomas Robinson, Camp at Oswego, Sep. 28, 1755, *ibid.*, MHS; James Glen to De Lancey, May 17, 1755, Gratz Collection (Colonial Governors), HSP.

[56] [anon] *State of the British and French Colonies in North America* (London, 1755), 37, Columbia University Special Colls.

[57] George A. Cribbs, "The Frontier Policy of Pennsylvania," *Western Pennsylvania Historical Magazine*, II (1919), 100–3; Dillon, *Oddities of Colonial Legislation*, 317. In 1757, 13,000 men were reportedly serving in a local, voluntary capacity in frontier garrisons or on patrol. Forts were located ten–twelve miles apart.

[58] Lawrence H. Gipson, ed., *Lewis Evans: To Which is Added Evans' 'A Brief Account of Pennsylvania'* [and *'Essays'* (1756) by Evans] (Philadelphia, 1939), 192.

[59] Petition and Remonstrance of the Merchants Trading with Virginia and Maryland, Jan. 1, 1757, PRO, CO, Vol. 18, LC.

[60] See Chapters 8 and 9; Brown, "Cherokee Chiefs," *Chronicles of Okla.*, XVI (1938), 6–8; Alden, *John Stuart*, 39–41; Hamer, "Anglo–French Rivalry," *NCHR* (1925), 306–13.

[61] Gov. Dobbs to the Board of Trade, Nov. 26, 1755, *NCCR*, V, 475.

[62] Dinwiddie to Earl of Halifax, June 20, 1757, Virginia Misc. Papers, Box 1, LC; Koontz, *The Virginia Frontier, 1754–63,* 67.

[63] Sharpe to Dinwiddie, Sep. 26, 1756, *Md. Archives*, VI, 488. Sharpe to Pitt, Oct. 22, 1757, *Pitt Corr.*, I, 121; High, "Horatio Sharpe" (Ph. D. diss.), 64; Schlesinger, "Maryland's Share in the Last Intercolonial War," *Md. Hist. Mag.*, VII (1912), 265–77.

[64] Sharpe to John Sharpe, Sep. 15, 1756, *Md. Archives*, VI, 485.

[65] Washington to Dinwiddie, June 1756, Fitzpatrick, ed., *Washington Writings,* I, 394. A Pa. officer thought Pa. ought to have a universal militia law, which would better enable the garrisoning of forts on the frontier and would allow provincials to carry the war into enemy territory. (Capt. Jos. Shippen, Jr. to Edward Shippen, Jan. 19, 1757, "Mil. Letters of Capt. Jos. Shippen," *PMHB*, XXXVI, 408.)

[66] Dinwiddie to Washington, Oct. 19, 1757, Hamilton, ed., *Letters to Washington*, II, 215; Hunter, *Forts on the Pa. Frontier*, 198, 208.

[67] Gov. Pownall to Pitt, June 8, 1758 and Sep. 30, 1758, *Pitt Corr.*, I, 265 and 360, resp.

[68] Stevens *et al., Bouquet Papers*, II, iii.

[69] "Plans of Operating on the Mississippi, Ohio . . .," Feb. 1, 1758, James, ed., *Forbes Writings*, 36.

[70] Forbes to Pitt, Oct. 20, 1758, Parkman transcripts, XLII, MHS.

[71] Forbes to Bouquet, Oct. 25, 1758, Stevens *et al.*, *Bouquet Papers*, II, 585; Pitt to Governors of Va., Md., and Pa., Jan. 23, 1759, *Pitt. Corr.*, II, 15.

[72] Pitt to Gen. Amherst, Mar. 10, 1759, *ibid.*, 64; Amherst to Pitt, June 19, 1759, *ibid.*, 122; Lt. Gov. De Lancey to Pitt, Oct. 28, 1759, *ibid.*, 203–4; Pitt to Governors of Pa., Md., Va., N.C., and S.C., Jan. 7, 1760, *ibid.*, 236.

[73] Pitt to Gen. Amherst., June 14, 1760, *ibid.*, 302.

[74] Stanwix to Pitt, Mar. 17, 1760, Parkman transcripts, XLIII, MHS; Carr, "Defense of the Frontier" (Ph. D. diss.), 8. For the role of Rogers' Rangers in this assignment, see John R. Cuneo, *Robert Rogers of the Rangers* (New York, 1959), Chapter 11.

[75] Morton, *Colonial Virginia*, II, 823.

[76] Amherst to Gov. Fauquier, July 2, 1761, PRO, WO:34, XXXVII, LC.

[77] Amherst to Pitt, May 4, 1761, *Pitt. Corr.*, II, 426.

[78] Sipe, *Indian Wars of Pa.*, 439–40. See chapter 9.

[79] Carr, "Defense of the Frontier" (Ph. D. diss.), 158.

[80] Bailey, *Ohio Company*, 222, 225. Precedent for Bouquet's order of 1761 and the Proclamation of 1763 can be found in the authority given to the Governors of S.C. and Ga. in 1759 to prevent settlers from going south of the "Alabamaha." Board of Trade to the Lords of the Committee, Apr. 27, 1763, Boyd, ed., *Susquehannah Company Papers*, II, 213–4.

[81] Conference at Easton, Aug. 31, 1761, Sylvester Stevens and Donald H. Kent, eds., *The Papers of Henry Bouquet: Indian Affairs, 1758-65*, mimeograph (Harrisburg, 1943).

[82] *Pennsylvania Journal*, Dec. 8, 1763; Morton, *Colonial Virginia*, II, 740–41. By the Proclamation of 1763, however, governors could grant lands to naval officers who had served in the Louisbourg and Quebec campaigns.

[83] E.g., Bouquet's refusal to allow Thomas Cresap's plan in 1760 of settling Germans and Switzers in the Ohio Valley. Morton, *Colonial Virginia*, II, 740–41. In 1763 there was much talk of the proposed establishment of a colony (New South Wales) on the Ohio under the proprietorship of the Prince of Wales. *Georgia Gazette*, June 9, 1763.

[84] Charles L. Mowat, "The Enigma of William Drayton," *Florida Historical Quarterly*, XXII (1943), 7ff. Witness the establishment of government in East Florida and the efforts at greater royalization of the colonies in the pre-Revolutionary War decade.

[85] Alfred O. Aldridge, *Benjamin Franklin: Philosopher and Man* (Philadelphia, 1965), 147.

[86] [anon.], *The Expediency of Securing Our American Colonies by Settling The Country Adjoining the River Mississippi . . .* (Edinburgh, 1763), in Clarence W. Alvord and Clarence E. Carter, eds., *The Critical Period, 1763–65* (Springfield, 1915), 142–43.

[87] William Smith to Major Gates, Nov. 22, 1763, Gates Papers, I, 140, NYHS.

CHAPTER XI

BOUNDARY DISPUTES

Perhaps no other area brought the colonies into greater confrontation with each other than did the troublesome boundary disputes. These controversies provided a constant irritant that would raise eventually the whole question of authority over disputed land claims and the public domain. At face value it would appear that these disputes only contributed negatively toward union. But in addition to calling attention to the over-all problem of need for higher authority over land disputes, the contention over boundaries led to involvement of intercolonial committees of arbitration, colonial agents in London, the Board of Trade, committees of the Privy Council, and the Privy Council as a Supreme Court of Appeals. Enmity generated from boundary troubles hindered cooperation in military affairs during the colonial and Indian wars. For the purposes of this chapter the form of attempts to arrive at solutions will be noted primarily rather than the details of the disputes and litigation.

Rhode Island and Massachusetts

By its charter of 1663 Rhode Island was granted the territory three miles to the east and northeast of Narragansett Bay. Plymouth Colony also laid claim to the area. In 1664 the royal commissioners, investigating the New England governments, decided upon Narragansett Bay as the boundary between the two colonies until further determination by the crown. After Plymouth was incorporated into Massachusetts, the original claims were reasserted, while the crown did nothing to clarify the issue. Both Rhode Island and Massachusetts reinforced their claims by stating that they had settled and placed forts in the area.[1]

In 1694 the town of Attleboro was founded in the disputed area. The boundary question rose to a boiling point in 1731 when the town attempted to levy and collect taxes.[2] Rhode Island forbade any exercising of authority or levying of taxes by the town until the boundary should be finally determined. Commissioners were appointed by Rhode Island to meet with any that Massachusetts might name, and if negotiation were unsuccessful the case should be sent to England, provided the inhabitants of the disputed area contributed £ 200 toward expenses and the other parties £ 4000. This stipulation, however, was soon repealed.[3]

In January 1731 Massachusetts appointed commissioners. The decision of the commissioners of both colonies was to be final. But the Rhode Island commissioners would not agree with Massachusetts' insistence upon the "Patauckett" River as the boundary. In the succeeding two years, the Massachusetts committee was continued and, without any negotiation with Rhode Island, the General Court instructed agent Francis Wilks in England to "take all possible Care that no Determination be made which may affect Property in the Settlements of the Boundaries. . . between this province and the Colony of Rhode-Island." Meanwhile, Massachusetts officials were ordered to exercise jurisdiction over Attleboro and to arrest all persons attempting to enforce the authority of Rhode Island.[4]

Three commissioners from each colony met in 1733, but they could not agree; therefore it was decided to have commissioners from "neighbouring Provinces" to serve as umpires.[5]

Since neither colony could agree on the umpires, Rhode Island decided to appeal to the King. The petition reached the Privy Council in December 1734, and then it went to the Board of Trade, where it stayed until May 1738. The Board ordered both parties to appoint commissioners from neighboring provinces to settle the line and the governors of both colonies to keep the peace. Francis Wilks, the Massachusetts agent, had unsuccessfully tried to have the earlier order of the royal commissioners of 1664 stand and the Rhode Island petition dismissed. Eventually, the Board of Trade found the whole matter of boundary disputes so time-consuming that it refused to consider any petition against a previous decision by the Board regarding boundaries or other special matters from the colonies – and the Privy Council also announced that it would hear no petitions or appeals from decisions of the Board of Trade unless agents gave bond for the expenses involved. The Board of Trade, however, in sending the case back to the colonies, did stipulate that the five oldest councilors of New York, New Jersey, and Nova Scotia should constitute a commission of arbitration.[6]

One other attempt was made by the two colonies to settle the controversy themselves, but again they disagreed, and the question was turned over to the royal intercolonial commission.[7]

The arbitration commission met April 7-30, 1741 at Providence. Daniel Updike and William Bollan argued for Rhode Island and John Read, Samuel Wells, and William Shirley for Massachusetts. The judgment rendered on June 30 said the 1627 grant of the Council of New England to Plymouth and the 1629 grant to William Bradford were invalid because one corporation could not create another; the 1664 order by the royal commissioners had been intended only as a temporary expedient. Most of the disputed territory was given to Rhode Island. In 1742 both colonies appealed; but the Board of Trade dismissed both appeals in 1744, and again when they were submitted two years later. On May 28, 1746 the king-in-council finally confirmed the decision. Five Massachusetts towns were ceded to Rhode Island.[8] Thus recourse to an intercolonial commission from colonies not party to the dispute had brought about an effective determination.

Rhode Island and Connecticut

The Narragansett country – between the Mystic and Pawcatuck Rivers – was a source of violent contention between Massachusetts, Connecticut, and Rhode Island. The king's commissioners in 1665 took over the disputed territory as a temporary special preserve for the crown, naming it the "King's Province." But Connecticut continued to claim not only this tract but also all land to the Narragansett Bay, according to its charter grant. Unfortunately Rhode Island's charter had also included the Narragansett country. The New England Confederation and special commissions had tried unsuccessfully to settle the dispute. During the period of the Dominion of New England, Governor Andros repudiated Connecticut's claim.

With Connecticut appealing Andros's decision, the Attorney General of England rendered an opinion in the colony's favor. In 1698, an attempt of the two colonies to settle a line failed. Then the dispute was appealed to England, with Henry Ashurst acting as agent for Connecticut and Captain Joseph Sheffield for Rhode Island. But the two colonies did not wait for a Board of Trade decision, and in 1702 appointed commissioners, who reached an agreement in 1703. In 1714, commissioners were appointed to survey the line – from the "middle channel of Pawquatuck River, alias Narragansett River" at the "mouth of Ashaway River," and from there in a straight line to the southwest corner of the Warwick grant and then due north to the Massachusetts border. The commissioners, however, did not finish the survey, and when they met again, not until 1720, they disagreed, and the dispute was referred to the Board of Trade. The Board's report to the Privy Council accepted Rhode Island's position but recommended that the charters of both colonies be annulled and both colonies be annexed to New Hampshire. From 1724-8, Rhode Island and Connecticut appointed commissioners with plenary powers to determine the line – and in the meantime the king-in-council accepted the line of 1703 and 1714.[9] Thus the two corporate colonies, with their independent charters in danger by a protracted boundary dispute, settled the matter themselves.

Massachusetts and Connecticut

The boundary relations between Massachusetts and Connecticut posed two major problems: the boundary line at Woodstock, Suffield, Enfield, Simsbury, and Windsor and, secondly, the jurisdiction over the Mohegan country.

Referrals to intercolonial commissions would eventually lead to a settlement of the boundary line. In 1694 the two colonies considered a meeting of commissioners, but Massachusetts begged off until a future time because the joint prosecution of the war "against the common Enemy" was deemed more urgent then "the adjusting of Lines." The reply of the Massachusetts General Court also reveals the delicacy of intercolonial action. Professing a willingness to negotiate an "orderly decision" on the boundary line, the General Court considered it best to wait for the lessening of Indian hostilities:

> It is easy to conjecture what effect it will have abroad, that disputes should now be raysed betwixt Neighbours and fellow Subjects about Lines and boundaries and be neglectful of common Interest, which the Enemy stands ready to decide the controversy by attempting the possession of the whole, we would hope asserting of your Authority for the restraint and Suppressing of any exorbitant and unwarrantable actions attempted by any of the people within your Government will prevent any inconvenience by the deferring of your Affayre. We shall take alike care effectually to restrain any of ours, who upon conviction of their being Aggressors therein shall be proceeded against with the severity of Law.[10]

In 1695 both colonies appointed commissioners,[11] but, meeting in the following year, they could not decide upon a method to run the line, so that the Massachusetts Governor "resolved to assert and maintain their Line anciently run by men of approved and unquestioned Skill which fully takes in your Town [Windsor?]."[12] Connecticut, desiring to end the controversy once and for all, sent John Butcher and William Whiting to survey the line according to the boundaries of the Massachusetts Charter. The northern line was put at 42° 4' (present line today 42° 3'), but Massachusetts contended the starting point was too far north. Meanwhile, Connecticut settlers moved into lands at Enfield and Suffield over the protests of Massachusetts.[13]

In 1700 Connecticut commissioners drew up proposals for a determination of the line from the two colonies, but a bi-colony surveying team in 1702 could not reach agreement.[14] A letter from the crown arrived urging an immediate solution in order to "continue that good Neighbourhood which all Her Majesties good Subjects owe to each other."[15]

In 1708 Connecticut appointed commissioners with full power to meet those appointed by Massachusetts to determine the boundary – if Massachusetts refused the joint survey, an appeal would be made to the crown. Massachusetts reacted negatively and both colonies petitioned to the home government. But Connecticut was soon discouraged from seeking a settlement in England: the colony's agent, Henry Ashurst, died, the Mohegan controversy called for attention, bringing an appeal was expensive, and, as noted in the dispute with Rhode Island, the independent status of the colony was under fire in England.[16]

Commissioners from the two colonies in 1713 awarded Massachusetts all of her old border towns, even though they dipped south of the line into Connecticut. "Equivalent lands" – improved lands in western Massachusetts and in New Hampshire – were given to Connecticut as compensation. Of the disputed territory Connecticut received only a small tract near Windsor.[17]

The towns ceded to Massachusetts, however, were dissatisfied and wished to be included in Connecticut. In 1747 Connecticut appointed a committee to hear petitions from Enfield, Woodstock, and Suffield. It was decided that the 1713 decision should hold, having been ratified by the assemblies of both governments: namely Windsor to remain within the jurisdiction of Connecticut and Woodstock, Suffield, and Enfield under Massachusetts.[18] But in 1749 Massachusetts took up the controversy, appointing three commissioners.[19] Connecticut responded, and subsequently commissioners of the two colonies met irregularly throughout the eighteenth century – with a compromise reached in 1804.

Although the Mohegan case was an intra-territorial dispute in Connecticut, it brought on intercolonial arbitration.

The case grew out of a jurisdictional grant conferred upon John Mason, Deputy Governor and agent for Connecticut, by Uncas, Chief of the Mohegans, in 1659. Mason surrendered his authority to Connecticut in in 1660. The lands involved took in roughly the northern two-thirds of New London County and the southern two-thirds of Windham County. Connecticut claimed both property and jurisdictional rights. Since Mason's turning over the territory was under a cloud of illegality, the Mohegans brought suit.[20] In 1705 Governor Dudley of Massachusetts, at the head of a royal commission appointed by the Privy Council,[21] tried the case *ex parte,* since Connecticut objected to the legality of the commission. Judgment was rendered in favor of the Indians, restoring to them four tracts of land which they had been deprived of – north of Lyme and a tract within the township of New London. Since a necessary royal command was not forthcoming, the decision was not enforced.

Henry Ashurst, the agent for the colony, appealed to the Privy Council in February 1706, basing Connecticut's claims upon conquest and Uncas having submitted to the colony's authority. On June 10, 1706, the Privy Council appointed Governor Cornbury of New York as a commissioner to further hear the dispute; the Board of Trade named the other members of the commission – the eleven members of the New York Council. This commission of review did not change the decision of 1705.

When the Mohegans began to complain of new trespass on their lands, Connecticut appointed a committee in 1720 to settle claims between landholders and the Indians. The committee's report to quiet the claims for the time being was ratified by the Assembly. The colony-appointed guardian of the Mohegans, John Mason, of the same name as his forebearer, unsuccessfully in 1723 and 1725 made applications to the Assembly for redress, which led Connecticut to replace Mason with new guardians. Nevertheless, Mason accompanied the Mohegan chief, Mahomet, to England in 1735 where Mason pleaded the case of the Indians before the Board of Trade. Acting upon the Board's advice, the Privy Council in April 1737 established a new commission of review – to consist of the Governor and Council of New York and the Governor and Assistants of Rhode Island (five to be a quorum and no appeal).

On May 24, 1738 the royal commission – two New York Councilors and the Governor and six Assistants of Rhode Island – convened at Norwich, Connecticut. Disagreeing with the Rhode Island majority, the New York members withdrew. The Rhode Island commissioners then declared the Indians as the rightful owners of the lands, except for one tract – thereby reversing the judgment of 1705. Samuel and John Mason, sons of the late guardian, appealed to the king-in-council as did the New York members to the Board of Trade. In

1741 a new commission of review was ordered, with the New York and New Jersey Governors and Councils to make up the commission.

Six commissioners convened at Greenwich, Connecticut on May 4, 1743 and ordered parties to appear at Norwich on June 28. President Colden considered the proceedings as a re-hearing much like a chancery review, open to an entire re-examination of the case. The commissioners, however, were soon divided on the sovereignty status of the Indians. Eventually, on August 16, the commissioners issued a decree that the 1705 decision was null and void, except for lands confirmed to the Mohegans by the Assembly in 1721. An appeal from the Mohegans remained dormant from 1746 to 1756, when the Privy Council rejected it. Not until 1773 did the crown get around to affirm the judgment of 1743.[22]

Massachusetts and New Hampshire

Bad blood had long existed between the settlers of New Hampshire and the parent colony. King William's War stimulated the granting of lands by both colonies, and frequently these were the same lands. To the New Hampshire point of view, as later stated in a petition to the crown:

> one special circumstance which in effect determined the said disputes was that the people of the Massachusetts being much more numerous than those of N. Hampshire (at least 40 to one), would rate assess and tax the persons who were settled really within the Province of New Hampshire and to the publick charges in the Massachusetts, and by their power and numbers destrain [sic] for such taxes and even carry off and imprison the New Hampshire inhabitants for pretended trespasses and try them and their causes in the Courts in the Massachusetts, where to plead to the jurisdiction (when the partys themselves were to be the sole Judges in the matter) was to no manner of purpose.

Since the tax and fine for trespass amounted to five or ten shillings, it was not large enough a sum to appeal to England; "nor could a young settler possibly bear the expense of an appeal, and if he had, it would only have settled the status of his own land." New Hampshire made efforts in 1705, 1711, 1713, and 1715 to have commissioners of both colonies meet to settle the boundary, but not until 1719 did commissioners meet at Newbury, Massachusetts. This effort, however, came to naught because the Massachusetts commissioners insisted on extending the northern boundary of the colony to cut off the eastern towns of New Hampshire. At the heart of the dispute was the drawing of a line parallel to the Merrimac River – which the king-in-council in 1677 said should be three miles north of the river, but which the Massachusetts Charter of 1691 did not mention.[23]

Other attempts in the 1720's to set up a commission of the two colonies failed, and the colonial agents did not make much headway in England. Royal instructions to Governor Belcher in 1730, however, recommended to the assemblies of the two colonies to appoint commissioners from the neighboring governments. Massachusetts named three men, and New Hampshire, finding two of the three acceptable, named only the Governor of Rhode Island. But New Hampshire protested Massachusetts's giving plenary authority to the commissioners contrary to the royal instructions which had said that final determination was up to the crown. Thus negotiations broke up before the meeting could take place.[24]

Petitions from the colonial agents in 1732-3 finally led to the Privy Council, on recommendation of the Board of Trade, appointing an intercolonial commission to consist of the five eldest councilors from New York, New Jersey, Rhode Island, and Nova Scotia – five of whom would constitute a quorum. From August to October 1737, nine commissioners met at Hampton, New Hampshire, with Philip Livingston as President. With cooperation from Massachusetts, it was not necessary for the commission to act *ex parte*.[25] The commission decided to keep the three-mile parallel and where the line was in doubt it should be run from such point due west until it met another colony. Both colonies appealed to England, and the controversy was a factor in naming a separate governor for New Hampshire.[26] Both provinces were commanded to appoint surveyors to mark boundaries according to the 1737 decision. Massachusetts refused to comply. A final judgment of the crown in 1739 gave the whole disputed area to New Hampshire plus a fourteen-mile tract in width mostly west of the Merrimac, which New Hampshire had never claimed.[27] Thus again a long-standing boundary dispute was settled by a royal review commission.

New York, Pennsylvania, and New England

The New York-Connecticut boundary dispute developed from the early Dutch boundary line and the overlapping and ambiguity of the colonial charters. Rye had become part of Connecticut in 1665 and Bedford also seceded from New York in 1697. Connecticut's efforts to set up a bi-colony commission in 1698 failed. The king-in-council in 1699 confirmed Bedford and Rye as under Connecticut jurisdiction, and ordered a survey of the line in 1700. New York, however, refused to accept the boundary, which led Connecticut to appeal to the king.[28]

Eventually both colonies agreed in 1719 to appoint commissioners to survey the line, but not until after a long correspondence did the colonies begin the survey, which was soon discontinued because of the ensuing differences of interpretation. In 1731 a joint survey was completed, to which both colonies agreed.[29]

Between 1750 and 1755 several petitions were submitted to the Connecticut legislature, most notably from the Susquehannah Land Company, to settle or colonize lands beyond the Hudson. The Company challenged the jurisdiction of the Penns to land lying within the sea-to-sea claims of the Connecticut Charter. Protests of William Johnson on behalf of the Iroquois and the Penns influenced the crown and the Board of Trade to refuse to act upon the request. William Johnson advised the crown to close the frontier, and in January 1763 the Board of Trade recommended banning all western settlement, which was fixed into policy by the famous Proclamation later in the year.[30]

At the end of King George's War, Governor Wentworth of New Hampshire began to grant lands west of the Connecticut in defiance of the New York boundary. In 1749 he asked Governor Clinton of New York to define the boundary, but at the same time erected a settlement at Bennington, thirty-five miles west of the Connecticut. Clinton's successor, Cadwallader Colden, and Wentworth agreed that both sides should appeal to the king. Wentworth immediately petitioned, but Colden, thinking he had such a perfect case, delayed his appeal until 1753. Meanwhile, Wentworth went against an agreement he had with Colden not to allow any further settlement in the disputed area, and he proceeded to grant some three and a half million acres between Lake Champlain and the Connecticut River. In 1763 Colden issued a proclamation asserting New Yorks's claim to territory and jurisdiction west of the river. The following year the king-in-council confirmed the New York claim to the Connecticut River boundary – and the struggle for an independent "Vermont" was on.[31]

The boundary dispute between New York and Massachusetts stemmed from conflicting charter rights, and especially from the grant to the Duke of York of all land west of the Connecticut River. The violence over the claims is aptly told in Irving Mark's *Agrarian Conflicts in New York* and need not concern us here.

In 1739 Massachusetts unsuccessfully attempted to have commissioners appointed from both colonies to settle the dispute.[32] Again in 1752 New York declined to meet with commissioners appointed by Massachusetts. When disturbances quieted, New York appointed commissioners, but acting Governor James De Lancey held them back on grounds that "I cannot send Commissioners to meet to debate upon they know not what."[33]

Massachusetts speculators continued to encroach upon Livingston Manor and Van Rensselaer property; by the end of February 1755 a vigilante war raged on the disputed border.

In 1757 Governor Charles Hardy of New York presented the matter to the Lords Commissioners for Trade and Plantations.[34] Lieutenant Governor Colden in September 1763 sought a royal determination of the dispute and he warned that the home government had a vested interest in the outcome:

> The New England Governments are formed on republican principles and these principles are zealously inculcated on their youth, in opposition to the principles of the Constitution of Great Britain. The Government of New York, on the contrary, is established, as nearly as may be, after the model of the English Constitution. Can it then be good Policy to diminish the extent of Jurisdiction in His Majesty's Province of New York, to extend the power and influence of the others.[35]

New York and New Jersey

Contention over the New York-New Jersey boundary was rooted in the 1664 proprietary grant to Lords Berkeley and Carteret from the Duke of York.[36] Surveyors of both New York and East New Jersey ran a line which was approved by both governments in the 1690's.[37] In 1719 both colonies appointed commissioners to re-determine the line. The New York commissioners refused to complete the boundary, claiming faulty instruments, although a western terminus was decided upon.[38]

Recurring border strife embittered relations between the two colonies. In February 1748 New Jersey passed an act for running the boundary according to the unfinished survey of 1719 subject to royal approval. The New York Assembly, however, instructed its agent in England, Robert Charles, to secure a disallowance of the New Jersey law. Ferdinand John Paris, the New Jersey agent, tried to offset Charles's tactics. After holding up a decision for four years in order to obtain documentation, the Board of Trade in 1753 decided that New Jersey could not unilaterally resolve disputes concerning royal grants. The act for running the boundary line was disallowed.[39]

With severe rioting in Orange County, Governor Belcher requested the crown for a determination of the boundary. Lieutenant Governor De

Lancey in the meantime refused to cooperate with Belcher in preserving the peace or running a temporary line. In March 1754 De Lancey obtained a vote from the New York legislature to take the whole northern section of New Jersey into New York, and he issued a proclamation accordingly. Convinced of the validity of the New York claim, the legislature also voted to ask the king to set up a commission to settle the dispute. This act, however, was disallowed in June 1755 because it was contrary to the policy already established that boundary questions involving private property should go to the king-in-council in the form of an appeal.[40]

Further petitions by Governor Belcher and the East Jersey proprietors were to no avail. In December 1762 New York passed an act to submit the controversy to the king, and in June 1763 New Jersey did the same. In the meantime New York and New Jersey appointed their own boundary commissioners.[41] The crown did an about face from its earlier position and approved the boundary referral legislation. Thus the way was open for a royal review commission (which convened at Hartford, July 1769-July 1770) to settle the dispute.

Pennsylvania and Maryland

Proprietary holdings interested the Baltimores in boundary disputes even though Maryland was a royal colony from 1691 to 1715. Charles, third Lord Baltimore, in 1708 and 1709 petitioned the Queen to nullify an order-in-council of 1685, which had given Pennsylvania an outlet to the sea and had divided the peninsula between the Chesapeake and Delaware bays at midpoint west from Cape Henlopen, with Maryland allocated lands west and south of the line. Both petitions were denied. Actually the charters of both colonies had assumed a boundary line at the fortieth parallel – but no one knew its precise location. During Queen Anne's War, settlers in the disputed area had irritated both proprietaries in their refusal to pay taxes or quitrents. Periodically after the war, violence erupted; thus in 1723 Hannah Penn, executrix for the Penn lands, and Charles, fifth Lord Baltimore, concluded an agreement for eighteen months that no one be molested.[42] But attempts to exercise authority by both colonies over the disputed area again produced violence.

In 1732 Charles, Lord Baltimore and John, Thomas, and Richard Penn agreed to run the boundary from Cape Henlopen fifteen miles south of Philadelphia and to establish a joint commission to survey the line. During the cold winter the commissioners met at New Castle, which was to be the center for an arc twelve miles in radius to form the northern boundary of the Delaware counties. Faulty deeds, poor maps, and illness of the commissioners hampered the survey. Conferences lasted until November 24, 1733. The presiding commissioner, Governor Samuel Ogle of Maryland blamed the Pennsylvania commissioners, of whom the Pennsylvania Governor was one, for not cooperating.[43]

Since the matter had reached an impasse, Lord Baltimore renewed his claims to the Lower (Delaware) Counties on Pennsylvania's side of the transpeninsular line. The Board of Trade remained noncommittal towards the dispute, but the crown advised the Penns to bring suit in equity to protect their claim to the Lower Counties, and on June 21, 1735 a bill was filed in "His Majesty's High Court of Chancery" against Lord Baltimore.[44]

Outrages continued along the border. A newspaper item of 1737 reflects the extent of the border war:

> We hear that in the Jarrs happening lately between the Inhabitants of that Province *[Pennsylvania]* and those of *Maryland* several have been killed and wounded and that the Governor of *Maryland* has issued a Proclamation, offering 100 l. *per* Head reward for taking 4 Pennsylvania Men named in the Proclamation, of which *Samuel Smith Esq.* Sheriff of Lancaster County, is one.[45]

In 1738 the crown persuaded the litigant parties to come to an agreement to stay the violence and to work out a temporary settlement.[46] Commissioners and surveyors were appointed, but nothing came out of their meeting from December 5, 1738 to May 4, 1739.[47]

Fresh fuel was added to the fire when a decision was finally rendered in the chancery suit in 1750, which went against Maryland in supporting the 1732 agreement. Charles, Lord Baltimore died in the same year, and his successor, Frederick, and Thomas Penn entered into the controversy with verve.[48]

Commissioners of the two colonies now met intermittently. At New Castle, from November 15–28, 1750, they agreed upon the exact center of the line but failed to decide whether the center was to be the radius or the periphery; they also had to determine the precise location of Cape Henlopen in order to run the transpeninsular boundary and to set up a tangent for the north-south line. William Parsons and John Watson, surveyors for the Penns, and John Emory and Thomas Jones for Lord Baltimore were directed to go immediately to Cape Henlopen and commence a survey at a point on Fenwick Island. Meeting near Fenwick Island from April 22–29, 1751, the commissioners disagreed on the true location of Cape Henlopen, but they did consent to run a line due west from a point on the verge of the main ocean. As the line approached Chesapeake Bay, the commissioners again disagreed and adjourned.[49]

In 1760 seven men from each colony, including the governors, were appointed to run the boundary lines. The commissioners held a series of meetings: at New Castle, November 18, 1760; Chester Town in Kent County, Maryland, March 25–June 26, 1761; New Castle, October 19, 1761 to April 30, 1762; the house of Solomon Turpin near the "fifteen mile post," July 29–30, 1762; New Castle, September 14–17, 1762, April 29–30, July 15–23, and November 30–December 10, 1763.[50]

With general agreement reached on the bounds, the Penns and Frederick, sixth Lord Baltimore gave the surveying task to two of the best surveyors in England, who arrived in Philadelphia on November 15, 1763, and immediately began their work. In 1764, the "gentlemen commissioners" from Pennsylvania and Maryland inspected and accepted the arc of the northern boundary of the Lower Counties and also the north-south line with Maryland. At the end of 1764, Charles Mason and Jeremiah Dixon were ready to begin the survey of the east-west Pennsylvania-Maryland line – the proprietors having agreed to run the boundary along a latitude circle fifteen miles south of Philadelphia.[51] The settlement of this east-west line was long overdue. The disputed area at the Susquehanna River had been the scene of recurring violence, going back to the bloody encounters of the 1730's, known as the "Conojacular War."[52]

Virginia and North Carolina

Dispute over the Virginia-North Carolina boundary arose over a no-man's land fifteen miles wide between the colonies. The area presented problems not only in conflicts over land titles but also over trade and cattle ranging.

The first offer to settle the boundary by a joint commission was made by the Virginia House of Burgesses in 1705 in a resolution:

> That the Best way to prevent any further Encroachments being made by the Government of *North Carolina* on the Inhabitants of This Colony, is to Make provision as soon as possible for Laying out and Ascertaining the Boundaries between this Government and that of *North Carolina* and That Commissioners be Appointed and Impowered by his Excellency with the Advice and Consent of the Council to Treat with Such Commissioners as Shall be Appointed by the Government of *Carolina* for Effecting The Same.[53]

North Carolina refused to accept the offer of negotiation, and instead began to run the dividing line "without the least notification" to the Virginia authorities. Virginia ordered the halting of any further "surveys or entrys" by North Carolina "for any of the lands in controversy."[54]

In 1709 the Lords of Trade recommended that Virginia and North Carolina establish a joint commission to survey the disputed boundary. Thus North Carolina appointed John Lawson and Edward Mosely and Virginia named Nathaniel Harrison and Philip Ludwell. A squabble over the exact location of the starting point, Weyanoke Creek (North Carolina held this to be the Nottoway River and the Virginians, Wicocon Creek), and the civil war in Carolina between the followers of Thomas Cary and Lieutenant Governor Edward Hyde brought an end to their meeting.[55]

The first real step toward settlement came in 1715 when Governor Spotswood and Governor Charles Eden of Carolina agreed upon a compromise plan to run the line. The proposal was forwarded to the Board of Trade and the proprietors. The proprietors informed the Governor of North Carolina to appoint commissioners but apparently failed to notify the Board of Trade, and crown approval was withheld until more definite information could be secured.[56]

Spotswood frequently sought the Carolina Governor as well as the Board of Trade to settle the boundary as quickly as possible because of the anarchy in the contested area,

> for I am of opinion that it were much better for both Governments to lose the Land in controversy than to leave undecided, for as it is impossible to restrain people from seating themselves on that Land, where they live without either Religion or Government. It may be very difficult when their numbers increase to reduce them again to either.[57]

The Virginia Governor threatened on occasion to proceed with the boundary survey unilaterally and to use force to remove all persons "seated there without any lawful Authority."[58] Spotswood also feared that if word should be spread of the value of the frontier, such as "that there are gold and silver mines in these parts towards the Mountains," there would be such a population boom that it would be difficult to settle the boundary line let alone the jurisdiction.[59] Indeed as one contemporary Virginian in a tract published in 1724 said, the "disputed bounds" was "an asylum for the runagates of both countries."[60]

In 1727 the crown approved the compromise plan of 1715. Thereupon North Carolina appointed a commission consisting of

Christopher Gale, Edward Moseley, William Little, and John Lovick, and Virginia appointed William Byrd, William Dandridge, and Richard Fitz-William. In addition were the surveyors: Alexander Irvine and William Mayo for Virginia and Samuel Swan and commissioner Edward Moseley for North Carolina. Or let William Byrd himself introduce the commissioners:

> They therefore appointed Steddy (William Byrd) and Merryman (Nathaniel Harrison), Commissioners, on the part of Virginia to Execute that Order, and Astrolabe (William Mayo) and Capricorn (John Allen, whom Irvine replaced) to be the Surveyors. But Merryman dying, Firebrand (Richard Fitz-William) and Meanwell (William Dandridge) made Interest to fill his Place. Most of the Council enclin'd to favour the last, because he had offered his Services before he knew that any pay wou'd belong to the Place. But Burly (Rev. James Blair) one of the Honorable Board, perceiving his Friend Firebrand wou'd lose it, if it came to the vote, propos'd the Expedient of sending 3 Commissioners, upon so difficult and hazardous an Expedition. To this a majority agreed, being unwilling to be thought too frugal of the Publick Money. Accordingly they were both joined with Steddy in this commission. . . . (North Carolina) named Jumble (Christopher Gale), Shoebrush (John Lovick), Plausible (Edward Moseley), and Puzzle Cause (William Little), being the Flower and Cream of the Council of that Province.[61]

Thus begins the most famous journal of a boundary survey in America and an early classic in hilarity, which the reader can easily avail himself of.

Suffice it to say here that the joint commissioners met at Coratuck Inlet on March 5, 1728, with the Virginians conceding to the North Carolina interpretation. By March 14, the team reached the Dismal Swamp. Then they proceeded to the Meherrin River, a distance of seventy-three miles from the starting point, whereupon, because of the climate and snakes, the survey was suspended. It resumed on September 20. Although a bitter dispute ensued over the line above the Roanoke (North Carolina had instructed the commissioners not to go beyond thirty or forty miles above the river, but the line now reached fifty miles), the commissioners continued the survey. Finally the line was terminated in the Alleghenies at Peter's Creek, 237 miles from its origin.[62]

In 1746 Virginia sent Colonel Joshua Fry and Peter Jefferson, with forty men, on an exploratory tour west of Byrd's line. In 1749 Fry and Jefferson for Virginia and William Churton and Daniel Weldon for North

Carolina were appointed commissioners to continue the survey, which they did to the Holston River opposite Steep Rock.[63]

North Carolina and South Carolina

An initial mistake of the Carolina proprietors in setting up separate governments was the reference to the boundary line at Cape Fear instead of the Cape Fear River. As the settlements at Albemarle and South Carolina expanded toward each other it became necessary to establish a definite border. Runaways and debtors escaping from one area to the other aggravated the problem.

In 1721 South Carolina, now a royal colony, instructed its agents in London, Francis Yonge and John Lloyd, to urge that North Carolina be put under the jurisdiction of South Carolina or, if this were not feasible, to secure royal approval to run the boundary from the head of the North Branch of the Cape Fear River due west parallel to Virginia. South Carolina again in 1725 petitioned the King to settle the boundary, but without result. After North Carolina was made a royal colony in 1729, the new Governor, George Burrington and the new South Carolina Governor, Robert Johnson, met with the Board of Trade, where they reached an agreement on a line from thirty miles southwest of Cape Fear River to run parallel at that distance along the whole course of the river. Commissioners from both colonies were to run the line. Burrington and Johnson, however, soon fell out over an additional provision inserted by the Board of Trade that the Waccamaw River was to be the boundary if it was within thirty miles of the Cape Fear River – the mounts of the two rivers were about fifty miles apart but the rivers moved to within a thirty-mile distance.

It was not until 1735 that the governors of both colonies appointed commissioners, who met for the first time on April 23 at a residence near Brunswick on the Cape Fear River. After six weeks negotiation, the commissioners agreed to a line: thirty miles due west from Cape Fear, then northwest to the thirty-fifth parallel and then due west to the "South Seas." If the line came within five miles of the Pee Dee River it should run along that river to five miles distant from the thirty-fifth parallel, which it should then follow. The survey proceeded slowly, and in September the commissioners parted to determine separate lines. South Carolina sent a request to England to alter the agreement, while Governor Gabriel Johnston of North Carolina protested to the Board of Trade to ignore this petition.[64]

One reason the commissioners stopped the survey was because they had received no pay; North Carolina asked the Board of Trade for reimbursement. But in 1737 North Carolina agreed to pay her commissioners and work started again. The survey completed in 1737 to the thirty-fifth parallel and twenty-two miles northwest found the two colonies again at odds, and the survey was again interrupted. Both colonies continued to make land grants along the line. On lands belonging to Governor Dobbs in Anson County on Sugar and Reedy Creeks lawless persons organized into militia claiming to be under South Carolina jurisdiction. In 1747 Dobbs filed complaints with the Board of Trade.[65] Dobbs believed that no colonial commission could ever solve the dispute and hence he recommended that the crown should decide.[66]

When James Glen assumed the governorship of South Carolina, relations between South Carolina and North Carolina over the boundary became even more strained. Only about one hundred miles of a surveyed line (that of 1735) from the coast existed. Settlers from both colonies poured into the region of the Catawbas beyond the line. Glen, fearing an Indian war, accused Dobbs of surveying the Catawba towns. Dobbs wrote the Board of Trade in 1754 that Glen was trying to incite the Indians against North Carolina.[67] Dinwiddie of Virginia considered the Catawbas under his jurisdiction and since border disputes were related to Indian affairs the crown should exact a settlement.[68]

In 1759 Dobbs resumed petitioning the Board of Trade, but again without result. In 1762 he turned to South Carolina for joint action, which led to heated correspondence between the two governors, each charging the other with encouraging disturbances. Both colonies continued to issue land warrants in the disputed area. Commissioners from South Carolina and representatives of the Catawba nation met in Anson County in July 1762 to extend the line; Dobbs protested by proposing to suspend the survey. At the Augusta conference with the Indians, boundaries were agreed upon between Catawbas and South Carolina. The Board of Trade finally recommended on December 16, 1762 that a temporary line be established "until the propositions of both Provinces in respect to a final line of division can be fully considered and determined." Unlike his predecessor, Governor Boone of South Carolina was willing to cooperate with Dobbs in furthering the survey, which was resumed at the thirty-fifth parallel.[69] Again there were delays, due to the nonpayment of the commissioners and the lack of cooperation between the Governor and Assembly of South Carolina. In the 1760's Lieutenant Governors Tryon of North Carolina and Bull of

South Carolina went about their own ways in surveying the lines of their respective colonies – and the border in the western region was not definitively settled until the nineteenth century.[70]

Significantly, each of the major boundary disputes commented on here involved petitioning the crown for direction or determination in the settlement of a long-standing controversy. When it accepted responsibility, the home government responded usually by instructing the colonies to set up their own intercolonial commissions or by exercising the royal prerogative to constitute special review commissions from disinterested colonies. When proprietary rights were concerned, suits in equity proved too indecisive and too costly. The royal review commission, based upon the right of the crown to original jurisdiction in controversies between colonies, served as a vital precedent for both appellate jurisdiction and judicial review in the later application of federal judicial authority over the states.

NOTES

1 "Pleas of New Plymouth respecting the bounds fixed by their patent," May 15, 1694, *CSP*, XIV, 287.

2 Joseph H. Smith, *Appeals to the Privy Council from the American Plantations* (New York, 1950), 449; John Noble, "An Incident in 1731 in the Long Dispute of Massachusetts and Rhode Island over their Boundary Line," *MHSP*, 2nd Ser., XIX (1905), 21.

3 Arnold, *Hist. of R.I.*, II, 103. In 1724, R.I. also tried to get Mass. to negotiate a settlement. Commissioners appointed by R.I. at that time were: Col. William Coddington and Lt. Col. Thomas Frye. (–Oct. 1724, *RICR*, IV, 346.)

4 Noble, "Incident in 1731," *MHSP*, 2nd Ser., XIX (1905), 21–34. Pertinent documents relating to the dispute, 1731–34, are included here.

5 "Meeting . . . At the Court of St. James," Nov. 30, 1738, Miscellaneous Papers (Boundaries), MHS.

6 Smith, *Appeals to the Privy Council*, 449–51; Ferrell,"Massachusetts Colonial Agents" (Ph. D. diss.), 175–76.

7 Resolutions of the House, July 7, 1739 and Oct. 2, 1739, MA, Colonial, VI, 549 and 558, resp. Though six commissioners were named originally, Mass. appointed Graves Wells and John Chandler.

8 John H. Cady, *Rhode Island Boundaries, 1636–1936* (Providence, 1936), 16–17; Smith, *Appeals to the Privy Council*, 452–53; Foster, *Stephen Hopkins*, 161.

9 Clarence W. Bowen, *The Boundary Disputes of Connecticut* (Boston, 1882), 37–49; Arnold, *Hist. of R.I.*, II, 81.

[10] Gov. and Council of Mass. to Gov. and Council of Conn., Nov. 8, 1694, MA, Colonial, II, 225; Conn. Gov. to Gov. and Council of Mass., – 1695; *ibid.*, 232; *Mass. Acts and Resolves,* VII (1892), 93, Draft of a letter to Government of Conn., Dec. 12, 1695.

[11] S/ John Allyn, Sec., Hartford, Oct. 29, 1695, MA, Colonial, II, 237c; S/ William Bond for Mass. House of Rep., Dec. 3, 1695, *ibid.* Commissioners for Conn.–Col. Allyn, Maj. Fitch; for Mass.–Elisha Cooke, Elisha Hutchinson, and James Taylor.

[12] William Stoughton to Conn. Gov. and Council, June 16, 1696, *ibid.*, II, 58.

[13] Bowen, *Boundary Disputes of Connecticut*, 54–55.

[14] "Some proposals" of Mass. and Conn. commissioners, June 12, 1700, MA, Colonial, II, 26. William Pitkin, John Chester, and William Whiting drew up the report.

[15] Resolution of May 27, 1702, *ibid.*, 237; Letter of Mass. to Conn., Nov. 2, 1702, *ibid.*, II, 102. Appointed commissioners by the Conn. Gen. Ct.: John Butcher, Samuel Chester, and William Whiting. Members of the surveying party were: James Taylor (Mass.) and William Pitkin and William Whiting (Conn.).

[16] Bowen, *Boundary Disputes of Connecticut*, 56–58.

[17] Report of the commissioners, June 13, 1713, Belknap Papers, MHS. Mass. commissioners–Elisha Hutchinson and Isaac Addington; Conn. commissioners–William Pitkin and William Whiting; surveyors–John Chandler and Samuel Thaxter.

[18] Resolution of the Assembly, Dec. 11, 1747, MA, Colonial, IV, 24.

[19] Resolution of the Mass. Council, Jan. 9, 1749, *ibid.*, 33. Mass. commissioners were: Thomas Hutchinson, – Williams, and Timothy Dwight. In Jan. 1751, Mass. directed its agent to make a "humble Representation to his Majesty" against Conn. for departing from the agreement with Mass. on the boundary. *Mass. Acts and Resolves*, Jan. 17, 1751, XIV (1907), 460.

[20] On the theory that the Mohegans were a sovereign body.

[21] Since it claimed jurisdiction over suits between an Indian tribe and a colony.

[22] For a detailed tracing of the dispute and the problems of jurisdiction, see Smith, *Appeals to the Privy Council*, 418–42. Bowen briefly summarizes the case. Bowen, *Boundary Disputes of Connecticut*, 25–27.

[23] Commission of Dec. 19, 1719, MA, Colonial, III, 131; Petition of John Rindge, Agent for N.H. to the King (abstract), Apr. 16, 1733, *CSP*, XL, 75–77; Journal of the Council and Assembly, Dec. 18, 1705, Bouton, ed., *N.H. Provincial Papers*, III, 321; Jonathan Smith, "The Massachusetts and New Hampshire Boundary Line Controversy, 1693–1740," *MHSP*, XLIII (1910), 78–88; J.H. Smith, *Appeals to the Privy Council*, 443–48; Kimball, *Dudley*, 77. For the Allen claims and litigation, see Fry, *New Hampshire as a Royal Province*, 220–65. New Hampshire commissioners–Capt. Henry Dow, Maj. Joseph Smith, and James Philbrook; Mass. commissioners–Thomas Fitch, – Addington, –Davenport, Elisha Cooke, William Dudley, and John Gardiner.

[24] Journal of the House, Aug. 29, 1730, Bouton, ed., *N.H. Provincial Papers*, IV, 568ff.; Anna De Armond, *Andrew Bradford: Colonial Journalist* (Newark, Del., 1949), 75ff. N.H.–Mass. boundary documents are transcribed in the Force transcripts (Mass.–N.H. Boundary, 1731–42), LC.

[25] "By order in council . . .," –1737 (Mass.) Belknap Papers, MHS; Council of Trade and Plantations to Gov. Jonathan Belcher, Feb. 18, 1737, *CSP* XLIII, 42; Arnold, *Hist. of R.I.,* II, 117–18. For documents relating to the Mass.–N.Y. boundary dispute and the proceedings of the commissioners in their Aug. 1737 meeting, see "New York and the New Hampshire Grants," *NYHSC*, III (1870), 94–131.

[26] Wood, *Shirley*, I, 70–71.

[27] For the rapid settlement of New Hampshire towns during and after the French and Indian War by settlers from Mass., Conn., and R.I., see Lois K. Mathews, *The Expansion of New England*, reprint ed. (New York, 1962), 108–17. For a study of the surveys and the townships involved, see Samuel A. Green, "The Northern Boundary of Massachusetts in its Relation to New Hampshire," *AASP*, New Series, VII (1892), 22–29.

[28] Order by Governor and Council, June 17, 1698, R.C. Winthrop Collection, CSL; Gov. Benjamin Fletcher to Lords of Trade, June 25, 1697, *NYCD*, IV, 276; Representation of Mar. 14, 1699, *ibid.*, 626–27; "Confirmation of the Agreement," Mar. 28, 1700, *ibid.*, 628–30.

[29] Cadwallader Colden to Lt. Gov. Clarke, Feb. 14, 1738, E.B. O'Callaghan, ed., *The Documentary History of the State of New–York*, 4 vols. (Albany, 1849–51), IV, 178; Act of June 25, 1719, *The Colonial Laws of New York*, I (1894), 1042; *The New–York Gazette*, Dec. 30, 1734; William Smith, *History of New–York to 1732* (Albany, 1814), 275; Bowen, *Boundary Disputes of Connecticut*, 69–74. For the best general account see Dixon R. Fox, *Yankees and Yorkers* (New York, 1940), 117–45.

[30] *Providence Gazette*, May 14, 1763; Zeichner, *Connecticut's Years of Controversy*, 30–33. For Pennsylvania's protests against the Connecticut intrusions see Gov. Hamilton to the Gov. of Conn., Mar. 4, 1754, *PA*, 1st Ser., II, 120–21 and "Proclamation of the Pennsylvania Governor," Feb. 20, 1761, *PCR*, VIII, 566–67.

[31] Fox, *Yankees and Yorkers*, 157–61; Fry, *New Hampshire as a Royal Province*, 266–69. For correspondence and documents between N.H. and N.Y. on the boundary question, 1750–1773 see "Collection of Evidence . . .," *NYHSC*, II (1869), 281–98. Also see Irving Mark, *Agrarian Conflicts in Colonial New York* (New York, 1940), 116–29.

[32] Gov. George Clarke's Speech to the Gen. Assembly, Aug. 29, 1739, *Journal of the Legislative Council of N.Y.*, I, 732.

[33] Extract from letter of James De Lancey to Gov. Shirley, Dec. 18, 1753, MA, Colonial, IV, 423. The case of Mass. is stated in document of Dec. 18, 1753, *ibid.*, 424–37. See "The Memorial of Robert Livingston, Jr.," May 31, 1753, O'Callaghan, ed., *Documentary History of New York*, III, 739–49 and also "Collection of Evidence . . .," *NYHSC*, II (1869), 400–49; Act of July 4, 1753, *The Colonial Laws of New York*, III (1894), 912–13.

[34] Gov. Hardy's answer to address of the N.Y. Council, in *The New–York Mercury*, Feb. 28, 1757.

[35] Lt. Gov. Colden to the Lords of Trade, Sep. 26, 1763, *NYCD*, VII, 563–65.

[36] See New York and New Jersey Boundary Papers, I, NYHS; Smith, *Appeals to the Privy Council*, 454–63; Fisher, *New Jersey as Royal Province*, 210–39.

[37] Minutes of the Council of N.Y., Feb. 22, 1694, *NJA*, 1st Ser., II, 106.

[38] President Lewis Morris of N.J. to Peter Schuyler, President of the Council of N.Y., Mar. 31, 1720, *ibid.*, IV, 446–47.

[39] Varga, "Robert Charles," *WMQ*, 3d Ser., XVIII (1961), 221–24.

[40] For James Alexander's role as a "surveyor-councillor" in the boundary dispute, over a period of forty years, see Henry N. MacCracken, *Prologue to Independence: The Trials of James Alexander, American, 1715–56* (New York, 1964), 24–30, 96–102, 116–19.

[41] Fisher, *New Jersey as a Royal Province*, 228–29. N.Y. commissioners (1763)–John Cruger, Henry Holland, Frederick Philipse, Benjamin Kissam, John Morin Scott, and William Bayard; N.J. commissioners (1764)–Gov. Franklin, Andrew Oliver, Peter Randolph, Peyton Randolph, and Richard Corbin.

[42] Levin C. Baily, "Maryland's Boundary Controversies," reprint from *The Daily Record*, June 23, 1951 (speech delivered at the Md. State Bar Assoc., June 22, 1951), 9; Tolles, *James Logan*, 115, 170; Lincoln, *Revolutionary Movement in Pa.*, 55.

[43] *South Carolina Gazette,* Nov. 18, 1732; Hugh Jones, *The Present State of Virginia From Whence is inferred a short view of Maryland and North Carolina*, ed. Richard L. Morton (Chapel Hill, 1956), 27–30.

[44] *Pennsylvania Gazette*, Oct. 16, 1735; Burton A. Konkle, *The Life of Andrew Hamilton*, 1676–1741 (Philadelphia, 1941), 60. Pertinent documents are found in *PA*, 2nd Ser, VII and XVI and *PCR*, IV and V.

[45] *South Carolina Gazette*, Jan. 15, 1737.

[46] Proceedings of the Council of Md., May 28, 1738, *Md. Archives*, XXVIII, 145–48; James Veech, *The Monongahela of Old* (Pittsburgh, 1910), 231.

[47] Gov. Bladen to Gov. Thomas, Mar. 9, 1747, Gratz Collection (Colonial Governors), HSP; Ettling Revolution Papers, (Benjamin Chew Papers), 1738–39, HSP. Commissioners for Pa.–Richard Peters and Lawrence Growden; Md.–Lewis Gale and Samuel Chamberlaine.

[48] . . . May 10, 1732, Ettling Revolution Papers (Mason and Dixon Papers), HSP; Gov. Samuel Ogle to Gov. Hamilton, Nov. 30, 1749, *ibid.*, (Penn Papers: Official Correspondence), HSP.

[49] Meeting of the commissioners . . ., 1750 and 1751, *ibid.*, (Chew Papers), HSP; *New-York Evening Post,* Feb. 18, 1751. Commissioners present at Newcastle, Nov. 15–28, 1750:

Md.	Pa.
Benedict Calvert	William Allen
Edmund Jennings	Thomas Hopkinson
Robert Henry	Richard Peters
John Ross	Thomas Cookson
	Ryves Holt
	Benjamin Chew
	Tench Francis

Commissioners present at session near Fenwicks Is., Apr. 22–29, 1751:

Md.	Pa.
Benedict Calvert	William Allen
Robert Henry	Richard Peters
George Plater	Ryves Holt
John Ross	Benjamin Chew
	Tench Francis

See Dreer Collection (Letters of Members of Colonial Conventions), HSP for relatively unimportant correspondence between Pa. governors and the boundary commissioners. J.W. Jordan's "Penn versus Baltimore," *PMHB,* XXXIX (1915) contains biographical sketches of the two Pa. surveyors (pp. 1–3); Gipson, *Lewis Evans,* 46–51 recounts Evans' efforts in researching the Baltimore claims in N.Y. records.

[50] Richard Peters to –, Oct. 9, 1760, Chalmers Collection, I, NYPL; Meetings of the commissioners, Nov. 19, 1760– December 10, 1763, *passim*., Ettling Revolution Papers (Chew Papers), HSP; Sharpe to Calvert, Dec. 22, 1760, *Md. Archives*, IX, 480; Sharpe to Hamilton, Mar. 15, 1762, *ibid*., XIV, 33. The personnel serving variously as commissioners during this period (usually five attending of the seven required for each colony) were:

Md.	Pa.
Gov. Horatio Sharpe	Gov. James Hamilton
Benjamin Tasker	William Allen
Edward Lloyd	Richard Peters
Daniel Dulany	Lynford Lardner
Robert Henry	Benjamin Chew
John Ridout	Thomas Hopkinson
-------Malcolm	Ryves Holt
John Leeds	William Coleman
Stephen Berndley	Rev. John Ewing
Rev. John Barclay	
George Stewart	

[51] John H. Latrobe, *The History of Mason and Dixon's Line* (Oakland, Del., 1882), 30–32; Mason A. Hughlett and William F. Swindler, "Mason and Dixon: their Line and its Legend," *American Heritage*, XV (1964), 28–29.

[52] Kenneth P. Bailey, *Thomas Cresap: Maryland Frontiersman* (Boston, 1944), 31–47. Norkus, "Francis Fauquier" (Ph. D. diss.), 191–98. Gov. Fauquier of Va. had referred the western boundaries of Va. and Pa. to the Board of Trade and had recommended that the crown should appoint commissioners to settle the question. In December 1761, however, the crown forbade the governors from granting lands in Indian territory where Indians were protected by treaties.

[53] *JHB–Va*. (1702–12), May 2, 1705, 103–4.

[54] President and Council of Va. to the Council of Trade and Plantations, Oct. 26, 1706, *CSP*, XXIII, 281–82. In 1699 an Order in Council had instructed Dep. Gov. Harvey of N.C. to name commissioners to settle the boundary with Virginia. Two N.C. commissioners–Daniel Akehurst and Henderson Walker–went to Williamsburg, but the Va. Council did not consider Harvey the legal Governor and refused to treat with his appointees. William K. Boyd, ed., *William Byrd's Histories of the Dividing Line betwixt Virginia and North Carolina* (Raleigh, 1929), xvii–xviii.

[55] Gov. Spotswood to Gov. Hyde, Dec. 15, 1710, *NCCR* I, 750; Memorial from Boone and Barnwell, Nov. 23, 1720, *ibid*., II, 395; Dodson, "Spotswood" (Ph. D. diss.), 323.

[56] Council Journal, Jan. 23, 1724, *NCCR*, II, 517; Dodson, "Spotswood" (Ph. D. diss.), 325–27; Morton, *Colonial Virginia*, II, 427–28.

[57] Spotswood to the Lord Commissioners for Trade and Plantations, Apr. 5, 1717, *Spotswood Corr*., I, 229.

58 Spotswood to the Council of Trade, Mar. 6, 1711, *ibid.*, 60 and to the Lords Commissioners of Trade, July 21, 1714, *ibid.*, II, 70.

59 Spotswood to the Board of Trade, May 15, 1712, *ibid.*, I, 160.

60 Jones, *Present State of Virginia*, ed. Morton, 89.

61 Boyd, ed., *Byrd's Histories*, "The Secret History . . .," 13–19. This is perhaps the best edition of both the "Secret History" and the more reserved "History of the Dividing Line," both of which are paired page by page in this edition.

62 For a good summary but otherwise not too accurate biography, see R.C. Beatty, *William Byrd of Westover* (Boston, 1932), 127–35.

63 Wheeler, *Hist. of N.C.*, I, 144; Burke Davis, "Joshua Fry" *A Williamsburg Galaxy*, (New York, 1968), 53–54. The line was completed in 1778 when it reached the Tennessee River.

64 Marvin L. Skaggs, *North Carolina Boundary Disputes Involving her Southern Line (The James Sprunt Studies*, XXV [Chapel Hill, 1941]), 28–41; Marvin L. Skaggs, "The First Boundary Survey between the Carolinas," *NCHR*, XII (1935), 218–32; Carter, "James Glen" (Ph. D. diss.), 97ff.; Gov. Burrington to Lords of Trade and Plantations, Feb. 20, 1732, *NCCR*, III, 336; Ashe, *Hist. of N.C.*, I, 254ff.; Wheeler, *Hist. of N.C.*, I, 43; Sherman, *Robert Johnson*, 125–29; Wallace, *South Carolina: A Short Hist.*, 157. N.C. commissioners–Robert Holton, Matthew Rowan, and Edward Moseley; S.C. commissioners–James Abercrombie, Alexander Skene, and William Walters.

65 Skaggs, *North Carolina Boundary Disputes* 41–46.

66 Attig, "William Henry Lyttleton" (Ph. D. diss.), 97.

67 Carter, "James Glen" (Ph. D. diss.), 95–97; Sirmans, *South Carolina,* 300.

68 Koontz, *Dinwiddie*, 267.

69 *South-Carolina Gazette,* Aug. 27, 1763; Board of Trade Journal, Dec. 16, 1762, *NCCR,* VI, 754; Skaggs, *North Carolina Boundary Disputes,* 46–55.

70 Gov. Dobbs to the Board of Trade, Mar. 29, 1764, *NCCR*, VI, 1037; Skaggs, *North Carolina Boundary Disputes*, 68–75. N.C. sought to pay the commissioners out of the King's quitrents.

CHAPTER XII

COMITY

Although the imperial system instilled a large measure of uniformity in government and institutions of the colonies, the fact that each colony was a separate state posed the need of harmonizing laws and policies with each other.

Two early plans of union advocated the establishment of common practices among the colonies. Penn's Plan of Union called for a single value for coinage in all the colonies, a colonial mint, uniform laws to deal with runaways and fraudulent debtors, uniform naturalization proceedings, and uniform control over marriage.[1] The anonymous Virginia Plan of 1701 suggested that the home government provide some means for deciding all controversies between colony and colony, extradition of criminals, servants, and debtors, and adjusting all disputes concerning trade.[2]

It was Penn also, who initiated a governors' conference in New York in November 1700 to bring about greater uniformity in laws and policies among the colonies – the only conference of this kind held in the colonial period. Penn met with Bellomont of New York, Nicholson of Virginia, and Blakiston of Maryland. The main result was the submitting of reports by Penn and Bellomont to the Lords of Trade dealing principally with the need for standardization of colonial laws.[3]

In every colony there was similarity in legislation and methods for apprehending and punishing runaways – deserters, debtors, servants, slaves.[4] But much bad feeling arose over the apathy of one colony in harboring escapees from another. Particularly the problem was severe in the southern colonies where there were wide open spaces of cheap or free land and no one to ask questions. Or one could flee into the Spanish borderlands. Even the movement of respectable persons – particularly en masse – seeking new lands or lower tax rates caused intercolonial friction: it drained the economy of one colony and often brought a squatter and dissident population to another. In an aggravated situation in 1714, when a large exodus headed for Virginia because of the Indian hostilities, Governor Spotswood issued a proclamation to arrest anyone coming into Virginia without a passport from North Carolina.[5]

A problem recurring in the colonial wars was the evasion of military service by fleeing to another colony. In 1693 Governor Fletcher complained that the neighboring colonies "Harbour all our Deserters;"[6] Governor Hamilton of East Jersey in 1696 noticed that "severall of our youth" had gone to the southern colonies "to be free from detachments;"[7] and Governor Fitch at a later time echoed complaints of other governors that "Opulent Neighbours" were giving large bounties to "Induce our Men upon our Borders to go into the Immediate Service of other Governments."[8] In 1697 the crown, having been informed "of the undue methods practised in some of his Colonies for seducing the Inhabitants from others," urged the southern governors to

> take care that effectual Laws be made in each of their respective Governments against the receiving and harbouring not only of Deserters, but also of such Fugitives as leave any of his Plantations contrary to the Laws provided for that purpose in each plantation respectively . . . .[9]

The New London conference in 1711 took up the matter of desertion, upon the request of the New York Council, and, as a result, Massachusetts was censored for encouraging the harboring of deserters.[10] For the most part the colonies complied with royal directives not to "entertain" deserters from the royal navy or army.[11]

In each of the three wars of the eighteenth century, Rhode Island was the worst offender as a receptacle for deserters from the other northern colonies.[12] Rhode Island, however, in 1758 did attempt to make amends by passing an act that any person deserting "His Majesty's Service in this, or either of the neighboring governments in New England" should be fined £ 500.[13] Governor Hopkins of Rhode Island called for uniform legislation among the colonies: "it might be of Service if each of the Colonies, concerned in the present Expedition [1755], were to pass Laws, prohibiting men's traveling, who appear in Common Character, without obtaining Leave so to do, under Hand of some proper Officer. Should your Assembly [Massachusetts] think fit to do any Thing of this Sort, the Assembly here will readily follow so usefull a Step."[14]

Enlistment of indentured servants by officers of the crown long caused general opposition in the colonies. In 1756 Parliament passed an act that the king's officers could enlist any indentured servant in any colony regardless of any colonial law; but it did provide that owners could be compensated as two justices of the peace should decide.[15] Pennsylvania, Maryland, and Virginia, however, prohibited servants from enlisting ir military service during the French and Indian War unless first consent had been obtained from their masters. The New England colonies for the most part complied with the British policy – with these colonies also compensating owners for the time their servants were on military duty.[16]

Laws governing slavery varied only in degree in the colonies. Although colonial legislation was severe against those aiding and abetting fugitive slaves,[17] little action was taken by the colony governments to apprehend escapees – the burden of recovery of slaves was a private matter, with the master expected himself to enlist the aid of local officials. Newspaper advertisements gave notice to the possibility that a slave, or other escapee, had crossed colonial boundaries and called upon authorities "in the Neighbouring Governments" to assist in apprehending a fugitive.[18] South Carolina long complained of escaped slaves being aided by people of neighboring colonies. Georgia and South Carolina did work out agreement on the recovering of fugitive slaves; in rare instances, where criminals were involved, Georgia permitted a *posse comitatus* of Carolinians to cross into Georgia.[19] The colonies also had laws forbidding anyone from receiving Indian slaves from another colony.[20] By mid-century most colonies – north and south – were acting in concert by levying prohibitive duties on the importation of slaves or otherwise totally excluding their importation.[21]

No rules or procedures were established binding the colonies to any general extradition policy. What laws were passed concerning fugitives were simply communicated by a colony to its neighbors.[22] Nevertheless, the request of one governor to another to return any notorious runaway was usually honored. Thus in 1748 Governor Clinton made arrangements to send a deputy sheriff from New York City to Philadelphia to convey a prisoner via water from Trenton, with Governor Belcher providing security while the prisoner was in New Jersey.[23]

What sense of a general economic community existed was attributable mainly to intercolonial business ties. Organization of many enterprises cut across colonial lines. Merchants with an intercolonial stake in business developed concern for the affairs of other colonies.[24] Trading relations at the principal ports were intertwined in both coastal and ocean trade, and thus prices varied simultaneously from one port to another.[25] But colonial rivalries persisted, and by 1763 there was much need for uniform legislation and policy affecting trade. It is surprising, however, that virtually no efforts were made to reach a commercial entente among any of the colonies. It was a rare instance when Governor William Shirley attempted to have commissioners meet from Massachusetts and Connecticut to work out a common accord on commercial problems.[26]

It seemed to be a consensus in the colonies that Great Britain should encourage colonial manufacturing. Governor Dudley wrote in 1709 that it was "derogating" that Great Britain "Should have their whole Dependance upon us for all Trade and Supply's, and yet not do the least Service as Dependants nor Allyes for us."[27] Or reiterating the same view in a more popular vein, a letter to the publisher in the *Weekly Rehearsal* asked in 1735:

> And how can it be reasonably expected but that Poverty and Vice must creep in amongst us, when we are taking Pains to graft Pride in our Children's Hearts, before they are taught how to maintain it? Here is a fine Country, that flows with plenty of Provisions for the Belly, but little Improvement for the Back .... And how can any one be called a Lover of this Country, and see so plain a Road and not put his Hands to the Plow: .... We must consider as we grow larger in Body, we should grow ripe in Trade, or else tell me how or in which Way we can be employed some Years hence .... for every Pair of Stockings made here we are so much the Richer ....[28]

As John Mitchell wrote in 1757: "The thing that breeds a jealousy between Britain and her colonies is not power, but manufactures, in which they interfere with one another."[29]

Benjamin Franklin, Cadwallader Colden, Stephen Hopkins and many others in the colonies and in England at mid-century argued the necessity of removing all restraints on American production and trade if both the mother country and the colonies were to prosper. Some English writers, by the 1760's, felt that Britain and America would profit economically by a complete separation.[30]

The prevalence of illicit trade pointed to the need of uniform policy and enforcement in trade regulation. Not until the last colonial war was the full force of the British navy used and absenteeism in the customs service ended to bring about some effectiveness in the enforcement of British navigation and trade laws.[31] But the colonists still found various ways to carry on illicit trade, including goods under "flags of truce," for which it was known that even several governors of the colonies were bribed. One of the many problems was the duplicity of authority, colonial as well as British. For example, three separate authorities were responsible for the colonial supervision of trade in the Delaware Valley alone: Pennsylvania, Delaware, and New Jersey.[32]

Colonial governors had powers to interdict commerce in a colony port, the success of which depended upon the cooperation of other governors. Embargoes were levied chiefly in wartime and in a few instances to protect domestic industries or when there was a threatened scarcity of food or other essential commodities. In wartime, embargoes were usually issued in concert by several or more governors against trade with the enemy, and frequently, but not always, were in response to a directive from the crown. In five colonies governors could declare embargoes without first obtaining legislative enactment, although they had to follow certain legal conditions.[33] This exercise of a "police power" in commerce is significant, therefore, because it demonstrates a local executive authority in commerce, which required a pooling of action in the various colonies to be effective.

Throughout the colonial period all the colonies levied tonnage duties, except for Delaware and New Jersey. Originally these duties were referred to as "powder" or "castle" money because they were applied to defense and fort building. In the eighteenth century they were used chiefly for maintaining lighthouses and other similar maritime purposes. Usually a colony made the duties more liberal for ships of neighboring colonies and those engaged in the coastal trade than for other shipping.[34]

Levying impost duties, Adam Smith once said, is one of the "great engines for enriching the country."[35] Mercantilist policies of one colony affecting the commerce of another certainly had a negative force toward union, but, in the long run, the chaos of trade rivalries actually gave an impetus for stronger ties of union. Most colonies levied impost duties during some period of their history, both for revenue and encouragement of shipping and trade.

The imposts of the New England colonies, with the exception of Massachusetts, were largely restricted to liquors and Negroes; in New York, liquors and cocoa. On several occasions Massachusetts imposed discriminating duties against neighboring colonies as a form of retaliation, but these laws were short-lived. In 1697 Massachusetts passed a law placing double duties on enumerated goods coming from England, and in 1718 an act levied a double charge upon all commodities from England. This practice was disallowed in 1719.[36]

Because New Jersey and Delaware did not engage extensively in maritime trade, these colonies employed other means of taxation than levying impost duties. Before 1723 Pennsylvania levied impost duties, but after that time until the French and Indian War, Pennsylvania had virtually free trade. Tariffs of Pennsylvania were usually of a retaliatory nature, in response to discriminatory duties on the colony's exports placed by Maryland, New York, New Jersey, Delaware and Virginia.[37]

Virginia's commercial restrictions sought mainly to reduce competition from tobacco planting in North Carolina.[38] North Carolina levied retaliatory imposts upon naval stores, liquors, and foodstuffs coming from other colonies. At mid-century South Carolina and North Carolina were in a tariff war to control trade that followed the inland waterways.[39]

All colonies, except Delaware and Rhode Island, at some time levied export duties, but by 1750 such levies were retained only by New York, Maryland, South Carolina, and Virginia. Eight colonies had duties on exportation of furs, including all the southern colonies only Virginia and South Carolina with any degree of consistency, but by mid-century most of these colonies had lifted these levies because of the decline of the fur trade. The only other prominent area in which colonies levied export duties was timber going to other colonies rather than shipments to England.[40]

A drastic solution for the intercolonial economic rivalry would have been for Parliament to take from the assemblies their powers of taxation over trade and to impose imperial duties at American ports. An anonymous Virginian had written in 1701 that "To redress the Grievances that one Plantation may suffer by another" there should be "the Setling an equal Liberty of Trade" and to obtain this end a "General Law" needed to be passed that could decide and adjust all controversies over trade and commerce in the colonies.[41] If the colonies were unwilling to work out any uniformity in tariff regulations, they could scarcely be expected to favor a universal tariff under imperial auspices. But, for the sake of providing for military security, they could accept the raising of incidental revenue in connection with trade regulation. Richard Jackson, the agent for Connecticut and Pennsylvania in London, said he could not argue against Great Britain levying revenue in the colonies "for the Support of British Troops," but he contended that "it should be built on a foundation consistent with the Constitutions of the Colonies."[42] Here was the key to the impending crises between the colonies and the mother country.

The lack of uniform currency pointed to the need for some central means for stabilizing monetary evaluation. One is familiar with the increasing issue of paper currency by the colonies in the eighteenth century and particularly the insufficient restraint in Rhode Island and the paper money struggles in Massachusetts and the Carolinas. Rhode Island seemed all the more eager to issue paper money when neighboring colonies withdrew paper currency from circulation, which led to retaliation in the form of banning notes from Rhode Island.[43] As early as the 1730's depreciated Rhode Island currency making its way into Massachusetts shook the financial structure of that colony and helped to create an impasse in relations between the governor and legislature.[44] Rhode Island bills of credit also undermined the currency of New York.[45] Nor did New York or Massachusetts honor New Hampshire paper in the 1750's.[46] New Jersey sought to discourage influx of paper money from its neighbors as a law of 1732 indicates:

> That no Person or Persons within this Province, shall ask, demand, take or receive any Advance on the Paper Currency of *Pennsylvania* or *New York* for the Paper Currency of this Province . . . .[47]

But, over-all it was difficult for a colony to enforce a prohibition or limitation on currency from another colony because of the interlinking of trade and business.

The necessity of using money as a medium of trade led to some attempts by the colonies to set up standards of currency evaluation. For example, the relatively stable paper money of the middle colonies was received at fixed ratios in colonies from New England to Maryland.[48] New Hampshire, Connecticut, and Rhode Island followed Massachusetts's evaluation of foreign coins – thus providing "a uniform legal measure of value that governed the transactions between Boston and the other New England towns."[49] Because the need for specie in Virginia was less demanding than elsewhere, the colony exercised a stabilizing influence in adhering closely to evaluation of foreign coins comparable to that of England – and therefore Virginia did not raise the value of coins until other colonies had done so.[50]

Until the colonists discovered the panacea of paper money, recommendations went to the Board of Trade for establishing some means for a colonial coinage system. Lord Bellomont suggested in 1700 that the home government declare a standard coin to be used at uniform value throughout the colonies and that a mint for "small silver" be set up in New York.[51] About the only response of the Board of Trade was to advise the colonial governors to urge upon their assemblies

> that it is absolutely necessary to settle a true and uniform standard in order to prevent clipping and coining, and other deceits in the trade, by crafty and designing men, by which means fair and honest dealing will be settled among yourselves, and with your neighbours, and trade established upon a solid foundation agreeable to equity and justice.[52]

Governor Belcher in 1734 argued that more bounties on American manufactures – by both the colonies and the home government – would "bring the Ballance of Trade in our Favour, which will of Course fix the standard of Money among us."[53]

Had the British government lent its efforts to create a central monetary system in the colonies instead of singularly limiting currency expansion, much of the chaos and crises in fiscal matters affecting imperial-colonial relations could have been averted. As it was, the colonists themselves chiefly directed their interest in monetary reform to justify the issuance of paper currency[54] rather than to bring uniformity.

One of the most important areas of a growth of comity was the loose adaptation of the colonies of an English legal system, minus the proliferation of courts and jurisdictions in England.

In the judicial system some uniformity depended upon the imperial tie. Judicial appointments at the various levels supposedly were to receive royal sanction.[55] The chain of review and appellate jurisdiction manifested by the king-in-council had effect upon uniform judicial practice in the colonies, but it is a subject better discussed elsewhere. It may be well, however, to point out that complaints as well as appeals of colonial laws could be brought before the Privy Council on any phase of governmental administration in the colonies.

Although governors were instructed to set up certain courts, this was not always done. For example, no effort was made in South Carolina, with an exception during Robert Johnson's administration, to establish a court of exchequer.[56] In none of the New England colonies was there a chancery court or any court invested with powers to try cases in equity in the early eighteenth century, although courts of equity were found in most of the royal colonies elsewhere. Thus in New England, as had been the experience under the Puritan governments of the seventeenth century, the practice developed of petitioning the legislative courts for relief. These courts

> transact this Business by Orders or Resolves, without the Solemnity of passing Acts for such purposes, which Orders or Resolves are not sent home for the Royal Assent. And by these kind of Orders, They have extended the Exercise of this Power, beyond what a Court of Chancery ever attempted, to a degree even to the suspending public Laws.

The main complaint here was the encroaching on power of administration of estates.[57] Thomas Pownall suggested that greater uniformity in colonial judicial decisions could be obtained through establishing circuit courts of appeal empowered to hear all appeals of law and equity and to regulate inferior courts and standards of procedure.[58]

The colonial charters similarly offered an element of legal uniformity in their grants of customary rights of Englishmen and stipulation that laws passed should conform to the laws of England.[59] But the colonists were on their own in forming their local judicial systems. Out of the disparity of colonial justice grew a concern for technical rules of common law,[60] and expansion of fundamental English liberties,[61] and, as one author contends for Virginia, a greater "judicial recognition of the principles of popular rights by the administration of popular justice."[62]

It perhaps can go without saying that the colonists purposively fitted English common and statute law into their own law, but, as Professor Chafee once cautioned, this may have been done, as there were more frequent evidences of this intent in the later colonial period, in order to bolster the Revolutionary movement against taxation. "And yet colonial law could not be overwhelmingly new law," says Chafee. "Nobody can get outside himself to do his thinking, even after he has tossed for weeks on the Atlantic. No doubt, new surroundings do eventually produce new thoughts, but these do not wholly drive out deeply-rooted attitudes and customary methods of handling practical difficulties. It takes too much trouble to discard everything you know and start all over again."[63]

From the earliest period of settlement, the colonists generally applied principles of law which they had been accustomed to in England to their own legal system – witness, for example, the guarantees of personal rights in the early Mosaic code of Massachusetts. Some colonies at an early date declared English common law to govern in cases not provided for by colonial legislation. The adaptability and selectivity in the colonial legal system to English law and practice is attested to by a resolution of the Maryland Assembly in 1739:

> Resolved further that this Province hath always hitherto had the Common Law, and such General Statutes of England as are not restrained by words of Locall Limitation in them, and such Acts of Assembly as were made in the Province, to suit it's particular Constitution as the Rule and standard of it's Government and Judicature, such Statutes and Acts of Assembly being Subject to the like Rules of Common Law or equitable Construction, as are used by the Judges in Construing Statutes in England . . . .[64]

Or we might also allow for the reasonable accuracy of an observation by the Governor of Rhode Island:

> They doe allow the Laws of England to be pleaded in all cases without partiality (as well for strangers as for serving their own turns) where their own Laws do not extend to; the various circumstances of time and place and people doe often make it necessary to enact and establish Laws different, though not repugnant to the Laws of England.[65]

As time went on, and the colonies became more settled communities, colonial law even more so took on the semblances of English law doctrine and practice.

Naturalization restrictions were gradually lowered in the colonies until they approached a degree of uniformity, although, of course, rights conferred by one colony did not extend beyond its borders. But the distinction of citizenship vis-à-vis of one colony with another was gradually being erased, whereas persons once admitted to citizenship had no difficulty in renewing their rights in another colony. The practice of debarring Hugenots and other foreign dissenters was diminishing until most of the colonies permitted resident foreigners to become British subjects. Typical of colonial legislation in this area was a Massachusetts Act in 1730 which stated that all foreign born inhabitants could "hold and enjoy all the privileges and immunities of his majesty's natural born subjects."[66]

The growth of a uniform postal service, itself a product of improved roads and transportation, aided intercolony comity. Thomas Neale secured a royal patent for running a postal service in 1692 for a period of twenty-one years. Neale's deputy in America, Andrew Hamilton, conferred with various colonial governors to set up uniform regulations and subsidization.[67] He also requested the provincial assemblies to "ascertain and establish such rates and terms as should tend to quicken maintenance among the neighboring colonies and plantations, and that trade and commerce might be better preserved."[68] Soon Hamilton, with the cooperation of the legislatures, had a regular postal system underway from Portsmouth, New Hampshire to Philadelphia. Since at this time most of the mail from the southern colonies went directly to England and Europe, Hamilton did not consider it necessary to link the northern and southern colonies.[69] In 1695, however, a regular post was established from the Potomac River to Philadelphia, with John Perry as post rider at a salary of £ 50 a year; Perry was required to make eight trips a year in addition to carrying all public messages.[70]

Lieutenant Governor Nicholson of Virginia in 1690 had written to the Lords of Trade that a post should be established between Virginia and New England "for we have little intelligence from our neighbors, and to send messengers is tedious and costly."[71] Virginia eventually entered Neale's postal system for carriage of letters only in Virginia.[72] Maryland, however, refused to join. In 1699 Hamilton reported that letters between Virginia and the northern colonies did not exceed one hundred letters a year. In 1718 Virginia refused to accept the postal rates set by the crown on grounds that this was taxation without representation; but in 1752 the colony joined the postal system.[73] Parliament in 1711 set up a postmaster general in England with deputies for the different colonies, and eventually the colonial post office was under the direct responsibility of two deputy postmasters.

The story of the colonial post office or the role played by such prominent deputies as Alexander Spotswood, William Bradford, and Benjamin Franklin need not concern us here. Needless to say, the colonial wars brought about an urgency for news, and the far-flung military operations increased the range of postal services. In 1755 there was a regular post between Philadelphia and Winchester; although postal service between Virginia and Charleston, South Carolina was improved, there was no definite postal system linking the two until 1769.[74] But thanks to the indefatigable colonial post riders, colonial Americans received news from all sections of the country. The increase in the number of newspapers paralleled the expansion of the postal service. Importantly, the average American now read newspapers reflecting an urban, cosmopolitan culture,[75] which henceforward would be a springboard for American nationality.

As Americans, by 1763, were living in closer contact with each other, they were aware of the vast similarities in their institutions and life, and could also assess the value of harmony and uniformity.

NOTES

1 Bronner, *William Penn's Holy Experiment,* 220–21.

2 Wright, ed., *Virginia Plan of 1701,* xxi.

3 Originally the governors had planned to meet in Philadelphia. Council of Trade and Plantations to Governor Blakiston, Sep. 20, 1699, *CSP,* XVII, 443; Evanson, "Nicholson" (unpubl. MA Thesis), 62–65; Beatty, *William Penn as Social Philosopher,* 90–94.

4 Abbot E. Smith, *Colonists in Bondage,* 1607–1776 (Chapel Hill, 1947), 275.

5 Gov. Burrington to the Lords of Trade and Plantations, Feb. 20, 1732, *NCCR,* III, 337; *JHB–Va.* (1695–1702), Sep. 27, 1701, 315; "Journal of the Earl of Egremont," Mar. 16, 1739, *GCR,* V, 137–38; Gov. Henderson Walker to Gov. of Va., 1699, quoted in Ashe, *Hist. of N.C.,* I, 150, 194; Morton, *Colonial Virginia,* I, 427; Crabtree, *N.C. Governors,* 24–25.

6 Col. Fletcher to William Blathwayt, Feb. 14, 1693, Miscellaneous Blathwayt Papers (photostats), NYHS.

7 Gov. Hamilton of E. Jersey to Gov. Fletcher of N.Y., Aug. 28, 1696, *NJA,* II, 115.

8 Gov. Fitch to Pitt, Apr. 10, 1758, *Pitt Corr.,* I, 222.

9 Council of Trade to the Lords Proprietors of Carolina, Feb. 9, 1697, *NCCR,* I, 475.

10 Proceedings of the Congress held at New London, June 21–22, 1711, *NYCD,* V, 257–61.

[11] Spotswood to the Council of Trade, Mar. 9, 1714, *CSP*, XXVIII, 303.

[12] Col. Dudley to Earl of Nottingham, Dec. 19, 1703, Bancroft transcripts, NYPL; *Mass. Acts and Resolves,* IX (1902), Feb. 8, 1710, 106–8; Hanna "New England Military Institutions"(Ph. D. diss.), 110. An early complaint of harboring deserters was lodged against Conn., E. and W. Jersey by N.Y. (Fletcher to Sec. John Trenchard, Nov. 19, 1694, PRO, CO. Vol. 1082, LC.) The high tax levies in Mass. particularly during war spurred inhabitants to move elsewhere. (E.g., Gov. Dudley to the Council of Trade and Plantations, Mar. 1, 1709, *CSP,* XXIV, 235.)

[13] "Act to prevent the detaining or secreting soldiers," June 17, 1758, *RICR,* VI, 155.

[14] Hopkins to Phips, Sep. 5, 1755, MA, Colonial, VI, 631.

[15] Address of Gov. R.H. Morris in *Pennsylvania Gazette,* Feb. 19, 1756; Cheesman A. Herrick, *White Servitude in Pennsylvania* (Philadelphia, 1926), 247–49. For a discourse by Governor Shirley on the question of property rights versus prerogative authority concerning enlistment of indentured servants, see Shirley to Sharpe, Feb. 29, 1756, *Md. Archives,* XXI, 106–111.

[16] Sachs, *et al., The Enterprising Colonials,* 87–88.

[17] Such laws were stringent in the northern colonies, but less so than in the south. For examples of fines upon ship captains for taking slaves out of a colony, see Jeffrey R. Brackett, *The Negro in Maryland: A Study of the Institution of Slavery* (Baltimore, 1889), 82; and Lorenzo J. Greene, *The Negro in Colonial New England, 1620–1776* (New York, 1942), 129–30. On uniformity of machinery of slave control, also see Greene's study, Chapter 5, and Edwin V. Morgan, "The Status of the Slave under the English Colonial Government," *Papers of the American Historical Assoc.,* V (1891), 337–50.

[18] E.g., see "Declaration of the Governor" in *R.I., Gazette,* Oct. 11, 1732.

[19] Instructions to Francis Yonge and John Lloyd, Sep. 19, 1721, *NCCR,* II, 448; Sherman, *Robert Johnson,* 124–25.

[20] E.g., *The Statutes at Large of Pennsylvania,* II (1896), 237. Because of the threatened influx of Indian slaves from the Carolina Indian war, Connecticut in 1715 prohibited importation of Indian slaves from anywhere in the colonies. Order of Gov. and Council, July 8, 1715, *CCR,* V, 516.

[21] Edward McCrady, "Slavery in the Province of South Carolina, 1670–1777," *Annual Report of the ANA for 1895* (Washington, 1896), 666; Edgar J. McManus, *A History of Negro Slavery in New York* (Syracuse, 1966), 125.

[22] Brackett, *Negro in Md.,* 82ff.

[23] Gov. George Clinton to President Palmer, Sep. 12, 1748, *PA,* 1st Ser., II, 16. On New York's request for the assistance of Pennsylvania in the return of Indian slaves captured by the Senecas, see A.W. Lauber, *Indian Slavery in Colonial Times . . .* (*Columbia University Studies . . .,* LIV [New York, 1913]), 224.

[24] Harrington, *New York Merchants,* 206–7, 218–22, 227; Michael Kraus, *Inter-colonial Aspects of American Culture on the Eve of the Revolution* (New York, 1928), 18–22; Williams S. Sachs, "Interurban Correspondents of a National Economy Before the Revolution: New York as a Case Study," *New York History,* XXXVI (1955), 324–30. For a bitter comment on the Boston hegemony see Gov. Pownall to Pitt, Sep. 30, 1758, *Pitt Corr.,* I, 358.

[25] See Kraus, *Inter-colonial Aspects,* 29–39; Carlos R. Allen, Jr., "Travel and Communication in the Early Colonial Period, 1607–1720"(unpubl. Ph. D. diss.,

University of California, 1956), 26; Emory R. Johnson *et al.*, *History of Domestic and Foreign Commerce of the United States* (Washington, D.C., 1915), I, 76; Curtis Nettels, "The Economic Relations of Boston, Philadelphia, and New York, 1680–1715," *Journal of Economic and Business History,* III (1930–1), 185–91. James Glen, *A Description of South Carolina* (London, 1761), in Chapman J. Milling, ed., *Colonial South Carolina: Two Contemporary Descriptions* (Columbia, 1951) specifically discusses trade between S.C., New England, New York, and Pa. Early South Carolina trade channels are outlined in Gov. and Council of Carolina to the Council of Trade and Plantations, Sep. 17, 1709, *CSP*, XXIV, 466–68.

26 William Shirley to Roger Wolcott, Sep. 22, 1753, *Wolcott Papers (CHSC,* XVI [1916]), 374–75. Connecticut appointed Jabez Hamlin and John Ledyard as commissioners for such a meeting. MA, Colonial, IV, 49.

27 Dudley to Winthrop and Leverett, Mar. 25, 1709, Gurdon Saltonstall Papers, MHS.

28 *The Weekly Rehearsal* (Boston), Apr. 7, 1735.

29 John Mitchell, *The Contest in America Between Great Britain and France with its Consequences and Importance* (London, 1757), reprint, 1965, xxiii.

30 Lt. Gov. Colden to Pitt, Dec. 27, 1760 and Gov. Hopkins to Pitt, Dec. 20, 1760, *Pitt Corr.*, II, 381 and 377, resp.; Letter of Lt. Gov. Clarke (1736) quoted in George W. Edwards, *New York as an Eighteenth Century Municipality, 1731–76* (Port Washington, N.Y., 1917), 94; "Observations on the Case of the Provinces. . ., *New York Gazette,* July 14, 1729; "OBSERVATIONS concerning the Increase of Mankind, Peopling of Countries, &c." *FP,* IV, 229, Klaus Knorr, *British Colonial Theories, 1570–1850* (Toronto, 1944), 115–17.

31 Arthur M. Schlesinger, *The Colonial Merchants and the Revolution, 1763–76,* reprint ed. (Atheneum, 1968), 48.

32 Beer, *British Colonial Policy,* 74.

33 For efforts of the governors to concert embargoes on an intercolony basis in each of the colonial wars, see Margaret Morriss, "Colonial Trade of Maryland, 1689–1715," *JHUS,* XXXII (Baltimore, 1914), 93; Evanson,"Nicholson"(unpubl. MA Thesis), 62; "Letters from Gen. Oglethorpe to the Trustees of the Colony and Others, 1735–1744," *GHSC,* III (Savannah, 1873), 33; "American Participation in the War of Jenkins' Ear," *Ga. Hist. Quarterly,* XI (1927), 129–55, 191–215; F.T. Nichols,"The Braddock Expendition" (unpubl. Ph. D. diss.), 205; Root, *Pa. Relations,* 77–79; Dickerson, *American Colonial Government,* 335; Victor L. Johnson, "Fair Traders and Smugglers in Philadelphia, 1754–63," *PMHB,* LXXXIII (1959), 13–16, 128–29; Beer, *British Colonial Policy,* 78; Rossiter Johnson, *A History of the French War* (New York, 1882), 256; Arnold, *Hist. of R.I.*, II, 335; Osgood, *American Colonies,* 120–21, 168–69. Also see pertinent documents: Simon Bradstreet to Gov. Robert Treat, June 28, 1690, CA, Colonial Wars, II, 100; Council of Trade and Plantations to Mr. Secretary Hedges, Feb. 1, 1706, *CSP*, XXIII, 35; *EJCC-Va.*, II, June 10, 1701, Apr. 25, 1702, June 22, 1702, April 10, 1703, 147–48, 230, 236, 257, 313 and III, Feb. 5, 1706 and Apr. 17, 1719, 139 and 498; *Boston News-Letter,* May 22, 1704 in *Weeks, Hist. Digest,* 75; Proclamation (Boston), Oct. 30, 1705, PRO, CO, Vol. 863, LC; Extract of a Letter from St. Augustine by Capt. Kipp, July 25, 1736, *New-York Gazette,* Aug. 30, 1736; Thomas Broughton to Gov. of Va., Feb. 5, 1737, Gratz Collection, Governors, HSP; The Lords of Admiralty to the Lords Justices, Sep. 26, 1743, *Lewis Morris Papers, NJHSC,* IV (1852), 171; Mr. Corbett to the several

governors of his Majesty's Colonies, Privy Council Orders (copy), Aug. 19, 1743, CHS; *South Carolina Gazette,* June 25, 1753; Jonathan Law to Shirley, July 16, 1746, *Law Papers* (*CHSC*, XIII [1911]), II, 263; *Virginia Gazette,* Mar. 7, 1755 (Proclamation of Mar. 6.); Gov. Charles Hardy to the Lords of Trade, June 19, 1756, *NYCD,* VII, 117; Alexander Colden to Cadwallader Colden, May 8, 1756, CP, V (1921), 73; H. Fox to Sir Charles Hardy, Aug. 14, 1756, PRO, WO, Vol. 30, LC; *Md. Archives,* XXXI, 121, May 22, 1756; Additional Instrs. to William Denny, July 5, 1756, *PA*, 8th Ser., VI, 4399; Loudoun to Horatio Sharpe, Mar. 2, 1757, Dreer Collection, XLV, LIII, HSP; Loudoun to Pitt, June 17, 1757, *Pitt. Corr.*, I, 78; Isaac Norris to William Denny, June 15, 1757, Loudoun Papers (Huntington Lib.), microfilm in Pa. St. Archives, Harrisburg. Gov. William Denny to Loudoun, June 18, 1757, *ibid.*; William Pepperrell to Gov. Denny, June 6, 1757, *ibid.*; Sharpe to William Sharpe, July 6, 1757, *Md. Archives,* IX (*Sharpe Corr.*, II), 50; Sharpe's Order to the several Officers of the Customs, June 27, 1757, *Md. Archives,* XXXI, 229; "Remonstrance of the Merchants," June 14, 1757, *PA* 8th Ser., VI, 4571; (Agent) James Abercromby to Samuel Swann, May 13, 1757, James Abercromby Letter Book, Va. State Lib.; (Gen) James Abercromby to Gov. Denny, May 8, 1758, Emmet Collection, #4421 NYPL; Abercromby to Gov. De Lancey, May 8, 1758, *ibid.*, #1723; Pitt to Abercromby, Jan. 11, 1758, *Pitt Corr.*, I, 59; James De Lancey to Gov. Denny, July 12, 1758, Ebenezer Hazard Collection, N.Y. Records, LC; Abercromby to Pitt, Mar. 16, 1758, *Pitt Corr.*, II, 208; John Blair to Pitt, June 29, 1758, *ibid.*, I, 288; Lt. Gov. Colden to Pitt (Abstract), Oct. 27, 1760, *ibid.*, II, 348–9; Gen. Amherst to Gov. of R.I., May 7, 1762, *RICR,* VI, 318.

34 "An Act for granting His Majesty a Duty of Tonnage... [Pa.]," –May, 1758, (Newspaper Abstracts), *NJA*, 1st Ser., XX (IV), 206; *The Colonial Laws of New York,* II (Albany, 1894), 843–44; Johnson, *Domestic and Foreign Commerce,* I 56–7, 63; Harrington, *New York Merchants,* 276–80; Gipson, *British Empire,* X, 85.

35 Quoted in E.A.J. Johnson, "Some Evidence of Mercantilism in the Massachusetts Bay," *NEQ,* I (1928), 391.

36 *Ibid.;* "Reasons why the revenue of N.Y. was not so great, 1692–97 as in 1687," *CSP,* XVII, 29; Johnson, *Domestic and Foreign Commerce,* I, 57; Harrington, *New York Merchants,* 276–80.

37 Petition of the Proprietors of East New Jersey, Mar. 9, 1699, *CSP,* XVII, 94–5; Friedelbaum, "Bellomont" (PH. D. diss.), 182–84; "Proposals of William Penn to the House of Lords...," –Apr., 1697, *CSP,* XV, 471–73; Nettels, "Economic Relations of Boston, Phila., N.Y.," *Journal of Economic and Business Hist.,* III (1931), 196–97; Johnson, *Domestic and Foreign Commerce,* I, 57–58. To follow further the course of retaliatory legislation between Pa. and Md., see Gary B. Nash, "Maryland's Economic War with Pennsylvania," *MHM,* LX (1965), 236ff.; Charles H. Lincoln, *The Revolutionary Movement in Pennsylvania, 1760–76* (Philadelphia, 1901), 55ff.

38 Mr. Fitzwilliam to the Council of Trade and Plantations, Mar. 12, 1731, *CSP,* XXXVIII, 57; *JHB-Va.* (1702–12), May 25, 1706, 203; F.W. Clonts, "Travel and Transportation in Colonial North Carolina," *NCHR,* III (1926), 23; Nettels, "Economic Relations of Boston, Phila., N.Y.," *Journal of Economic and Bus. Hist.,* III (1931), 201.

39 "Considerations Humbly Offered..." [by an anonymous North Carolinian], May 19, 1704, in Hart, ed., *American History Told by Contemporaries,* II, 248; "Gov.

James Glen's Answers to the Lords of Trade," ed. Plowden C.J. Weston in *Documents Connected with the History of South Carolina* (London, 1856), 82; Marvin L. Skaggs, "North Carolina Boundary Disputes Involving her Southern Line," *The James Sprunt Studies,* XXV (1941), 15–16; Leila Sellers, *Charleston Business on the Eve of the American Revolution* (Chapel Hill, 1934), 34.

[40] Paul C. Phillips, *The Fur Trade,* I (Norman, Okla., 1961), 313; Andrews, *Colonial Period,* IV, 105; Harrington, *New York Merchants*, 279–81; Johnson, *Domestic and Foreign Commerce,* II, 60–61.

[41] Wright, ed., *An Essay on Government* (1701), 47–48.

[42] Richard Jackson to Franklin, Dec. 27, 1763, *FP*, X, 415.

[43] George L. McKay, *Early American Currency,* (New York, 1944), 45.

[44] Gov. Shute's Speech to the Assembly, *Weekly Rehearsal* (Boston), Nov. 19, 1733. Particularly the land bank and currency troubles of Gov. Shute.

[45] Report of Resolutions of House of Commons, Mar. 12, 1750, Bancroft transcripts (England and America), NYPL.

[46] Fry, *New Hampshire as a Royal Province.* 404.

[47] *American Weekly Mercury* (Philadelphia), Dec. 19, 1732, quoting a law enacted by N.J. A resolution passed the Pa. House with Pa. to prevent counterfeit bills from being admitted into Pa. (Order of the House, Mar. 31, 1727, *PA,* 8th Ser., III 1809.)

[48] Sachs *et al., The Enterprising Colonials,* 120.

[49] Nettels, "Economic Relations of Boston, Phila., and N.Y.," *Journal of Economic and Bus. Hist.*, III (1931), 194.

[50] William Z. Ripley, *The Financial History of Virginia, 1609–1776 (Columbia University Studies . . .,* IV [New York, 1893]), 144–45.

[51] Beatty, *William Penn as a Social Philosopher,* 91–92.

[52] Council of Trade and Plantations to Gov. Dudley, Feb. 4, 1706, *CSP*, XXIII, 44.

[53] Gov. Belcher's speech to the House of Rep., *New-England Weekly Journal,* June 3, 1734, concerning request for premiums on "Cultivation of the Lands, as on Hemp and other Naval Stores, and on English Grain." An act for bounties on hemp and flax passed the N.H. Leg. *The Weekly Rehearsal* (Boston), May 26, 1735.

[54] E.g., see the writings of Franklin, Hugh Vance, or a tract written by an anonymous Carolinian, *An Essay on Currency* (1734), fascimile (Charleston, 1950).

[55] As Spotswood noted, in the courts of Virginia during his time "the General Court and Courts of Oyer and Terminer, the Court of Vice Admiralty and the County Courts . . . no one Justice has ever been appointed by me without such Advice" of the Council. Spotswood to the Lords Commissioners of Trade and Plantations, Feb. 7, 1716, *Spotswood Corr.*, II, 192–93. Before 1718 all colonial laws were referred by the Board of Trade to the Attorney General and Solicitor General. Thereafter the Board of Trade appointed a legal adviser to serve as a standing counsel. In 1751 the Board of Trade recommended to the Council Committee "the framing a new body of good and well digested laws in all the colonies." Francis K. Fane, *Reports on the Laws of Connecticut* (1733–41), ed. Charles M. Andrews (–[Acorn Club], 1915), 32–37.

[56] Smith, *South Carolina as a Royal Province,* 82.

[57] [Thomas Pownall?], "The state of the government of Massachusetts as it stood in the year 1757," Massachusetts Miscellany, LC.

[58] Schutz, *Pownall*, 188.

[59] Zechariah Chafee, "Colonial Courts and the Common Law," *MHSP*, LXVIII (1947), 134–35.

[60] Paul Reinsch, "English Common Law in the Early American Colonies," *Bulletin of the University of Wisconsin,"* No. 31 (Madison, 1899), Thjis study takes a different view from Chafee in stressing indigenous origins of American common law. Also for a brief essay on colonial adaptation and interpretation of the principles of Magna Carta and the common law, see Lawrence H. Leder, *Liberty and Authority: Early American Political Ideology, 1689–1763* (Chicago, 1968), Chapter 6. The Reinsch and Goebel essays have been most recently reprinted in David H. Flaherty, *Essays in the History of Early American Law* (Chapel Hill, 1969). See Part Three of this volume for further details on comparison of the colonial legal systems in the eighteenth century.

[61] E.g., the origins of the Fifth Amendment; see Leonard W. Levy, *Origins of the Fifth Amendment* (New York, 1968).

[62] George L. Chumbley, *Colonial Justice in Virginia* (Richmond, 1938), 155.

[63] Chafee, "Colonial Courts," *MHSP*, LXVIII (1947), 137–38.

[64] Assembly Proceedings, May 1–2, 1739, *Md. Archives*, XL, 284.

[65] "Reply of the Governor and Company of Rhode Island . . . to the charges exhibited, Mar. 26, 1705," Feb. 1, 1706, *CSP*, XXIII, 34.

[66] Joseph Willard, "Naturalization in the American Colonies," *MHSP*, IV (1860), 349, 352. For a comparison of the two "species" of naturalization operating in the colonies–English and colonial–see Cora Start, "Naturalization in the English Colonies in America." *Annual Report of the Amer. Hist. Assoc. for 1893* (Washington, 1894), 317–28. A New York law of 1715 was typical–declaring all persons of foreign birth and "being alive in this colony," after taking a loyalty oath, to be citizens. Act of July 5, 1715, *The Colonial Laws of New York,* I (1894), 862. The famous Parliamentary Act of 1740 gave citizenship to residents of seven years. For statistics of persons in the colonies naturalized under this Act, see M.S. Giuseppi, *Naturalizations of Foreign Protestants in the American and West Indian Colonies . . .* (Manchester, 1921).

[67] Proclamation of Gov. Andros of Va., Jan 12, 1693, Bancroft transcripts (American Colonies), NYPL; Howard Robinson, *The British Post Office: A History* (Princeton, 1948), 167–68.

[68] Quoted in William Smith, "The Colonial Post-Office," *AHR*, XXI (1916), 211.

[69] *Ibid.*, 266, 268.

[70] Gatke, "Plans of American Colonial Union" (Ph. D. diss.), 81; "An Act Encouraging a Post Office." *MHSC*, 3d Ser., VII, 51–52 lists rates to points from Boston, i.e.:

6 pence a letter, to or from	R.I.
9 pence a letter, to or from	Conn.
12 pence a letter, to or from	N.Y.
15 pence a letter, to or from	Pa.
2 shillings a letter, to or from	Jerseys

----	Md. and Va.
3 pence a letter, to or from	Salem
4 pence a letter, to or from	Ipswich and east of Salem
6 pence a letter, to or from	Piscataqua, etc. in proportion

[71] Lt. Gov. Nicholson to Lords of Trade, Aug. 20, 1690, quoted in Gatke, *ibid.*, 80.

[72] *Ibid.*, 81; *JHB-Va.* (1660–1693), Mar. 17, 1693, 430.

[73] Smith, "Colonial Post-Office," *AHR,* XXI (1916), 268.

[74] *Ibid.*, 261-68; Robinson, *British Post Office,* 168–70; Harry M Konwiser, *Colonial and Revolutionary Posts* (Richmond, 1931), 21; "Post Office Department Records," *MHSC,* 3d Ser., VII (1838), 84–87; Colden to James Alexander, May 20, 1729, *NJA,* 1st Ser., V, 237–43; Franklin to James Wright, July 9, 1759, *FP,* VIII, 412–14 and 336n., 413–14n.

[75] For American symbols in the colonial press, see Richard L. Merritt, "The Colonists Discover America: Attention Patterns in the Colonial Press, 1735–75," *WMQ,* 3d Ser., XXI (1964), 270–87.

CHAPTER XIII

PATRIOTISM

If the colonies could not effectively unite "for their common defense and security against their enemies, and how sensible soever each colony has been of that necessity," asked Franklin of critics of America in 1760, "can it reasonably be supposed there is any danger of their uniting against their own nation, which protects and encourages them, with which they have so many connections and ties of blood, interest and affection, and which 'tis well known they all love more than they love one another?" But Franklin foresaw that the "most grievous tyranny and oppression" could drive the colonies into union.[1]

Franklin did not perceive at the time that another force could also contribute to the creation of an American nation. What C. M. Andrews has called the "silent revolution" – Americanization – was taking form.[2] Within a very few years after Franklin's observation, the colonist was beginning to be aware that he was a new man, a British American, as is evident in the majority use of native rather than British symbols in the colonial press after 1763.[3]

It was the fact that because they were Englishmen, the colonists were constructing a new nationality; as special protectors of English liberties, they sought an accomodation of a diverse population, an open-ended society, unrestrained pursuit of special and private interests, and geographic mobility – reverse elements from the rise of nationality in Europe but nevertheless important ingredients of a new American nationality. The more the colonists developed a maturity in their political institutions, the more they began to see their history in perspective – an inheritance of English and natural rights, forming a society of free men. American political tracts appealed to the legacy of Magna Carta and all the liberties of the British Constitution.[4] Theses presented at college commencements increasingly stressed the origins of government from the free consent of men in a state of nature, the rights of kings deriving from the popular will, and the necessity of majority rule.[5] The colonists were finding that a perspective and appreciation of the past is indispensable to freedom and that likewise it is a basis of nationality.

An English culture provided for an intercolonial solidarity. A seaboard people of English origins held political and social control, while other racial elements were largely confined to the frontier. The idea of universal public education was spreading,[6] even if the attainment of this goal outside of New England belonged to a distant future. Diffusion of public knowledge, which soon became the practical aim of a proliferation of societies formed during the American Enlightenment, received an early impetus in Cadwallader Colden's proposal in 1729 for a central library in New York to serve that colony and neighboring colonies.[7] Intercolonial family and merchant ties contributed to social cohesion, while at the same time enlarged the sphere of action and mobility. In religion, there was emerging a sense of common purpose transcending colonial boundaries.[8] A new evangelical ministry brought the common people into "spiritual contact" with congregations of other provinces. As John C. Miller has said: "In a sense, the Great Awakening was a nationwide movement before a nation had been formed and its contribution towards making the nation that later came into being is perhaps not the least of its influences."[9]

Along with the growth of Americanization came the feeling, to some, of pride and joy in being an American. Thus the homesick John Dickinson wrote his mother in 1754:

> But notwithstanding all the diversions of England, I shall return to America with rapture. There is something surprizing in it, but nothing is more true than that no place is comparable to our native country. It is some strange affection nature has implanted in us, for her wise ends. America is, to be sure, a wilderness, and yet that wilderness to me is more pleasing than this charming garden. I dont know how, but I dont seem to have any connections with this country; I think myself only a traveller, and this the inn. But when I think of America, that word produces a thousand pleasing images; it is endeard by my past pleasures there, by my future prospects; that word includes my Honoured Parents, my dear relations, my friends and every thing that makes life valuable. I can bear a comparison between it and any other place. Tis rude, but it's innocent. Tis wild, but it's private. There life is a stream pure and unruffled, here an ocean briny and tempestuous. There we enjoy life, here we spend it. And indeed, till I see it again, I shall not be so happy as I think it possible to be on earth . . . .[10]

If the idea of "country" was not receiving the generic connotation as was "American," yet "country" by mid-century was beginning to mean something more than a particular colony. In patriotic essays published in New England during the 1730's "my country" meant New England.[11] The groupings of the colonies according to interests in trade, Indian affairs, the colonial wars, and westward expansion contributed to the growth of regional identity.

Defending one's home against foreign invasion could be easily translated into the protection of the peculiar distinctiveness of a people. John Wise on his return from the Phips expedition of 1690 could speak of the spirit of fighting to preserve the New England way.

> There are men Enough in New England that will offer themselves as Volunteirs in this Service for their King, country, and nation. Only They pray, and hope They may bee resetled in the Enjoyment of their Auntient Charter rights and priviledges which were the Sole inducement to Their fathers, at their own proper costs and charge, to subdue a Wildernesse, and Inlarge the Dominions of the Crown of England.[12]

And a half century later an anonymous Virginian could broaden the appeal:

> The Earl of Loudoun, like another Fabius, is watching the Motions of the French to the Northward, and all the Northern Colonies are in Motion to assist him. and shall that Colony which calls itself the most dutiful and loyal; which has been so frequently fired with Resentment and Indignation at the Encroachments and Depredations of the French; and offered the Lives and Fortunes of it's People to defend his Majesty's just Rights; shall the eldest and, I am persuaded, the richest Sister of all the British Colonies, sit supine and negligent; and, like a proud Boaster be only big in Words, while her younger Sisters are gaining Laurels in the Field, and Credit and Reputation with their common Sovereign? No, my Friend! let it not be said; but let yours and every Patriot Spirit be roused and really fired with Resentment and indignation against the cruel Ravagers of their Country.[13]

The real and imagined dangers from a foreign power served as a catalyst for national consciousness. Even the Scottish rebellions were interpreted in America as French invasion of British territory.[14] Americans shared in British pride over French defeats in Europe, although the colonies usually had to be prompted by royal order to hold days of public thanksgiving celebrating the military victories[15] — for success in colonial arms, however, there was no such hesitation. A theme of letters of the colonial governors in the last colonial war was that the people should "unite as one Man" and trust in "His Majesty's gracious Favour and princely Protection."[16] Assistance from the mother country would raise in the colonies "an Emulation, which shall Exceed in duty and Obedience to their Sovereigns Commands."[17] Victory over the French would establish a new order of the ages of liberty and peace under a benevolent sovereign. As the Virginia Council put it in 1755:

> We may reasonably hope to see the Peace of *America* Settled upon a Foundation that will not be shaken for Ages yet to come. –
>
> To drive the *French* from our Borders to maintain the just Rights of the Crown and to reestablish the Tranquillity of the British empire in North America are views that must warm the Patriots Breast . . . .[18]

The French threat in the French and Indian War was considered one of survival – a war against barbarians and the possibility of Americans being driven "into the Sea."[19] Washington wrote that nothing could keep him from resigning his commission except the "imminent danger to my country."[20]

A large dose of religious bigotry fanned patriotic ardor. Pepperrell's expedition in 1745 was personally blessed by George Whitefield who gave the army a motto for their flag: "*Nil desperandum, Christo Duce* – Nothing is to be despaired of, Christ being the leader." Most of the officers were chosen from church deacons and one soldier carried an axe to cut down images and crosses of the French churches.[21] In 1692 the Massachusetts General Court warned that if Connecticut persisted in refusing to cooperate with the other New England colonies as Connecticut had done in scuttling the New England Confederation two years before, Christ and Country would be threatened:

> You cannot be unsensible that not onely the whole of their Majesties interests in this part of their Dominions but also the Interest of Christ here is in danger of being exposed unless God raise up a Spirit to joine with one heart and Shoulder in the Opposing of this Common Enemy.[22]

Samuel Sewall in 1706 prayed that "God will speedily bring forward a glorious Reformation in New Spain, and cause the Kingdoms of this New World to become the Kingdoms of our Lord and of his Christ."[23] Appeals to the common mission of church and state intended to strike up colonial unity. Royal governors did not miss this opportunity.

> In this critical situation let us his Majestys faithful subjects of the Colony of North Carolina shew that we are true sons of Britain whose ancestors have been ever famous for defending their valuable religion and liberties, and that we are still Inspired with the same spirit of Liberty, and are determined to support our Religious, and civil rights, and hand them down to our Posterity
>
> . . . .
>
> Let us then behave like generous brave men and true christians [and] for a little while confine our appetites and luxuries and part with a reasonable part of our wealth to preserve the Remainder and our happy Constitution in church and state to our latest posterity. This

> will shew the Gallic Monarch, and his insatiable ministry that we are not to be Intimidated or to be bullied out of our rights and that if he should Insist upon his Romantic scheme of surrounding, confining, and enslaving us, that we will Jointly and Unanimously support our valuable religion Liberties and Properties with our lives and fortunes, and that whilst we behave like brave men and true Christians we are sure of the protection of God our Messiah and that we will not only be happy in this world but to endless Ages.[24]

The sense of desperation of the last colonial war especially evoked religious hatred. Following Braddock's defeat a mob almost tore down "the Mass House" in Philadelphia, and night watchers had to be appointed in Lancaster to prevent attacks upon Catholic property.[25] The Acadians forcibly relocated in Pennsylvania and elsewhere were kept under close surveillance and denied civil liberties. In Virginia, Hugenot immigrants, because they refused to take an oath of supremacy and allegiance, were forbidden to possess firearms or a horse valued over £ 5.[26] Daniel Dulany of Maryland noted in 1755: "The clamors against Popery are as loud as ever. One of our priests had like to have fallen into the hands of the army when the troops were at Alexandria, and if he had, I believe he would have been hanged as a spy."[27] New England troops, befitting a New Model Army even in the last colonial war at Albany, had constant prayers and psalm singing and two sermons a week, and as one observer enviably commented on the discipline, they "are in the very best Frame of Mind for an Army, looking for Success in a Dependance upon Almighty God and a Concurrence of Means. Would to God, the New-England Disposition in this Respect were catching."[28]

A feeling of the superiority of virtue in America combined with military confidence to bring about pride in being an American. Especially the two expeditions and victories at Louisbourg in 1745 and 1758 involved a good deal of propaganda and public acclaim on the superiority of the "Character of British Subjects."[29] Governor Clinton saw a significance in the first Louisbourg victory in that "we shall no longer sit still as unconcerned Spectators; nor be content that the neighbouring Colonies alone . . . unassisted by us, reap the Glory of a Conquest so considerable . . . ."[30] There was also the idea that honor within the empire had to be earned. Governor George Thomas in addressing the Pennsylvania House of Representatives in 1740 noted:

> From His Majesty's Royal Virtues, and His impartial Regard for all His Subjects, I agree with you, that we have Reason to hope for a Share of His Protection with His other Subjects in *America*: But should we

> declare we are unwilling to be at any Expence, or to expose our Persons to any Danger, and at the same time implore the Assistance of our Mother Country, I fear we shall rather expose ourselves to Derision and Contempt, than obtain its Compassion or Protection.[31]

The *New-York Mercury* in July 1755 expressed much the same opinion:

> God grant us all that Success against our perfidious Enemies, which we have Reason to expect from Armies conducted by Generals of *unwearied* Industry, and Vigilance for the Service of their Country, and an *animated* Zeal, for the Rights and Dignity of the British Crown.[32]

Taking Canada was a project that all Americans could become emotionally involved in, especially in light of the traditional wars against France by the mother country and the religious prejudice against Catholics. In 1711 all the colonies adopted resolutions to the Queen asking that another expedition be sent against Canada.[33] Pressures had built up by the time of the last colonial war. "Canada, my Lord, Canada must be demolished," exhorted a prominent New Yorker. "Delenda est Carthago, or we are undone."[34] Many could echo the view of Charles Lee that "I hope we shall have no peace 'till N. America is ours."[35]

What was yet scarcely realized was that, once the French were removed from Canada and the Spaniards from Florida,[36] the colonies would lose a source of particular irritants among themselves and, with security along the borders, they could afford to pursue an independency with the mother country, which could now supplant the enemy as the "outside threat." If the colonies "had any ambitious views," noted an anonymous writer in 1759, "a strong colony, of a natural enemy to England, on their borders, would be the only article that would render an attempt of independency truly dangerous."[37] In the same year a worried Frenchman made the same observation:

> Although the lack of cooperation among the English colonies, and the division of the English forces may have been very favorable for Canada, is it to these causes only that should be ascribed the safety of that colony, and should those two causes have been regarded as purely the fruit of chance?
>
> The lack of cooperation of their colonies is doubtless a weakness on their side; but that lack of cooperation will be much more prevalent if several of their colonies are exposed to attack. By abandoning Canada we would give up the points of attack which can most inspire them with fear and uneasiness; as a result they will have more opportunity for acting with security, union, and cooperation.[38]

Franklin mused that from an imperial viewpoint it would be advantageous to leave Canada in the hands of the French. British Canada would create a market for American manufactures and commerce. But by restoring Canada to the French "we may have occasion constantly to employ, in time of war, a fleet and army in those parts" and "the French may, by means of their Indians, carry on . . . a constant scalping war against our colonies, and thereby stint their growth; for, otherwise the children might in time be as tall as their mother."[39]

The quest for territory was posed in terms of extending English freedoms. Thus Robert Livingston, Jr. wrote in 1760: "God Grant we may Soon take all Canada, and keep it while the world Stands, that we may be relieved from Sundry pette Tyrants who, rule with a rod of Iron the best Subjects the King of Great Britain has in all his Kingdoms."[40] The Massachusetts Council in 1761 resolved referring to the conquest of Canada: "This event gives us the greater joy as we have contributed so largely to effect it . . . . To our relation to Great Britain we owe our present freedom. No other Nation upon Earth . . . could have delivered us from the Enemy we had to contend with."[41] Taking the Ohio country was viewed as an opportunity to establish freedom of conscience and other English freedoms,[42] and some of the colonial resolutions, such as that of the Virginia Council in 1755, had the air of a "spread eagle nationalism:"

> The Great and important Business of the *Ohio* we have always considered in a National Light not as *Virginians* but as Britons, and what Difficulties will not a Briton surmount what Dangers will he not encounter when he is engaged in the Glorious cause of his King and Country.[43]

The colonists were learning how to sell a war effort by combining appeals to patriotism and freedom. Witness a few verses from a recruiting song for the Maryland Independent Company in 1754:

> Over the Hills with Heart we go,
> to fight the proud insulting Foe;
> Our Country calls, and we'll obey
> Over the Hills, and far Away
>
> . . . .
>
> No Popery nor Slavery
> No arbitrary Pow'r for me.
> But Royal George's righteous Cause
> The Protestant and British Laws.
>
> . . . .

Who'er is bold, who'er is free
Will join and come along with me;
To drive the French without delay,
Over the Hills, and far Away.[44]

Perhaps it is the fate of a democracy, where the preponderant majority governs, to have nationalism linked with militarism. As De Tocqueville later pointed out the truism, when the majority has made up its mind to go to war there is no swerving from the projected goals. The colonial wars, in stirring up patriotism of the majority of the population, can be estimated a major factor in promoting a sense of national purpose. That the colonies were often at odds with each other and did not always wholeheartedly support war measures is another question; in sentiment – even to the extent of "my country; right or wrong"– they were united.

Thus the idea that the colonial wars were fought for freedom did not take into account the right publicly to resist a war effort. When the victory at Louisbourg was celebrated in Philadelphia in 1745 with the fanfare of toasts, cannon, "Bonfires, Illuminations, and other Demonstrations of Joy," a mob gathered and broke the windows of houses that were not lighted.[45] In 1755, in Milford, Connecticut, one Edward Cole was publicly whipped and branded for having published a "scurrilous Letter" which tended "to beget Ill-will, and breeding a Disunion in the several Governments in America, the contrary of which, at this Time, and present Situation of our Affairs, is much wanted."[46]

The colonial wars demonstrated the tendency of democracy to be reduced to mobocracy in wartime. British authorities had not learned the modern techniques of manipulating popular deomocracy. They feared the tendencies towards levelling and anarchic factiousness. Governor Shirley blamed democratic government getting out of hand for the mob action over the impressment of sailors in 1746.[47] Cadwallader Colden reported in 1754 that "the Inhabitants of the Northern Colonies are all so nearly on a level, and a licentiousness, under the notion of liberty, so generally prevails, that they are impatient under all kind of superiority and authority."[48]

The possibilities of developing a plebiscatory democracy to serve the national interest were not foreseen by royal placemen; rather democracy to them meant Whiggish party divisions struggling for power, the anathema of true patriotism. "From the Moment that Men give themselves wholly up to a Party," an essayist wrote in *The Independent Reflector* of February 22, 1753, "they abandon their *Reason*, and are led Captive by their *Passions* . . . . A disinterested Love for their Country, is succeeded by an intemperate Ardor; which naturally swells into a political Enthusiasm; and from that, easy is the Transition to perfect Frenzy."[49] To one observer American democracy lacked a frame of reference; there were not "the Loyal and Jacobite, the Governor and Country-Whig and Tory, or any religious sectary denominations" – only the debtor versus the creditor.[50] Colonel Henry Bouquet lamented the want of aristocracy and merit in American democracy, which he found honored only power and wealth.[51]

The colonists of 1763 were loyal British Americans, but that loyalty would now come at a price, to be calculated in the gains and benefits from the empire befitting a people matured in their English liberties. They would no longer tolerate economic and political restrictions from abroad. By going with the tide of colonial maturity, the British government may have been able to perfect a national political incorporation of the colonies under the imperial system; by going against it, collective secession would be inevitable. The colonists themselves would find that patriotism and federalism were not incompatible.

NOTES

1 "The Interest of Great Britain Considered . . ." (1760), *FP,* IX, 90.

2 Charles M. Andrews, *Colonial Background of the American Revolution* (New Haven, 1924), 178 and Chapter 4.

3 Richard L. Merritt, *Symbols of American Community, 1735–1775* (New Haven, 1966), 125.

4 E.g., see "The Philopatrios Essays on the Cherokee Wars, Gadsden to the Gentlemen Electors of the Parish of St. Paul," Feb. 5, 1763 in Richard Walsh, ed., *The Writings of Christopher Gadsden, 1746–1805* (Columbia, S.C., 1966), 29–50. For the development of a "Whig conscience" among American colonial historians, see H. Trevor Colbourn, *The Lamp of Experience: Whig History and the Intellectual Origins of the American Revolution* (Chapel Hill, 1965), chapters 2 and 3.

5 James J. Walsh, *Education of the Founding Fathers of the Republic: Scholasticism in the Colonial Colleges* (New York, 1935), 118, 169.

6 Marcus Jernegan, *Laboring and Dependent Classes in Colonial America, 1607–1783* (Chicago, 1931), 4.

7 Cadwallader Colden to James Alexander, May 20, 1729, *NJA*, 1st Ser., V 237–43. Colden's plan was endorsed by the Society for the Propagation of the Gospel in Foreign Parts.

8 E.g., see H.J. Cadbury, "Intercolonial Solidarity of American Quakers," *PMHB,* LX (1936), 362–74.

[9] J. C. Miller, "Religion, Finance, and Democracy in Massachusetts," *NEQ,* VI (1933), 29-58.

[10] Dickinson to his mother, May 25, 1754, 274–75, H. Trevor Colbourn, ed., "A Pennsylvania Farmer at the Court of King George: John Dickinson's London Letters, 1754–56," *PMHB,* LXXXVI (1962).

[11] Shipton, "The New England Frontier," *NEQ,* X (1937), 27. For early definitions of "American" and American patriotism, see Calhoun Winton, "Jeremiah Dummer: The 'First American'" *WMQ*, 3d Ser., XXVI (1969), 105–8.

[12] Green, ed., "Sir William Phips's Expedition . . .,*MHSP,* XV (1902), 318.

[13] Letter S/ 'Philopatria' [Richard Bland?] to Washington, Hamilton, ed., *Letters to Washington,* I, 394.

[14] John Rutherford to Daniel Horsmanden, Feb. 19, 1748, Horsmanden Papers, NYHS; "The humble Address of the Governor and Council of the Province of Maryland," Aug. 13, 1746, *Md. Archives,* XXVIII, 364–65.

[15] E.g., the circular letter of the Board of Trade, Aug. 2, 1704, ordering the celebration of the battle of Blenheim. See Arnold, *Hist. of R.I.,* II, 15.

[16] Belcher to Shirley, Apr. 4, 1754, Belcher Letter Book, MHS; Belcher to Dinwiddie, Apr. 8, 1754, *ibid*.; Gov. William Greene to Thomas Robinson, Apr. 17, 1755, Parkman transcripts, XL, MHS.

[17] Benning Wentworth to Sir Thomas Robinson, Dec. 13, 1754, PRO, CO, Vol. 15, LC.

[18] H.R. McIlwaine, ed., *Legislative Journals of the Council of Colonial Virginia*, May 5, 1755, III (1919), 1132.

[19] Belcher to Gov. Morris, July 9, 1755, Belcher Letter Book, MHS; Belcher to Sir John St. Clair, Sep. 3, 1755, *ibid.*

[20] Bradley, *Fight with France for North America,* 205.

[21] De Normandie, "Sir William Pepperrell," *MHSP*, XVII (1903), 89; Johnson, *History of the French War,* 158.

[22] Joseph Addington (Boston) to Gen. Ct. of Connecticut, May 7, 1692, CA, Colonial Wars, II, 157.

[23] Samuel Sewall to Joseph Lord, Feb. 6, 1706, "Sewall Letter Book," *MHSC,* 6th Ser., I, 325. See Cotton Mather, *Decennium Luctuosum* [The Sorrowful Decade] . . . *Remarkable Occurrences in the Long War . . . with the Indian Savages* (1699) in Charles H. Lincoln, ed., *Narratives of the Indian Wars, 1675–99 (Original Narrative Series* [New York, 1913]), 215–77 and *passim* for the belief in the triumph of New England Puritan virtues in war and peace.

[24] Speech of Gov. of N.C. to Council and General Assembly, Dec. 18, 1754, *NCCR*, V, 224–25.

[25] Extract of a letter of a Gentleman in N.Y. to his friend in Boston, July 27, 1755,*Virginia Gazette*, Sep. 5, 1758; Nichols,"The Braddock Expedition" (Ph. D. diss.), 447.

[26] Morton, *Colonial Virginia,* II, 688–89.

[27] Daniel Dulany, "Military and Political Affairs in the Middle Colonies" (1755), *PMHB,* III (1879), 27.

[28] Extract of letter . . .,July 27, 1755, *Virginia Gazette.* Sep. 5, 1758.

[29] *New Hampshire Gazette,* Aug. 25, 1758; Arthur H. Buffington, "The Canada Expedition of 1746," *AHR*, XLV (1940), 563.

[30] Gov. Clinton's Speech to Council and Assembly of N.Y., June 25, 1745 in *The New-York Evening Post,* July 1, 1745.

[31] *American Weekly Mercury* (Philadelphia), Jan. 22, 1740.

[32] *The New-York Mercury,* July 7, 1755.

[33] Arnold, *Hist. of R.I.,* II, 45.

[34] [Livingston], *Review of the Military Operations,* 163.

[35] Charles Lee to Miss Sidney Lee, Dec. 7, 1758, *Charles Lee Papers, NYHSC,* IV (1871), I, 18.

[36] Spanish Florida had been held in contempt by South Carolinians because it had been a "Den of Thieves and Riffians! Receptacle of Debtors, Servants and Slaves! Bane of Industry and Society!" Report of the committee to Enquire into Causes of the Disappointment in the Late Expedition . . . (1741), *JCHA-SC,* III, 84.

[37] *South-Carolina Gazette,* Jan. 12, 1759.

[38] "Memoir of Etienne de Silhouette on Migration Proposed from Canada to Louisiana, Feb. 1759," Pease, ed., *Anglo-French Boundary Disputes, IHSC,* XXVII (1936), 261–62.

[39] "Humourous Reasons for Restoring Canada," from the *London Chronicle,* Dec. 27, 1759 in Crane, ed., *Franklin's Letters to the Press,* 13–14.

[40] Robert Livingston, Jr. to Abraham Yates, Feb. 8, 1760, Abraham Yates Papers, NYPL.

[41] Mass. Council to Gov. Bernard, Feb. 8, 1761, PRO, WO: 34, XXVI, LC.

[42] *South-Carolina Gazette,* Jan 12, 1759.

[43] McIlwaine, ed., *Legislative Journals of the Council of Colonial Va.,* May 5, 1755, III, 1133.

[44] "A recruiting Song for the Maryland Independent Company written by an officer of the company, Sep. 1754." *Md. Mag. of Hist.,* III, 1–2. Not until the eve of the Revolution did British policy in the west, according to a recent study, generate patriotism in Virginia hostile to Great Britain. This was done by Lord Dunmore's announcing the sale of public lands at auction at quintupled prices. Thad W. Tate, "The Coming of the Revolution in Virginia: Britain's Challenge to Virginia's Ruling Class, 1763–76," *WMQ,* 3d Ser., XIX, 338.

[45] *Pennsylvania Gazette* extract, July 18, 1745, *FP,* III, 57.

[46] *Pennsylvania Gazette,* Dec. 11, 1755.

[47] Brown, *Middle Class Democracy in Mass.,* 55.

[48] Colden to Halifax, Aug. 3, 1754, Pargellis, ed., *Military Affairs in North America,* 19.

[49] *The Independent Reflector,* Feb. 22, 1753, ed. Milton M. Klein (Cambridge, 1963), 143. For the fear of "democratical despotism" in the colonies, see Bernard Bailyn, ed., *Pamphlets of the American Revolution, 1750–76,* I (Cambridge, 1965), chapter 7 of the Introduction, "The Contagion of Liberty."

[50] Douglass, *A Summary, Historical and Political* (1755), I, 535.

[51] Bouquet to Miss Ann Willing, Jan. 15, 1761, in George H. Fischer, "Brigadier-General Henry Bouquet," *PMHB,* III (1879), 141–42.

CHAPTER XIV

AN EVALUATION

Ideas and institutions of government are shaped through the cauldron of time and experience. Jefferson's adage that "all experience hath shown, that mankind are more disposed to suffer, while evils are sufferable, than to right themselves by abolishing the forms [of government] to which they are accustomed" is no less true than Plato's comment that "necessity is the mother of invention." Ideas become reality when they have undergone the trial and error of competition, and when alternatives prove unfeasible. Thus was the case of the road to union in the American colonies. Rivalries and jealousies had to be shown more burdensome than cooperation. Forms of loose cooperation had to be tried before discarded.

If a single judgment can be made of the course of American union before 1763 it would be that the colonies were not ready for union but unconsiously were being thrust towards it. The alternatives facing the colonies by 1763 were that they should continue to go along as they pleased – at their discretion honoring or refusing commitments imposed upon them by the crown – or be caught up in a new, reorganized imperial system. Habit would prove stronger than the will to bend into a stringent imperial mold. The precipitousness of British policy after 1763, however, would leave the colonists no choice but to stir themselves out of their lethargy and to take action to insure their autonomy. But, in accepting as the only alternative to allow the fruition of their own political destiny, the colonists were not yet aware that insistence upon a dichotomous imperial-colonial constitution would inevitably lead to general resistance. It was true that a major theme in the political history of the colonies was the struggle between the governors and their assemblies – between the royal prerogative and the legislative right of the colonies. But before 1763 this contest was localized to the colonies individually.

There could be no united protest as long as the colonies were succeeding in making their assemblies little Parliaments. As spoiled children, the colonists could go about their own way, with only slight inconveniences and occasional rebuffs from the mother country. Advantages were to be had from the protection and paternalism of the imperial system; and when imperial controls seemed too demanding, they could be circumvented. But, at mid-century, the colonies were now in a stage of adolescence, as Franklin and others were pointing out, and would soon outgrow parental authority. The advance to maturity would be more inviting than when the colonies had needed the assistance of the mother country to fight a common foreign enemy in America. With the awakening to divergent paths and the need to take action to defend a complete autonomization of the American governments, then and only then, would the colonies realize the immense potentiality of cooperation and unity, which they had so lackadaisically pursued for over a century.

Intercolony cooperation in almost every instance was inspired or directed either by the home government or by the royal governors or magistrates in the colonies. The royal government asked cooperative support from the colonies rather than compelled it. When the immediate benefit to an individual colony was substantial, there was compliance. But there was always the reluctance to extend a colony's resources beyond its sphere of interest. Because the colonial assemblies claimed a constituency of the people, whereas the crown servants could not, except of the broader base of Englishmen at large, they were hesitant to bestow either gifts or power to the machinations of the royal placemen. Disunity was not viewed as injurious to a particular colony because it was the function of the empire – not a colony – to look after the external interests of the whole.

Military union afforded the most viable form of intercolony cooperation. There were always good intentions, expressed on the surface at least, of a colony doing its share towards the general security. War crises called for pooling efforts to the extent of warding off the enemy and protecting the colonies from invasion, and sometimes the colonists felt it to be in their own interests to join in aggressive war. A sustained attempt, however, to drive the enemy out of America proved too demanding upon the conservative colonists, who enjoyed the relative isolation of Indian and topographical barriers. The American militiaman was also the honest husbandman, who could only spare his time at intervals between harvesting and planting. Few military offensives were mounted in the warmer seasons – a factor in itself explaining failure of many hastily prepared cooperative expeditions against the enemy. Yet occasionally the thrill to war fever would lift the colonist out of his boredom, and especially if he were a New Englander, he was apt to feel the cause of glory to a Protestant king and country. Enthusiasm would bring on large-scale participation, but the hardships of military life and the inability of a fighting force to remain long periods in the field or to patiently lay siege to an enemy stronghold soon dampened the spirits of the fighting men. Confusion, overlapping authority, inadequate planning, and misunderstandings in performance of pledges made harassed the supply of an army in the field.

Colonial governments supporting a war effort or simply bowing to token assistance requested by royal authority all too willingly thought in terms of other people's money: floating paper issues or depending upon reimbursement from the crown. The idea of a general fund, coming out of fixed colony revenues, though constantly proposed by serious thinkers on the subject, was anathema to the colonists. Legislatures, more often than not, using the power of the purse to gain control over the policy making functions of the governor and council, usually voted initial appropriations but refused to extend sufficient funds to sustain a military effort. Particularly in the southern colonies, which in most instances were remote from the war zone, the governors sought to meet the responsibility of raising a fighting force to cooperate with other colonies, while the assemblies were bent upon retrenchment.

From the first colonial war on, the crown took charge of a requisition system – for supplies, men, and finances – by issuing instructions to the colonial governors, whose duties then were to fulfill the quotas and to coordinate the use of the colonies' resources. The problems besetting the system were the same as those of the more familiar loose Confederation of 1781. It was one thing to require contributions, another to get them. The multitudinous orders-in-council and instructions from the Board of Trade could not be enforced if assemblies were recalcitrant. Indeed, the whole problem of effective coordination of the colonies in contributing to a war effort was the failure of the British government to develop coercive powers in the colonies. If the legislatures could have their price for support, the British government could have made demands also. But it was an age of blundering politicians and bureaucrats, who were totally negligent of the opportunities presented by imperial rule. The colonies came to depend on British assistance, first in men and matériel and then to an increasing amount in financial aid as well – if this assistance had been withheld in time of crises until the colonists fulfilled their obligations, imperial authority in the colonies would have been enhanced. Unfortunately, the greater stake in empire in America belonged to England – not to the colonies – and this was always an ace up the sleeve for the colonists. Nevertheless, a vigorous contending for colonial rule by the home government would have made for more responsible government in the colonies and a more healthy imperial relationship. Opportunity went by default from the crown throughout the period and each time it did, opportunity diminished.

No objection was raised by the colonists to a unified command system. If an intercolonial force was to be led in the field who better could command than a professional soldier appointed from abroad? Fearing the idea of a captain general in the seventeenth century, the colonists were willing to tolerate one in wartime when empires could be won in the New World. Unfortunately, however, it took until the last colonial war before the home government ceased to dally around with the appointment of one of the royal governors, who could never divest himself of his political role, to have the chief command. Though the colonial governor chosen was usually professionally trained, he could only stir the rivalry of the other governors. Nevertheless, the colonists were not opposed in principle to military union in wartime under a crown-appointed commander. The crown also made the mistake of making a governor commander in chief only on a regional basis and usually for a specified campaign. Had there been experimentation with a permanent commander in chief of a military union – if not an establishment – continued in peacetime, by 1763 the colonists might have been prepared for a regular military establishment, which when tried was to be so offensive to their sensibilities. In reality a royal governor designated commander in chief could only command militia of a neighboring colony in wartime and then he was dependent upon the willingness to cooperate of that colony's governor and assembly. The military union attempted under Fletcher, Bellomont, and Dudley was totally unsuccessful. In the last two colonial wars governors as commanders in chief were given charge of expeditionary forces only and did not have the right to order out the militia of a colony other than their own.

The intercolonial congress coordinated executive functions in external matters, namely in war preparations and operations and in Indian diplomacy. Commissioners came from the governors and councils, rarely from the assemblies. In fact the congresses bore the semblance to royal commissions. The war conference fell into disuse with the establishment of the supra-commanders in chief and a line of military command in the colonies. Loudoun preferred to deal with the colonial governments unilaterally; Amherst pushed the role of the commander in chief to attend to general planning and command, leaving details to subordinates like the Quartermaster General to be worked out individually with the colonial governments. The increased paternalism of the last colonial war, when the British government undertook substantial provision of matériel, funds, and manpower, lessened the necessity of colonial governments concerting the war effort. But the active participation and concern of British authorities in itself spurred colonial support to some degree.

The intercolonial war conference was of value when governors, as commanders in chief, unsure of their powers, had to cater to the sense of importance of other governors. However unsuccessful this means of intercolonial cooperation was, it nevertheless established the principle of shared responsibility on the part of colonies participating – a principle to be the basis for later standing committees in the Continental Congress and the idea of the Committee of States to meet when Congress was not in session (as a means of cooperative unity it was discredited along with the Confederation).

The Indian conference – hardly ever more than a powwow called by a single governor to protect the immediate frontiers of a particular colony– never developed into a means of useful intercolonial cooperation. Like the war conference giving way to unified military authority, the growth of Indian diplomacy through intercolonial congresses was nipped by the imperialization of Indian affairs in the offices of the northern and southern superintendents. A failure of colonial conduct of Indian affairs had been the difficulty of securing ample funds for Indian gifts. Under imperial departments, Indian gifts could be supplied out of the royal treasury.

Only in relation to boundary disputes did intercolonial commissions of arbitration develop. In most instances, disputes were not settled until a royal commission of disinterested parties from colonies not involved in the dispute was created, and authorities at Whitehall and Westminister both adopted the practice of letting the decisions of these royal commissions be final.

A certain amount of idealism characterized plans of union. This was also true in conceptions of establishing a frontier barrier, whether as a line of communication or as a chain of settlements of immigrants or veterans. Such plans went beyond practicality and the capacity and inclinations of the colonists. It is worthy of note that most ideas of union involved the creation of a third party, usually in the form of an intercolonial agency or assembly that would be a liaison between king and Parliament and the colonies. Ideas of cooperation – if not union – remained on a regional basis until the end of the Seven Years War, when even this concept broke down, with the colonies contributing locally as adjuncts to the king's forces rather than through a cooperative agency. The ending of cooperative control of military affairs paved the way for the centralization of a war executive, first to be given trial by the crown, and then by the colonies in the American Revolution.

By 1763 the colonists were also discovering similarities in life and institutions. Aggravations and rivalries still remained – but the colonists were now more aware of them and that solutions called for uniformity and standardization. A void in a centralizing authority existed, and the colonists were mindful of the continuing consequences for the failure of harmonizing policies of individual colonies. Unity could only be imposed through the erection of some central means to coordinate and even fuse the colonial interests. To the colonies such means should be built from the bottom up, representing consensus of various constituencies, not emanating from an apex of authority in England.

A central representative authority, not a cooperative magistry, could only bring the colonial assemblies together to work towards a common end. The long experience in haphazard cooperative action culminating at a time a new imperial system was being proposed compelled the colonists to take stock of the future. If the colonists could not accept a thorough imperialization of colonial affairs, they would, nevertheless, have to build resistance in kind, not on cooperation but on union.

ABBREVIATIONS

AASP	*Proceedings of the American Antiquarian Society*
AHR	*American Historical Review*
APSR	*American Political Science Review*
CA	Connecticut Archives
CHS	Connecticut Historical Society
CHSC	*Collections of the Connecticut Historical Society*
CL	Clements Library
CP	*Cadwallader Colden Papers*
CSL	Connecticut State Library
CSP	*Calendar of State Papers, Colonial Series, America and West Indies* (PRO), ed. J. W. Fortescue *et al.* Page numbers cited.
EJCC-Va.	*Executive Journals of the Council of Colonial Virginia*, ed. H. R. McIlwaine
FP	*The Papers of Benjamin Franklin*, ed. L. W. Labaree
GCR	*The Colonial Records of Georgia*, ed. A. D. Candler
GHSC	*Collections of the Georgia Historical Society*
HSP	Historical Society of Pennsylvania
IHSC	*Collections of the Illinois State Historical Society*
JCHA-SC	*Journal of the Commons House of Assembly*, South Carolina, ed. A. S. Salley
JHB-Va.	*Journal of the House of Burgesses of Colonial Virginia*, ed. H. R. McIlwaine
JHUS	*Johns Hopkins University Studies in Historical and Political Science*
LC	Library of Congress
MA	Massachusetts Archives
MHS	Massachusetts Historical Society

MHSC	*Collections of the Massachusetts Historical Society*
MHSP	*Proceedings of the Massachusetts Historical Society*
MVHR	*Mississippi Valley Historical Review*
NCCR	*The Colonial Records of North Carolina,* ed. W. L. Saunders
NCHR	*North Carolina Historical Review*
NEQ	*The New England Quarterly*
NJA	*New Jersey Archives*
NJHSC	*Collections of the New Jersey Historical Society*
NYCD	*Documents Relative to the Colonial History of New York,* ed. E. B. O'Callaghan
NYHS	New York Historical Society
NYHSC	*Collections of the New York Historical Society*
NYPL	New York Public Library
PA	*Pennsylvania Archives*
PCR	*Colonial Records of Pennsylvania*
PMHB	*The Pennsylvania Magazine of History and Biography*
PRO, CO*	Public Record Office, Colonial Office
PRO, WO*	Public Record Office, War Office
PSQ	*Political Science Quarterly*
RICR	*Records of the Colony of Rhode Island,* ed. J. R. Bartlett
VMHB	*The Virginia Magazine of History and Biography*
WMQ	*The William and Mary Quarterly*

*refers to photostat collection in the Library of Congress

BIBLIOGRAPHY

I. MANUSCRIPTS

Ann Arbor, Michigan

William L. Clements Library
- Clinton-Glen Correspondence, 1750–52 (microfilm)
- Selections from Amherst Correspondence (microfilm)

Boston

Massachusetts Archives, State House
- Colonial Series
- Military Series

Massachusetts Historical Society
- Jeremy Belknap Papers
- Miscellaneous Papers (Boundaries)
- Parkman transcripts – Public Record Office (Great Britain): America and West Indies – New England
- Sedgwick Papers
- Gurdon Saltonstall Papers
- Charles E. French Collection
- Jonathan Belcher Letter Books
- William Shirley Papers
- Barrett Wendel Papers on Relations Between Massachusetts and New Hampshire
- Jacob Wendell Papers
- Miscellaneous Boundary Collection, XI–XII
- William Pepperrell Papers

Harrisburg, Pennsylvania

State House
- Loudoun Papers (microfilm from collection at Huntington Library, San Marino, California)

Hartford

Connecticut Historical Society
- Colonial Agents Letters
- Jonathan Trumbull, Sr. Papers
- Privy Council Orders, 1743–75 (copies)
- Elisha Williams Papers
- Roger Wolcott Papers

Connecticut State Library
- Connecticut Archives: Colonial Wars
- Robert C. Winthrop Collection
- Jonathan Trumbull Papers

New York City

New York Historical Society
- Daniel Horsmanden Papers
- Joseph Dudley Miscellaneous Manuscripts
- Miscellaneous Blathwayt Papers (photostats)
- New York and New Jersey Boundary Papers, I
- Horatio Gates Papers, Box I
- Benjamin Pomroy Miscellaneous Manuscripts
- William Alexander Papers
- Amherst Miscellaneous Manuscripts

New York Public Library
- Emmet Collection
- Chalmers Collection (R.I., Va., Carolina, N.Y., Pa., Phila., Md., Conn.)
- N.Y. Colony Manuscripts, Letters of Governors
- Bancroft transcripts: England and America, 1620–1761
  - England and America, 1761–63
  - American Colonies, I and II
  - Colonial Documents, 1748–64 (6 vols.)
  - Thomas Penn's Letters
  - Massachusetts Papers (letters of Shirley and Willard)
  - Virginia Papers, 1756–68
- Sir William Pepperrell Miscellaneous Manuscripts
- S.G. Drake, Chronicles of the Indians

William Shirley Miscellaneous Correspondence
Abraham Yates Papers

Richmond, Virginia

Virginia Historical Society
Lee-Ludwell Papers

Virginia State Library
James Abercromby Letter Book

Washington, D.C.

Library of Congress

Public Record Office (photostats)

Colonial Office 5: America and West Indies

Vol. 9	Canadian Expedition, 1710–13
10	Original Papers: New England, 1710–52; New Hampshire, 1711–52; Mass. Bay, 1710–42; Rhode Island, 1709–42
13–20	Correspondence of Colonial Governors, 1742–62
44–45	Louisbourg Expedition
46–47	French and Indian War, 1755–56
48–64	Military and Naval Correspondence, 1756–63
719–21	Secretary of State: Original Correspondence, 1689–1780
860–65	Board of Trade Original Correspondence, Letters with Enclosures from the Governor of Maryland, 1698-1712
1081–96	Board of Trade Original Correspondence, Letters with Enclosures from the Governor of New York, 1696–1752
1233–34	Board of Trade Original Correspondence, Letters with Enclosures from the Governor of Pennsylvania, 1690–1767
1305–45	Board of Trade Original Correspondence, Letters with Enclosures from the Governor of Virginia, 1691–1781

War Office 34: Amherst Papers, Correspondence with Governors or Government of:
24 New Hampshire and Rhode Island
25-27 Massachusetts
28 Connecticut
29-30 New York
31 New Jersey
32-33 Pennsylvania
34 Maryland
38-39 Sir William Johnson
44 Brigadier General John Forbes
47 Virginia and South Carolina Officers
71-74 Correspondence with Secretaries of State and Government Departments in England
83 Miscellaneous Papers and Letters to Commander in Chief

Belknap Papers (Force transcripts)
I Correspondence of Governor Shirley with Governor Wentworth
II Correspondence of Theodore Atkinson and John Thomlinson (agent for N.H.)
III Miscellaneous Papers
Ebenezer Hazard Collection, N.Y. Records
Massachusetts Miscellany: "The state of the government of Massachusetts as it stood in the year 1757" (by Thomas Pownall?)
Massachusetts Papers: Jeremiah Dummer to Timothy Lyndal, April 12, 1721; New Hampshire Boundary, 1731–42 (Force transcripts)
Personal Miscellany: Horatio Sharpe Correspondence; Robert Hunter Morris Correspondence
Sir Jeffrey Amherst Letters (transcriptions of W.B. Sprague Collection, Albany)
Adam Stephen Papers

II. NEWSPAPERS

(Microfilm and microcard collections of the Institute of Early American History and Culture, Williamsburg, and Southern Illinois University)

The New-York Evening Post, 1744–51

South-Carolina Gazette, 1742–63

Pennsylvania Journal, 1742–63

New-York Weekly Journal, 1733–51

New-York Gazette, 1726–44, 1752–63

The New-York Mercury, 1750

The American Weekly Mercury (Philadelphia), 1719–46

Pennsylvania Gazette, 1728–63

Rhode Island Gazette, 1732–33

Providence Gazette, 1762–63

New London Summary Weekly, 1758–63

Georgia Gazette (Savannah), 1763

The New-England Courant, 1721–27

The Weekly Rehearsal (Boston), 1731–35

Boston Evening Post, 1735–63

New-England Weekly Journal (Boston), 1727–41

New Hampshire Gazette, 1756–64

Virginia Gazette (scattered issues in Va. Hist. Soc.), 1756–64

III. UNPUBLISHED THESES*

Allen, Carlos R., Jr."Travel and Communication in the Early Colonial Period, 1607–1720." California, 1956.

---

*Ph.D. Dissertations, except when MA thesis designated.

Attig, Clarence J. "William Henry Lyttleton: A Study in Colonial Administration." University of Nebraska, 1958.

Baer, Harold M. "The Equality of States as a Theory of Britain and America: Imperial Structure at the Time of the American Revolution." Harvard, 1925.

Beyer, Richard L. "Robert Hunter, Royal Governor of New York." Iowa (MA), 1927.

Buffington, Arthur H. "The Policy of the Northern English Colonies towards the French to the Peace of Utrecht." Harvard, 1925.

Calloway, James E. "Disallowances of Colonial Legislation, 1696–1737." Indiana, 1953.

Carr, Paul "The Defence of the Frontier, 1760–1775." State University of Iowa, 1932.

Carter, Mary F. "James Glen: Governor of Colonial South Carolina." California (Los Angeles), 1951.

Dodson, Leonidas "Alexander Spotswood, Governor of Virginia." Iowa, 1927 (pub. 1932).

Evanson, Chellis N. "Sir Francis Nicholson, 1690–1705." Iowa (MA), 1930.

Ferguson, William W. "The Development of Home-Made Governments in New England." Indiana, 1938.

Ferrell, Clyde M. "The Massachusetts Colonial Agents in England." Wisconsin, 1923.

Fiore, Jordan D. "Francis Bernard." Boston University, 1950.

Friedelbaum, Stanley H. "Bellomont: Imperial Administrator." Columbia, 1955.

Gatke, Robert M. "Plans of America Colonial Union, 1643–1754." American University, 1925.

Giddens, Paul H. "The Public Career of Horatio Sharpe." Iowa, 1930.

Hammelef, John C. "British and American Attempts to Coordinate the Defenses of the Continental Colonies to Meet French and Northern Indian Attacks, 1643–1754." Michian, 1955.

Hanna, Archibald, Jr. "New England Military Institutions, 1693–1750." Yale, 1951.

Harlow, Ralph. "The Development of the Standing Committee System in the Colonial and State Legislatures, 1750–1790." Yale, 1913.

High, James H. "Reluctant Loyalist: Horatio Sharpe." California (Los Angeles), 1951.

Kemmerer, Donald L. "The Struggle for Self-Government in Colonial New Jersey, 1664–1738." Princeton, 1934.

McCain, James R. "The Executive in Proprietary Georgia, 1732–52." Columbia, 1914 (pub. 1914).

Nichols, F.T. "The Braddock Expedition." Harvard, 1946.

Norkus, Nellie. "Francis Fauquier." Pittsburgh, 1954.

Rogers, Sara B. "The Rise of Civil Government and Federation in Early New England." Yale, 1894.

Rolland, Siegfried. "Cadwallader Colden." Wisconsin, 1952.

Sanford, Charles L. "The Days of Jeremy [Jeremiah] Dummer, Colonial Agent." Harvard 1952.

Zimmerman, John. "Benjamin Franklin: A Study of Pennsylvania Politics and the Colonial Agency, 1755–1775." Michigan. 1956.

IV. PRINTED SOURCES

Adams, Charles F., ed. *The Works of John Adams.* Vol. I. Boston, 1850.

"Additional Belcher Papers, 1732–49." *MHSP*. XLIV (1911), 189–212.

The American Magazine, or A Monthly View of the Political State of the British Colonies. Publication No. 39 of the Facsimile Text Society (1741), New York, 1937.

An Account Showing the Progress of the Colony of Georgia in America (1761). *American Colonial Tracts,* I (5). Rochester, 1897.

Andrews, Charles M., ed. *Reports on the Laws of Connecticut* (by Francis K. Fane), 1733–41. The Acorn Club, 1915.

An Essay on Currency (1734). Facsimile, Charleston, 1950.

"A Ranger's Report of Travels with General Oglethorpe, 1739–42," in Mereness, Newton D., ed. *Travels in the American Colonies,* 218–236. New York, 1961.

Bailyn, Bernard, ed. *Pamphlets of the American Revolution, 1750–76.* Vol. I. Cambridge, 1965.

Balch, Thomas, ed. *Letters and Papers relating Chiefly to the Provincial History of Pennsylvania.* Philadelphia, 1855.

Barrow, Thomas S., ed. "A Projection for Imperial Reform: 'Hints Respecting the Settlement for our American Provinces'" (1763, William Knox probable author), *WMQ*, 3d Ser., XXIV (1967), 108–126.

Bartlett, John R., ed. *Records of the Colony of Rhode Island.* Vols. III-VI. Providence, 1858–61.

Borden, William. *An Address to the Inhabitants of North-Carolina* (1746) in Boyd, William K., ed. *Some Eighteenth Century Tracts concerning North Carolina,* 67–92. Raleigh, 1927.

Bouton, Nathaniel, ed. *Documents and Records relating to the Province of New Hampshire,* Vols. II-VI. Manchester, 1868–72.

Boyd, Julian P., ed. *The Susquehannah Company Papers.* Vols. I and II. Ithaca, 1962 reprint of 1930 ed.

Boyd, Mark F., translator. "The Seige of Saint Augustine by Governor Moore of South Carolina in 1702 as Reported to the King of Spain by Don Joseph de Zuniga y Zerda, Governor of Florida." *Florida Historical Quarterly.* XXVI (1947–49), 345–52.

———, ed. "John Rutherford's 'The Importance of the Colonies to Great Britain . . ." (1761). *NCHR.* II (1925), 351–86.

———, ed. *William Byrd's Histories of the Dividing Line betwixt Virginia and North Carolina* (contains *The Secret History of the Line*). Raleigh, 1929.

Brock, R.A., ed. *The Official Letters of Alexander Spotswood. Colls.* of the Va. Hist. Soc. 2 vols. (I and II), Richmond, 1882 and 1885.

———, ed. *The Official Records of Robert Dinwiddie. Colls.* of the Va. Hist. Soc. 2 vols. (III and IV). Richmond, 1883–84.

Browne, William H. *et al.*, eds. *Archives of Maryland.* Vols. II–LVIII. Correspondence of Governor Sharpe contained in Vols. VI, IX, XIV, and XXXI. Baltimore, 1883-1935.

Candler, Allen D., ed. *The Colonial Records of the State of Georgia*. Vols. I and II. Atlanta, 1904.

Carroll, B.R., ed. *Historical Collections of South Carolina . . . from its First Discovery to its Independence.* 2 vols. New York 1836.

Carter, Clarence E., ed. *The Correspondence of General Thomas Gage with the Secretaries of State and with the War Office and the Treasury, 1763–1775. Yale Historical Pubs.*, XI–XII. New Haven, 1931–32.

Channing, Edward *et al.*, eds. *The Barrington-Bernard Correspondence, 1760-1770. Havard Hist. Studies.* XVII. Cambridge, 1912.

Clarke, William. *Observations on the Late and Present Conduct of the French with regard to their Encroachments upon the British Colonies in North America together with Remarks on the Importance of these Colonies to Great-Britain.* Boston, 1755. Columbia University Special Collections.

Cleland, Hugh, ed. *George Washington in the Ohio Valley.* Pittsburgh, 1955.

Cohen, Sheldon S., ed. "The Diary of Jeremiah Dummer." *WMQ*. 3d Ser., XXIV (1967), 397–422.

Colbourn, H. Trevor, ed. "A Pennsylvania Farmer at the Court of King George: John Dickinson's London Letters, 1754–56." *PMHB.* LXXXVI (1962), 241–86, 417–53.

Colden, Cadwallader. *The History of the Five Indian Nations of Canada* (1747). 2 vols. New York, 1922.

—

The Letters and Papers of Cadwallader Colden. NHYSC. 9 vols. (L-LVI, LXVII-LXVIII). New York, 1918–37.

"Collection of Evidence in Vindication of the Territorial Rights and Jurisdiction of New York against Massachusetts and New Hampshire and the People of the Grants who are commonly called Vermonters." (1779). *NHYSC.* II (1869), 279–528.

Coulter, E. Merton., ed. *The Journal of William Stephens, 1741–43.* 2 vols. Athens, Ga., 1958.

Crane, Verner W., ed. *Benjamin Franklin's Letters to the Press, 1758–75.* Chapel Hill, 1950.

Darlington, Mary C., ed. *History of Colonel Henry Bouquet and the Western Frontiers of Pennsylvania, 1747–64.* Pittsburgh, 1920.

De Filipis, M., trans. and ed. "An Italian Account of Cherokee Uprisings at Fort Loudoun and Fort Prince George, 1760–61." *NCHR.* XX (1943), 247–58.

De Forest, Louis E., ed. *Louisbourg Journals, 1745.* New York, 1932.

Dillon, John B., ed. *Oddities of Colonial Legislation in America.* Indianapolis, 1879.

Douglass, William. *A Summary, Historical and Political of the First Planting, Progressive Improvements and Present State of the British Settlements in North-America.* 2 vols. Boston, 1755.

Duane, James. "State of the Evidence and Argument in Support of the Territorial Rights and Jurisdiction of New York Against the Government of New Hampshire and Massachusetts." (1784 brief). *NYHSC.* III (1870), 1–144.

Dulany, Daniel. "Military and Political Affairs in the Middle Colonies" (1755). *PMHB.* III (1879), 11–31.

Dunbar, John R., ed. *The Paxton Papers.* The Hague, Neth., 1957.

Easterby, J.H., ed. *The Journal of the Commons House of Assembly* (South Carolina). 9 vols. Columbia, 1951–1962.

The Expediency of Securing Our American Colonies by Settling the Country Adjoining the River Mississippi . . ., (1763) in Alvord, Clarence and Carter, Clarence E., eds. *The Critical Period, 1763–1765. IHSC.* Springfield, 1915.

"Expedition Against Crown Point." *Maryland Hist. Mag.* IX (1914), 249–52.

Extracts from American Newspapers, Relating to New Jersey. 5 vols. *New Jersey Archives.* 1st Ser., XI, XII, XIX, XX, and XXIV. Paterson, N.J., *1894–1902.*

The Fitch Papers: Correspondence and Documents during Thomas Fitch's Governorship, 1754–66. 2 vols. *CHSC.* XVII and XVIII (1918-20).

Fitzpatrick, John C., ed. *The Diaries of George Washington, 1748–99.* Vol. I. Boston, 1925

——————, ed. *The Writings of George Washington.* Vols. I and II. Washington, D.C., 1931.

Flick, Alexander C. *et al.*, eds. *The Papers of Sir William Johnson.* 13 vols. Albany, 1921–62.

Ford, Worthington C., ed. *Broadsides, Ballads &c Printed in Massachusetts, 1639–1800: Check List. MHSC.* LXXV. Boston, 1922.

Fortescue, J.W. *et al.*, eds. *Calendar of State Papers, Colonial Series, America and West Indies* (PRO). Vols. XIII–XLIII. London, 1901–63.

Gipson, Lawrence H., ed. *Lewis Evans: To Which is Added Evans' "A Brief Account of Pennsylvania"* (1756). "Essays" by Evans also included. Philadelphia, 1939.

Grant, James. "Journal of the March and Operations of the Troops Under the Command of Lieut. Colonel Grant of the 40th Regiment Upon An Expedition from Fort Prince George Against the Cherokees." *Fla. Hist. Quarterly.* XII (1933), 26–36.

Green, Samuel A., ed. "Sir William Phips's Expedition to Canada: The Narrative of John Wise." *MHSP.* 2nd Ser., XV (1902), 281–320.

Greene, Jack P., ed. *The Diary of Colonel Landon Carter.* Vol. I. Charlottesville 1965.

--------, ed. "Martin Bladen's Blueprint for a Colonial Union: 'Reasons for Appointing a Captain General for the Continent of North America.'" *WMQ.* 3d Ser., XVII (1960), 516–30.

Hamer, Philip M., ed. *The Papers of Henry Laurens.* Vol. I. Columbia, S.C., 1968.

Hamilton, Stanilaus M., ed. *Letters to Washington and Accompanying Papers.* Vols. I–III. Boston, 1898–1901.

Hardin, William, ed. "James Mackay (with correspondence of)." *Ga. Hist. Quarterly.* I (1917), 77–98.

Harriss, Frances L., ed. *Lawson's History of North Carolina* (1714). Richmond, 1937.

Hart, Albert B., ed. *American History told by Contemporaries.* Vol. II. New York, 1899.

Hastings, Hugh, ed. *Orderly Book and Journal of Major John Hawks on the Ticonderoga-Crown Point Campaign under General Amherst.* New York, 1911.

Hening, William W., ed. *The Statutes at Large being a Collection of all the Laws of Virginia from the First Session of the Legislature in the Year 1619.* Vols. III–VI. Philadelphia, 1819–23.

Hewatt, Alexander. *An Historical Account of the Rise and Progress of the Colonies of South Carolina and Georgia* (1779). 2 vols. Reprint ed., Spartanburg. S.C., 1962.

"The Hinckley Papers: being Letters and Papers of Thomas Hinckley, 1676–1699." *MHSC.* 4th Ser., V (1861), 1–308.

Hoadley, Charles J., ed. *The Public Records of the Colony of Connecticut.* Vols. IV-XI. Hartford, 1850–80.

Hopkins, Stephen. *A True Representation of the Plan Formed at Albany in 1754, for Uniting All the British Northern Colonies*. . . (1755). *R.I., Hist. Tracts,* No. 9. Providence, 1880.

Hutchinson, Thomas. *The History of the Colony and Province of Massachusetts Bay.* Ed. by Lawrence S. Mayo. Vols. II and III. Cambridge, 1936.

"Instructions of Queen Anne to Colonel Samuel Vetch for the organization of a Colonial Contingent for the conquest of Canada, 1708," *PMHB.* XXXVIII (1914), 335–45.

"Intercepted Letters to the Duke de Mirepoix, 1756." *Annual Report of the AHA for 1896.* Washington, D.C., 1897. 660–703.

Jacobs, Wilbur R., ed. *Indians of the Southern Colonial Frontier: The Edmond [Edmund] Atkin Report and Plan of 1755.* Columbia, S.C., 1954.

James, Alfred P., ed. *Writings of General John Forbes.* Menasha, Wisc., 1938.

Jensen, Merrill *et al.*, eds. *English Historical Documents.* Vol. IX. New York, 1955.

Jones, Hugh. *The Present State of Virginia From Whence is inferred a short view of Maryland and North Carolina.* Ed. by Richard L. Morton. Chapel Hill, 1956.

Jordan, John W., ed. "Penn *versus* Baltimore: Journal of John Watson, Assistant Surveyor to the Commissioners of the Province of Pennsylvania, Dec. 13 – Mar. 18, 1750–51." *PMHB*. XXXIX (1915), 1–47.

"Journal of the Lieut. Governor's [Spotswood] Travels and Expeditions Undertaken for the Public Service of Virginia." *WMQ*. 2d Ser., III (1923), 40–45.

"Journal of John Barnwell." *VMHB*. V (1898), 391–402 and VI (1899), 42–55.

Journals of the House of Burgesses of Virginia. 1659–1765, 9 vols. 1907–14.

Journal of the Legislative Council of New York. 2 vols. Albany, 1861.

"Journal of the Proceedings of the Congress held at Albany, in 1754." *MHSC*. 3d Ser., V (1836), 5–74.

Kennedy, Archibald. *The Importance of Gaining and Preserving the Friendship of the Indians to the British Interest* (1752). Franklin Collection, Yale U.

Kimball, Gertrude S., ed. *Correspondence of William Pitt when Secretary of State with Colonial Governors and Military and Naval Commissioners in America*, 2 vols. New York, 1906.

————, ed. *The Correspondence of the Colonial Governors of Rhode Island, 1725–75*. 2 vols. Boston, 1902–3.

Kinard, Margaret, ed. "John Usher's Report on the Northern Colonies, 1698." *WMQ*. 3d Ser., VII (1950), 95–106.

Klingberg, Frank, ed. *The Carolina Chronicle of Dr. Francis Le Jau, 1706–17. U. of Calif. Pubs. in History*, LIII. Berkeley, 1956.

Labaree, Leonard W., ed. *The Papers of Benjamin Franklin*. 1706–1763. 10 vols. New Haven, 1959–66.

The Law Papers: Correspondence and Documents during Jonathan Law's Governorship, 1741–50. 3 vols. *CHSC.* XI, XIII, XV (1907–14).

Lawson, Murray, ed. "An Act for the Better Regulation of the Indian Trade, 1714." *VMHB.* LV (1947), 329–332.

Leder, Lawrence H., ed. "Dam'me Don't Stir a Man: Trial of the New York Mutineers in 1700." *The New-York Hist. Soc. Quarterly.* XLII (1958), 261–83.

———, ed. *The Livingston Indian Records, 1666–1723.* Gettysburg, Pa., 1956.

The [Charles] Lee Papers. Vol. I (1754–76). *NYHSC.* IV (1871).

"Letters Relating to the French and Indians." *Md. Hist. Mag.* IV (1909), 344–53.

"Letters from General Oglethorpe to the Trustees of the Colony, Oct. 1735 – Aug. 1744." *GHSC.* III (1873), 1–157.

Lincoln, Charles H., ed. *Correspondence of William Shirley, 1731–1760.* New York, 1912. 2 vols.

[Livingston, William]. *A Review of the Military Operations in North America, from the Commencement of the French Hostilities on the Frontiers of Virginia in 1753, to the Surrender of Oswego, on the 14th of August, 1756; in a Letter to a Nobleman. MHSC.* 1st Ser., VII (1801), 67–163.

Livingston, William *et al. The Independent Reflector or Weekly Essays on Sundry Important Subjects More particularly adapted to the Province of New-York* (1752–53). Ed. by Milton M. Klein. Cambridge, 1963.

Logan, Deborah, ed. *Correspondence of William Penn and James Logan and Others, 1700–50.* 2 vols. Philadelphia, 1870 and 1872.

McAnear, Beverly, ed. "An American in London, 1735–36: The Diary of Robert Hunter Morris." *PMHB.* LXIV (1940), 164–217, 356–406.

———, ed. "Personal Accounts of the Albany Congress of 1754." *MVHR.* XXXIX (1953), 727–46.

McCulloh, Henry. *Miscellaneous Representations relative to Our Concerns in America* (1761). *Some Eighteenth Century Tracts concerning North Carolina.* Ed. by William K. Boyd, pp. 141–56. Raleigh, 1927.

McCulloch, William. *Proposals for Uniting the English Colonies on the Continent of America So as to enable them to act with Force and Vigour Against their Enemies* (1757). Harvard University Library.

McDowell, William L, Jr., ed. *Colonial Records of South Carolina: Documents relating to Indian Affairs, May 21, 1750–Aug. 7, 1754.* Columbia, S.C., 1958.

McIlwain, Charles H., ed. *Peter Wraxall: An Abridgement of the Indian Affairs Contained in Four Folio Volumes Transacted in the Colony of New York, 1678–1751.* Cambridge, 1915.

McIlwaine, H.R., ed. *Executive Journals of the Council of Colonial Virginia, 1680–1739.* 4 vols. Richmond, 1925–30.

Manross, William W., compiler. *The Fulham Papers in the Lambeth Palace Library: Calendar and Indexes.* Oxford, 1965.

"Witham Marshe's Journal of the Treaty Held with the Six Nations by the Commissioners of Maryland, and other Provinces, at Lancaster, in Pennsylvania, June, 1744." *MHSC.* 1st Ser., VII (1800), 171–201.

The Acts and Resolves of the Province of the Massachusetts Bay. Vols. I–XVII. Boston, 1869–1910.

Massachusetts Royal Commissions, 1681–1774. Pubs. of the Colonial Society of Massachusetts. II. Boston, 1913.

Mather, Cotton. "*Decennium Luctuosum* . . . Remarkable Occurrences in the Long War . . . with the Indian Savages . . . 1688 to . . . 1698" in Charles H. Lincoln, ed. *Narratives of the Indian Wars, 1675–99. Original Narrative Series of American History,* pp. 171–300. New York, 1913.

Memoirs of Robert Stobo of the Virginia Regiment. Pittsburgh, 1854.

Mereness, Newton D., ed. *Travels in the American Colonies* (1961) reprint, New York, 1961.

"Military Letters of Captain Joseph Shippen of the Provincial Service, 1756–58." *PMHB*. XXXVI (1912), 367–68, 385–463.

Milling, Chapman J., ed. *Colonial South Carolina: Two Contemporary Descriptions by Governor James Glen and Doctor George Milligan* (1761). Columbia, S.C., 1951.

Minutes of the [Pa]. Provincial Council. Vols. I–IX. Harrisburg, 1838–52.

Mitchell, John. *The Contest in America between Great Britain and France with its Consequences and Importance.* (1757). Reprint, 1965.

Moody, Robert E., ed. "Massachusetts Trade with Carolina, 1686–1709." *NCHR*. XX (1943), 43–53.

Moore, Francis. "A Voyage to Georgia Begun in the Year 1735." *GHSC.* I (1840), 79–152.

The Colonial Laws of New York. Vols. I-IV. Albany, 1894.

Niles, Rev. Samuel. "A Summary Histroical Narrative of the Wars in New England with the French and Indians in the Several Parts of the Country." *MHSC.* 4th Ser., V (1861), 309–589.

O'Callaghan, E.B., ed. *Documents relative to the Colonial History of the State of New York.* Vols. III–X. Albany, 1853–58.

———, ed. *The Documentary History of the State of New York.* 4 vols. Albany, 1849–51.

Osgood, Herbert L. *et al.*, eds. *Minutes of the Common Council of the City of New York, 1676–1776.* 8 vols. New York, 1905.

Papers of Lewis Morris, 1738–1746. NJHSC. IV. Newark, 1852.

"Papers Relating to the Expeditions of Colonel Bradstreet and Colonel Bouquet in Ohio, A.D., 1764." *Western Reserve and Northern Ohio Historical Society.* Tracts No. 13 and 14 (Feb., 1873).

Pargellis, Stanley, ed. *Military Affairs in North America, 1748–65: Selected Documents from the Cumberland Papers in Windsor Castle.* New York, 1936.

Pease, Theodore, C., ed. *Anglo-French Boundary Disputes in the West, 1749–63. IHSC.* XXVII (1936).

———— and Jenison, Ernestine, eds. *Illinois on the Eve of the Seven Years' War, 1747–55. IHSC.* XXIX (1940).

The Statutes at Large of Pennsylvania. Vols. II–VI (1682–1766). 1896.

Pennsylvania Archives. 9 Series. Omitting Series 5, 6, 7, 9: 77 vols. Harrisburg and Philadelphia, 1852–1949.

Pennsylvania Colonial Records. 16 vols. Philadelphia, 1852–53.

Pitt, John, ed. *Correspondence of William Pitt, Earl of Chatham.* Vol. I. London, 1838.

"Post Office Department Records." *MHSC.* 3d Ser., VII (1838), 48ff.

"Report of the British Board of Trade and Plantations, Dec. 1703." *NYPL Bulletin.* XI (1907), 469–97.

"Report of the Committee Chosen by the General Assembly Respecting the Foregoing Plan of Union, Oct. 1754." *MHSC.* 1st Ser., VII (1800), 207–9.

Rogers, Robert. *Reminiscences of the French War.* (1765). Concord, N.H., 1831.

Salley, AS., ed. *Commissions and Instructions from the Lords Proprietors of Carolina to Public Officials of South Carolina.* 1685–1715. Columbia, S.C., 1916.

————, ed. *Journal of the Commissioners of the Indian Trade of South Carolina, Sep. 20, 1710–Apr. 12, 1715.* Columbia, S.C., 1926.

————, ed. *Journal of Colonel John Herbert, Oct. 17, 1727–Mar. 19, 1728.* Columbia, S.C., 1936.

Saunders, William, ed. *The Colonial Records of North Carolina.* Vols. I–VI. Raleigh, 1886–88.

Sewall, Samuel. "Letter Book." *MHSC.* 6th Ser., I and II (1878 and 1888).

———. *Papers.* 3 vols. *MHSC.* 5th Ser., V, VI, VII.

Severall Proceedings in the two late Sittings of Assembly [Pa.], on the Affair of raising Money, Men, etc. for the Expedition now on foot against the Spanish West-Indies (1740). [anon.] Columbia University Special Collections.

Smith, Samuel. *The Colonial History of New Jersey* (1765). Reprint. Trenton, N.J., 1890.

[Smith, William?]. *An Historical Account of the Expedition Against the Ohio Indians under the Command of Henry Bouquet . . . to which are annexed Military Papers* (London, 1766). Reprint. Cincinnati, Ohio, 1868.

The Statutes at Large of South Carolina. Vols. II–IV. Columbia, S.C., 1837–38.

State of the British and French Colonies in North America (1755). [anon.] Columbia University Special Collections.

Stevens, Sylvester K. *et al.*, eds. *The Papers of Henry Bouquet.* Vol. II *(The Forbes Expedition).* Harrisburg, 1951.

———,eds. *The Papers of Henry Bouquet: Indian Affairs, 1758–65. Northwest Pennsylvania Historical Series.* Mimeographed. Harrisburg, 1943.

———, eds. *Wilderness Chronicles of Northwestern Pennsylvania.* Harrisburg, 1941.

Tailfer, Patrick *et al. A True and Historical Narrative of the Colony of Georgia in America* (1741). *American Colonial Tracts,* I. Rochester, N.Y., 1897.

The Talcott Papers: Correspondence and Documents during Joseph Talcott's Governorship, 1724–41. 2 vols. *CHSC.* IV and V (1892 and 1896).

Tilghman, Harrison, ed. "Letters between the English and American Branches of the Tilghman Family, 1697–1764." *Md. Hist. Mag.* XXX (1938), 148–75.

Towle, Dorothy S., ed. *Records of the Vice-Admiralty Court of Rhode Island, 1716–52. American Legal Records,* III. Washington, D.C., 1936.

"Union of the British American Colonies as Proposed in the Year 1754 and reports of a Committee Chosen by the General Assembly, Respecting the Foregoing Plan of Union." *MHSC.* 1st Ser., VII (1800), 203–14.

Walsh, Richard, ed. *The Writings of Christopher Gadsden, 1746–1805.* Columbia, S.C., 1966.

"Meshech Weare's Plan for Colonial Union, 1754." *NYPL Bulletin.* I (1897) 149–50.

Webster, J. Clarence, ed. *The Journal of Jeffrey Amherst, 1758–63.* Chicago, 1931.

Weeks, Lyman H. and Bacon, Edwin M., eds. *An Historical Digest of the Provincial Press, 1704–1707. Massachusetts Series.* Vol. I. Boston, 1911.

Weston, Plowden C.J., ed. "Answers of James Glen, Governor of South Carolina, to the Queries from the Right Honourable the Lords Commissioners for Trade and Plantations." (1755). *Documents Connected with the History of South Carolina* (London, 1856), 61–99.

Whiston, James. *The Causes of our Present Calamities in reference to the Trade of the Nation fully discovered.* (1691). Columbia University Special Collections.

Whitehead, William A. *et al.*, eds. *New Jersey Archives: Documents relating to the Colonial History of the State of New Jersey.* 1st Ser., II–XXIV. Trenton, N.J., 1881–1902.

Whitworth, Charles, ed. *The Political and Commercial Works of Charles D'Avenant* (1771), Vols. I and II. Virginia State Library.

Williams, Samuel C., ed. *Lieutenant Henry Timberlake's Memoirs, 1756–65.* Marietta, Ga., 1948.

Correspondence of Fitz-John Winthrop. MHSC. 6th Ser., III (1889).

The Wolcott Papers: Correspondence and Documents during Roger Wolcott's Governorship, 1750–54. CHSC. XVI (1916).

Wright, Louis B., ed. *An Essay Upon the Government of the English Plantations on the Continent of America* (1701); *An Anonymous Virginian's Proposals For Liberty Under the British Crown, With Two Memoranda By William Byrd.* San Marino, Calif., 1945.

Wynne, John A. *A General History of the British Empire in America* (1770). 2 vols.

Wynne, Thomas H., ed. *William Byrd's History of the Dividing Line and Other Tracts.* 2 vols. Richmond, 1866.

V. SECONDARY SOURCES

Abbot, W.W. *The Royal Governors of Georgia, 1754–75.* Chapel Hill, 1959.

Adams, James T. *Revolutionary New England, 1691–1776.* Boston, 1923.

———. "The Unexplored Region in New England History." *AHR.* XXVIII (1923), 673–61.

Alberts, Robert C. *The Most Extraordinary Adventures of Major Robert Stobo.* Boston, 1965.

Alden, John R. *John Stuart and the Southern Colonial Frontier,* Ann Arbor, 1944.

———. *General Gage in America.* Baton Rouge, La., 1948.

———. "The Albany Congress and the Creation of the Indian Superintendencies." *MVHR.* XXVII (1940), 193–210.

Aldridge, Alfred O. *Benjamin Franklin: Philosopher and Man.* Philadelphia, 1965.

Anderson, Niles. "The General Chooses a Road–The Forbes Campaign of 1758 to Capture Fort Duquesne." *West. Pa. Hist. Mag.* XLII (1959), 109–38, 241–58, 383–401.

Andrews, Charles M. *The Colonial Period of American History.* Vol IV. New Haven, 1966. Reprint.

———. *Colonial Background of the American Revolution.* New Haven, 1924.

———. "Colonial Commerce." *AHR.* XX (1915), 43–63.

———. "Anglo-French Commercial Rivalry, 1700–50." *AHR.* XX (1915), 539–56, 761–80.

Andrews, Matthew P. *History of Maryland.* New York, 1929.

Appleton, Marguerite. "The Agents of the New England Colonies in the Revolutionary Period." *NEQ.* VI (1933), 371–87.

Armor, William C. *Lives of the Governors of Pennsylvania.* Philadelphia, 1872.

Arnade, Charles W. *The Seige of St. Augustine in 1702. University of Fla. Soc. Sci. Monograph Series,* No. 3. Gainesville, 1959,

Arnold, Samuel G. *History of the State of Rhode Island and Providence Plantations, 1636–1790.* 2 vols. New York, 1878.

Ashe, Samuel A. *History of North Carolina.* Vol. I. Greensboro, 1908.

Bailey, Kenneth P. *The Ohio Company of Virginia and the Westward Movement, 1748–92.* Glendale, Calif., 1939.

———. *Thomas Cresap: Maryland Frontiersman.* Boston, 1944.

Baily, Levin C. "Maryland's Boundary Controversies." Speech delivered to Md. State Bar Assoc. Reprint from *The Daily Record,* June 23, 1951.

Baker-Crothers, Hayes. *Virginia and the French and Indian War,* Chicago, 1928.

Barker, Charles A. *The Background of the Revolution in Maryland. Yale Hist. Pubs.,* XXXVIII. New Haven, 1940.

Barnes, Viola F. *The Dominion of New England: A Study in British Colonial Policy*. Reprint. New York, 1960.

Barrow, Thomas C. *Trade and Empire: The British Customs Service in Colonial America 1660-1775.* Cambridge, 1967.

Beatty, Edward C.O. *William Penn as a Social Philosopher.* New York, 1939.

Beatty, R.C. *William Byrd of Westover.* Boston, 1932.

Beer, George L. *British Colonial Policy, 1754–65.* Reprint. New York, 1933.

Belknap, Jeremy. *The History of New-Hampshire.* 3 vols. 1812.

Bell, Whitfield and Labaree, L.W. "Franklin and the 'Wagon Affair,' 1755." *Procs. of the Amer. Phil. Soc.,* CI (1957), 551–58.

Bennett, W.H. *American Theories of Federalism.* Tuscaloosa, Ala., 1964.

Bird, Harrison. *Battle for a Continent.* New York, 1965.

———. *Navies in the Mountains: The Battles on the Waters of Lake Champlain and Lake George, 1609–1814.* New York, 1962.

Black, William J. "Maryland's Attitude in the Struggle for Canada." *JHUS.* 10th Ser., VII (1892).

Bond, Beverley W. Jr. "The Colonial Agent as a Popular Representative." *PSQ.* XXXV (1920), 372–92.

Bowen, Clarence W. *The Boundary Disputes of Connecticut.* Boston, 1882.

Brackett, Jeffrey, R. *The Negro in Maryland: A Study of the Institution of Slavery.* Baltimore, 1889.

Bradley, A.G. *The Fight with France for North America.* Westminister [Eng.], 1900.

Branch, E. Douglas. "Henry Bouquet: Professional Soldier." *PMHB.* LXII (1938), 41–51.

Brewster, William. *The Pennsylvania and New York Frontier.* Philadelphia, 1954.

Bridenbaugh, Carl. *Cities in Revolt; Urban Life in America, 1743–1776.* Reprint. New York, 1964.

Bronner, Edwin B. *William Penn's Holy Experiment.* New York 1962.

Brown, John P. "Eastern Cherokee Chiefs." *The Chronicles of Okla.,* XVI (1938), 3–35.

Brown, Richard B. *The South Carolina Regulators.* Cambridge, 1963.

Brown, Robert E. *Middle-Class Democracy and the Revolution in Massachusetts, 1691–1780.* Ithaca, 1955.

Brown, Stuart E., Jr. *Virginia Baron: The Story of Thomas 6th Lord Fairfax.* Berryville, Va., 1965.

Bruce, Philip. A. *History of Virginia.* Vol. I. New York, 1924.

———. *The Virginia Plutarch.* Vol. I., Chapel Hill, 1929.

Buffington, Arthur H. "The Canada Expedition of 1746." *AHR.* XLV (1940), 552–80.

———. "The Policy of Albany and English Westward Expansion." *MVHR.* VIII (1922), 327–66.

Burns, James J. *The Colonial Agents of New England.* Washington, D.C., 1935.

Burns, John F. *Controversies between Royal Governors and their Assemblies in the Northern American Colonies.* Boston, 1923.

Burrage, Henry S. *Maine at Louisbourg in 1745.* Augusta, Maine, 1910.

Cadbury, H.J. "Intercolonial Solidarity of American Quakers." *PMHB.* LX (1936), 362–74.

Cady, John H. *Rhode Island Boundaries, 1636–1936.* R.I. Tercentary Commission, 1936.

Caldwell, Norman W. "The Southern Frontier During King George's War." *The Journal of Southern History.* VII (1941), 37–54

Carter, Clarence E. "The Office of Commander in Chief: a Phase of Imperial Unity on the Eve of the Revolution" in R.B. Morris, ed., *The Era of the American Revolution,* pp. 170–213. Reprint. New York, 1965.

———. "The Significance of the Military Office in America, 1763–75." *AHR.* XXVIII (1923), 475–88.

Caruso, John A. *The Appalachian Frontier.* Indianapolis, 1959.

Chafee, Zechariah, Jr., "Colonial Courts and the Common Law." *MHSP.* LXVIII (1952), 132–59.

Chalmers, George. *An Introduction to the History of the Revolt of the American Colonies* (1782). 2 vols. Boston, 1845.

Chapin, Howard M. *Privateering in King George's War, 1739-48.* Providence, 1928.

Chumbley, George L. *Colonial Justice in Virginia.* Richmond, 1938.

Clark, Charles B. "The Career of John Seymour, Governor of Maryland, 1704–1709." *Md. Hist. Mag.* XLVIII (1953), 134–59.

Clarke, Desmond. *Arthur Dobbs, 1689–1765.* Chapel Hill, 1957.

Clonts, F.W. "Travel and Transportation in Colonial North Carolina." *NCHR.* III (1926), 16–35.

Cohen, Sheldon S. "The Diary of Jeremiah Dummer." *WMQ.* 3d Ser., XXIV (1967), 397–422.

Colbourn, H. Trevor. *The Lamp of Experience: Whig History and the Intellectual Origins of the American Revolution.* Chapel Hill, 1965.

Connell, Brian. *The Plains of Abraham.* London, 1959.

———. *The Savage Years.* New York, 1959.

Conner, Paul W. *Poor Richard's Politicks: Benjamin Franklin and His New American Order.* New York, 1965.

Cook, George A. *John Wise.* New York, 1952.

Cooke, Charles S. "The Governor, Council and Assembly in Royal North Carolina." *The James Sprunt Hist. Pubs.* XII (1912), 1–40.

Corbett, Julian S. *England in the Seven Years' War.* 2 vols. New York, 1907.

Corkran, David H. *The Cherokee Frontier: Conflict and Survival, 1740–62.* Norman, Okla., 1962.

Cort, Rev. Cyrus. *Colonel Henry Bouquet and his Campaigns, 1763 and 1764.* Lancaster, Pa., 1883.

Coulter, E. Merton. *Georgia: A Short History.* Chapel Hill, 1947.

Cowie, Leonard W. *Henry Newman: An American in London, 1708–43.* London, 1956.

Crabtree, Beth G. *North Carolina Governors, 1585–1958.* Raleigh, 1958.

Craig, Neville B. *Lecture upon the Controversy between Pennsylvania and Virginia about the Boundary Line.* Pittsburgh, 1843.

Crane, Verner W. "Projects for Colonization in the South, 1684–1732." *MVHR.* XII (1926), 23–35.

———. *The Southern Frontier, 1670–1732.* Reissue. Ann Arbor, 1959.

Cribbs, George A. "The Frontier Policy of Pennsylvania." *Western Pa. Hist. Mag.* II (1919), 5–35; 72–106, 174–98.

Crouse, Maurice A. "Gabriel Manigault: Charleston Merchant." *The S.C. Hist. Mag.* LXVIII (1967), 220–31.

Daniell, Jere R. "Politics in New Hampshire under Governor Benning Wentworth, 1741–67." *WMQ.* 3d Ser., XXIII (1966), 76-105.

Davidson, Robert. *War Comes to Quaker Pennsylvania, 1682–1756.* New York, 1957.

Davis, Burke. *A Williamsburg Galaxy.* New York, 1968.

DeArmond, Anna U. *Andrew Bradford: Colonial Journalist.* Newark, Del., 1949.

DeNormandie, James. "Sir William Pepperrell." *MHSP.* XVII (1903), 87–90.

DePeyster, Frederick. *The Life and Administration of Richard, Earl of Bellomont.* New York, 1879.

De Vorsey, Louis, Jr. *The Indian Boundary in the Southern Colonies, 1763–1775.* Chapel Hill, 1966.

Dickerson, Oliver M. *American Colonial Government, 1696–1765: A study of the British Board of Trade in its relation to the American Colonies, Political, Industrial, Administrative.* Reprint. New York, 1962.

————. *The Navigation Acts and the American Revolution.* Philadelphia, 1951.

Dietze, Gottfried. *The Federalist: A Classic on Federalism and Free Government.* Baltimore, 1960.

Dill, Alonzo. "Eighteenth Century New Bern: A History of the Town and Craven County, 1700–1800, Part IV, Rebellion and Indian Warfare." *NCHR.* XXII (1945), 293–319.

Dixon, W. Hepworth. *A History of William Penn.* New York, 1902.

Dorn, Walter L. *Competition for Empire, 1740–63.* New York, 1940.

Douglas, Charles H. L. *The Financial History of Massachusetts. Columbia University Studies . . .*, I. New York, 1940.

Downey, Fairfax. *Louisbourg: Key to a Continent.* Englewood Cliffs, N.J., 1965.

Downs, Randolph C. *Council Fires on the Upper Ohio.* Pittsburgh, 1940.

Drake, Samuel D. *The Border Wars of New England.* New York, 1897.

Duer, William A. *The Life of William Alexander, Earl of Stirling with Selections from his Correspondence. NJHSC.* II (1847).

Dunn, Richard S. *Puritans and Yankees: The Winthrop Dynasty of New England, 1630–1717.* Princeton, 1962.

Edwards, George W. *New York as an Eighteenth Century Municipality, 1731–1776.* Port Washington, N.Y., Reprint, 1967.

Edgar, Lady. *A Colonial Governor in Maryland: Horatio Sharpe and His Times, 1753–1773.* New York, 1912.

Egerton, H.E. *Federations and Union within the British Empire.* Oxford, 1911.

Ervin, Samuel J., Jr. "The Provincial Agents of North Carolina." *James Sprunt Hist. Pubs.,* XVI (1917), 61–77.

Ettinger, Amos A. *James Edward Oglethorpe.* Oxford, 1936.

Everett, Edward G. "Pennsylvania's Indian Diplomacy, 1747–1753." *The West. Pa. Hist. Mag.,* XLIV (1961), 241–56.

Ezell, John S. *Fortune's Merry Wheel: The Lottery in America.* Cambridge, 1960.

Fant, H.B. "The Indian Trade Policy of the Trustees for Establishing the Colony of Georgia in America." *Ga. Hist. Quarterly.* XV (1931), 208–22.

Fisher, Edgar J. *New Jersey as a Royal Province, 1738–76. Columbia University Studies. . .,* XLI. New York, 1911.

Fisher, George H. "Brigadier-General Henry Bouquet." *PMHB* III (1879), 121–43.

Fisher, Sidney G. *Pennsylvania: Colony and Commonwealth..* Philadelphia, 1897.

Fiske, John. *Old Virginia and Her Neighbours.* 2 vols. Boston, 1897.

Fitz, Virginia White. "Ralph Wormeley: Anonymous Essayist." *WMQ,* 3d Ser., XXVI (1969), 586–95.

Flaherty, David H., ed. *Essays in the History of Early American Law.* Chapel Hill, 1969.

Flippin, Percy S. "The Royal Government in Georgia, 1752–1776." *Ga. Hist. Quarterly.* XIII (1929), 128–53.

———. *The Royal Government in Virginia, 1624–1775. Columbia University Studies . . .*, LXXXIV. New York, 1919.

Forbes, Gerald. "The International Conflict for the Lands of the Creek Confederacy." *Chronicles of Okla.* XIV (1936), 478–98.

Foster, William E. *Stephen Hopkins, Rhode Island Statesman. R.I. Historical Tracts.* No. 19. Providence, 1884.

Fox, Dixon R. *Caleb Heathcote: The Story of a Career in the Province of New York, 1692–1721.* New York, 1926.

———. *Yankees and Yorkers.* New York, 1940.

Franklin, W. Neil. "Pennsylvania-Virginia Rivalry for the Indian Trade of the Ohio Valley." *MVHR.* XX (1934), 463–80.

Freeman, Douglas S. *George Washington.* Vols. I–III. New York, 1949–51.

Frothingham, Richard. *The Rise of the Republic of the United States.* Boston, 1886.

Fry, William H. *New Hampshire as a Royal Province. Columbia University Studies . . .*, XXIX. New York, 1908.

Gamble, Thomas. "Colonel William Bull–His Part in the Founding of Savannah." *Ga. Hist. Quarterly.* XVII (1933), 111–126.

Giddens, Paul H. "Maryland and the Earl of Loudoun." *Md. Hist. Mag.* XXIX (1934), 268–94.

Gipson, Lawrence H. *The British Empire Before the American Revolution.* Vols. I–X. New York, 1936–61.

———. "Connecticut Taxation and Parliamentary Aid preceding the Revolutionary War." *AHR.* XXXVI (1931), 721–39.

———. *Jared Ingersoll: A Study of American Loyalism in Relation to British Colonial Government. Yale Hist. Pubs.*, VIII. New Haven, 1920.

———. "Massachusetts Bay and American Colonial Union, 1754." *AASP.* LXXI (1961), 63–92.

———. "Thomas Hutchinson and the Framing of the Albany Plan of Union, 1754." *PMHB.* LXXIV (1950), 6–35.

Giuseppi, M.S. *Naturalization of Foreign Protestents in the American and West Indian Colonies (Pursuant to Statute* 13 *George* II 7). *Pubs. of the Hugenot Soc. of London,* XXIV. Manchester, 1921.

Goebel, Dorothy B. "The 'New England Trade' and the French West Indies, 1763–1774; A Study in Trade Policies." *WMQ.* 3d Ser., XX (1963), 331–72.

Gordon, Thomas F. *The history of Pennsylvania, from its discovery by Europeans to the Declaration of Independence in 1776.* Philadelphia, 1829.

Graeff, Arthur D. "The Relations between the Pennsylvania Germans and the British Authorities, 1750–76." *Pa. German Soc. Procs.* XLVII (1939).

Green, Samuel A. "The Northern Boundary of Massachusetts in its Relation to New Hampshire." *AASP.* New Series, VII (1892), 11–32.

Greene, Evarts B. *The Provincial Governor in the English Colonies of North America.* Reprint, New York, 1966.

Greene, Jack P. "The Opposition to Lieutenant Governor Alexander Spotswood, 1718." *VMHB.* LXX (1962), 35–42.

———. *The Quest for Power: The Lower Houses of Assembly in the Southern Royal Colonies, 1689–1776.* Chapel Hill, 1963.

Greene, Lorenzo J. *The Negro in Colonial New England, 1620–1776. Columbia University Studies*. . ., No. 494. New York, 1942.

Griffen, William B. "Spanish Pensacola, 1700–1763." *Fla. Hist. Quarterly.* XXXVII (1959), 242–62.

Hall, Clayton C. *The Lords Baltimore and the Maryland Palatinate.* Baltimore, 1902.

Hall, Hubert. "Chatham's Colonial Policy." *AHR.* V (1900), 659–75.

Hall, Michael G. *Edmund Randolph and the American Colonies, 1676–1703.* Chapel Hill, 1960.

Hamer, P.M. "Anglo-French Rivalry in the Cherokee Country, 1754–57." *NCHR.* II (1925), 303-22.

———. "Fort Loudoun in the Cherokee War." *NCHR.* II (1925), 442–58.

Hamilton, Edward P. *The French and Indian Wars.* Garden City, N.Y. 1962.

Hanna, Charles A. *The Wilderness Trail.* 2 vols. New York, 1911.

Harkness, Albert, Jr. "Americanism and Jenkins' Ear." *MVHR.* XXXVII (1950), 61–90.

Harper, Lawrence A. "The Effect of the Navigation Acts on the Thirteen Colonies" in R.B. Morris, ed., *The Era of the American Revolution,* pp. 3–39. Reprint. New York, 1965.

Harrington, Virginia D. *The New York Merchant on the Eve of the Revolution.* New York, 1935.

Hart, Albert B., ed. *Commonwealth History of Massachusetts.* Vol. II (1689–1775). New York, 1928.

Herrick, Cheesman A. *White Servitude in Pennsylvania.* Philadelphia. 1926.

High, James. "The Earl of Loudoun and Horatio Sharpe, 1757–58." *Md. Hist. Mag.* XLV (1950), 14–32.

Hildeburn, Charles R. "Sir John St. Clair, Baronet, Quarter-Master General in America, 1755–67." *PMHB.* IX (1885), 1–14.

Hotblack, Kate. *Chatham's Colonial Policy: A Study in the Fiscal and Economic Implications of the Colonial Policy of the Elder Pitt.* New York, 1917.

Howard, C.N. "The Military Occupation of British West Florida, 1763." *Fla. Hist. Quarterly.* XVII (1939), 181–99.

Hughson, Shirley C. *The Carolina Pirates and Colonial Commerce, 1640–1740. JHUS.* 12th Ser., V–VII (1894).

Huidekoper, Frederick. *The Sieges of Louisbourg in 1745 and 1758.* Washington, 1914.

Hunter, William A. *Forts on the Pennsylvania Frontier, 1753–58.* Harrisburg, 1960.

Jacobs, Wilbur R. "Edmond Atkin's Plan for Imperial Indian Control." *Journal of Southern Hist.* XIX (1953), 311–20.

————. *Wilderness Politics and Indian Gifts: The Northern Colonial Frontier, 1748–1763.* Reprint, Lincoln, Neb., 1966.

James, Alfred P. *The Ohio Company: Its Inner History,* Pittsburgh, 1959.

———— and Stolz, Charles M. *Drums in the Forest.* Pittsburgh, 1958.

Jenkins, Howard M. *Pennsylvania: Colonial and Federal.* Philadelphia, 1903.

Jernegan, Marcus. *Laboring and Dependent Classes in Colonial America.* Chicago, 1931.

Johnson, E.A.J. "Some Evidence of Mercantilism in the Massachusetts Bay." *NEQ.* I (1928), 371–95.

Johnson, Emory *et al. History of Domestic and Foreign Commerce of the United States.* Vol. I. Washington, D.C., 1915.

Johnson, Rossiter. *A History of the French War.* New York, 1882.

Johnson, Victor L. "Fair Traders and Smugglers in Philadelphia, 1754–1763." *PMHB.* LXXXIII (1959). 125–49.

Kammen, Michael G. *A Rope of Sand: The Colonial Agents, British Politics and the American Revolution.* Ithaca, 1968.

Katz, Stanley N. *Newcastle's New York: Anglo-American Politics, 1732–53.* Cambridge, 1968.

Keith, Charles P. *Chronicles of Pennsylvania from the English Revolution to the Peace of Aix-la-Chapelle, 1688–1748.* 2 vols. Philadelphia, 1917.

Ketcham, Ralph L. "Conscience, War, and Politics in Pennsylvania, 1755–57." *WMQ.* 3d Ser., XX (1963), 416–39.

Keys, Alice M. *Cadwallader Colden: A Representative Eighteenth Century Official.* New York, reprint, 1967.

Kimball, Everett. *The Public Life of Joseph Dudley, 1660–1775. Harvard Hist. Studies,* XV. New York, 1911.

Knorr, Klaus E. *British Colonial Theories, 1570–1850.* Toronto, 1944.

Konkle, Burton A. *George Bryan and the Constitution of Pennsylvania, 1731–91.* Philadelphia, 1922.

----------------. *The Life of Andrew Hamilton, 1676–1741.* Philadelphia, 1941.

Konwiser, Harry M. *Colonial and Revolutionary Posts.* Richmond, 1931.

Koontz, Louis K. *Robert Dinwiddie: his career in American Colonial Government and Westward Expansion.* Glendale, Calif., 1941.

————. *The Virginia Frontier, 1754–63.* Baltimore, 1925.

Kraus, Michael. *Intercolonial Aspects of American Culture on the Eve of the Revolution.* New York, 1928.

Labaree, Leonard W. "Benjamin Franklin and the Defense of Pennsylvania, 1754–57." *Pennsylvania History.* XXIX (1962), 7–23.

—————. *Royal Government in America: A Study of the British Colonial System before 1783.* New Haven, 1930.

Lanning, John T. "American Participation in the War of Jenkins' Ear." *Ga. Hist. Quarterly.* XI (1927), 129-55.

Latrobe, John H.B. *The History of Mason and Dixon's Line.* Oakland, Del., 1882.

Lauber, Almon W. *Indian Slavery in the Colonial Times within the Present Limits of the United States. Columbia University Studies . . .*, LIV. New York, 1913.

Leake, James M. *The Virginia Committee System and the American Revolution. JHUS.* Series XXXV, No. 1. Baltimore, 1917.

Leamon, James S. "Governor Fletcher's Recall." *WMQ.* ed Ser., XX (1963), 528–42.

Leder, Lawrence H. "The Glorious Revolution and the Pattern of Imperial Relationships." *New York History.* XLVI (1965), 203–11.

————. *Liberty and Authority: Early American Political Ideology, 1689–1763.* Chicago, 1968.

————. *Robert Livingston, 1654–1728, and the Politics of Colonial New York.* Chapel Hill, 1961.

Lee, Lawrence. *The Lower Cape Fear in Colonial Days.* Chapel Hill, 1965.

Lefler, Hugh T. *History of North Carolina.* Vol. I. New York, 1956.

Lemisch, Jesse. "Jack Tar in the Streets: Merchant Seamen in the Politics of Revolutionary America." *WMQ.* 3d Ser., XXV (1968), 371–407.

Levy, Leonard W. *Origins of the Fifth Amendment.* New York, 1968.

Lewin, Howard. "A Frontier Diplomat: Andrew Montour." *Pennsylvania History.* XXXIII (1966), 153–86.

Lilly, Edward P. *The Colonial Agents of New York and New Jersey.* Washington, D.C., 1936.

Lincoln, Charles H. *The Revolutionary Movement in Pennsylvania, 1760–76. University of Pa. Series in Hist.,* No. 1. Philadelphia, 1901.

Long, Breckinridge. *Genesis of the Constitution of the United States.* New York 1926.

Long, J.C. *Lord Jeffrey Amherst.* New York, 1933.

———. *Mr. Pitt and America's Birthright.* New York, 1940.

Lonn, Ella. *The Colonial Agents of the Southern Colonies.* Chapel Hill, 1945.

McCain, James P. *Georgia as a Proprietary Province.* Boston, 1917.

McCormac, Eugene I. *Colonial Opposition to Imperial Authority During the French and Indian War. Univ. of Calif. Pubs. in History,* I. Berkeley, 1911.

MacCracken, Henry N. *Prologue to Independence: The Trials of James Alexander, American, 1715–56.* New York, 1964.

McCrady, Edward. *The History of South Carolina, 1670–1719.* New York, 1901.

———. "Slavery in the Province of South Carolina, 1670–1770." *Annual Report of the AHA for 1895.* Washington, D.C., 1896. 631–673.

McKay, George L. *Early American Currency.* New York, 1944.

McLaughlin, Andrew C. *The Foundations of American Constitutionalism.* New York, 1932.

McManus, Edgar J. *A History of Negro Slavery in New York.* Syracuse, 1966.

Main, Jackson T. *The Upper House in Revolutionary America, 1763–88.* Madison, Wisc., 1967.

Mark, Irving. *Agrarian Conflicts in Colonial New York, 1711–1775.* New York, 1940.

Mason, A. Hughlett and Swindler, William F. "Mason and Dixon: their Line and its legend." *American Heritage.* XV (1964), 23–29, 93–96.

Mathews, Lois K. "Benjamin Franklin's Plans for a Colonial Union, 1750–1775." *APSR.* VIII (1914), 393–412.

———. *The Expansion of New England.* Reprint, New York, 1962.

Mauduit, Israel. *A Short View of the History of the New England Colonies, with respect to their Charters and Constitutions.* London, 1776.

Mereness, Newton D. *Maryland as a Proprietary Province.* New York, 1901.

Merrens, Harry R. *Colonial North Carolina in the Eighteenth Century.* Chapel Hill, 1964.

Merritt, Richard L. *Symbols of American Community, 1735–75.* New Haven, 1966.

———. "The Colonists Discover America: Attention Patterns in the Colonial Press, 1735–75." *WMQ.* 3d Ser., XXI (1964), 270-87.

Middleton, Arthur P. *Tobacco Coast.* Newport News, Va. 1953.

Miller, E.J. "The Virginia Committee of Correspondence, 1759–70." *WMQ.* XXII, 1st Ser. (1914), 1–19.

Miller, John C. "Religion, Finance, and Democracy in Massachusetts," *NEQ.* VI (1933), 29–58.

Milling, Chapman J. *Red Carolinians.* Chapel Hill, 1940.

Montgomery, Thomas L. *Report of the Commission to Locate the Site of the Frontier Forts of Pennsylvania.* 2 vols. Harrisburg. 1916.

Morgan, Edwin V. "The Status of the Slave under the English Colonial Government." *Papers of the AHA.* V (1891), 337–50.

Morgan, William T. "The Five Nations and Queen Anne." *MVHR.* XIII (1927), 169–89.

Morriss, Margaret S. *Colonial Trade of Maryland, 1689–1715. JHUS.* Ser. XXXII (No. 3), 1914.

Morrow, Rising Lake. *Connecticut Influences in Western Massachusetts and Vermont.* New Haven, 1936.

Morton, Richard L. *Colonial Virginia.* Vol. II. Chapel Hill, 1960.

Mowat, Charles L. "The Enigma of William Drayton." *Fla. Hist. Quarterly.* XXII (1943), 3–33.

Mowat, Clarence A. "The Southern Brigade: A Sidelight on the British Military Establishment in America, 1763–75." *The Journal of Southern Hist.* X (1944), 59–77.

Mulkearn, Lois. "Why the Indian Treaty of Logstown, 1752." *VMHB.* LIX (1951), 3–20.

Murdock, Kenneth B. *Increase Mather: The Foremost American Puritan.* Cambridge, 1925.

Namier, L.B. "Charles Garth and His Connexions." *English Historical Review.* LIV (1939), 443–70, 632–52.

Nash, Gary B. "Maryland's Economic War with Pennsylvania." *Md. Hist. Mag.* LX (1965), 231–44.

Nettels, Curtis. "The Economic Relations of Boston, Philadelphia, and New York, 1680–1715." *Journal of Economic and Business History.* III (1930–31), 185–215.

Newbold, R.C. *The Albany Congress and Plan of Union of 1754.* New York, 1955.

Nixon, Lily L. *James Burd: Frontier Defender, 1726–93.* Philadelphia, 1941.

Noble, John. "An Incident in 1731 in the Long Dispute of Massachusetts and Rhode Island over their Boundary Line." *MHSP.* XIX (1905), 20–34.

Nolan, J. Bennett. *General Benjamin Franklin.* Philadelphia, 1956.

Norkus, Nellie. "Virginia's Role in the Capture of Fort Duquesne." *The West. Pa. Hist. Mag.* XLV (1962), 291–308.

O'Conor, Norreys J. *A Servant of the Crown in England and in North America, 1756–61: John Appy* . . . . New York, 1938.

Olson, Alison G. "The British Government and Colonial Union, 1754." *WMQ.* 3d Ser., XVII (1960), 22–34.

————. "William Penn, Parliament, and Proprietary Government." *WMQ.* 3d Ser., XVIII (1961), 176–95.

Osgood, Herbert L. *The American Colonies in the Eighteenth Century.* 4 vols. Reprint, Gloucester, Mass., 1958.

————. "The Proprietary Province as a Form of Colonial Government." *AHR.* II, 31–55 and III, 244–65.

Owings, Donnell M. *His Lordship's Patronage: Offices of Profit in Colonial Maryland. Studies in Md. Hist.,* No. 1. Baltimore, 1953.

Palfrey, John G. *History of New England.* Vols. IV and V. Boston, 1890.

Pargellis, Stanley M. *Lord Loudoun in North America.* New Haven, 1923.

Parkman, Francis. *The Conspiracy of Pontiac and the Indian War after the Conquest of Canada.* 2 vols. New Library Edition, X–XI. Boston, 1899.

————. *A Half Century of Conflict: France and England in North America.* 2 vols. New Library Edition, VI–VII. Boston, 1898.

————. *Count Frontenac and New France under Louis XIV.* New Library Edition, V. Boston, 1903.

Parsons, Usher. "Sir William Pepperrell" in Freeman Hunt, ed., *Lives of American Merchants,* I, 101–68. New York, 1858.

Peckham, Howard H. *The Colonial Wars, 1689–1762.* Chicago 1964.

———. *Pontiac and the Indian Uprising.* Reprint, Chicago, 1961.

———. "Speculations on the Colonial Wars." *WMQ.* 3d Ser., XVII (1960), 463–72.

Perry, Charles E. *Founders and Leaders of Connecticut.* New York, 1934.

Peters, Samuel. *General History of Connecticut* (1781). New York, 1877.

Phillips, Paul C. *The Fur Trade.* Vol. I. Norman, Okla., 1961.

Pole, J.R. *Political Representation in England and the Origins of the American Republic.* New York, 1966.

Pound, Arthur. *Johnson of the Mohawks.* New York, 1930.

Proper, Emberson E. *Colonial Immigration Laws.* Reprint, New York, 1967.

Proud, Robert. *The History of Pennsylvania in North America . . . 1681, till after the Year 1742.* 2 vols. Philadelphia, 1797–98.

Rand, James H. *The Indians of North Carolina and Their Relations with the Settlers. The James Sprunt Hist. Pubs.,* XII. Chapel Hill, 1913.

Ranny, John C. "The Bases of American Federalism." *WMQ* 3d Ser., III (1946), 1–35.

Raper, Charles L. *North Carolina: A Study in English Colonial Government.* New York, 1904.

Reese, Trevor R. *Colonial Georgia: A Study in British Imperial Policy in the Eighteenth Century.* Athens, Ga., 1963.

Reich, Jerome R. *Leisler's Rebellion: A Study of Democracy in New York, 1664–1720.* Chicago, 1953.

Reinsch, Paul. *English Common Law in the Early American Colonies. Bulletin of the University of Wisconsin,* No. 31. Madison., 1899.

Richards, Henry M. *The Pennsylvania-German in the French and Indian War. Pa. German Soc. Procs.*, XV. Lancaster, Pa., 1905.

Riker, Thad W. "The Politics Behind Braddock's Expedition." *AHR.* XIII (1908), 742–52.

Riley, F.L. *Colonial Origins of New England Senates. JHUS.* 14th Ser., III (1896).

Ripley, William Z. *The Financial History of Virginia, 1609–1776. Columbia University Studies . . .*, IV. New York, 1893.

Rivers, William J. *A Sketch of the History of South Carolina to the Close of the Proprietary Government by the Revolution of 1719.* Charleston, 1856.

Robinson, Howard. *The British Post Office: A History.* Princeton, 1948.

Root, Winfred T. *The Relations of Pennsylvania with the British Government, 1696–1765.* New York, 1912.

Sachs, William S. "Interurban Correspondents of a National Economy Before the Revolution: New York as a Case Study." *New York History.* XXXVI (1955), 320–35.

——— and Hoogenboom, A. *The Enterprising Colonials: Society on the Eve of the Revolution.* Chicago, 1965.

Sachse, William L. *The Colonial American in Britain.* Madison, 1956.

Sanford, Ezekial. *History of the United States before the Revolution.* Philadelphia, 1819.

Sawtelle, William. "Thomas Pownall: Colonial Governor and Some of His Activities in the American Colonies." *MHSP.* LXIII (1930), 233–87.

Schlesinger, Arthur M. *The Colonial Merchants and the American Revolution, 1763–76.* Fascimile edition. New York, 1939.

———. "Maryland's Share in the Last Intercolonial War." *Md. Hist. Mag.* VII (1912), 119–49, 243–67.

Schutz, John A. "Imperialism in Massachusetts during the Governorship of William Shirley, 1741–56." *The Huntington Library Quarterly*. XXIII (1960), 217–36.

———. "Secession Politics in Massachusetts, 1730–41." *WMQ*. 3d Ser., XV (1958), 508–20.

———. *Thomas Pownall: British Defender of American Liberty*. Glendale, Calif., 1951.

———. *William Shirley: King's Governor of Massachusetts*. Chapel Hill, 1961.

Sellers, Leila. *Charleston Business on the Eve of the American Revolution*. Chapel Hill, 1934.

Sherman, Richard P. *Robert Johnson: Proprietary and Royal Governor of South Carolina*. Columbia, S.C., 1966.

Shipton, Clifford K. "The New England Frontier." *NEQ*. X (1937), 25–36.

Shy, John. *Toward Lexington: The Role of the British Army in the Coming of the American Revolution*. Princeton, 1965.

Sipe, Chester H. *The Indian Wars of Pennsylvania*. Harrisburg, 1929.

Sirmans, M. Eugene. *Colonial South Carolina: A Political History, 1663–1763.* Chapel Hill, 1966.

Skaggs, Marvin L. "The First Boundary Survey between the Carolinas." *NCHR*. XII (1935), 213–32.

———. *North Carolina Boundary Disputes involving her Southern Line. The James Sprunt Hist. Pubs.,* XXV. Chapel Hill, 1941.

Slick, Sewell E. *William Trent and the West.* Harrisburg, 1947.

Smith, Abbot E. *Colonists in Bondage, 1607–1776.* Chapel Hill, 1947.

Smith, Jonathan. "The Massachusetts and New Hampshire Boundary Line Controversy, 1693–1740." *MHSP*. XLIII (1910), 77–88.

Smith, Joseph H. *Appeals to the Privy Council from the American Plantations*. New York, 1950.

Smith, W. Roy. *South Carolina as a Royal Province, 1719–76.* New York, 1903.

Smith, William. "The Colonial Post–Office." *AHR*. XXI (1916), 258–75.

----------------. *History of New York to 1732.* Albany, 1814.

Sollers, Basil. "The Acadians (French Neutrals) Transported to Maryland." *Md. Hist. Mag.* III (1908), 1–21.

Sosin, Jack M. *Agents and Merchants: British Colonial Policy and the Origins of the American Revolution, 1763–75*. Lincoln, Neb., 1965.

————. *The Revolutionary Frontier, 1763–83*. New York, 1967.

Start, Cora. "Naturalization in the English Colonies in America." *Annual Report of the AHA for 1893,* pp. 317–28. Washington, D.C., 1894.

Steele, I.K. "The Board of Trade, The Quakers, and Resumption of Colonial Charters, 1699–1702." *WMQ*. 3d Ser., XXIII (1966), 595–619.

Stitt, Robinson W. "Virginia and the Cherokees: Indian Policy from Spotswood to Dinwiddie" in Darrett B. Rutman, ed., *The Old Dominion: Essays for Thomas P. Abernethy.* Charlottesville, Va., 1964. pp. 21-40.

Stone, William. *The Life and Times of Sir William Johnson, Baronet.* 2 vols. Albany, 1865.

Stourzh, Gerald. *Benjamin Franklin and American Foreign Policy*. Chicago, 1954.

Tanner, E.P. "Colonial Agencies in England." *PSQ*. XVI (1901), 24–49.

————. *The Province of New Jersey, 1664–1738. Columbia University Studies . . .,* XXX. New York, 1908.

Tate, Thad W. "The Coming of the Revolution in Virginia: Britain's Challenge to Virginia's Ruling Class, 1763–76." *WMQ*. 3d Ser., XIX (1962), 323–43.

Thayer, Theodore. "The Army Contractors for the Niagara Campaign, 1755–56." *WMQ*. 3d Ser., XIV (1957), 31–46.

———. *Israel Pemberton, King of the Quakers.* Philadelphia, 1943.

———. *Pennsylvania Politics and the Growth of Democracy, 1740–1776.* Harrisburg, 1953.

Tolles, Frederick B. *James Logan and the Culture of Provincial America.* Boston, 1951.

Trelease, Allen W. *Indian Affairs in Colonial New York: The Seventeenth Century.* Ithaca, 1960.

Ubbelohde, Carl. *The Vice Admiralty Courts and the American Revolution.* Chapel Hill, 1960.

Van Every, Dale. *Forth to the Wilderness: The First American Frontier, 1754–74*. New York, 1961.

Varga, Nicholas. "Robert Charles: New York Agent, 1748–70." *WMQ.* 3d Ser., XVIII (1961), 211–35.

Veech, James. *The Monongahela of Old.* Pittsburgh, 1910.

Wade, Herbert T. *A Brief History of the Colonial Wars in America.* New York, 1948.

Wainwright, Nicholas B. *George Croghan: Wilderness Diplomat.* Chapel Hill, 1959.

———. "Governor William Denny in Pennsylvania." *PMHB*. LXXXI (1957), 170–98.

Waller, G.M. "New York's Role in Queen Anne's War, 1702–13." *New York History.* XXXIII (1952), 40–53.

———. *Samuel Vetch: Colonial Enterpriser.* Chapel Hill, 1960.

Walsh, James J. *Education of the Founding Fathers of the Republic: Scholasticism in the Colonial Colleges.* New York, 1935.

Walton, Joseph S. *Conrad Weiser and the Indian Affairs of Colonial Pennsylvania.* Philadelphia, 1900.

Warden, G.B. "The Proprietary Group in Pennsylvania, 1754–64." *WMQ.* 3d Ser., XXI (1964), 367–89.

Weaver, Glenn. *Jonathan Trumbull: Connecticut's Merchant Magistrate, 1710–85.* Hartford, 1956.

Webb, Stephen S. "William Blathwayt: From Popish Plot to Glorious Revolution." *WMQ.* 3d Ser., XXV (1968), 1–21.

———. "William Blathwayt, Imperial Fixer: Muddling Through to Empire, 1689–1717." *WMQ.* 3d Ser., XXVI (1969), 373–415.

———. "The Strange Career of Francis Nicholson." *WMQ.* 3d Ser., XXIII (1966), 513–48.

Wheeler, John H. *Historical Sketches of North Carolina.* Vol. I. Baltimore, 1964, reprint.

Whitney, Edson L. *Government of the Colony of South Carolina. JHUS.* XIII (1895), 9–121.

Whitton, F.E. *Wolfe and North America.* Boston, 1929.

Wickwire, Franklin B. *British Subministers and Colonial America, 1763–83.* Princeton, 1966.

Willard, Joseph. "Naturalization in the American Colonies." *MHSP.* IV (1860), 337–64.

Williams, Basil. *The Life of William Pitt, Earl of Chatham.* Vol. I. Reprint. New York, 1966.

Winton, Calhoun. "Jeremiah Dummer: The First American." *WMQ.* 3d Ser., XXVI (1969), 105–8.

Wood, George A. *William Shirley*. Vol. I. *Columbia University Studies* . . ., XCII. New York, 1920.

Woodward, Carl R. *Ploughs and Politics: Charles Read of New Jersey and His Notes on Agriculture, 1715–74.* New Brunswick, 1941.

Wright, Louis B. *The Atlantic Frontier.* New York, 1947.

Zeichner, Oscar. *Connecticut's Years of Controversy, 1750–76.* Chapel Hill, 1949.

Zimmerman, John J. "Benjamin Franklin and the Quaker Party, 1755–56." *WMQ*. XVII (1960), 291–313.

INDEX